Wilhelm Hohenzollern

The Last of the Kaisers

Wilhelm Hohenzollern

BISMARCK AND THE EMPEROR

Wilhelm Hohenzollern

The Last of the Kaisers

By

Emil Ludwig

Author of "Napoleon," etc.

Translated from the German
by
Ethel Colburn Mayne

Blue Ribbon Books, Inc.
New York City

Printed and Bound by The Cornwall Press, Inc., for
Blue Ribbon Books, Inc., 448 Fourth Ave., New York City

Printed in the United States of America

To
His Subjects

Acknowledgments are due to PROFESSOR H. W. CARLESS DAVIS, *of Oxford University, for reading the translation of this book and giving valuable advice.*

PREFACE

THIS book is a portrait of William the Second—no more: it presents neither his epoch, nor the whole story of his life.

That it is too soon for such a delineation can scarcely be maintained; in the seven years since his abdication the pace of events, the overthrow of accepted forms of government, have brought to light a greater quantity of relevant documents than seven decades would hitherto have afforded us. In these years, some twenty volumes of German memoirs, together with the remarkable series of German Foreign Office Papers, have laid bare the greater part of what had been kept secret until now. To the illumination thus obtained, even the solitary missing link—a volume from Prince Bülow's pen—could add but little.

Of William the Second, then, we know in these days not too little, but too much. His chronicler must forget the full extent of his own knowledge—the details seen and heard by him, as a contemporary; he must sacrifice a hundred anecdotes of which historians in the future will assuredly make use. For fairness' sake, at any rate, we here design *to let no adversary of the Emperor bear witness,* but to construct our portrait wholly from his own deeds and words, together with the reports of those who stood in close relation to him, and who give strikingly similar answers to the psychical questions involved. In the following pages neither Socialist nor alien voices will be heard—only the voices of the Emperor, his relatives and friends, his Chancellors, Ministers, and Generals, his courtiers and officials.

All these documents and reports are to be found in well-known works. As sources, they have sometimes been quoted more fully than was desirable for the flow of the narrative; in such special instances the present chronicler has often felt obliged to repress his more summary judgment in favour of the individual opinions of eye-witnesses, thus guarding himself against the reproach of a one-sided interpretation. The one liberty occasionally taken by the author has been the modulation of indirectly reported conversations into dialogue form. There is but a limited appeal to the oral testimony of participators in the events. The War-years, to which the youngest reader can bear witness, receive the least extended treatment—for they were merely the logical epilogue to the psychological prologue.

In short, this is an attempt to trace from the idiosyncrasies of a monarch the direct evolution of international political events—from his essential nature, the course of his country's destiny. Hence there is a twofold purpose in this presentation of the story of one human being's life:—

The realization of what may befall a mentally gifted, physically disabled young man, inspired by the best intentions, when after an adolescence fruitful in stern experiences he suddenly attains to power, and finds no one who will speak the truth to him. It is so that the Law of Succession may too early lead a youth, untaught, untrained, to that exalted station where, surrounded by Court-flatterers, he all too easily becomes an overweening autocrat. Further, it will be seen that for thirty years this monarch's own opinions, own volitions, decided all great national problems for his country; that no vital question, whether in peace or war, was ever answered without consulting him—no, nor ever answered against his will.

Then there will stand before us the figure of a man with whom an able family came to perdition—only because he never met with such resistance from his people as in time would have matured him.

E. L.

ABBREVIATIONS FOR THOSE WORKS MOST FREQUENTLY CITED

AKTEN, Die diplomatischen, des Auswärtigen Amtes (Die Grosse Politik der europäischen Kabinette 1871-1914). Band I-XXV. Berlin, 1921-25. Deutsche Verlagsgesellschaft für Politik und Geschichte . . . . **A**

BISMARCK. Gedanken und Erinnerungen. Band III. Stuttgart, 1921. J. G. Cotta'sche Buchhandlung Nfl . . . . **B**

DOKUMENTE, Die deutschen, zum Kriegsausbruch. Berlin, 1919. Deutsche Verlagsgesellschaft f. Politik u. Geschichte . . . . . . **D**

ECKARDSTEIN, Hermann Freiherr von. Lebenserinnerungen und politische Denkwürdigkeiten. Leipzig, 1919-20. Band I-III. Paul List Verlag . . . . **Eck**

EULENBURG-HALLER, Prof. Dr. Johannes, Philipp Eulenburg-Hertefeld. Berlin, 1924. Gebrüder Paetel **E2**

EULENBERG-HERTEFELD, Fürst Philipp zu. Aus 50 Jahren. Berlin, 1923. Gebrüder Paetel . . **E**

HOHENLOHE, Prinz Alexander von. Erinnerungen.
Frankfurt-a-M., 1925 . . . . . . **Al**

HOHENLOHE-SCHILLINGSFÜRST, Fürst Chlodwig zu.
Denkwürdigkeiten. Stuttgart, 1907. 2. Bd.
Deutsche Verl.-Anst. . . . . . **Ho**

LUCIUS VON BALLHAUSEN. Bismarcks Erinnerungen. Stuttgart, 1920. J. G. Cotta'sche Buchhandlung Nfl. . . . . . . **L**

MOLTKE, Helmuth von. Erinnerungen, Briefe,
Dokumente 1877-1916. Stuttgart, 1922 . . **M**

SCHWERTDFEGER, Bernhard. Die politischen und
militärischen Verantwortlichkeiten im Verlaufe
der Offensive von 1918. Band II der vierten
Reihe im Werk des Parlamentarischen Unter-
suchungsausschusses. Berlin, 1925. Deutsche
Verlagsgesellschaft f. Politik u. Geschichte . **S**

TIRPITZ, Alfred von. Erinnerungen. Leipzig,
1919-20. K. F. Koehler. . . . . **T**

WALDERSEE. Denkwürdigkeiten Generalfeld-
marschalls Alfred v. Waldersee. Stuttgart, 1922-
23. Deutsche Verl.-Anst . . . . **W**

ZEDLITZ-TRUTZSCHLER, Graf Robert v. Zwölf Jahre
am deutschen Kaiserhof. Stuttgart, 1923.
Deutsche Verl.-Anst. . . . . . **Z**

CONTENTS

CONTENTS

WILHELM HOHENZOLLERN

BOOK I

VOCATION

"It would be of the first importance to know something of his secret history, especially the influences predominant in his earliest youth, and how he came to believe that good intentions are sufficient for a successful reign."—*Johannes von Müller on Joseph II.*

CHAPTER I

1   1859–1887

PANIC swept through the room of travail; women gathered round the new-born child in perturbation and dismay. The first rejoicings in the Crown Prince's Palace at Berlin—rejoicings that it was a boy, and the succession thus assured to the third generation—had died out; for there lay the eighteen-year-old mother, a mere girl, in deathlike unconsciousness, and here lay the child, to all appearance lifeless. Vain were the efforts of doctor, nurse, and waiting-woman to animate it by swinging and slapping; Destiny hesitated for an hour and a half before deciding to turn the motionless substance into a human being.

At last it stirred; but in the confusion and anxiety about mother and child, in the excitement borne on the thunder of salvoes into the hushed sick-room, nobody thought to examine closely the person of this royal heir. Not until the third day was it perceived that the left arm was paralysed, the shoulder-socket torn away, and the surrounding muscles so severely injured that in the then state of surgical knowledge no doctor would venture to attempt the readjustment of the limb (L. 74). Moreover, it at first appeared to be more than a local disability: the left leg reacted but slightly,

3

and the child suffered pain in the left ear and corresponding side of the head.

For this physically disabled boy, named Friedrich Wilhelm Victor Albrecht, and called Fritz until he was six years old, Nature seemed to have designed a private life; and as a brilliant intelligence was soon made manifest, that life might well have been an intellectual one in which he would have been distinguished and happy, sheltered from fear of humiliations. But he had been born in the Palace of Potsdam, christened in the historic wooden cradle—a Prussian Prince and more, for as the future ruler of the land he was irrevocably destined to one profession. A soldier he must become— that was demanded of him by the secular tradition of his fathers.

Who can refuse sympathy to the boy, as he duly sought by self-discipline, and under the stern tutelage of his teachers, to do his utmost towards supplying that which Nature had denied him? His crippled arm was subjected to electric treatment which caused him extreme torture, until the attempt to strengthen the paralysed limb was abandoned, and the boy trained to simulate some use of it. Cleverly did he learn to support his left arm in his belt or pocket, to let the reins slip into his left hand from his normal right one, to handle his horse in every sense without the aid of a groom; but in this way the right arm became so over-developed and heavy that frequently, when riding, it caused him to lose his balance, and slide off on that side.

An incurable disability in the left arm [writes his tutor Hinzpeter] was a very particular hindrance to his physical and psychical development, and one which the utmost skill and care would have been powerless to remove, had not the child himself co-operated with an unusual energy of resolution. He was confronted with the task of overcoming a natural sense of bodily helplessness, and the timidity inseparably connected with it.

Thus did a boy grow up who could not but be beset, by reason of an infirmity for which he was in nowise to blame, with a dread of those who were stronger than he, and a corresponding tendency to seclusion; and it was this boy who was obliged to display instead the spirited intrepidity which is the soldier's virtue—who must moreover make a greater show of energy than most officers, since he would have to stand one day before the people, unabashed, unruffled, the chief personage on all occasions, "every inch a king." How should a child undergo a training such as this, entirely directed to pretence, without some spiritual risk? The only way of salvation would have been for him to make a drastic separation of the show from the reality, and while cynically flaunting the purple, build himself an inward realm wherein bodily weakness should be no dishonour.

But to such a compromise the boy's character was strongly opposed. "While he was still a remarkably handsome but very girlish-looking lad," continues his tutor, "one was struck by the resistance called forth in him by any sort of pressure, any attempt to form his deeper nature." It was only by the aid of etiquette and an unwearied zeal that something had been achieved in externals, and this contributed to make the direction of the boy's more intimate self supremely difficult.

The gentlest mental discipline was resisted to the utmost by that elusive nature. . . . The strife with this disastrous incapacity for concentration is always one of the most exacting duties of those who are entrusted with a Prince's education. And in this instance, where the nature was so essentially refactory, it was formidable indeed. Only the most extreme severity . . . availed to overcome the resistance, until the awakened self-consciousness summoned to its aid the boy's own will, and soon removed all my difficulties. But even from the powerful pressure of the moral forces, now in their normal development, the nature of the adolescent Prince would constantly shake itself free.

When after an Emperor's accession to the throne his tutor, writing as his clear-sighted friend, makes public use of such strong expressions, it is evident that he has had to combat in his pupil an unusual degree of defiance and self-will. Whether these traits of character will be refined into dignity and self-reliance, or debased into arrogance and despotism, is the problem of their possessor's destiny. If he is to hold rule over others, it may become, as well, the problem of a nation's destiny; the great ancestor of this young Prince "Frederick" had been, when he came to the throne no better equipped in character, and it was only by the hammering of circumstance that he was shaped into a man.

Like that Frederick, this William experienced a father's harshness; and to it was added the cold-heartedness of a despotic mother from whom he inherited too much self-will and frigidity to be able to get on with her. The ambitious Victoria, daughter of the powerful Queen of England and her sagacious consort, could not forgive the imperfection of this child, especially as she regarded her husband's blood as less illustrious than her father's. Racial feeling bore down maternal feeling; instead of compassion, she cherished in her heart a secret grudge against her misshapen son, precisely because he *was* her first-born, and openly displayed a preference for her healthier children. Never through all his life does a child forget a slight of this nature, especially when inflicted before those who are his inferiors in rank. Sooner or later it will be avenged.

In years to come his defiance deepened the estrangement, but the boy's heart was originally embittered through the mother's own shortcoming; his impressionable young mind was poisoned, his political ideas were inevitably coloured by an instinctive opposition to those of his parents.

The strong-minded mother led her weak husband whither she would; and though the external suggestions were highly favourable to the father, the boy's heart, thus repulsed, was obdurate against them. For just as he was learning his drill at Potsdam, the palace and the town, the land and all Europe, were ringing with the swift and overwhelming conquests of his father and grandfather, marching on Paris. When Prince William, then twelve years old, opened out a newspaper or an illustrated journal, on every page he beheld his father *in excelsis,* throned on his horse, the handsome, somewhat effeminate head bowing from the lofty saddle; and the glowing boy would read of, would see depicted, the scene in the Hall of Mirrors at Versailles when his father sank on one knee before his grandfather, doing homage to him as the new-made Emperor. True, that ever at their side would stand the adamantine figure of the Chancellor; but as nobody told the children what malignities and insults were being perpetrated in those French palaces, their imaginations were inevitably peopled with heroic figures like those in the old sagas and ballads. War and victory, vanquished France and the German Empire, were as a picture-book in this small soldier's eyes, and he called the principal personages in it by the titles of father and grandfather.

Thus, misled by a romantic precedent, he early learnt to regard the history of his land as that of his family alone; and even as a boy he could not be insensible to the gulf between ruler and subject when he looked down from the balcony where he stood between mother and grandmother, and saw father and grandfather ride up the Linden in dazzling procession, acclaimed by a people inherently less liberty-loving than submissive, who now could adulate not only their liege lords but the lords of battle. And when soon afterwards, as a boy of fifteen, he went with his brother to live at Wilhelmshöhe, how could he help peopling the lofty apartments with the figures of Napoleon and his last devoted followers, who had languished here six months in imprisonment, bereft of power through the genius of the King of Prussia? Who was there to point out to the youth that all this had sprung from the brain of a Junker out of Pomerania, and that it was due entirely to the strength and devotion of a courageous people? The grace of God lay visibly upon his grandfather's brow, and in the boy's ears resounded the intoxicating music of "To arms! To arms!"

From the English quarter came a change of wind. Victoria, the Crown Princess, resolute to bring up her sons after the precepts of her father, broke for the first time in history through the Prussian régime, and sent them from their cadet-drill to the Lyceum at Kassel, where they would sit in the class-room with civilians' sons, and see life out of uniform. The plan proved abortive. Prince William needed only to perceive such an intention, and at once he set himself to disappoint it; the more "liberal" his parents would have him, the more unapproachable he became. At Kassel he was soon "quite the future Emperor. . . . This overbearingness," said Caprivi later, "would never have set in if he had been brought up in the good old fashion with a few companions."

From Hinzpeter we have only a private observation on those two years at Kassel; he wrote to his patron, who had recommended him to the Court: "You have no conception of what an abyss I have looked into!" (Al. 368, from a letter to Sir R. Morier). Later, he said that the Emperor had "never learnt the first duty of a ruler, hard work" (E. 231). When the Prince left at eighteen he was awarded, though he was distinctly more gifted than the majority of his companions, only tenth place out of seventeen in the school examination, with the laconic comment: "Satisfactory."

And yet his master emphatically extols him. For what distinguished the Prince, especially as an officer, was the struggle against his infirmity. Here lay all his ambition, all his achievement. When he for the first time rode at the head of his Hussars before his formidable grandfather and the uncle who was so renowned a horseman, both were amazed; and when the old man said: "Well done! I could never have believed you could do it!" the Prince was inspired with an instant confidence in his ability to overcome his infirmity, and be as strong and valiant as his forebears and comrades. "Never," writes Hinzpeter, "was a young man enrolled in the Prussian army who seemed so physically unfitted to become a keen and brilliant cavalry-officer. The few who then could estimate the significance of this victory of moral force over bodily infirmity, felt justified in their proudest hopes for this royal personage."

In reality, the moral victory over his physique was his destruction. If this was the greatest of days for the youthful Prince, riding in glittering uniform upon a galloping horse under the morning sunlight at the head of his regiment before his astonished elders, it was but the prelude to countless parades and processions, resounding orations, and men-acing gestures, whereby he endeavoured for a decade to im-pose upon his inmost consciousness.

2

Before the octogenarian Emperor stands the eighteen-year-old grandson in the mantle of an order of knighthood; to-day, on attaining his majority, admitted into the Most Noble Company of the Black Eagle, he swears before his grandfather "to maintain the honour of the Royal House, and guard the Royal privileges." On the same day in Janu-ary he enters as first lieutenant the First Regiment of Guards, in which at the age of ten he had begun his military career. Opening the newspaper in the evening, he reads:

This figure, in the bloom of its youth, gives promise to our Emperor, the father of his people, for the duration of all that he has undertaken and achieved. With every succeeding year the eyes of the world will dwell on Prince William with keener expecta-tion. It is more than a portent, it is a guarantee for his future career, that to-day, through his strenuous energy, he has attained the goal held forth to the flower of our German youth as the final guerdon of their early training.

When soon afterwards he visited a Saxon mine, Rübe-zahl stepped forth from between the layers of coal and il-luminated by Bengal lights, declaimed: "Good luck to you! A thousand times good luck—I, Rübezahl, Spirit of the Mines, exultingly repeat and will repeat it. Welcome among us, Hohenzollern Prince! Rejoice, ye hills; rejoice, ye vaulted caverns! Noble Prince, the star of Germany! Protect our mines, at home and afar!" How could this fail to go to his head?

As a student at Bonn in February, 1878, invited to the carnival at Cologne, he finds a mummer dressed as a

General confronting him in the dizzy circle; the gentleman is presented as the editor, Grieben. The Prince at once clinks glasses, and with a dexterous allusion to "this fellow-soldier, who daily leads thousands to the strife," raises a cheer—William the Second's first public speech, arousing some uneasiness, and cautiously commented on by the Press. People were asking: "Is this to be another War-Lord?"

He was not to be that. . . . Yet, going to Paris for Easter, he looked at everything they showed him, but was drawn and held by Versailles as by nothing else. How should he have any foreboding that in that very Hall of Mirrors where, seven years earlier, his fathers had glittered, there would one day be signed and sealed, at a less gorgeous but more terrible table, the ending of his own Imperial reign? The vainglory in these pompous paintings of mighty monarchs struck an answering chord; to strive after their image was a dream of glory and of power more congenial to his soul than such a homely ideal as his grandfather's, whose Prussian parsimony made him alternately derisive and angry.

Even in later life he never depreciated the French; rather was he drawn to them, through many a year, by a sense of inward affinity. It was from his French tutor Ayme that he first learnt the achievements of this nation; on that subject they once came into conflict.

"You could," said the Prince one day when they were talking of the recent war, "you could have paid from ten to fifteen milliards!" Then after a pause, smiling, "Well, next time!"

"Next time," answered the Frenchman gravely, "it will not be we who shall have to pay."

"So much the worse for you, for you'll never squeeze such a sum out of us!"

Ayme replied, and this time very sharply, that it would be abominable if the Germans, after their good haul, were to declare in defeat that they could pay nothing. "That reminds one of the adventurer who, after winning in the card room, hurries away as soon as he begins to lose."

On this the Prince's face grew dark, he looked at me with angry eyes for quite a while; then he said coldly: "You have put a detestable interpretation on my little joke. I never thought your nation capable of plundering Germany in war. Such a war would be nothing but colossal robbery. The whole thing is entirely contrary to my ideas. Of course these conflicts are really brought about by the intrigues of ambitious ministers, who will do anything to stay in power. They ought to be obliged to fight it out personally, that would keep them off adventures, and save much innocent blood. For the rest, I shall take care never again to jest with you on this subject.

Afterwards the Prince tried to bury the hatchet by great amiability.

This is the first significant dialogue of the young William which has come down to us; all the elements are there. He starts by being tactless; next, driven into a corner, gives an unworthy retort; and when sharply taken to task, becomes unapproachable all of a sudden. Then, however, he makes a well-considered pronouncement on the danger and criminality of wars, to which, in principle, he held all his life; finally he seeks, by personal charm, to atone for his princely arrogance. The ideas are good, the behaviour uncertain: vacillating between intimacy and class-consciousness, he repels and invites—a youth who is perpetually at odds with his own duality.

In his father the Prince could have studied, though in a very modified degree, some kindred characteristics; and that the two had a suspicion of this affinity in their weaknesses was from the first a reason for mutual distrust. When the young man of twenty-one returned to his parental home from his Potsdam garrison, the antagonisms in the family became sharply apparent. The Prince now looked with clearer vision on his parents—what did he perceive in them?

Nobody ever sustained the tragi-comic part of all Crown Princes for a longer time and in a more powerless position than did this Frederick William who now, at fifty, still without serious occupation, languished in semi-thraldom, with no control over his time or finances, and even in his ideas continually checked by the octogenarian father and his oldest minister. And were even these ideas truly his own? This not wholly Prussian Hohenzollern, fond of display, despotic of temperament, his Caesarist tendencies aggravated by long inactivity, this Prince who held the doctrine of the Divine Rights of Kings, felt obliged to entertain Liberal opinions because they were urged on him by a passionate and vehement consort, as the higher conception of a man's, a prince's, duty. He was proud to have for wife the interesting daughter of a powerful Queen, but mortified because she was unpopular; and though his victorious father might extol him in public as a "great general," he knew well enough that he had never been anything of the sort. He tried to forget his position in long and frequent journeys.

The Crown Prince, one of the keenest observers at Court [remarks Waldersee at this time], is naturally disappointed at having to wait so long for the throne. Ten years—nay, fifteen years ago, he thought it unfair of Providence to let his father live so long. Influenced by his ambitious consort, he made many plans for the future, which were much inspired by Liberal ideas. . . . 'The Chancellor, whom the Crown Princess cannot, and the Crown Prince therefore must not, endure, gains in prestige daily. . . . In this way the Crown Prince's position is made very difficult. The intellectual superiority of the Princess has proved a great misfortune. She has turned a simple-minded, gallant, honourable Prince into a weak-minded man devoid of self-reliance, no longer open-hearted, no longer Prussian in his ideas. Even of his steadfast faith she has robbed him. . . . His grown-up children have no illusions about the true state of affairs. . . . The father's weakness will be the measure of the son's self-will. . . . If the Emperor lives much longer, the Crown Prince will go to pieces altogether. Even as it is, he has attacks of profound depression, and no confidence in the future.

The military relations between father and son (who in the meantime, at twenty-five, had been promoted major) sharpened the conflict between them.

Often—writes Waldersee of the manœuvres in 1884—[the Crown Prince] displayed great vehemence, for the most part over unimportant matters, things which were chiefly personal; unfortunately he imagines that due deference is purposely withheld from him. . . . The fact that Prince William has been summoned to head-quarters, which means to join his father, was completely ignored. The Crown Prince never once asked him, "Where is my son?" or "What is he doing?" When the latter, as constantly happened in the course of the manœuvres, returned to my head-quarters, his father behaved as if he scarcely knew he was there, but took much notice of Prince Henry, who was on his staff. Prince William, however, allowed no one to see how much he felt this unfriendliness from his father.

Is it surprising? This forcible-feeble man was possessed with the foreboding, frequently expressed, that he had not long to live; it was intensified by the more than patriarchal longevity of a still vigorous father, who might well see a hundred; how could he escape the thought that his might be the generation to be skipped? Must not the time-honoured grudge against an heir have been sharpened by the sense that *his* would in all human probability have a much shorter probation? For these last twenty years, what had been given him to do? Manœuvres, openings of exhibitions, and the like. At the inauguration of a Council of State in the year 1884, he advanced to the great chair which looked so like a throne, and read an address. "On this occasion he showed so little tact and dignity as somewhat plainly to underline his distaste. He spoke in an expressionless voice, constantly drawing a deep breath, as if it were extremely uncongenial to him" (W. 245).

When his father's long life exacerbated him beyond endurance, he revenged himself on his son. At a Guards' dinner in the beginning of 1885 he took occasion—

rather, he let himself go, and represented his son to all the officers and guests as an immature and injudicious person. The Prince controlled himself but was infuriated. The universal opinion is that he behaved very well, and the Crown Prince incredibly badly. . . . The parents are now intent on getting up a scandal, and provoking an open rupture (W. 255).

Yet for the humiliated Prince it was a matter for rejoicing when he had only his father to contend with. "When my father is alone, all goes well enough. But now for the change of wind!" he said to Waldersee, when his mother was expected home after a visit to England.

Victoria, acclaimed in Berlin when she arrived as a bride of eighteen, in twelve years saw nothing but mistrust all round her. Now, after the war of 1870, Court and Society, imbued with exaggerated patriotism, complained that she spoke English in her household, called herself Vicky, her son William, associated with English scientists; that her cookery, her servants, her table appointments were English. As though averse from everything Old-Prussian, North-German, she encouraged those democrats—like Virchow and Helmholtz—whose views assorted with her English outlook; this was looked upon as anti-military, as calculated intrigue against the Court of the hide-bound old monarch. A dilettante, with her finger in everyone's pie, telling the artists how they were to paint, scenting from afar the New Century, but never going deeply into any social or even feminist questions—she was all for show, just as her son was, and for that very reason was his enemy.

"A combination of remarkable intelligence and Coburg cunning, with a fine education and iron will, together with covetousness and a lack of Christian faith": this judgment of Eulenburg's is too severe, for it ignores the energy and pride which were her best qualities; also the difficulty of a position between two countries which was afterwards to embarrass her son himself. The long exclusion from the throne, the succession to which would not even mean for her the loss of her father, must have been the more irksome to this imperious nature, her hostility against this (to her ideas) barbarian country the keener, because it had taken the bloom of her years and had given her nothing in return. "If your father should die before I do," she said to her son, "I shall leave at once. I will not stay in a country where I have had nothing but hatred—not one spark of affection" (E. 136).

The son had long known that his mother was unchangeably an Englishwoman; but from the eighties onward he was convinced "that she consciously worked for English as against Prussian and German interests" (W. 239). Immediately all his defiance and hostility were concentrated on everything that she loved and cherished; at the age of twenty Prince William, out of opposition to his mother, first became definitely hostile to England. About that time he made a particular study of the war in the Sudan, and showed "a strong prepossession against England" (W. 247). Prince Herbert Bismarck, especially, summed him up well on this point when he said: "Prince William can never hear enough against England. . . . If his mother comes to the throne, it is all up with Germany anyhow" (E. 176). But at the same time the Minister Lucius perceived behind this parade of dislike "a great unconscious attraction towards England."

For a decade his heart vacillated between these emotions of aversion, admiration, and jealousy; for a lifetime it thrilled with this personal hate and love for his mother's country, the outcome of which was to decide the destiny of his nation.

The first open quarrel was kindled by this flame. The father and mother, instigated by the aging English Queen, whose interests were anti-Russian, were set upon their daughter's betrothal to the Prince of Bulgaria; it had even come to an exchange of rings between the girl and this Battenberg Prince, when Bismarck interposed on the Tsar's behalf, and instantly found Prince William on his side. A violent scene between mother and son ensued at the beginning of 1885; it was thought desirable to remove him from Potsdam. "If the Crown Prince were suddenly to become Emperor, there would be nothing for it but to transfer the Prince to a distant garrison" (W. 258).

Meanwhile the Prince honestly tried to win his parents over by various achievements. He was now in the middle twenties, he was even himself a father, for at two-and-twenty

he had taken to wife the Holstein Princess who had been
assigned him. After this he was twice sent to Russia, and on
his return "most warmly received in all quarters, even by
his parents. They have been obliged to hear too much approval of him, to be able any longer to treat him as a spoilt,
ungrateful son. They are jealous of him" (W. 242).

About this time there fell some terrible words from Victoria's lips. "You can scarcely imagine," she said to an
Austrian nobleman, "how I admire your handsome, intelligent, and graceful Crown Prince when I see him beside my
uncouth, lumpish son William" (Corti, *Alexander von Battenberg,* p. 328). Spoken by a woman brought up as a
Princess, spoken to a foreigner, in full consciousness that her
words would be repeated in Vienna, and from Vienna would
penetrate into all the Courts of Europe. So deep in the
mother's heart lay the unnatural antipathy for her partly
deformed son.

3

Far from Potsdam, in quite another continent, stands
on the Linden at Berlin the palace of the old Emperor.
Augusta, in the eighties, instituted little intimate evenings
at the so-called Bonbonnière. Here would gather a few old
ministers and other nobles; professors too were invited—
Curtius, who excavated Olympia, Hofmann, the authority
on aniline dyes—and there would be no suite at all, for in its
absence consisted the hostess's holiday. On these evenings
she was quit for once of the painted, padded Count Per-
poncher, of the parchment visage of old Albedyll; Plessen
distributed elsewhere the amiabilities proper to an aide-de-
camp, and Goltz, the Adjutant-General, now quite in his
dotage, was free to slumber. The Empress would be rolled

in, sitting in her invalid-chair, and established at a little table round which she would invite the guests to take their places; on her left would be a vacant chair for the Emperor. Tea, mandarines, ices, an exiguous glass of wine. It was the general amazement that she, with her feeble voice and hands in which the teacups rattled, should still care to appear in the world. After a while the Emperor would enter. He was near ninety by that time. His overcoat thrown open, for he usually came from the theatre, he would welcome every guest individually and cordially, then take a chair, unceremonious, cheerful, as always. Except for the hardness of hearing, which had begun to make conversation difficult to him, one might have taken him for a vigorous septuagenarian. A nonagenarian, he had brought down his twenty-six head of deer at his last shoot.

His favourite stories were of his youthful days. Once at the Bonbonnière he told of his being, as a lieutenant, at the Tsar's banquet after the victory of Leipzig, and there having been asked why he took no lobster. "I said I didn't know how one ate it, for in my parents' house I had never looked a lobster in the face" (Al. 348).

The guests sit attentive; we too listen with amazement. Here is a King who has sat at table with Alexander the First, who knew Talleyrand, and entered Paris with him after Waterloo; and beside him is a Queen who had talked with Goethe, known Charles Augustus, and in the March days of 1848 had fought her House's battle in this very palace—and yet neither has ever changed. She still tries to rule him, he still courteously refuses to be ruled; and if he does know a lobster now when he sees one, he still inquires every other day for the remains of yesterday's bottle of champagne. . . . It was upon this simplicity that his innate dignity was most surely based; for "he stands in the centre like a rock, the roaring billows round him, exalted high above the pitiful strife beneath. His prestige increases daily, nowadays, because he is a man who knows no guile, who cannot be approached by intriguers" (W. 285).

And in the closing years of his life, when war again seemed imminent, he said to old Albedyll: "I will take the command again, myself; my son will be with me. How far I shall get God only knows; it won't be far, but I shall go with the others" (W. 315).

Not a thousand yards away lies the domain of him who weighs in the balance these questions of war and peace— Bismarck, the grim central figure of all three Courts; but he too, as it were, creates for himself quite another world. True, he is sure of his old master; but even for *him* the dictator is occasionally too much, and when the head of the Cabinet one day perceives the Emperor to be enraged after the Chancellor's speech, and impulsively counsels him to let the man go if he will not yield to His Majesty's will, the Emperor replies: "In spite of all my gratitude, I *have* thought of it before now. His arrogance is often almost beyond bearing. But the Fatherland needs him too badly."

Augusta can never entirely forgive this man the splendour of her two crowns, because it is he to whom, in fact, she owes them both. It vexes the imperious old woman to realize that her masterfulness must yield the palm to this stranger's. Even in these years of the eighties, she has had to suffer Bismarck's admonition against agitating the Emperor by seeking to influence him. "I never," writes Bismarck, "had seen the Empress look so handsome in the last decade of her life as at that moment. She drew herself up, her eyes blazed with such fire as I never encountered before or since. She broke off our interview, left me standing, and said afterwards: 'Our most gracious Chancellor of the Empire is very ungracious to-day.' "

Such inside information was eagerly retailed by the Berlin Court-folk from the Chamberlain down to the humblest lackey; no frown or grumble of the old master but the grandson heard of it, and he might well have joined, out of his marked fear and respect for his grandparents, in the general hostility against the omnipotent Chancellor, to whom he was in no way personally attracted. But hatred for his parents drew the Prince to Bismarck's side.

It had already become history, but had been kept from the youth as from all subjects—how in the conflict of 1863 his father had publicly dissociated himself from his grandfather's, the King's, *coup d'état.* Now, however, grown-up, and lavishly supplied by his contemporaries with any sort of material against his father, Prince William heard not only of such revolts, but in the more fearless historical publications could even read besides that it was his mother who at that time had, under English pressure, urged his father to this step, "so as to safeguard her children's future." With the eagerness of aspiring youth, the son now read and heard of the whilom aspirations of his own father.

Yet in his heart of hearts he was not for his father, but against him. His father's advanced opinions were not to his taste, the anti-democracy of Bismarck's sphere was congenial; in a book about him, the Prince at that time underlined all Bismarck's most royalist pronouncements, and everything against England. To the passage in Bismarck's speech of that same year, 1863, in which he alluded to the birthday of "our youngest Prince," and emphatically told the Landtag that the Prussian monarchy was not yet ripe to form a mere decoration in the constitutional structure, the Prince appended, "and it never will be if that 'youngest Prince' can prevent it" (L. 292).

Thus his earliest political ideas were biassed by his hostility towards his parents; that was why he made himself the mirror of Bismarck. And had not "blood and iron" prevailed against England's Liberal dogmas? The Prince delighted in hearing from eye-witnesses how his proud father had to bend his will to that of his grandfather, or of how Bismarck had asked the sullen Crown Prince why he held aloof from the sessions of a Government which after all would "in a few years" be his own? Whereupon the Crown Prince, even then embittered, drew himself up most haughtily, suspicious that the evil genius of Prussia was intent on paving his way to serve the new King also.

Even to-day [wrote Bismarck thirty years afterwards] I seem to see the head flung back, the cheek reddening, the look at me over the left shoulder. I controlled my own wrath, thought of Carlos and Alba, and answered that I had spoken in an access of dynastic emotion. . . . I knew I should never be [his servant].

One seems to see the pair. At the end of a coldly glittering palatial room, or perhaps right at the door, this minister, now approaching fifty, colossal, already nearly bald, scarce two years at the helm of affairs, as yet unrenowned, the best-hated man in Prussia and proud to be so, and nevertheless in full assertion of genius, upborne by the arrogance which attributed the salvation of this dynasty to himself. Near by, no less gigantic, a man in the early thirties, blonde as can be, and very dandified—the heir to the throne, his opponent, and yet possessed by the same thought: "When will the sceptre change hands?" The minister, a stranger, wishes the King who trusts him a long life; the son and heir, like other Crown Princes before him, is torn by conflicting emotions—indeed for him there is no longer any conflict.

"Is it possible!" reflects Son William, when he hears such stories. To-day, after more than twenty years, can these be the same three men who, in the self-same places, actuated by the same suspicions and predilections, watch one another unceasingly, trustful and malevolent, recalcitrant and submissive? The old master still obeys the same counsellor, the master's son still hates him; but in the interval the power of that stranger, who rules the destinies of royal houses and divides them against themselves, has secretly and uncannily waxed to an autocracy; in his brain is shaped the fate of Europe, his renown has reached from pole to pole, and he, whose might no law pronounces to be permanent, is fixed more firmly on his throne than are the members of a family protected by the Law of Succession!

Obscure emotions, compounded of pride and fear, contend in the young Prince's heart when he is in the presence of the Chancellor. Amid the conflicting currents which distract the royal house, this stranger is the only man whom none dares to assail.

4

In view of the immaturity as well as the inexperience of my eldest son, together with his tendency towards over-bearingness and self-conceit, I cannot but frankly regard it as dangerous to allow him at present to take any part in foreign affairs.

With these words the Crown Prince sought, in the autumn of 1886, to veto the employment of his son in the Foreign Office, which Bismarck had caused the old Emperor to ordain. But what had he to take as the Chancellor's reply? That in the royal family the paternal authority must yield to the monarchical. Once again he knew himself defeated—he who might succeed to the throne to-morrow, and the day after dismiss this paid official!

For he knew well that Bismarck's will alone had inspired the order which would reveal State-secrets to the Prince, and prepare him for every contingency of the future. Was the old man trying to put the Prince under an obligation, to turn the unfavourable situation between father and son into one favourable to himself? Did it not look as if the aim was to supersede him, the Crown Prince? And here he was on the Riviera, in perfect health, a man approaching sixty, hailed as a Prince by all the world, the heir to one of the most powerful of kingdoms; yet, for all that, prevented by this eternal minister from forbidding to his own unripened son the thing that seemed to him a danger!

Nevertheless it was precisely then that Bismarck and the Crown Prince seemed to make some *rapprochement*. Since with every added year, every indisposition of the aged ruler, the sceptre seemed more likely to change hands, these two men had to consider coming events which were already the topic of Court gossip. When at this time the Crown Prince asked the Chancellor if in the event of a change he would remain, he was answered by the condition: No parliamentary government, and no foreign influence in policy. Despite the unmistakable allusion to England, the Crown Prince answered, with a gesture corresponding to his words: "Of course not."

Prince William saw all this at close quarters; we know what he thought of it, for Waldersee, his personal friend, records the deliberations of this group with constant reference to the young Prince's rôle.

I consider the Chancellor and the Crown Princess together simply an impossibility, so long as we are not openly allied with England. How is the Chancellor to conduct foreign policy when the future Empress, initiated in all these matters by the weakness of her husband, is English at heart? But on the other hand, whom can the Crown Prince take for Chancellor? There is no one available! . . . It could not last a month; then would come collapse and chaos. . . . I am convinced that his fall would mean complications at home and abroad, probably war. The great game of intrigue grows more transparent every day. It is a question of who is to be master in the Imperial Court of the future. The Bismarcks, father and son, propose to rule alone, and flatter themselves they can manage the Crown Princess. . . . If the Crown Prince comes to the throne [Bismarck] will easily make a pretext of, or actually force on, such differences of opinion as will enable him to resign. His son will go with him—to resume office under Prince William, on whom everyone is calculating (W. 251 *seq.*).

Uncanny—this conviction in those around him of the early death or abjuration of a man who has been waiting thirty years, who is in perfect health, and not yet sixty!

All these calculations and desires found their way to the ears, to the heart of the Prince; and sooner than with other heirs to a crown his fancy began to hover round the thought of his father's death. This drew him into yet closer relations with the powerful Chancellor, who played with him in masterly fashion. The old minister knew how the jealous father watched every visit paid him by the son. He personally initiated him into foreign affairs, called him his most important coadjutor, for the whole Foreign Office was in fact no more than Bismarck's workshop; and only at one name did the Chancellor hesitate. "When the name of Privy Councillor Holstein was mentioned," the Prince wrote afterwards, "I seemed to hear in his tone a sort of warning against that man. He called him later on the man with the hyena-eyes, from whom I should do well to hold aloof."

But the Prince's zeal quickly faded; he visited but fitfully the Ministry now open to him, "ready for anything exciting, but with no liking for continuous work, for real knowledge." And besides this: "It was thought unfitting for the Prince, now in command of a regiment, to be so often and so long absent from Potsdam" (W. 267); of this the old Emperor, too, disapproved. For the most part he was shooting or abroad, in Vienna, in Scotland, and again in Vienna.

Soon his adherence to the House of Bismarck began to waver, at first not of his own accord. In the beginning of 1886 the Chancellor had certain reasons for approaching the Crown Prince, and consequently Victoria, whom at heart he despised.

She is no Catherine, [he said;] put to the test, she shows cowardice. She wants to be popular . . . to seem Liberal, to perplex people with paradoxes—no more. About twenty years ago she told me that the Prussian nobility were servile because they were poor, that in Birmingham alone there was more silver plate than in all Germany . . . and that she believed I should love to be a King or the President of a Republic. I answered: "Doubtless England is much richer; but Prussia, in compensation, has many valuable qualities. And as to the danger of a Republic, that is still far from Germany. Possibly our children and grandchildren may see it—but only if the Monarchy abandons its own cause" (L. 396).

Prophetic, stinging words! When he spoke of abandoning its own cause, he was alluding to the Crown Princess's Liberalism, for he could not then have dreamed by what strange ways, a generation later, his prophecy would reach its fulfilment. At the moment his aim was, for international purposes, to win over the ruling spirit of Potsdam. Now that his policy was inclining towards England, his distrust of the Englishwoman necessarily decreased, since he could make direct use of her correspondence with London for the furtherance of his aims.

Every means to that end he pressed into his service.

The Chancellor is now on the best of terms with the Crown Prince and Princess. . . . The consequence is that she, bent as she is on attacking and humiliating her son, claims the Chancellor's co-operation to this end. It will be a bitter disillusionment for him, but perhaps a useful experience (W. 288).

The Prince's disillusionment was severe. In the vortex of intrigue, standing between the hostile Courts, and dependent on the moods of the enigmatic, and even more inflexible than enigmatic, Chancellor to whom he had hitherto reverentially adhered, and whom he had sought to please above all others, he now saw once for all that he too was no more than a pawn in the master's game, and felt himself pushed aside in favour of his detested mother. This young man would have had to be an expert in the art of diplomacy, an initiate in the shifting sphere of high politics, the confidant of Bismarck's soaring schemes, if he were not to be confounded by such an experience. But as he was, young and inexperienced, no less sensitive than unstable, he could see in this *chassez-croisez* nothing but a revulsion of the Chancellor's, and on Herbert's side especially a kind of betrayal. Bismarck's enemies did their part in confirming these views. For in truth everyone suffered and groaned under the yoke of the omnipotent man; and with smiles of glee they wrote and whispered to

each other that at last Prince William was getting over his
craze for Bismarck. When at that time it was one day
rumoured that Bismarck was dead, and the Prince, hasten-
ing to Berlin, heard from the Minister von Scholz joyous
démenti: "No; he is still with us," very coldly did the Prince
rejoin: "No one is irreplaceable. Of course he will be
needed for some years. After that, his functions will be
divided; the monarch must himself take a larger part in
them."

Meanwhile Bismarck sought to provide him with a
serious adviser, who should instruct him in the arts of government; but the Prince rejected the gentleman on the
ground that "when he was a boy, he had seen Rübezahl
wearing just such an unkempt beard." But the adviser
chosen by himself withdrew at his own request after a few
weeks, because he "could not instil a sense of the importance of earnest application, nor reconcile himself to an idle
Court existence."

Nevertheless the Prince had his successes, especially
abroad; his two missions to the Tsar went off admirably, he
was lauded for tact and geniality, knowledge of the Russian
language, and a certain charm. In conversation he was
versatile; "he talked with much animation, and was enthusiastic about Wagner's music and military manœuvres"
(L. 213). But at the same time Waldersee, who was devoted to him, complains of indignant letters about utterly
trivial circumstances, and of great difficulty in persuading
him to estimate people reasonably. Moreover, even as a
mere Prince, he gave birthday presents of his own bust,
wrote under his photograph the untimely words: *"Oderint
dum metuant,"* and under one sent to England: "I bide my
time." Ominous signs of a restive self-confidence.

He was far from well, it is true; frequently prevented by ear-aches from appearing on great occasions; in the spring of 1886 vertigo and sickness led to the grave diagnosis "that there is some risk of the brain being affected" (W. 292). Soon afterwards the sound ear was attacked; the tympanum had to be pierced—all this endangered his mental balance.

From his twenty-third to his twenty-eighth year the Prince's life was divided among three circles. He was a husband, was yearly made a father, and on the birth of his first-born son expressed the hope that he might follow in the footsteps of his great-grandfather. Rumours and reports of conjugal infidelity in those years are contested not only by his friends, but by the psychologists, for to the Prussian virtues of which he was so proud that kind of fidelity peculiarly belongs; and though Bismarck ascribes to him a strong vein of sensuality, this is but scantly attested outside his domestic relations.

One thing only is certain—that even in this youthful period he preferred the society of men to that of women, and liked to amuse himself in the Guards Club with his Potsdam brother-officers. Bismarck looked with disapproving eyes on this way of life and desired other influences for him; for, as he says, an heir to a throne, consorting with young officers of whom the most gifted have probably a keen eye to their official future, is only in very rare instances likely to find such an environment a good preparation for his future career. "I deeply deplored the limitations of this early intercourse" (B. 5). The attempt to transfer him to Berlin proved abortive, despite Bismarck's pressure, by reason of the old monarch's parsimony, which refused to allow him a fitting establishment. So did a Prussian virtue prevent the Prussian heir-apparent from undergoing the discipline appropriate to his situation.

What his brother-officers admired in him was the energy with which he had surmounted his infirmity, and taught himself to be a fine horseman and a fine shot. For he was urgent to outdo them all. When his bride came in procession along the Linden to the Palace on the wedding-day, he was standing in the courtyard in command of the bodyguard, "and commanding with such enthusiasm that her entry seemed to be a matter of no other interest in his eyes" (L. 203). Again, laying the foundation-stone of the new Reichstag, he "wielded his trowel so vigorously that there was general acclamation" (L. 296). His intimates alone knew the degree of nervous energy demanded of him by this display. "The poor Prince," writes Eulenburg, "is much incommoded by his paralysed left arm. His loader has to lean his right arm on a long pole, thus serving the Prince as a support for the rifle. Not every buck will put up with this!" (E. 137).

Only those who can appreciate this lifelong struggle against the congenital weakness will be fair to him when the future Emperor is seen to strain too far, or lose, his nervous energy. The perpetual struggle with a defect which every newcomer must instantly perceive and he, for that very reason, the more ostentatiously ignore—this hourly, lifelong effort to conceal a congenital, in no way repulsive, stigma of Nature, was the decisive factor in the development of his character. The weakling sought to emphasize his strength; but instead of doing so intellectually, as his lively intelligence would have permitted, tradition and vainglory urged him to the exhibition of an heroic, that is to say a soldierly, personality. And everything combined to strengthen the delusion: his forefathers' martial glory, his parents' depreciation, his opposition to their Liberal ideas; and above and before all, the innate vanity inherited from his father, and frequently characteristic of the family —this and these it was which drove him all his life to seem what he was not.

5

The Prince preferred the third group—that of his brother-officers—to the other two. Whom did he choose for friends? Hinzpeter, his tutor, was his adviser; but he was too old, and socially too far removed, to be called his friend. Even General Waldersee, in the middle fifties, could not be the bosom friend of a young man in the middle twenties; but the choice of him as confidant is significant.

Among the Generals of the previous generation, who had held the highest Prussian commands in three victorious campaigns, Count Waldersee was perhaps the only one who was deficient in the virtues of Moltke, Roon, and Blumenthal—straightforwardness, reticence, austerity; and who, because of this, was given over to intrigue, political wirepulling, and consuming ambition, all of which were in accordance with his crafty nature. His diary, invaluable as an indication of William's opinions, rich in spitefulness and knowledge of the world, yet for all that wearing a sanctimonious mask which is particularly in evidence on birthdays and in illness, is the earliest document of a type of Prussian officer which originated with him, and was in the next thirty years to be summoned to decisive power— that is to say, to the Cabinet of the monarch.

This first Court-General, who was also the originator of "aide-de-camp politics," very swiftly gained a pernicious influence over the Prince. His policy was ruled by Bismarck's—which means that he was always on the other side. Thus when old Moltke wanted to retire, and appointed Waldersee, his protégé, as Quartermaster-General, Bismarck desired someone else for the position. What was the result for Waldersee? A deadly feud with the Bismarcks. When, on the other hand, Bismarck discovered that Waldersee was playing-up to the Prince for the future Chancellorship, what was the result for the Bismarcks? A deadly feud with Waldersee.

Hence Waldersee concentrated all his energy on embroiling Herbert Bismarck with Prince William, Herbert being Foreign Secretary and on good terms with the Prince. Again, Waldersee suggested hostility towards Russia, because Bismarck's plans were pro-Russian; at the same time systematically undermining the Prince's confidence in Bismarck's greatness as a statesman. Yet simultaneously he struck up a sudden friendship with Privy Councillor Holstein, whom shortly before he had designated as "one of Bismarck's sorriest tools"; but this was a critical moment, and he divined that Holstein was beginning to revolt against the Chancellor.

Amid all this, his diary will invoke—on Good Friday or some other day of humiliation, or in tedium of a watering-place—the faithful love of his devout wife, who was a connection of Prince William; and from the welter of personalities, Court-gossip, lesser and larger treacheries, there will suddenly shine forth a pious gleam: "how Marie will rejoice in my spiritual transformation," or how from henceforth "he will strive, not after honours and earthly things, but to prepare himself for the next world." Such was the mentor chosen by the Prince.

His bosom friend was entirely different. Prince William

had a stern adolescence behind him; native coldheartedness had been reinforced by his early experience. Neither father nor mother, neither brothers nor sisters, had shown him that warmth of affection which calls forth the best attributes of youth; in his extremely uninspiring marriage he had later found no sedative against the hell of the home-life he knew. It is certain that he never was in love. Whether his nature was inherently incapable of devoted affection for a woman, or whether, fearing out of egotism to abandon himself to feeling, he followed the fashion of his time and group, wherein there was abundance of male friendships, not necessarily perverted—certain it is that at twenty-seven Prince William for the first time lost his heart.

Having from his childhood up obeyed the strictest Prussian ordinances, in his horror of betraying any physical inferiority, and possessed by the constant fear of not truly shining as an officer, the passive side of his nature now demanded its compensation. Suppressed sentimentality needed a field for ardour, fancy yearned for an artistic friendship. Music and song, lyric poetry and mystic speculations, nordic sagas and southern sunlight, the lofty presentation of heroic figures, draped in glittering mantles: all, in short, that Richard Wagner gave him, he now sought among his fellow men. And he found it all in Count Philip Eulenburg, to whom he was most fervently attached for thirty years.

This remarkable, many-sided man, whose nature is more plainly revealed to us in his Memoirs than he would have desired, was above all else an actor. His powers of adaptation were so great that he himself records the caustic comment of a friend: "If all his dear pals were to be brought together at one time, there would be a big fight." And speaking of his father and uncle, he adds: "I was like both in the exercise of my social talents, but I was an actor and they were sincere." Even his gifts were those of an effeminate nature, vacillating in half a dozen directions; and having been as a young man uncertain whether to decide for music, painting, architecture, or poetry, he finally realized that all his talents, combined as they were with rank and training, could find no more dazzling field for display than in diplomacy.

During those agitated years of inward conflict and overflowing productiveness, stimulated by the artistic life of Munich . . . I would flee in desperation to the lake, leap from the boat into the azure flood, or ply my fishing-rod for many a dreamy hour, until, remote from strife, I drew from Nature's greatness, from the blue-green waters, from my poetical and musical projects and fancies, a kind of tranquillity.

And it is not only the dilettante, but the actor, who writes as it were, with guilelessly uplifted eyes: "Even as a child I was possessed by measureless compassion . . . to help was ever my dearest joy." The man who, with an appearance of complete naïveté, can so depict himself in memoirs written decades later, is looking back upon a life in which the false note was unheard by others, and finally even by himself.

A tall supple figure, indefinite features, eyes which in Bismarck's opinion were enough to spoil the best breakfast, large soft hands, a Narcissus-like grace of bearing, alike in diplomatic uniform and Guards' full-dress, brilliantly witty, a store-house of anecdotes told in a beautiful, slightly veiled voice, able to improvise gracefully at the piano, to turn a rhyme, mimic a fellow-creature, put style into a letter; above all, so pliant that any friction with other natures was precluded . . . a personality imbued with no less sagacity than insincerity, its glitter at the same time oxidized by an unconquerable dread of responsibility —here is the seductive picture of an aristocratic Cagliostro, formed to bewitch the young Prince, twelve years his junior, as the embodiment of all human graces, the epitome of all artistic achievement, set forth before his eyes in the person of a living man.

Such was the first impression. And when we delete the superlatives without which such natures can neither exist nor write, there remains a great deal of truth in Eulenburg's statement: "The Prince's affection for me was an ardent one . . . my musical performances drove him into almost feverish raptures." The nordic ballads and roseate songs of sentiment—twin products of the Eulenburgian Muse— it would delight the Prince to hear

by the hour together . . . always sitting beside me and turning the pages . . . and he loved to greet me, when we met on shooting-mornings in the forest, with turns and phrases from my verses. I have had many a ravished listener to my performances, but hardly ever have I inspired such ravishment as in Prince William. And as at the same time I familiarly frequented Bismarck's house, was an officer in the Prince's adored Guards, and (alas!) was profoundly initiated in the byways of politics, I can understand that the young Prince should have felt as if looking deep into a cup filled with a draught whose ingredients were delightful to his palate.

It is in such an enervating atmosphere that the vanity of an idolized tenor, and the folly of his idolizing devotee, will thrive and grow. And yet we cannot be angry with this Count who was the first to open the gates of the garden of Romance to the young man who had been forced into the part of hard-bitten Prussian Prince, and now was taking leave of an adolescence poor alike in love and in the dreams of youth.

CHAPTER II

TOO SOON

1   1887–1888

SUDDENLY a prodigious hope dawned for the Prince. When in the March of 1887 all Germany was flocking round the old Emperor, now concluding the fabulous ninth decade and approaching centenarianism, the Crown Prince, in the delivery of his speech, showed signs of hoarseness. A week later the courtiers were whispering the word of terror in the ante-rooms. By May the trouble in the throat had gone so far that six German physicians met in consultation, each a renowned specialist, among them Virchow and Bergmann, already, as Liberals, familiar figures in the sick man's household. Though Virchow's opinion was undecided, they resolved to try laryngotomy: that is to say, the external operation on the throat, attended with no risk either to life or articulation, which at the worst may render the voice rough and husky. The operation was to take place on the twenty-first of May, the patient and his consort fully acquiescing. Bergmann in particular, who was to operate, hoped much from Frederick William's constitution; moreover, statistics showed seventy per cent. in favour of success.

On the evening of the twentieth there arrived at the Palace of Potsdam Sir Morell Mackenzie, a prominent

English specialist, not very highly esteemed by the majority of his colleagues, but whose work was not unknown to Germans. With him stepped Fate into the House of Hohenzollern.

Ever since William's unhappy birth, Victoria had stubbornly clung to the nonsensical idea that the German physicians were to blame for her son's disability. This *idée fixe* induced her—so all her surviving friends agree—to underline her distrust of German therapeutics by calling in an Englishman for her husband. And since it was owing solely to his erroneous treatment of the patient that premature death ensued and that Prince William's accession was thus brought about, with that misfortune of that one paralysed arm are indirectly but indissolubly connected the most grievous political consequences. So, as in a classical tragedy, we watch this doomed dynasty, and with it the German people, move under the terrible hand of Necessity from one snare of the Olympian powers to the next; and with passionless logic there follows upon an apparently trivial oversight at the birth of a Prince the darkening of his counsels, the premature death of his father, his too-early accession, and everything which, resulting therefrom, destroyed the security of millions of men.

Mackenzie, after his first brief investigation, pronounced that the trouble was not malignant, that the operation would be dangerous and superfluous, and maintained to Victoria and the German physicians—and a few days afterwards to other persons (L. 390)—that he could "definitely cure the Crown Prince in six or eight weeks, if he will come with me to my clinic in England like an ordinary mortal." Upon this, the patient withdrew his consent to the operation. The removal of a single specimen of tissue by the Englishman caused injuries to the larynx, which the German doctors attributed to maladroit handling.

The abandonment of the operation undoubtedly resulted in aggravation of the cancer, and death in the course of a year. The result of a timely operation would in all probability have been survival for years, possibly for decades—thus setting another man on the throne of Prussia, and with him another course of policy. In their official statements to the nation, after the death of the sufferer, two physicians wrote:

Professor Gerhardt:

No statistics are adequate to measure the probability, in this individual case, of a permanently favourable issue. For in no other was the disease so early perceived—I might go so far as to say, while actually in germ. The physical condition of the illustrious patient was the best imaginable; every kind of prophylactic was present or procurable.

Professor Bergmann:

The operation which we proposed was no more dangerous than that for inserting a tube, which in any event, if our diagnosis of cancer was correct, the Crown Prince would undoubtedly have had to undergo in course of time. Thus what we had proposed was nothing more than would sooner or later have become inevitable.

At the same time Bismarck wrote in his unmistakable style an article in the *Norddeutsche Allgemeine Zeitung*, the purport of which was that Mackenzie now declared that he too had quite clearly recognized the disease from the first, but that the Crown Prince had confided to him that he did not wish to be pronounced incurable, but on high moral and practical grounds desired to reign for a short time. A perversion of the truth! There existed no constitutional law whereby incurable disease excluded the heir-apparent from the throne of Prussia.

On the other hand, he gave us clearly to understand that he would not assume the sceptre if it were established beyond question that he was incurably attacked by cancer; which was in accordance with his fine unselfish way of thinking. As this was known, those who (for motives over which we had no control) desired to bring the Emperor Frederick, even though incapacitated for government, to the throne, made it their object to deceive the exalted patient as to his condition. It is now established beyond question that an unimportant English physician of Radical political opinions took upon himself to play the Privy Councillor, and interfere directly in the history of the German nation.

By this semi-official declaration Bismarck, before all the world, displayed his old enemy Victoria as nothing less than the indirect cause of the premature death of her husband; he plainly hinted that she preferred to be the widowed Empress rather than the wife of an abjuring Prince, the victim of cancer. Her character, and her behaviour during the illness, lend some colour to this view of her ill-considered proceedings. It is true, moreover, that external pressure was brought to bear on her; and Bismarck himself details the English influences, wholly beyond his control, which urged the necessity of keeping the Crown Prince available for the succession, because his anti-Russian views were of infinite value to England (L. 97). But we must do Victoria the justice to say that she was certainly no tigress, but much the reverse—an emotional affectionate woman; and therefore not to be blamed for hoping against hope that her husband's life might be saved.

She stands indicted, nevertheless, for serious indiscretion. She summoned from her native land an undistinguished physician, simply because she attributed a shortcoming of Nature to the physicians of the land she had adopted. Or did she wish, in love and sympathy, to conceal his doom from her husband? On this supposition she should have sought, before the German doctors gave their opinion, to forbid their utterance of the fatal word; even that attempt, though condemned to failure, would have saved her in the eyes of posterity. If the Englishman spoke the truth, the Crown Prince then, for the first time in his life, came to a decision alone and in secret, hiding from his consort that on which for thirty years their mutual hopes had centred. But since the doctor described himself as "the confidant of both Their Highnesses," how much more likely was he to be hers, who had caused her countryman to be instructed beforehand in London, who was the first to speak with him at Potsdam, giving her wishes to be known or at any rate perceived! And had she not really something to fear from her son, if he, whom for so long she had morally ill-treated, should come to power before she did?

The course of events, moreover, sustains Bismarck's indictment. Through all that year Victoria maintained the fiction that the Crown Prince was only slightly ailing, that he was better, that he would soon be well—not only by numerous despatches and protests to the public at large, whom on political grounds there was perhaps good reason to delude; but with her personal friends and with her children she acted this part for thirteen months, during which her husband was visibly failing at her side. Immediately after the fateful decision in June came her mother's Jubilee. Was she to be absent from that? And was her eldest son to bask in that reflected glory? No—and against the advice of her most trusted friends Victoria forced her suffering, already wellnigh voiceless husband to ride high upon his horse in the London procession, in the hope of silencing by that parade the whisperings of rumour.

During this English sojourn Mackenzie declined to permit a prolonged supervision of the patient by Professor Gerhardt, and concealed the growth of the tumour from sufferer and physicians alike. "Whoever brought about the absence of Gerhardt, is responsible for the fatal turn of events," says Bergmann (whose documents in Buchholtz's biography we here follow). Then the English party prevented the Crown Prince's return to Berlin, and they wandered, without German physicians, from one spa to another; yet when one considers the unremitting care shown by Victoria during all this time, one is again persuaded that she really thought it impossible her husband could be suffering from cancer.

At the beginning of November, a sudden change for the worse. A sojourn at San Remo, decisive position taken up by the doctors, *communiqué* in the *Reichsanzeiger* that the heir to the throne was attacked by cancer; nevertheless an operation was not to take place, for the patient did not desire it, and moreover it was probably too late. "Prince William is entrusted with the Regency."

From this day forward the Prince's every nerve was strained. He was now in point of fact Crown Prince, and had only to await the speedy departure of a nonagenarian, and a fatally stricken, forerunner. And now the hatred of the parents for their son reached a commensurable intensity. Thirty years of waiting—and then, Nothingness! And this crude boy was to step into the vainly longed-for sovereignty like an idle stroller—not one hour of patience or of struggle! Frederick's Regent? Then already he was looked upon as dead? "I am not yet an idiot, or incapable!" exclaimed the sufferer, when he heard of his relegation.

But soon afterwards, relapsing to the acceptation of his doom, his musings were on death and God alone. The life-long patience he had practised he resolved to keep unto the end; and when a few days after the tidings, his eldest son arrived at San Remo, and the mother, standing on the steps, attempted to dismiss him, he perceived his father smiling to him from the terrace (L. 402). Henceforward, in these his last moments, we shall see the Crown Prince's former arrogance but rarely blaze forth.

Victoria, on the contrary, was no less overwrought than her son. "The circumstances are enough to raise one's hair," was the Prince's account on his return; his mother was declaring the German doctors to be humbugs and trying to hunt them away; "she treated me like a dog" (W. 333). A high-placed officer, coming from San Remo, described her in Waldersee's presence as "nearly out of her mind. It is even thought that she is intriguing with Orleans against Berlin." But at Christmas she wrote home: "We were very cheerful, and indeed we had no reason for depression, for your father is getting on well. The only sad thing is the great age of your grandparents" (E. 155). How cold they are, these phrases! What must the youthful son, who in-dignantly showed them to his friend, have thought of woman's capacity for feeling when he read such a letter from his mother's hand?

The same tone in Berlin. While the people's prayers were demanded for the heir-apparent's recovery, Society was dancing every night. Eulenburg depicts the general consternation at the change for the worse as prodigious; but "the Lucullus supper" at Borckhardt's, where the conversation turned exclusively on the sufferer and on Victoria's shortcomings, "lasted from seven o'clock till midnight." Even his daughter Victoria danced through half the night, and declared: "It's all fuss about Papa."

Only the old, old Emperor cannot sleep. He never speaks of his son, but he thinks of him, feels himself deprived of his natural prop, and as he is just expecting a visit from the Tsar, repeats over and over again to himself, in the night-watches, the things he is to say and wants to say to him. "A dream in which the Tsar, with no one to receive him, stood waiting in the railway station, distressed him so much that he frequently told us of it" (E. 146). Where is my son? the old man muses. Who will take my place? inquires his sense of duty, with its ninety years upon it. For he knows that the times are very dark, that war and peace are once more in the balance.

Towards Christmas Bismarck for the first time brings the Prince into the Council Chamber. In a circle round the ninety-yeared Emperor sit Moltke, eighty-seven; Bismarck, seventy-two; Albedyll, sixty-three; Waldersee, fifty-six; with them Prince William, slim and restless, a youth who to-morrow may be all-powerful. In the freshly critical situation the Emperor desires to hear his Councillors' opinion about the war on two fronts, begins to talk about old times, and how loth he would be to draw the sword against the Tsar. "I said to him, 'If you were to make war upon us in alliance with France, you would be the stronger and could annihilate us. But, believe me, Europe would not suffer it to happen.'"

With silent consternation the circle hears these dangerous veracities from its supreme war-lord, reckoning the effect of such words at the Russian Court, where it is said that Prussia is feared. "I felt an icy shiver down my back," writes Waldersee. For the rest, the old man declares that if it comes to the worst he intends to go to the Western front. The gentlemen under eighty think "What absurdity!" "Go to war with a nonagenarian Emperor, a dying Crown Prince, and a Field-Marshal of eighty-seven!" (W. 345).

The Emperor treats the Prince "like a child" (E. 155), and bids him not talk about the proceedings. What does the Prince learn from this conference?

2

When his father's disease declared itself, he began to brood feverishly: he seemed to hear the approach of distant beating drums, the drums of power. In those days he opened his heart to his friend, who was staying with him. After he had listened to "Phili's" ballads, he took him into his "delightful bedroom," as the effeminate Eulenburg calls it, declared that the German doctors' diagnosis was correct, and spoke

gravely, but without any warmth of feeling. His father has always been a stranger to him, his mother is the Englishwoman hostile to the Fatherland; and his inheritance from that mother—a strong, inflexible will—now turns, in his devoted love for that Fatherland, against her to whom he owes its strength. I said to the Prince that the thought appalled me, that I held it to be an infinitely difficult task for so young a man to succeed the great old Emperor. The Prince was silent. His position is unalterably this . . . that the reign of the Crown Prince, that is to say, the Crown Princess, would mean the ruin of Germany.

Then, on the November evening of his return from San Remo, he talked very excitedly to the same friend about the question of the Regency; and when his brother Henry, who was heart and soul of the mother's party, vehemently opposed him, Prince William cried: "In any case it is very questionable if a man who cannot speak has any right whatever to become King of Prussia!" (E. 147). To his friend he said confidentially: "I am ready at any moment, I have thought out everything that I mean to do; at the decisive moment there's no time for thinking, so everything must be ready beforehand!" And when Eulenburg showed him, in his old castle, a screen on which the peoples were depicted as a mighty river flowing from antiquity to the Napoleonic era, William looked only at the little stream which represented Prussia, and said: "This shall be a very big one some day!" (E. 138). About the same time he said to Puttkammer when they were together at a shoot: "When *I* come on, I'll have no Jews in the Press"; and when the Minister happened to allude to the industrial ordinances: "Then we'll get rid of the industrial ordinances!" (L. 410).

How panting, burning, is the eager spirit! And how unbridled is the heartless impatience that anticipates the death of his two elders! Ignorant alike of the rights of subjects and of international affairs, yet firmly convinced of his vocation to be useful to his country—so much too early called to power, he is almost a pathetic figure as, in contemplation of world-history, his young eyes gaze on only Prussia: "*This* shall be a very big one some day!"

And already everyone he encountered began the work of destroying him. Secretly, writes Lucius, "All observers constantly remark upon his immaturity, which at the age of twenty-nine is truly extraordinary." But to himself and his intimates, who might repeat it to him, everyone loudly extolled his "firm character, and great promise for the future. . . . The very people who had been intriguing against the Prince now see that he will soon be Emperor, and are looking out for favours" (W. 327). His military rank, moreover, was prematurely enhanced by the impending crisis. At Christmas-time the old monarch was still refusing to promote his grandson, but later he yielded and made him a General on his twenty-ninth birthday. The Prince did not see that the order was instinct with distrust—he saw only that he, so young, had got so far; and began to tell himself that the promotion naturally ensued from his own qualifications.

The friend of his heart did nothing to enlighten him, did everything to destroy him the sooner by his adulation, for the Prince read any letter from this hand with something approaching worship. And he read in them that Eulenburg's children had said "how divinely handsome" the Prince looked in uniform; and that his friend, who writes like a lover, had at the New Year reception in Munich, surrounded by indifferent courtiers,

thought of Potsdam, of our sledge-drives, of our intimate companionship; and a sense of such ardent friendship came over me that suddenly I felt all the surrounding glitter as an unendurable affliction. How human is my nearness to you—and how it torments me to think that the social gulf between us, now bridged by our friendship, must inevitably become even wider, even deeper, when the Imperial Crown is yours!

Observe the tone—the dulcet idyllic tone—which this expert in adaptability could use as cleverly as that of cynical brilliancy in the society of older men; and always gracefully phrased, for everyone of these letters, which he selected for his Memoirs after many decades had gone by, are very intimate, written by his own hand, no copies taken; he prints them from the rough drafts he had preserved.

Incidentally, he advises his friend on high political matters, which his subtle pen contrived to mingle so skilfully with dreamy fancies and gossip about things of art that they would not be tedious to the eager recipient.

That he was intent on his own advancement would be nothing against him, if he did not so continually represent himself as despising place and worldly advantages. He writes, on his appointment to be Councillor to the Embassy: "I tell this to your Royal Highness in a spirit of pure friendship, because I know that it will give you pleasure to learn that I have obtained a position which will enable me to be of use to my beloved monarch, and the Fatherland— and that is my best reward." Whereupon his friend promoted him to Ambassador.

Such was the nature of the man of whom William said about this time to Hinzpeter: "My bosom friend Eulenburg, the only one I have!" (E. 2, 46). Nowhere was there anyone to guide the Prince, to counsel him—or even seek to warn him.

One man alone is incorruptible—him the Prince tries vainly to impress. When on the first night of Eulenburg's romantic drama he comes, all nervous agitation, to visit the Prince, he finds him bent over the rough draft of a proclamation to the German Princes for the day of his accession. It is only November, 1887; but the Prince is intent on having "everything ready before hand." Instead of hindering this literary labour, Eulenburg (by his own account) edits it for his friend. His friend sends it to Bismarck:

"I venture herewith to forward to your Serene Highness a paper which, in view of the not impossible contingency of the early or sudden demise of the Emperor and my father, I have drawn up. . . . It is a brief edict to my future col-

leagues, the German Princes of the Holy Roman Empire."
As it might not be agreeable to these princes to be subjected
to so young a master, they must be left no time for brooding
on the change. "So it is my idea that . . . this proclamation should be deposited, sealed, in every Embassy, and in
the event of my accession be at once handed by the Ambassadors to their respective Princes." He hopes that the
old uncles will not put a spoke in their dear young nephew's
wheel. . . . "As between nephew and uncle I can easily
humour these gentlemen by various little attentions. And
when I have once shown them the sort of man they have to
deal with, and got them under my thumb, they will obey me
the more good-humouredly. For obey me they must!"

This is the first constitutional effort of Prince William's
brain, and also the first document approved and edited by
Eulenburg. No one will ever know what cynical comment
Bismarck may have made to his son, as he perused the tactless, ignorant pages. Nor did they come alone.

Hard upon them followed a second composition, concerned with various socialistic activities of these Princes,
which he thought that Bismarck was opposed to:

My veneration, high as it is cordial, and my heartfelt attachment
to Your Serene Highness . . . I would be torn limb from limb
rather than put my hand to anything which could embarrass you
. . . this would—I mean, *should*—be sufficient guarantee. [If
war should come] you will not forget that here a hand and sword
are ready, those of a man who is very conscious that Frederick the
Great is his ancestor . . . and for whom his ten years' strenuous
military training has not been altogether in vain! For the rest,
Allerwege gute Zollere! [1] In most loyal friendship,

WILLIAM, PRINCE OF PRUSSIA.

---

[1] *Zollere* is a familiar way of speaking of the Hohenzollerns. This phrase
may therefore be rendered as "A Hohenzollern every time!" [Translator's
Note.]

The old man subtly smiles. The more extravagant the superlatives of veneration, the more doubtful he feels of the Prince's sincerity. Is he trying now to win him over by soft nothings? He gives himself six weeks before he answers the two letters with his own hand, for "my hand does not serve me so well for letter-writing as of old. Moreover, my answer had to be nothing less than an historical and political essay." He returns the proclamation to the Princes, "and would most respectfully advise that it be burnt without delay. . . . Even the single existing copy, which I kept most carefully locked up, may fall into the wrong hands." How much more dangerous would be some twenty copies! What would the Princes say on learning that the proclamation had been drawn up during the lifetime of reigning monarchs, and kept in readiness for their deaths? For the rest, he is there to protect their constitutional rights.

But I seek my surest support . . . In a monarchy whose representative is resolved, not only diligently to co-operate with me in the work of government during times of peace, but likewise at more critical periods to be ready, rather than yield, to die upon the steps of the throne, sword in hand, contending for his royal rights.

Then he ironically advises against any sort of participation in Christian-Socialist activities, and concludes with a cold acknowledgment of the "gracious confidence" shown him.

There he sits—the old man in his study at Friedrichsruh; it is January, the room is overheated; he must drive the steel pen with his own hand as he writes the eight-page letter to his master's heir, for not even to his son does he dare to dictate it. And, sitting there, he has a moment of pure insight. He warns the Prince against levity and indolence; and suddenly he seems to see him stand before his eyes in a moment of awful crisis, menaced in his rights, in his throne, and tells him solemnly that he had better die contending than give in! Ominous words, written by Bismarck, then seventy-three, to William the Second, immediately before his accession in the year of Our Lord 1888. What was to be their effect?

Instead of hearkening, the Prince brings the correspondence to a sudden end. In social affairs, he replies, his desire is to concede so far as to dissipate all mistrust. "If this fails, then woe to them whom I command!" A new note, this: a sudden fanfaronade! Then a courtly conclusion, as it were a bow, a clinking of spurred heels together—but there is a threat implied, based on the right which soon is to be his, the right to command while others "obey" him.

Meanwhile the sick man pants for breath beside the Mediterranean Sea. The old Emperor has fainting-fits. When the Crown Prince seemed like to suffocate on 9th February, and Mackenzie still refused to operate, an adjutant at last had the courage to confront him angrily with: "If you do not get Bramann here" (Bergmann's assistant, always in readiness) "you shall be summoned before a court-martial!" After vehement contention between Bramann and the Crown Princess, the patient underwent the operation for insertion of a tube, at which Bramann had to be both operator and anæsthetist, for Mackenzie was near to fainting and, as he said afterwards, "more dead than alive."

Between the old man sinking and his son expiring the final race begins—the last, the unseen, contest. Victoria trembles; "there is a strong current of popular feeling against her" (E. 146). She "scarcely seems a responsible being, so fanatically does she uphold the idea that her husband is not seriously ill" (W. 365). Prince William is beside himself, for he alone of all the children may not go to San Remo; he goes without warning, finds himself treated as in November, his mother demanding that he shall proceed to Rome, so as to confirm the better news of his father. Bismarck bids him come back.

What a state we should all be in [thus muses Waldersee] if the Emperor were now to be taken from us; the most horrible complications are indeed unavoidable. It is true that the Crown Prince cannot govern, but under pressure from his vehement consort he could do a lot of harm. And she, precisely because she knows that her rule must be a brief one . . . will seek to safeguard her future. The question is how far Prince William will suffer things to go.

A few days later, the worst comes to pass.

In his little room the old man lies upon his old camp-bed, in a white jacket with a red scarf round his neck; the Empress has been rolled in her chair to his bedside, members of the family and intimates are crowded in the narrow space; Prince William too stands near. The Emperor dies a soldier. In these last days of his life his fancy turns on war alone—war future and war past. "I am not afraid of war, if I am driven to it," he says as if to himself. He thinks he is talking to the Tsar: "I hope he won't break his word." Repeatedly they hear him speak of the war on two fronts; then of the Fourth Battalion and the tactics of the French. Now his mind recurs to the French campaign, but not the last one, which is scarce twenty years gone by; he is back at the War of Liberation; "and there he stopped. He spoke the names of several officers belonging to that period, who had been with him there" (W. 269).

When Bismarck hands him the order for prorogation of

the Reichstag, and says the "W" will suffice, he answers with his old sense of duty: "I'll sign the full name," but he cannot quite manage it. Then suddenly he takes Bismarck, who is bending close to his ear, for his grandson, addresses him as if he were Prince William, and says: "I've always been pleased with you. You've done everything well."

With this arresting confusion of identities in favour of his grandson, the life of William the First comes to an end.

3

"In my profound grief for my father, at whose death it was granted not to me, but to you, to be present, I make known on my accession my absolute reliance on your being a pattern to all others in loyalty and obedience."

With this ominous invocation to Berlin the moribund began his reign as German Emperor. Simultaneously it was announced that the new Crown Prince was not to be entrusted with the Regency, but that the Ministry of State would be called upon, if necessary, to exercise that function. Not until the answer came from Bismarck was it pointed out to him that in his hatred for his son he had sought to act unconstitutionally. The third day, on his homeward journey, he received Chancellor and Minister at Leipzig. The proceedings were subdued, all the conversation was in writing; the entry to Berlin, of which he so long had dreamed, was voiceless as himself; and behind the corpse of his father, on the hour-long transit, it was not he that marched, but—alone, in front of all the Princes—his son William, the true inheritor.

With his strong sense of allegory and gesture William —now Crown Prince—must have felt that this progress through the Tiergarten, cutting across the dumbly saluting

multitudes, was a symbol of succession. Not until the out-
lying Charlottenburg was reached did the son, through the
closed window, salute the dead father—the grandson, the
dying son.

In a little room at the Palace the Emperor Frederick
received the oath of allegiance from those nearest him; the
Lord Chamberlain went down upon one knee, the Ministers
kissed the new master's hand—even Bismarck. Before the
King of Prussia his arrogance was subdued—before him
alone. The patina of conceptions old as time, the sense of
dependence, long-implanted, ineradicable: these enforce that
kiss upon the hand which seems a contradiction of his inmost
being: it affronts his self-esteem in no wise, he feels like any
knight. True, his old master had caught him in his arms,
when on the seventieth birthday the Chancellor had bent to
kiss hands; he of to-day accepts the gesture, savouring perhaps the pseudo-victory over his ancient foe with the ultimate vibrations of his failing energy.

But the contest was over; he knew himself to be a flame
extinguished, and resigned all power to the dictator—even
extended that power, for his ideas confined themselves to
trifles such as the doing-away with epaulettes after the English fashion, and one of his earliest questions was: "Whose
likeness shall we choose for the new coins?" And when he
learnt that they could not be ready before Whitsuntide, it
was observed by Lucius that he clasped his hands together
with a woeful look, as though feeling that he would not live
to see them. The first desires of this Liberal were to make
new Barons, Counts, and Princes, so that Bismarck iron-
ized: "In order to remove the jealousy between the middle-
classes and the nobility, the Emperor wanted to ennoble his
entire people." When Bismarck himself was offered the

title of Duke, and Herbert that of Prince, he urgently begged that this proposal should be abandoned, and accounted for his disinclination with all his cynicism: "Why, if I had two million dollars, I would have myself made Pope!"

Beyond this playing at power, the Emperor had no strength to go. To the Minister Friedberg, of Jewish parentage, he gave the Black Eagle; but after at first refusing, he signed the Socialist decrees, and yielded likewise on a European question. Then his desire was that the Battenberg Prince should come, in pursuance of the old English project, to Berlin for his betrothal to their daughter; Bismarck, however, who just then dared do nothing to offend Russia, wished to postpone the arrangement, and in his mortal weariness the sufferer at once gave in. "The consequence was a frightful scene between the Emperor and Empress" (W. 382).

So full of strife and hatred, so vibrant with convulsive reverberations, was the life of this family, was the youth of William the Second.

But the old spell-binder now succeeded in winning over, in mastering, his deadly enemy. "I behave," he said to Lucius, "to the Empress like an enamoured dotard." That is to say, he put so much money in the excited woman's pocket that she never opposed him. Even the earliest days of her home-coming rustled with official papers. First, she made "exorbitant claims for her jointure" (W. 375): then was enraged because the old Emperor had remembered his grandsons, but not his grand-daughters, in his will; and most of all because he had left his entire private fortune—the twenty-two millions he had saved—in trust for the family, thus making it untouchable. Confusion and distraction ruled the day. Bismarck found a way out; the will did not speak of a trust, but of a "Crown Treasury" as administering the property. Legal opinion pronounced: "The son has power of disposal." Frederick at once made it over in equal parts to his wife and children (W. 403). With these eleven millions, which, according to other legal opinions, could have been sequestrated from Victoria, Bismarck broke down her opposition.

Thus were her revenues assured. Her honours were less so. There could be no question of a Coronation, and so the Englishwoman revived an Old-Prussian Custom—that of the Mourning-Court, at which she presided alone, thus savouring for once in her life the homage of the first men and women in the kingdom. Waldersee

was close to the throne as she approached it. . . . She tried to assume a regal bearing, flung her head back, and took the two steps not slowly, but as it were at a leap. Despite the black veil, from my sidelong viewpoint I could get a good look at her face; and reading it, my impression was that she revelled in being the centre of attention.

Bismarck let her have her own way. Although he admired the Emperor's endurance and reviled the roughness of the English doctors and nurses, he forbore to intervene. "If everything I am told is true, and not exaggerated, it would take a Royal Commission to protect the Emperor against the Empress" (Ho. 430). With wine and other stimulants she had him strung-up to make public appearances, at the conclusion of which he would utterly collapse; when a tent was pronounced needful for the asthmatic man to sleep in, she made him wait until an English pattern came from over the sea. When Mackenzie, who would use only his own tube, one day anxiously summoned

Bergmann to Potsdam, the latter found the Emperor suffocating. "In a few minutes the danger was removed by the insertion of the tube I had brought with me." Against the doctor's wishes, Victoria about this time obliged the invalid to drive in state to Berlin; finally, three weeks before his death, he was forced to assist at a wedding in Charlottenburg, where those sitting near him in the chapel could see and hear his piteous gasps for breath. "When he stood up, his tense bearing betrayed a fearful strain . . . then the Emperor left the chapel in three long strides. About a quarter of an hour later the guests saw him going by in an invalid-chair . . . he was in plain dress, utterly collapsed."

During these Hundred Days the hostility to their son mounted still higher; but this in itself contributed to strengthen his position. When in the early weeks there was again talk of his Regency, the attempt was frustrated, "because the wish to injure their son is clearly evident" (W. 372). But when the father, whom the son was scarcely even allowed to see, was obliged from sheer impotence to capitulate, the heir felt himself strong enough to make conditions. As the Liberal group, which reckoned on Frederick, was a small one, all hopes were increasingly fixed on the Crown Prince; and the consciousness of this liberated in him only too much of the mother's imperiousness and self-will (W. 402), inherited by her from her own mother, and now active in her son.

After all that he had undergone, and still had to undergo, in his home-life, no one can wholly blame the young man for the cold-heartedness of his anticipation, when, walking up and down with his intimates, he merely observed: "It's quite a good thing that my father has reigned for a while before me"; then talked circumstantially of formalities and persons.

precisely as Frederick had just been doing; and when Wal- dersee, unusually disturbed by such indifference, urged him to implore his father's blessing, the Prince replied: "Oh, I have *that* all right. . . . But my mother will never let me be alone with him" (W. 389).

About this time he said himself to his mother: "It would have been a good thing if Papa had been killed at Wörth" (which was nineteen years before).

"But, William, do you think nothing of the happiness he has had all the time—that I, that we all, have had?"

"No—even so, it would have been better" (Dohme, *Deutsche Revue,* 37, 84).

It is not lovable, but it is comprehensible, in a Prince who had had little happiness from his father in those twenty years; and who, moreover, liked other people to die in ro- mantic circumstances.

The invalid took a good turn; but the heir to the throne, with power coming ever nearer to his grasp, got haughtier every day. He gave Herbert Bismarck an appointment at the Palace for a quarter to two; when the latter drove in "at two minutes past the three-quarters, the Crown Prince drove past him, saluting," having left a message to say that he had to inspect his Hussars, and would His Excellency be at the Potsdam Station at ten minutes past five. So that their business would have had to be transacted in, at the most, three minutes. Then at the station, to Herbert: "I have no time to read documents." Herbert was not only Secretary of State, but had been for years his intimate friend; never before would the Prince, who had drunk deep with him through many a night, have dismissed him in a minute or two. But now, the Emperor's representative, he was prey to the old uncertainty of touch—he affected the overdriven young ruler; and with barely a word of apology, passed on after a casual salutation.

This avoidance of the son was aimed indirectly at the father; the Crown Prince declared that he would give Bismarck no voice in military matters, "and I think the good Herbert sets some store on the preservation of my friendship" (W. 375). On the Chancellor's birthday Prince William compared the situation to that of a storming regiment: "Their leader has fallen, the next in command, though severely wounded, yet rides fearlessly on." These words put the invalid beside himself; he wrote his son a savage letter (W. 384).

All this was in April. In May, when his father was on the point of death, the son went further still—he began to interfere in foreign affairs. Bismarck infuriated him; for when he took to covering the documents with marginal notes as Frederick the Great had been wont to do, the Chancellor begged him to desist, because such remarks had to be registered, and this obstructed business. Then in an official communication, edited by Waldersee, the Crown Prince warned the Chancellor against Russia: "Doubtless if at Versailles we had deprived France of her fortresses and her fleet we should not now be menaced by this dual danger." "That," continues the writer, administering a judicial censure to the old statesman, "that was, from a military point of view, mistaken, though from a political one . . . at the moment, the right course"; but since then the two neighbours had cherished aggressive intentions against Germany. In this communication, "I consider that I am offering most necessary aid towards the conduct of a pacific policy . . . William, Crown Prince of the German Empire and of Prussia." Over this signature Bismarck's pencil wrote in large letters the five cryptic words: "It would be unfortunate, if——"

Here we have it, issue joined already. The Crown Prince, who was Regent only for current affairs and not empowered either in this matter or a constitutional one to intervene at all, no longer clothes his communications, as heretofore, in the form of respectful interrogatories. He designates his aid as "necessary"; and thereupon the old statesman appends to the swaggering official signature a dark saying wherein he discloses all that he appears to conceal.

The Emperor, remote from these contentions, was dying daily. Two weeks before the end he went with Victoria to Potsdam, their old home. There he had been born, there their young married life had first flowered; and now, at the end of his course, an emaciated figure, voiceless, his face gone to nothing, his breath febrile; in possession of a crown for which the waiting had been too prolonged, and which he must renounce all hope of wearing—*now* the Emperor Frederick rechristens the New Palace with the name of "Friedrichskron.". . . . Shortly before, the old Queen had come over from England, desirous to guard her daughter's rights and look after her own; the son-in-law wrote her his welcome on a sheet of paper; she troubled him but little; he sat at the window and heard the multitudes gather round the Palace-gates. His daily written question was of the official reports of his state; he was particularly touched by the sympathetic comments in the French newspapers. Once he had his horses brought into the garden, and tried to feed them.

Up to the last days Victoria played her chosen part; at the end of May she was still denying that it was cancer. Two days before his death, when the Palace and all Germany were expectant of the end, the mother and son had a "violent scene": she would not suffer him to go near his father.

On the day before the Emperor died, Bismarck appeared at the Palace; Victoria led him into the sick man's room. He knew them both, and with a last effort of will he joined their hands and held them closely together with both his own. "To whom in the world"—so felt the dying man—"shall I entrust her? My life is over; now she will have enmity around her. This man here is the most powerful of all, let come what may; upon him she shall build." Not a sign that he wished to see, to bless, or even to admonish the heir to his crown. Bismarck was the last to receive Frederick's confidence—the only man to whom he would entrust his much-loved consort.

Scarcely had the two left his room before it was the old story: steel upon steel. Victoria declared that she required a castle on the Rhine as her jointure-house—that her son would have to consent. "But it must be a house," she added, while her husband's dying gasps could be heard through the door, "where I can pull down and build and arrange to my own taste, without consulting the Home Secretary." Bismarck, for his part, though he was moved, said to an intimate: "I can't go in for sentimental politics just now" (Ho. 473). He went to the future Emperor, found him "very rational," and made his own principles of action clear to him (L. 465). When, in the forenoon of the following day, he was communicating all this to the assembled Ministers, there came the tidings of the end.

4

For twenty-four hours the Palace—an eye-witness, Robert von Dohme, the Emperor Frederick's friend, gives this account—had been filled with hitherto unseen officers, who demanded quarters and rations; then, some hours before the end, the new Master of the Household hastened to promulgate the new ruler's orders: "No one in the Palace, including the doctors, to carry on any correspondence with outside. . . . If any of the doctors attempts to leave the Palace, he will be arrested." Dohme asked the old Master of the Household, already superseded, if the codicil regarding the Empress's inheritance, and above all the assignment of the sum for the landed property she desired, were in safe hands. "Fortunately Seckendorf had them in his desk; otherwise it would have been too late."

Shortly after eleven, death having but just occurred, the scene was thus transformed; it was as though a monarch had been murdered, and his hostile successor, long prepared, had seized upon the newly acquired authority.

Divisions of training-battalions approached the Palace at the double; round all the terraces was a regular system of guards with loaded guns. Major von Natzmer, one of the intruders of the night before, sat ready mounted, and the moment death was announced he galloped round the Palace, giving orders, inspecting guards. Suddenly the Hussars appeared at a trot; divisions established themselves at all the gates of the Park; the Palace was, in the military sense, hermetically sealed.

The doctors decided to summon Virchow to a post-mortem, and when the Surgeon-General was about to convey the despatch, the guard on the terrace ordered him to "Halt!" on pain of arrest. Anyone who wished to leave the Palace had to have a permit from the new master's aide-de-camp; telegrams had to bear his visâ.

Thus everyone—to the doctors, the brothers and sisters,

and even the mother of the new Emperor—was his prisoner. Vainly did the mother appeal to the young Empress; her son, suspecting that State-papers had for weeks been going to London, now stood sentry over the Palace in whose midst lay the dead Emperor.

For summoning of clergy, for a family-gathering, there was no time that day. "In the dead man's room . . . no ceremonial, no service . . . no thought of the religious aspect" (E. 169). The son, that he might indict his mother and grandmother, ordained the post-mortem; it ratified the German diagnosis of thirteen months ago. He himself walked up and down the park with Waldersee, again conversing of individuals. Soon afterwards he was handed a sealed envelope, which by tradition had to be delivered to every King of Prussia upon his accession. It contained an adjuration from Frederick William IV to all his successors, calling upon them to abrogate at once a form of government which had been wrung from him by force.[1] The new Emperor burnt the document (Z. 104). Was he so profoundly convinced of his duty to protect that form of government that he would fain keep from *his* successors any cognisance of the dead monarch's wish?

Even before the funeral, the son demolished the wish of his father's heart.[2]

In case [that father had written in his will, on the twelfth of April], in case I am . . . summoned hence, I wish to have set in evidence as my unbiassed personal opinion that I entirely ac-

---

[1] Frederick William IV, King of Prussia (1795–1861), was opposed to the unification of Germany, and refused the crown offered him by the German Princes. His mind became deranged before his death.—[Translator's Note.]

[2] For further information concerning the relations of the Princess Victoria with her husband's illness and with the selection as a medical advisor of Dr. Morell Mackenzie see note in the Appendix.

quiesce in the betrothal of your second sister with the . . . Prince Alexander of Battenberg. I charge you as a filial duty with the accomplishment of this my desire, which your sister Victoria for so many years has cherished in her heart. . . . I count upon your fulfilling your duty as a son by a precise attention to my wishes, and as a brother by not withdrawing your co-operation from your sister. Your affectionate Father (Hartenau-Archives, quoted by Corti, p. 336).

Two days after his father's death, the son not only broke off the engagement, in which proceeding he had Bismarck's veto to appeal to, but in his letter of apology to Battenberg he pointedly alluded to "the profound conviction previously held by my late deceased grandfather and father"; this, solely because the marriage was the wish of his mother's heart.

"With unprecedented haste" the funeral was organized. The dead man was clad in his uniform. Foreign princes were not invited; and while the chapel was being decorated, the coffin stood among the hammering workmen like a toolchest. At the entombment, the short path to the church was guarded by troops. "The troops were dignified, the clergy were laughing and chattering. Field-Marshal Blumenthal, with the Standard over his shoulder, reeling about, talking —it was horrible" (E. 169).

The populace was not allowed to come near. Nor did the new ruler remember his people in his maiden proclamations. On the first day went forth an Army and a Navy Order, long prepared and needing only to have the hour of his father's death filled in; the tone was somewhat over-virile, concluding with:

Thus we belong to each other—I and the Army—we were born for each other and will cleave indissolubly to each other, whether it be the Will of God to send us calm or storm. You will soon swear fealty and submission to me, and I promise ever to bear in mind that from the world above the eyes of my forefathers look down upon me, and that I shall have one day to stand accountable to them for the glory and honour of the Army.

Foreign countries were startled: though the new ruler might have warlike intentions, it was surely inconceivable that he would appear in arms on the opening day of his reign! As the European situation had for some time been threatening, the tone of foreign newspaper comments was uneasy. But the Emperor was not thinking of war when he wrote all this; he was thinking only of the Guards, the officers, the General Staff; for the thousandth time he was feeling, and more keenly than ever before, the eyes of all his soldiers fixed upon him. Would a critical glance fall on his arm? Would anyone notice how he passed the reins over? And so he was fain to pull on them the tighter— reins of the horse and reins of the government; "hard-bitten" was to be the first impression when that night his earliest imperial utterance should be discussed in clubs and messes, and next morning be recited in countless barrack-yards to the sound of the trumpet.

Three days later he did remember his people. All proclamations "he wrote himself, rejecting any one else's suggestions." In that to his people he led off again with a boast of his father's victories, but continued:

Summoned to the throne of my fathers, it is with eyes raised to the King of Kings that I assume the sceptre, and I vow before God to be to my people a just and merciful Prince, to do all things in piety and godly fear, to keep the peace, to promote the welfare of the country, to be a succourer of the poor and oppressed, a faithful guardian of the right. . . . Upon this fealty . . . I count, well knowing that with all my heart I shall requite it, as the loyal sovereign of a loyal people, both unwavering in devotion to their common Fatherland.

Germany heard these fine phrases, and was pleased. Many asked: "Is this a religious Prince, with his frequent appeals to God?" He was, in his way; for when here, and in countless future discourses, he appealed to his forefathers in heaven, who were looking down upon him—that represented his genuine belief. "Take my faith from me, and you take my King," said Bismarck, though his was a much more complex faith than William's, and it was only through the medium of love that he, who had been a pronounced atheist, became a believer. The principle is identical in both. Bismarck thus reconciled a subject's loyalty with his personal pride, William thus justified his regal arrogance; Bismarck could not have kissed the hand of his sovereign but for his belief in a divinely appointed order wherein he, for all his limitless self-esteem, came only second. William, as a Christian, could interpret that kiss, could interpret the power and the glory that were his, by the same means alone—that of a God-given order.

Unwittingly he misconstrued Charlemagne's reverential title of *Dei Gratia Imperator,* reversing its import; and while that Emperor of the past, kneeling to his God, thus read the meaning of his posture before Him to whom he owed all earthly power, this Emperor of the present, beholding men upon their knees before himself, held this to be so because he was ruler by the Grace of God. His overweening disposition, inherited from both parents, uncorrected by a sensible education, aggravated by the oppressions of his youth, inborn and ever guilelessly revealed—this had

a double use for God, and one use was a wrong use. **God**
was his shield against the megalomania which might have
made him claim equality with pagan deities; but likewise
against his people and those fellow-creatures, one and all,
who were not born like him to kingship, and so were not like
him endowed with authority by God. Throughout his royal
life, William the Second felt like a king of antiquity who was
High Priest as well, literally mediator between God and
People; and from this consciousness he drew the most far-
reaching inferences, especially with regard to kingdoms and
republics.

The Weisser Saal in the Palace at Berlin shone by his
orders, a week later, more brilliantly than it had ever shone
before in the history of Prussia. He had the Palace-Guard
dressed in the uniform of Frederick the Great's time; the
Knights of the Black Eagle were bidden to appear in their
scarlet mantles, so that he might wear one himself. Bismarck, who had refused to don this mantle, marched in his
cuirassier's uniform at the head of the Federal Council
(*Bundesrat*), who "followed him like lambs" (M. 145);
and when all were assembled he went himself to summon the
Emperor, thus playing Master of the Household for the day.
Enter the court-pages in their black knee-breeches, with
knots of crape at the knees; then the Insignia of State, then
Moltke alone, then the Emperor, in a long flowing crimson
mantle—no soldier, we perceive, but a legendary king; more
Eulenburg's than Waldersee's—this was his own idea, his
own decision.

Most grave he was, his head bent ceremonially; and soon
"he had another very effective gesture, when the Chancellor
handed him the King's Speech. He grasped it, set his helmet on his head with a vigorous hand, and flung his mantle

back; then, from his full height, he scanned the dumbly expectant audience." That was the great moment; he had been awaiting it through all the week. Now he began to read, at first indistinctly, delivering the phrases jerkily and laboriously. "Though the silence was like death, he could scarcely be heard." But gradually his voice obeyed him, he was speaking more fluently when he came to the most important passage, that in which Bismarck sought to redeem the rodomontade of the first Army Order by a doubly emphasized pacific tone.

On this first of ceremonial occasions his opposition to Bismarck was unmistakably made clear, though they were Bismarck's own words that he was reciting; for, records the younger Moltke,

when he came to the passage: "I am resolved to keep the peace with everyone, so far as in Me lies," he uttered the word "Me" on a note of such resonant beauty that it ran over the entire audience like an electric spark; there was so much in it—the full consciousness of sovereignty, and with that a ring as it were of warning: "But woe to him who shall dare to offend Me." An extraordinary sense of power and self-reliance made itself felt in that single word, so that there was a general shout of rapturous applause.

The only sceptic in that moment was the author of the phrase, for Bismarck had made the speaker continue:

My love for the German Army . . . shall never tempt me to disturb the tranquillity of the country, unless war is irremediably forced upon us by aggression. . . . Far be it from me to use this strength for aggressive purposes. Germany needs neither warlike glory nor acquisitions in any part of the globe, now that she has finally established her right to be a united and independent nation.

Though Bismarck wished in this way to leave no doubt of the desire for peace, unattended by any menace or admonition, he had hoped that the Press would not accentuate the passage. And accustomed to a strict decorum at such inaugurative ceremonies, he was taken by surprise when, against all precedent, the Emperor turned and shook hands with him after the Speech; but the logical chain of his emotions forged itself in the same moment, and for the first, and the last, time he kissed the hand of the third and youngest of his sovereigns. At this spectacle, applause again broke out (L. 470).

5

What had William solemnly sworn as Emperor, and immediately afterwards as King? What bounds were set to his authority by the Constitution of the Empire and the State? To whom was he responsible?

When he was twenty-three there had been promulgated an edict of his grandfather's, wherein Bismarck caused the King to say:

It is My determination that in Prussia no less than in the legislative bodies of My realm there shall be no question of the constitutional right possessed by Me and My successors to the personal direction of the policy of My Government, and that no colour shall be given to the opposite opinion, which holds that the . . . inviolability of the King's person, or the counter-signature required by My Royal Ordinances, has any bearing upon the independent nature of the Royal decisions.

Avidly had the Prince drunk in these phrases, to which he was only too soon to appeal; and his approbation of Bismarck had naturally been increased, when not long afterwards in Parliament he heard him hold forth upon this edict:

If the Emperor has a Chancellor who feels unable to counter-sign whatever represents the Imperial policy, he can dismiss him any day. The Emperor has a much freer hand than the Chancellor, who is dependent on the Imperial will, and can take no step without the Imperial sanction. . . . In this place I can put forth no ex-pression of opinion in which I do not know the Emperor to agree, and for which I have not his authority. . . . In the Constitution, the Minister is merely an almost negligible stop-gap. Whether this is in accordance with constitional theory or not, is entirely in-different to me. In principle the King decides upon the deep, smooth grooves in which alone the policy of Prussia, as part of the German Empire, can proceed. He ordains, by the light of his own convic-tions, how things are to be, and how the Prussian representatives of the Federated States are to be instructed; the part of the Minister is merely to execute, to formulate. The Royal Will is and remains alone decisive. The real, the actual, Prime Minister in Prussia is and remains His Majesty the King.

Before he now proceeded to swear allegiance to the two Constitutions, we may be sure that the young ruler perused them, or at any rate those portions which concerned himself; though he afterwards maintained that he was not acquainted with them at all. What did he find in these "Constitutional" documents, of one of which Bismarck was the author, while the other he had not failed to interpret in the sense most pleasing to the King? A tissue of contradictions, whereby the responsibility was perpetually shifted from the King to the Chancellor-Premier, and by him shifted back on the King, until in the inextricable meshes it expired once for all.

Actually no one in Prussia or Germany was responsible in the democratic sense which to-day prevails in all Euro-pean countries. In very truth, the Emperor-King was abso-lute; the only limitation to his authority was the right of the Houses to grant or refuse supplies; but even this had been set aside by Bismarck, who desired no "shadow-king." True, the Chancellor's counter-signature, which was necessary to the validity of the Imperial decrees, did make him responsible to the Parliament, but only on paper; no Parliament was empowered to remove from office, or even to censure, a Chancellor or Premier. "I shall stand in this place so long as I enjoy His Majesty's confidence": all the Imperial Chancellors and State Secretaries, all the Ministers in Prussia so spoke from the tribunes—and spoke no more than the truth. It was true that the Reichstag, together with the *Bundesrat,* had legislative rights; but the Emperor had the "Imperial-Competence," and invariably found a pliant Chancellor to countersign his decrees.

That this latter had to countersign his own appointment was the finishing touch to the blindman's-buff of responsibilities. Armed with a counter-signature, more easily and unconditionally obtained than, in a great business-house, the like would be by the most senior of its representatives, the Emperor could appoint and dismiss all State officials, could summon, open, prorogue, shut, and dissolve the Reichstag at his pleasure. The direction of international policy was entrusted to him alone: there was no Imperial Cabinet to be consulted; the Chancellor and the Foreign Secretary alone might advise, but must ultimately obey or see themselves replaced by one or another of their colleagues; the Federal Council was practically without influence, its sessional Committees were wellnigh an empty form.

Even that responsibility of the Chancellor's was confined to seeing that the Imperial decrees were in accordance with the Constitution and the Law; to introducing the measures, and taking all criticism on himself. On two important points the Emperor was even formally absolved from any counter-signature: personal expressions of opinion, and Army Orders, were signed by him alone. Relying only on himself, uncounselled if he so desired, fearing no contradiction, no impeachment, the Emperor declared war, concluded peace, held the supreme command in army and fleet; and thus could, acting by himself, compel the whole of his able-bodied subjects to take the field. True, it was necessary that the ever-pliant *Bundesrat* should concur in a declaration of war, but not if there ensued an attack upon the territory of the Empire, to which construction almost every instance lent itself; that the sovereign could make war even without money, in the refusal to grant which the rights of the Reichstag alone consisted, had been demonstrated by Bismarck.

And so the Emperor-King, in his oath, had sworn only to his own actual authority to decide all vital national questions "to the best of his ability"—and on what other principle does any reasonable human being proceed? None the less he remained, whatever the consequences, inviolable, unindictable, or, as it was expressed in other German National Constitutions, "hallowed." At the beginning of the twentieth century, in the Old and the New Worlds, there was—besides the Tsar and the Sultan—no one who possessed such authority as William the Second.

The man to whom he owed it must indeed have been persuaded both of the personal weakness of his sovereign and of his own position and power, when he risked calling himself a stop-gap. This anti-democratic idea was congenial to Bismarck only so long as he could conceal his own authority behind it; were a self-willed king to arrive, such theories were bound to recoil, with tragic retribution, on their propounder. Bismarck had not only, as has often been said, cut the constitution to his own figure, but still more to the tract-ability of the monarch whom his formula had endowed with such might.

But now, in the new ruler, the consciousness of documentary rights was united with a prodigious self-esteem; and thus, possessed by the idea that he was the instrument of God, too suddenly and much too early called to supreme power, a man of thirty fell a prey to all the dangers of infatuation, of delusion; William was driven to an ostentatious display of his authority by the wish—perpetual still, even though perhaps unconscious—to betray no sign of physical weakness.

Frederick the Great, as the young Fritz, was in a similar position: he too disabled, he too prematurely raised to power, victim of like perils, rushed into his first war out of vanity and thirst for fame; and only long afterwards began, through sufferings and defeats, to be a man—and later still, with whitening head, to be a great man. When on his accession the most courageous counsellor and friend his father had had, the old Dessauer, begged that place and authority, and in the impending war the supreme command, might be left to himself, the youthful Frederick rejected the petition in the arrogant words: "Authority in My land is possessed by the King of Prussia alone. . . . I reserve to Myself the appointment in question, that the world may not suppose that the King of Prussia enters the field with his preceptor at his side."

CHAPTER III

BISMARCK

1   1888–1890

IN the tribune of the Reichstag, four weeks before the
old Emperor's death, Bismarck is standing to speak.
To-day he is not contending with the Left, no one will
interrupt him, his opponent is invisible—Europe's greatest
statesman is speaking of Europe. We are still in February
1888: the peace of the Continent is endangered, the statesman knows it, the people feel it; but Germany is befogged,
and in the Council-Chamber everyone's eye is directed, in
the land everyone's thoughts are fixed, on the young Prince
who now stands in the royal box to hear the master-statesman. What is he going to say?

For the first time he dwells upon the imminent possibility
that Germany will have to fight on two fronts; he speaks
of the desire for peace, not of the certainty thereof; then
he sets forth the Balkan case for war and demonstrates its
futility:

Bulgaria, that little country between the Danube and the Balkans, is far from being an object of adequate importance . . .
for which to plunge Europe from Moscow to the Pyrenees, and
from the North Sea to Palermo, into a war whose issue no man
can foresee. At the end of the conflict we should scarcely know
why we had fought.

73

After this magniloquent phrase and its corollary, wherein he prophetically summed up the causes and effect of the World-War, the report has the comment: "Laughter."

Suddenly, in the middle of this speech (which lasted two hours) the man of seventy-three says: "Forgive me if I sit down for a moment. I am not now able to stand so long." At this moment, what are the sensations of the heir to the throne in the royal box? Are they not those of his own youth beside the Chancellor's enfeebled age—is it not clear in such a moment that Bismarck belongs to the grandfather's generation? But soon he stands up again, carefully balancing his adjectives as he depicts the relation of Germany to the individual powers, always as one who designs to tranquillize public opinion. Then he draws himself up in his old fashion, and the Chamber rings with his cry: "We Germans fear God, but nothing else in the world!"

Immense ovation, and the session closes—it was, so they wrote, a moment as great as that of July, 1870. Next day, the echo reverberates over Europe: Crispi wires pages of verbosity from Rome, Vienna is overjoyed, the Tsar sends a barrel of caviare as a token of gratitude. Only the orator himself is dissatisfied: "I am getting old, all the same; my ideas don't combine and kindle as they used." And of course it vexes him to have had to sit down. His photograph, taken that day in the Lobby, represents no giant now. This was his last European speech.

It was not, in the last analysis, spoken for the young man in the royal box, whose accession was still in the future, whose distrust of the Chancellor had for some time been evident. When the statesman chose that moment for unravelling the mighty skein of international relations, it was because he wished to show the world at large, as well as the Prince, that caught between threatening war and a change of sceptre, only one man could discover the right issue, and that man was he.

For simple objects, but by very complicated methods, Bismarck had in recent years conducted foreign policy, framing a system of treaties and conventions designed above all to restrain Austria no less than Russia from a single-handed attack in the Balkans, "for the German Empire is not called upon to stake the life and property of its subjects upon the furtherance of its neighbours' ambitions." To protect himself against Austria's Balkan adventures, he had the year before approached Russia anew: when in 1887 Austria refused to renew the Alliance of the Three Emperors, Bismarck had discovered a new form of insurance. Russia knew that she would never take the field against Austria only, that she would find Germany in arms if there were any attempt to strike at Austria in the Balkans; but on the other hand, if the Austrians attacked in the Balkans, the Germans would support the aggrieved Russians. In consideration of this, Russia undertook to remain neutral, if France should advance against Germany.

Bismarck called this his counter-insurance against Austria, having insured himself with Austria against Russia by the Triple Alliance. But the first object of the treaty was to obviate the mortal danger to his own country of having to fight simultaneously on the Eastern and Western fronts. At the end of an epoch dominated by the secret agreements of the European Powers, this system was a masterpiece; it might be called the gilt-edged security of divided alliances.

Hence, when in November 1887 the Tsar had come to

Berlin to see the old Emperor once more, he had, to Bismarck, disavowed all thought of an alliance with France; but had made a point of his jealousy of Austria. The Austrian frontiers were continually disturbed by Russian troops; at that time the German General Staff held war to be imminent, Waldersee even wished to provoke the conflict with France (W. 308). The military party was discontented because the old men desired peace; conversations were already begun with Vienna about the dispositions of the Austrian forces.

Bismarck's aim was to avoid war, though it were by threats. He made public the alliance with Austria of the year 1879, in order to intimidate Russia. He had to do this, because a nonagenarian war-lord was as impossible as a dying Crown Prince; he wished to do it, because otherwise his life-work was imperilled, "and the issue no man can foresee." His anxiety increased; he could get no rest without the aid of opiates, his brain seemed on fire. He had bound European Powers by treaties making them neutral or harmless; only one was outside the circle, that power which would never let itself be reckoned with, which had remained an unknown quantity in even Bismarck's calculations. For a whole decade he had caused his emissaries to knock at the door in London, and at last had designated as "the aim and object of German policy for ten years past" the joining of the Triple Alliance by England.

Then he took an entirely unwonted step; he approached England with an official offer of alliance. Now, in his old age, he for the first time deserted those byways of diplomacy trodden by him for five-and-twenty years; he reverted to the procedure of his youth, to frank unconcealed approach, and wrote to the English Prime Minister, Lord Salisbury, a long private letter, setting forth the advantages to all three Empires of an alliance of England with Germany, and ultimately with Austria. The alliance with England had at last come to represent in Bismarck's eyes the consummation of the Triple, in the form of a Quadruple, Alliance.

Before despatching it, he showed it to Prince William, and in a second document informed Salisbury of the Prince's "complete approval of the entire contents," thus indicating that the future too was addressing him—the ruler-to-be, whose views were spoken of as anti-English. Two months later, in January 1889, he directed his Ambassador (A. 4, f. 400) to say to Salisbury

that peace, which is equally desirable for both England and Germany, or even only delay, during which they would be able to organize their defences in a measure corresponding to the magnitude of the danger, could not be more certainly attained than by the conclusion of a treaty between Germany and England. . . . A secret convention, if anything of the sort were feasible, would give both Powers considerable security in the event of [another] war; but war could, in all probability, be obviated only by the conclusion of an open treaty.

This was Bismarck's legacy to the succeeding generation in Germany. Salisbury at first sent a polite but evasive reply: he feared that he was unlikely to gain the majority in Parliament, whose approval Bismarck desired; but he would "leave the agreement on the table without saying yes or no" (A. 4, 405).

So grave was Germany's, so precarious Europe's position when the two Emperors died. The High Command was in bellicose mood, the high officials of State were in perturbation, when they welcomed the new sovereign. He indeed said: "We must be prepared to fight the big war, even if we have to do it alone"; but he promised the Chancellor to give no provocation in any quarter; and, fervently desirous as he was of avoiding war altogether, he now sought to gain friends by personal intercourse. It was then that he began his visits to foreign rulers.

First to the Tsar—not to England; this, simply to defy his mother. But his grandmother wrote to the young Emperor, saying that his first visit should have been to her. When he showed the letter to Bismarck, and the Chancellor offered to draft a reply, William remarked, "I rather think I can manage to find for myself the middle course between sovereign and grandson." The old man stood dumbfounded.

The first visit to Petersburg seemed a success. Everyone praised his manners; what was actually said of him in private the Emperor was not to know for a long time —and that a critical time. The visits to Vienna, Rome, London, and the East were likewise tranquillizing in effect; public curiosity and interest regarding the impulsive young man were everywhere made manifest; and if heads were occasionally shaken in the Chancelleries, why, there was always Bismarck to rely upon.

2

The friendship between Emperor and Chancellor seemed a warm one. The Austrian Ambassador in Berlin speaks of a veritable "honeymoon of reverence and mutual understanding," though it is true that he refrains from drawing the horoscope of this union; even Bismarck himself, after the first Imperial visit to Friedrichsruh, is eloquent. "So considerate! . . . He was surprised that I had de-

layed breakfast for him till eleven o'clock . . . and had not
got up before nine, because he thought I slept late." And
Eulenburg tells how the Emperor once, with a courteous
gesture, made Bismarck precede him through a doorway.
From abroad he sent cordial dispatches; in the New Year
of 1889 he was "full of joy and confidence, since you are
still at my right hand, beginning the New Year with fresh
vigour. . . . May it long be vouchsafed me to work together with you."

But intimates knew better. In that same January his
uncle of Baden said: "The Emperor needs the Chancellor
for the present, to bring forward Army Bills" (Ho. 450);
and on the Prince's birthday the Emperor called for
Waldersee, Bismarck's enemy, that they might enter together with their congratulations. That was the first shock
for Bismarck. Keen-sighted though he was, had he, like
Danton, underestimated his danger? Certain it is that he
did not always take the measure of this young man.

When, for instance, there appeared a war-diary of the
Emperor Frederick's, the old man was beside himself at
the great sensation it caused, scented Liberal intrigues,
declared in the *Reichsanzeiger* that the undeniably authentic
document was apocryphal, and in the same number pub-
lished a drastic attack on Frederick and Victoria. It asserted that the then Crown Prince had not been informed
on confidential matters, because his father feared indiscretions at the Court of England. "The legend," he said
angrily, "that Frederick was a Liberal must be demolished!
Otherwise the Democrats may rise and delude the young
man into doing as his Martyr-Father did!" His agitation
over this affair struck Hohenlohe as that of "a man not
wholly sound," and the Grand-Duke of Baden said plainly;

"Many people begin to think that Bismarck is no longer quite right in the head" (Ho. 456).

But the Emperor, to whom such opinions were retailed, must surely have approved of Bismarck's action? On the contrary, he sprang another surprise. Certainly he too believed the diary to be genuine; indeed he attributed the whole thing to his mother and called it a woman's revenge (E. 238); nevertheless he perceived the growing embitterment in all classes, resulting from Bismarck's attack upon the editor. The Emperor's grudge against his father had, it is true, outlived that father's death; but he was resolved that the people should revere his memory—the monarchical idea demanded that. And, as a general thing, the masses must learn not to grumble. Fear of eruptions had disturbed him as Prince; as Emperor, he proposed to prevent them.

What sort of a deep menacing growl was this, underlying the fanfares? If there existed such lawless impulses, if there were masses of men who would fain overthrow the State, what would his constitutional rights avail the monarch? What antidote against this poison but religion? It was not with fire and sword that conflicts such as this were won; it was with God and good intentions. Obtuseness, and a kind of frigid piety, caused the Court-Chaplain Stöcker and his fervents to believe at this time that not the social system, but the soul of Labour, was decayed and breeding Socialism, and that it must be "healed by spiritual tendance, added to material succour." To these Christian-Socialist views the earliest converts had been the devout Countess Waldersee and her husband, through the Countess her devout niece, the then Princess William, and finally the Prince himself; in the end of 1887 meetings had been held in Waldersee's house to establish the "Spiritual Mission" in the different cities. The Press sounded an alarm, the Bismarckian organs were admonitory—upon which the Prince wrote to him, saying that he regarded this Mission to the cities "as the most effective deterrent to social democracy and anarchism."

The old man read this with a savage grin—little had *he* ever cared about the national well-being, piety he could not away with, the Black Coat in politics he had derided or combated throughout a lifetime. He wrote the Prince pages of admonition against clericalism—in vain.

Though condemned to political silence ever since the summer of 1885, Stöcker had latterly gained ground, and now had the mortification of reading in his enemy's organ a confidential letter written by himself, in his "pastoral" capacity, to one of the Conservative leaders.

The bonfires of revolt must be kindled round the *Kartell* [Bismarck's instrument of government] and their blaze be seen of all men. . . . If the [new] Emperor perceives that there is any intention to sow discord between him and Bismarck, he will at once draw back; but if in matters regarding which he is instinctively on our side, we nourish his dissatisfaction, we shall in that way confirm his principles, without personally vexing him.

The *Kreuzzeitung* had for some time been seeking to work upon the Emperor after this recipe.

He was soon to have his first opportunity of acting upon his humanitarian principles. Over a hundred thousand miners in the Ruhr came out on strike for higher wages. In the moment when Bismarck was laying before the Cabinet some strong emergency measures, there appeared, suddenly and unannounced, the Emperor in Hussar uniform and blustering mood, proclaiming: "The directors and shareholders must give in; the men are my subjects, for whom I am responsible. Yesterday I warned the Chairman of Committees in the Rhineland, telling them that if the industry does not at once grant an increase of wages, I shall withdraw my troops. Then, if the owners and directors have their villas burnt down and their gardens trampled on, they will sing a little smaller!"

Bismarck: "The owners are likewise, I think, Your Majesty's subjects?"

The Emperor, stung by this retort, laid bare the real reason for his excitement: "If no coal is being produced, our Navy will be helpless! We could not mobilize if there were a coal shortage. We are in such a precarious situation that if I were the Tsar I should instantly proclaim war against us."

Next day, to a delegation of the miners, in paternal mood:

Every subject has the Emperor's ear, as a matter of course. . . . You have put yourselves in the wrong, for your action is illegal . . . since the notices had not expired. . . . As to your demands, I shall examine them myself and let you know the result. But if . . . any connection with the social-democratic group should make itself apparent, I could not any longer estimate your desires by the light of my royal goodwill, for in my view every Social-Democrat is an enemy to his State and country. In such an event I should intervene with ruthless severity and use the power assigned me to its full extent—which is a considerable one!

Then to the employers, in courteous mood:

The men have made a good impression on me; they have no social-democratic sympathies. . . . After all, it is only human nature for everyone to try to earn as much as possible. The men read newspapers, they know the relation between their wages and the Company's profits, and claim to share more or less in the latter.

Bismarck, stunned by the Emperor's direct intervention, left him to himself at first; when it should become a question of legislating, *he* would take hold. And were his fundamental ideas so very far removed from the Emperor's? Neither the old man nor the young perceived the spirit of the age. Socialists and anarchists were identical; enemies of the State must be kept down—both were "all out" for that. For Bismarck it was no more than an intensification of his anti-democratic feeling; for William, a sentiment resulting from the attempt on his grandfather's life. But their methods of attack were worlds apart. Bismarck wanted to fight as he had always fought—with emergency measures, the lock-out, disfranchisement, and, if these failed, bullets. The Emperor wanted to attract the adherents of the new doctrines by protecting the status of the working-man; he addressed them as *"Ihr"* and *"Du,"* fancied himself in the part of father of his people, was anxious to distribute privileges without himself abjuring any —in short, he wanted "popular absolutism," after the fashion of Frederick the Great. Only he forgot that a century had gone by since then.

Both methods, resolutely carried out, could only have led to revolution: Bismarck's, through violent revolts which might be shot down once and twice, but not for ever; William's, through swift evolution of a movement which, feeling itself encouraged by the monarch and unopposed by the Law, would gradually encroach upon the Government and at last bring it to the ground.

Thus ensued a conflict between two mistaken methods,

wherein only one of the protagonists was thorough. Had this been an instance of a modern, democratically-inspired monarch opposed to a hide-bound Chancellor, it would have symbolized the encounter of youth and age, incarnated in the representatives of the two epochs, and we should have followed the contest with anxious sympathy. But here was a neurotic nature in revolt against obsolete methods, yet lacking the perseverance and courage to follow its own convictions. The Emperor wanted to reassure his conscience by an attempt; when that missed fire, he felt free to revert to his natural protection against danger—his Guards.

3

Bismarck was an oppression on the realm.

For a decade no political intelligence had dared to raise its head, unless prepared to defy him; thus the best brains in the Opposition were repressed, instead of ripening to potential authority. No official could develop under his rule, for all feared him who drew all things into his orbit, and decreed. Justly could the young Emperor say: "I have no Ministers; they are all Prince Bismarck's Ministers." If he interrogated one, or sought to stimulate another, always he was met by the embarrassed answer that the matter must first of all be laid before the Prince.

No longer had the latter any friends, nobody loved the old man. Even Roon and Moltke, with whom he stood depicted in bronze and on canvas before the nation, had drawn aloof from him. The War-Minister had died estranged from Bismarck; Moltke, egged on by Waldersee, had been furious when in the year 1888 Bismarck had taken on himself to make independent military proposals at Vienna (W. 356). When after this Moltke was invited to the Chancellor's, he found himself so badly placed, and the Princess so barely polite, that he left after dinner without any adieux. Next year, at his jubilee, he was offended by a cold, dictated congratulation from the Chancellor.

He has intimidated nearly everyone, so that none dares to express an independent opinion. He domineers in the administration, and suffers no opposition. . . . He wants to be master all round, and is no longer fit to be so. He is Foreign Minister and interferes with every one of the Home Ministers, paying no attention to the Chief's views; he is Prussian Prime Minister and Minister of Commerce, and regards the various Heads of Departments as his subjects; added to which he sits tight at Friedrichsruh, and is difficult to get at. . . . All complain of insufficient instructions, of having no real power of decision, and more particularly too of the Chancellor's duplicity (W. 2, 41).

Even his own family trembled before him—the only beings whom he loved and who loved him. Though everyone flattered him, the Princess's drawing-room grew steadily emptier; at Friedrichsruh especially, where they spent half the year, they led in their tasteless rooms, among gaudy cretonnes and diplomas of honour, the lives of small country gentry, seldom enlivened by company or music. When the old Prince in his obsolete coat, with a white neckcloth twisted round his throat instead of a cravat, lay on his chaise-longue, himself gigantic, his black dog gigantic, the pencil with which he laid about him on the Bills gigantic; when his small spouse, always pale, always coughing, sat by his side, her hair still partially dark above the diamond earrings, ever solicitous, as full of hatreds as he was himself— then woe betide the grown-up son if he disturbed them by an unconsidered word!

Terribly had the autocrat threatened his eldest son, when

he wanted to marry the beautiful Princess zu Carolath, who from her connections and repute was unwelcome to his father; he was ready, so Herbert reported to a friend, "to start with me for Venice, where the lady was, and so prevent me from entering into an engagement of marriage; for he said that it was more important to him than the whole Empire and all its affairs, and what remained to him of his life!" Inevitably this son, his life overshadowed by his father, his dream of love destroyed, showed an aggravated form of the inherited misanthropy; his native ruggedness, not to say rudeness, gained the ascendancy; and as he everywhere represented his father, he took that father's tyranny as his model, without possessing his fascination or the aureole of his legendary fame. And so Herbert too was hated.

The old man brooded with patriarchal intensity over the future of his progeny, and when he encouraged Herbert's friendship with the heir to the throne it was because he wanted to assure the future of his house against all contingencies. This is a cardinal clue to his actions in his last years of office—to bequeath the power which was only lent him, as the Mayors of the Palace had bequeathed it in the Middle Ages; to obtain by strategy the one thing that differentiated him from reigning princes; to leave his first-born the authoritative office to hold as securely as the Crown was held by these kings who, but for him, would scarcely have been kings at all.

Therefore his sons, as Secretary of State or President of Council, had to obey him as if they had been under age. The least thing infuriated the old man; if a servant said Count Bill was not in the house, and the father came across him afterwards, he would foam with rage, and waving his arms about: "Come here at once, I want you!" (E. 66).

So latent revolt was slowly seething among his principal officials; everyone panted for emancipation from the tyrant. Where would they more surely find it than with the new master? "It *must* improve," thought the Ministers of State, and were ready from the first to encourage every sign of dissatisfaction. And was it not more delightful to frequent a brand-new Court? Shooting-parties and balls, trips abroad, and processional entries—pleasanter to share in these than to tremble incessantly before the nods and frowns of the old misanthrope.

The Palace with its rows of glittering windows, with its Palace-Guard, its lines of sentries, Empress's Bodyguard, standards, weapons, Orders—everything in it was changed or renovated by the new master, everything ministered to the glory of the Highest, even the servants' children. Away with the ugly Old-Prussian dress-coat! How much more imaginative were knee-breeches, silk stockings, buckled shoes, three-cornered hats! Everyone extolled the new dress-regulations. What then can the Emperor have felt at the report of a session in which Bismarck cut down the scheme for the new Court dress, and moved an urgent representation against it? "Untimely, unfitting, politically detrimental, for this remarkable costume draws a distinction between Court-Society and all the rest of mankind. This expensive dress, worn in our country by none but lackeys, deprives its wearers of all dignity." "Easy to see" (thought the Emperor) "that he's nothing but a grumpy old man."

A royal train was needed for the constant journeyings. Twelve carriages, a saloon-carriage in three divisions; a large room in the centre, two smaller ones; blue silk upholstery, divan, chandeliers; a carriage for the Civil and Military Cabinets; royal kitchen, domestics. For the entries

—since the great German cities must all see their ruler at least once—body-guard, gold helmet, the Emperor always very serious, the ever-smiling Empress following him in an open carriage. The German people liked all this.

They willingly paid the price. Five months after his accession the monarch demanded an increase of six million marks a year in his stipend. What? Yet another objection from the Chancellor? Yes. He was

very much disturbed; he considered the demand as a whole untimely and exaggerated; he thought that the debate in the Landtag ought to last no more than five minutes, for any discussion would impair the prestige of the crown, and a rejection would oblige the Cabinet to resign (W. 2, 24).

Had one better wait a while? Had one not great expenses for the two widowed Empresses, for one's children? Unfortunately all the world knew how much the old Emperor had contrived to save.

In the second year, the Imperial yacht—four and a half millions, designated in the State paper as "pattern for the Grand Squadron"; but later, to the consternation of the representatives, described by the Kaiser at the launching as a pleasure-boat for himself and his family, whereof the armament was to serve "more as decoration." On his first trip to Vienna and Rome the Emperor took with him as presents: eighty diamond rings, a hundred and fifty silver orders, fifty breast-pins, three gold photograph-frames, thirty gold watches and chains, a hundred caskets, and twenty diamond-set Orders of the Eagle. That was the way to be popular everywhere.

So early as the second year, his friend and votary Waldersee declared that the zenith had been reached.

"Quite gradually there is growing a certain disillusionment; his frequent journeys, his restless activity, his numerous interests have their natural consequence in a lack of thoroughness. The Cabinet Ministers complain that they can only with difficulty obtain an audience, and that then everything has to be settled too cursorily and hastily. The Ministers feel that the Emperor ought to express a considered opinion on their proposals; this however he almost never does" (W. 2, 67). Even Hinzpeter, his prophet, exclaimed at a certain measure: "What do you say to *this* neuroticism? He gets more headlong every day!" (W. 2, 88).

As he was away from home more than half the year, usually for about thirty weeks, the description of his daily round in the shooting-season takes on an enhanced significance, especially as it comes from his friend Eulenburg. According to this he would shoot, in the summer of 1889 at Pröckelwitz, every day till about noon, then sleep till three.

Between three and four the Emperor attended to the private State papers which came to me in sheaves from Berlin. I was always with him at this time, laying the papers before him and discussing the business. Then dinner. Afterwards it would amuse the Emperor to look for thunderbolts in the garden—many were to be found under the gravel, most of which had been scattered there beforehand by Eberhard [Dohna] (E. 246).

Between three and four, then, all business had to be got through. When in the same year Eulenburg invited him to a shoot, he begged him to put crosses beside the names of such suggested guests as he did not approve of, and promised that "of course these crosses shall be concealed in the innermost recesses of my guileless heart." The list set forth the talents of the guests:

Hochberg: sings. Moltke: gambles. Hülsen: does conjuring-tricks. Varnbühler: draws caricatures. Herbert Bismarck: drinks. Dohna: mends shoes (sign of an exceedingly servile nature). . . . Dankelmann: shoots swallows with a bullet (E. 2, 49).

But the climax of jollity was reached in the evening "when Hülsen acted, in burlesque dumb-show, *The Glove of Schiller*." How astonishing the artlessness of these undergraduate diversions would have been to the subject who weekly perused the dogmatic solemnities and pompous rhetoric of the Imperial orations! Of a truth, these amusements had nothing of his Bavarian kinsman's romanticism, nothing either of a pernicious nature, for that a man should shoot down swallows struck no one in the circle as extraordinary. But the cobbling Count Dohna, who mingled thunderbolts with the gravel so that his Zeus should unearth these curiosities, does seem an omen of perilous things to come.

In such moods, amid dumb-shows, witticisms, and heroic ballads, the young monarch was easily led onward in the path of autocracy by his companions of the gun and glass. In such a mood it was that, over a luncheon-table, Waldersee with bland malignancy said to the Emperor: "Frederick would never have become the Great, if on his accession he had found and retained in power a Minister of Bismarck's authority and prestige" (B. 35).

That was as Iago's poisoned dart within Othello's breast.

4

A Crown-Council in the Palace at Berlin, January 1890 —the Emperor and Bismarck in uniform, the Ministers in their embroidered coats; on the left, near the Emperor, Bötticher with his pointed features and double eye-glasses, something between a cat and a bureaucrat. No one appears to know the reason for this Council-Extraordinary, such as William's predecessors have never before convened except on occasions of considerable danger, or for decisions of great importance. Bismarck, summoned from Friedrichsruh by wire, has vainly interrogated Bötticher on the agenda. Bötticher has been mute, though he is the only man who knows; even Herbert, Secretary of State, on asking the Emperor, has been left unanswered. A queer sensation for the Chancellor—never yet has his King taken him by surprise; at every session he has himself drawn up the programme, for wellnigh thirty years. What has the incalculable new ruler got up his sleeve? The effect is as if he "were planning an agreeable surprise for us all."

And indeed, for William this is a great moment. "I have chosen the birthday of the Great Frederick, because this Crown-Council is to be, historically, a very significant new departure." Two proposals, of which one is written by the Emperor's own hand, are read aloud by Bötticher. . . . "So *he's* being played off against me," thinks Bismarck of Bötticher, one of his oldest colleagues, a familiar friend, under many an obligation to him.

Protection of the working-man, no work on Sundays, no child labour: mere common-sense. After the reading the Emperor speaks:

The employers have squeezed the men like lemons, and then let them rot on the dung-heaps. And so the working-man has come to reflect that he is not a mere machine, and claims his share in the profits created by him. But his relation to the employer must be that of a colleague. These strikes are a proof that there is no sympathy whatever between the two parties; hence the increase of Social-Democracy. The modicum of truth which underlies that teaching will be forgotten, and the anarchists will gain the upper hand. Just as a regimental company goes to pieces if the captain takes no interest in it, so it is with industry. In the next strike the men will be better organized and more exacerbated; then there will be risings, which we shall be obliged to shoot down.

But it would be terrible if I had to stain the first years of my reign with the blood of my subjects. Everyone who means well by me will do his utmost to avert such a catastrophe. I intend to be *le roi des gueux!* My subjects shall know that their King is concerned for their welfare. . . . We must oppose International Social-Democracy with an international compact. Switzerland did not succeed in that. But if the German Emperor convokes a similar conference it will be quite a different affair. . . . My desires are based upon the information and deliberations of authoritative persons: Privy Councillor Hinzpeter, Count Douglas, von Heyden. . . . And so I have spent two nights in framing these proposals. I desire to have drafts, based upon these, of an edict worded in a spirit of warm goodwill, so that I may promulgate it on the day after to-morrow, which will be my birthday.

Is not this a modern monarch? A friend of the people, who inquires not of class or possessions? An enemy of the bureaucrats, with his ear open to every petitioner? The age of force and firearms has gone by. Reason and persuasion are to draw the classes together. In the van of civilization, President of a European Congress, marches the German Emperor in the twentieth century. What are the earliest effects? Has he carried away the Ministers? "With increasing bewilderment," says Lucius, "we sat and listened: who could have filled him up with these ideas?"

Bismarck knows who it is. The "authoritative persons," whom the Emperor has extolled as his constitutional advisers, are (he comments) Hinzpeter, "overbearing and clumsy, with careful avoidance of any responsibility"; Douglas, "a rich and fortunate speculator, who . . . by cultivating friendly intercourse with the Imperial children . . . had sought to obtain an influential position with the sovereign," and had written an enthusiastic article about him which he let him see before it was printed, thus gaining the title of Count. Then Heyden, at one time an official of the mines, now a painter, who "based his knowledge of the subject on his intercourse with an old miner from the Wedding region, whom he used as a model for beggars and prophets, and from whose conversation he then drew the materials for suggesting legislation in the highest quarters."

From these reflections he is recalled to his duty by the Emperor's inquiry as to his opinion. Slowly he rears his giant bulk, as slowly does he speak, with self-restraint, and puts the counter-question. In whose despite is the working-man forbidden to work on Sundays and at night—against whom or what is he verily being protected? Is it not against his own desire—his desire for work? His wage will decrease, his discontent proportionately increase. German industry will be depreciated by the deficit to the extent of fourteen per cent., hence will no longer be able to compete with the foreigner.

Indulgence will infinitely enhance the rapacity of the masses. Generally speaking, it is impossible to satisfy the working-man. Even the Tsar of Russia, with all his power, could not achieve it. God alone is capable of discharging that task to the working-man's satisfaction! But first of all we should consider the forthcoming elections: the owners would be irritated, the Socialists encouraged. . . . We should perplex the electors, when we ought properly to make them aware of the presence of an enemy in their midst. We should set foot upon a slippery path. I foresee peril to the monarchy.

Painful silence. Has the voice been heard? Is this only the contest between age and youth, self-preservation

and development? Has not the Emperor uttered the
slogans of the new epoch, the Chancellor those of the old?
Does he know nothing better against the threatening peril
than to invoke the Tsar and God? Or is it only that the
young ruler likes to intoxicate himself with fine phrases
about national well-being, while demanding inspired edicts
from his Ministers? Just now he controls himself; very courteously he says: "Of course I am very far from measuring
my insignificant experience against Your Serene Highness's
abundant knowledge." He can even quite see that the edicts
had better be discussed by the Ministry of State, not put
through in a hurry. But what he does require is mitigation
of the anti-Socialistic measures shortly to be renewed in the
Reichstag, and above all that the horrible right of the Government to proclaim a lockout shall be abjured. "Loyal
men, devoted to the King and Government, have begged me
to make my influence felt in this direction."

"Loyal men?" thinks Bismarck. "And what am I? The
neutrality of the throne will be endangered by such influences as these! If he undermines me like this at the elections,
my Kartell will be done for." And now he becomes
ferocious:

I should consider it a grave error to show even the appearance
of yielding to the Reichstag. Let us first stand firm; then deliberate
on what the Reichstag offers. To give in here and now is to take
the first fatal step; is to let the Reichstag lead us by the nose. . . .
I cannot demonstrate that such yielding will be fatal to Your
Majesty, but from long experience I believe it will. . . . If the bill
did not pass, we might have to dissolve, there would be a vacuum,
and the tide would rise higher and higher: then there might well be
collisions.

"Blood and iron!" thinks the Emperor. "Is not this old

man speaking as he has spoken for thirty years? Has he learnt nothing new?" And now he too grows excited: "It is precisely such catastrophes that I wish to prevent, instead of having to stain the first years of my reign with the blood of my subjects." The second time—this picture seems to flatter his imagination. But the old man braces himself:

"If there should be uproar and blood-shedding, Your Majesty, it will not be your fault, but that of the revolutionaries. We shall scarcely get through without blood, if we draw back. The later resistance sets in, the more forcible it will necessarily have to be."

The Emperor: "But anyhow, we must meet the Reichstag half-way!"

Bismarck: "That means capitulation. With my special knowledge, it is my duty to advise against this. Since I entered the Government, the royal authority has steadily increased. But such a retreat would be the first false step, and that in the direction of a temporarily convenient, but perilous parliamentary authority. . . . If Your Majesty attaches no weight to my counsels, I do not think that I can remain in my place."

So haughtily as this Bismarck had never spoken to his old sovereign. In claiming the enhancement of the royal authority as his achievement, he emphasizes his own authority and refuses to weaken the one by means of the other. Then he tenders his resignation. "Never!" the old Emperor had written on one of these requests, whereby Bismarck had always got his way in the end. Will the grandson answer him with the same word?

The grandson is silent, bites his lips, controls himself anew, only saying half aloud to Bötticher, with whom he has evidently talked it all over beforehand: "That puts me in a dilemma!" Pause. "I beg these gentlemen for their opinion."

Before the whole Cabinet, then, the old man has tendered his resignation; before the whole Cabinet the young man has left him unanswered and turned to the other Ministers. He could not have acted more adroitly, nor Bismarck more incautiously.

Silently the eight men sit around the oval green table. None sympathizes with the veteran whom all hate, all sympathize with the Emperor, whose good intentions, whose ardent impulses, are to expire under the hiss of that cold shower-bath. Yet not one, sitting here, directly interrogated, dares to speak out in the young ruler's defence. It is he who stands for power in the State, he alone gives and takes the portfolio of office; even the Chancellor he can dismiss, and has not returned a "No!" to the threat but now enunciated. But Bismarck's personality, and the fear of his wrath, are so potent that everyone takes his part—even Bötticher ventures only on a feeble effort at mediation.

The Emperor is furious; in open session he has been put down! Nevertheless he again controls himself, and when going, shakes the Prince by the hand.

Bismarck, as he drives home, is still more agitated. Now at last he realizes his mistake. For more than three months he has left the young ruler to his new friends, who are all the Chancellor's enemies. To Bötticher's cautious feeler in the autumn he had retorted by the haughty answer: "With my post, and in my position, I have no fear of ever having to go against my will." And now, is he to fear this after all? Did not the Emperor keep silence, when he laid down his conditions? To-day, indeed, he gave in, because the Ministers ratted in presence of their master—but to-morrow?

Bötticher, who has been proxy for Bismarck in Berlin, has been profiting by these months: he has always wanted to succeed him.

The temptations [wrote Bismarck afterwards in one of his verbose sentences] to which Bötticher was exposed, of turning to his own advantage the charm of novelty which the monarchical office possessed for the Emperor, together with my trusting weariness in affairs, was, as I now hear, much enhanced by feminine ambitions. His duty as a functionary was not to work for the subjection of an experienced Chancellor to the will of a youthful Emperor, but to support the Chancellor in his responsible position towards the sovereign.

The old man muses further, as he drives homeward. Only now is he to learn—how bitterly!—of the gossip rife in these three months: how Bötticher has told the Emperor that Bismarck can only keep going by the aid of morphia. Only now is he to measure the significance of all the rubs that have occurred. When Eulenburg in the summer hinted to his friend Herbert that the Emperor thought German policy too Russophile, Herbert said roughly: "My father has weighed the matter as a whole; amateurs and soldiers don't understand that sort of thing. If it doesn't suit him, we can both go." Whereupon Eulenburg changed the subject, wanted to pretend he had meant nothing, but retailed it all, word for word, to his Imperial friend. Soon this latter was abusive to Herbert about the Russian loan, saying that Bismarck ought to keep the bankers in order, that Bleichröder in particular was a dangerous man. "I have nothing to do with him," said Herbert angrily.

"What does that matter?" cried the Emperor. "He's for ever in and out of your father's house!"

Their last meeting had turned out very badly indeed.

WILHELM HOHENZOLLERN

The Tsar had just left after his visit; on the way back from the railway-station the Emperor told the Chancellor: "At Hubertusstock I stuck myself on the box of the barouche, and left my guest all the fun of the shoot." In full complacency over his adroit amiability, he awaited the applause to which he was accustomed. But Bismarck, calculating the effect upon a formal, misanthropic Tsar of these allurements of a German Emperor on the box of a barouche, preserved a studied silence.

The Emperor: "Well, you might give me some praise!"

What else could the old man do? Whereupon the Emperor: "I have told the Tsar that I intend to pay him a long visit at Spala."

Bismarck: "There might be certain drawbacks to that. The Tsar likes quiet and domestic life; Spala is only a little shooting-box," heaping up superficial objections, because he could not mention the deeper ones: "I was considering that the two exalted gentlemen would be constrained to a very close intercourse with one another . . . and thought it undesirable to bring unnecessarily into such confined and prolonged contact the distrustful defensiveness of the Tsar, and the aggressive blandishments of our own monarch."

The Emperor never dreamt of all this. It was his good pleasure to instal himself with the Tsar, whom he could not bear; and again he felt checked in his best impulses, again it was this old man who wanted to spoil everything—and in a sudden rush of defiant feeling he set down the Chancellor at his own house and drove on, instead of going in with him to the conference which they had arranged to hold.

Since that unpropitious parting in October the two had not set eyes on one another until the Crown-Council of to-day.

5

After the Crown-Council both champions felt defeated. The Emperor, wounded in his vanity, shook his fist in the War-Minister's face: "Why did you leave me in the lurch? You everyone of you looked just as if you'd been flogged! What had he said to you beforehand?" Bismarck lay ailing on his sofa, complained of the Ministers' alienation from him, talked of these things to everyone who would listen; the manly advice of his second son, to resign without delay, he angrily rejected; then again reviled Bötticher. During these weeks his moods and tempers were no different from those of his opponent, the monarch.

Two days after the Crown-Council, he suddenly made a most loyal declaration in the Cabinet: "The moods of a monarch are like good and bad weather; one takes an umbrella and gets wet all the same. I venerate in the Emperor the son of his forefathers, and my sovereign. . . . We could not possibly suffer a camarilla of irresponsible advisers. . . . So I think we will co-operate."

In the meantime the Ministers had secretly deserted him; and when in the following week, on the 31st, he opened a new session, all of them had made their arrangements. This day saw the beginning of the end of Bismarck. When he proposed a revision of the decrees, he met with opposition. Nobody had ventured on this at the Crown-Council, although the Emperor's eyes had sought the oval table round for aid; now, the monarch absent, Bötticher and the War Minister who had been threatened by the Emperor declared: "We must not displease the Emperor. . . . We must produce something that will satisfy His Majesty." This vote, as they knew, would become known to the Emperor, and would assure their careers.

Open opposition? And that upon no practical grounds?
The old man flamed forth: "For a Minister to conceal from
his sovereign that in his opinion he is entering upon a path
which will be perilous to the State, is half-way to high treason! If we are always to do only the Emperor's bidding,
eight subalterns would be as much good in our places as the
Ministry of State here present!" Silence. A division. Almost universal abstention. An awful moment! Would
he not now, in his fury, fling his shattered power at the
Imperial feet?

A stir—enter an aide-de-camp. For the second time the
monarch, unannounced beforehand, with clinking spurs appeared before the Session, which was quickly closed. Later,
Bismarck to the Emperor: "It was only in obedience to your
behest that I drafted these edicts, feeling, as a still active
functionary, constrained to do so. I decidedly advise against
this step, and would request that the papers be here and now
consigned to the flames." Never before had he spoken thus
—even as an inexperienced novice he had never ventured so
far.

"No, no!" cried the Emperor, and signed "with a certain
haste." The Chancellor refused his counter-signature.

The first draft announced a Social Conference of the
Powers; the second promised Labour a statute, soundly and
unrevolutionally conceived, whereby the workers

should, through their representatives, have a voice in the regulation
of such matters as affected them, thus directly watching over their
own interests in negotiations with the employers and the instru-
ments of Government . . . in order to facilitate a free and pacific
expression of their views.

By this proclamation the Emperor, signing alone, could
claim the distinction of having been the first monarch to

enunciate to all the world, thirty years before its establishment, the idea of the Industrial Council. Here, beyond question, he saw rightly; Bismarck, beyond question, wrongly.

Proudly that evening did he show the edicts to his guests, but laid bare his personal motives in the naïve words: "The men shall know that I think for them!" Next day, the democratic papers applauded the Emperor for at last lending an ear to new advisers. Nevertheless, the first effect was confusion. In several towns the men, appealing to the imperial words, demanded an immediate increase of wages; in the Rhineland the Miners' Union claimed instant expropriation of the mines in the workers' favour.

Despite all this, the Emperor was cock-a-hoop: "The old man is knuckling under! I'll leave him a few weeks to recover his breath—then I govern!" Bismarck, who did not hear these words to the group of intimates, divined the mood they expressed; and said at a laying of papers towards the end of February: "I fear I am in Your Majesty's way." The Emperor was silent—that meant he agreed.

Whereupon Bismarck, *à l'amiable* suggested the possibility of resigning all his Prussian offices, reverting to his old part of Foreign Minister. The Emperor nodded; then he asked, nowise embarrassed: "But—you would see the Army Bills through the Reichstag for me, anyhow?"

With wounded feelings the Chancellor left the Palace. When, next day, he hinted at his semi-retirement to his colleagues, he beheld them "silent, with varying expressions of countenance." Bötticher only, who had the succession to the Prussian offices in his pocket, put the question of statesmanship: "Suppose I were Premier, should I take precedence at Court before or after Major-General von Pape?"

Afterwards the old man said wearily to his son: "The Emperor wants to get rid of me . . . and my colleagues all say 'Ouf!' at the prospect, relieved and well-satisfied."

While the Emperor exulted, the Chancellor grew more and more dejected. The unheard-of was happening: Bismarck paid a visit to several of the officials at the Ministries, sat with the electrified gentlemen, and reviled the Emperor. It was as if he were wandering about in his fortress. Then he visited Moltke and Waldersee, and finally announced himself to the Empress Frederick, when he poured out his heart to his enemy against their common adversary.

Not until election day did he retrieve his old intrepidity. Now it was for the Emperor to tremble. By way of a demonstration, he had the troops on the alert that morning and held a parade in Tempelhof; here only, among his Guards, did he feel safe from the ominous stream of the hurrying masses, objects of his distrust. Result next morning: one and a half million red voting papers—the Socialists trebled.

While the Emperor in his turn grew more and more dejected, the old man was arming himself. The Emperor had lost his first election; this thought rejuvenated the champion hater, while the new situation spurred him to a fresh encounter. Now he could not resign, he told the Emperor; "after this election, the consequence of your edicts, we shall have to strengthen the laws against Socialism, bring forward the Big Army Bill—if necessary, alter the suffrage, and disfranchise the Socialists on the ground that they are enemies of the State."

The Emperor, in the ultimate throes of his conscience: "But I cannot reply to the desires of my subjects with matchlocks! I won't be called the Grape-shot King, like my grandfather!"

Bismarck, excitedly: "Better sooner than later. Social Democracy cannot be reformed out of existence—so some day it will have to be shot out of existence."

The Emperor, in complete disorder: "I will *not* wade in blood!"

Bismarck, adamantine: "Your Majesty will have to go in all the deeper, if you draw back now. At all events, I could not any longer shoulder the responsibility."

Uttering this third threat, the old man felt conscious of his strength, because he could read the Emperor's heart. He saw before him no philanthropist; only a conscience already appeased by its first futile gesture. Had not the Chancellor mentioned the Army Bill? thought the Emperor, and felt his Guards encircling him again. Eighty thousand men! And he caught Bismarck's hand at parting, reiterating Bismarck's favourite motto: "No surrender!" Now, because he needed the strong hand, the Emperor clung hard to Bismarck. Assuredly he would never love him—on the contrary: because he now believed him necessary, he began to hate him.

"He is almost impossible!" he complained to his friends. "He can't bear me even to express a wish or an intention. I reminded him of all I had sacrificed for him, my home-life. . . . I had to go through the most abominable scenes, because I trusted him, and my parents couldn't get on with him!" (E. 229). The Emperor thoroughly believed all this; though for years he had taken Bismarck's side only because his parents opposed him, he did believe in his "sacrifice" for the stranger.

At the same time he was irritated by the Chancellor's vacillation; moods and tempers were not permitted to *him*.

First he wants to go and then . . . takes back his offer; I won't put up with that game. I mean to set a definite term. . . . His monstrous arrogance has been the ruin of him; gradually he has got them all under his thumb, and it has spoilt him. But he'll find out his mistake with me! (W. 2, 105).

And Bismarck was no less ready to contend with him— first against the Socialists, then in single combat one against the other. While everyone in office, at Court, on the Staff, was intent on bringing him down at last, Bismarck himself, feeling his indispensability, took up the covert challenge; and that he might the better lay low the Ministers caused every copy of documents to bear an old Cabinet Regulation, whereby in the year 1852 Frederick William IV had forbidden to the Ministers any official intercourse with the monarch unless the Premier was present. It was thus that the two men fought for power.

But Bismarck was fighting, too, for his own life-work.

On sleepless nights, [he said afterwards,] I used to debate with myself whether I could endure it any longer, under him. My love for my country said: "You must not go. You are the only man who can keep that wilful nature in equilibrium." But I knew too the monarch's mental condition, which seemed to me potentially capable of bringing about the most deplorable developments. The spectacle which had been presented in Bavaria by Ludwig II passed off smoothly enough, but in a military State like Prussia a similar entertainment would have fatal effects.

Bismarck's diagnosis was at fault; the Emperor was never at any time mentally diseased, as Ludwig of Bavaria had been. He merely suffered, at certain periods, from intermittent nervous irritation, invariably followed by the characteristic depression—alarming enough at times, it is true. Thus he now gave vent to his rage against the Chancellor in a speech on the 5th March: "Those who desire to be helpful to me are cordially welcomed. But anyone who opposes me in the execution of my task, him I will shatter!"

And when a few days later he vainly sought to mediate between Bismarck and Bötticher, he chose the same evening for giving to the latter functionary the Black Eagle, a decoration which he had in no way earned, and for which Bismarck had been obliged to wait until after his first victorious peace. The rupture was in being; the crash was only a question of time. "I behave," said the Emperor on the 9th to Waldersee, "as if I didn't notice his grumpiness; I'm even dining with him shortly, so that people may think we're getting on all right." Instead of slaying him with one thrust of the lance, he sought to enfeeble the lion by petty pinpricks. And later, he did the like with lesser adversaries. He was no fighter.

6

But Bismarck was.

He was incapable of flight under fire. That he might master his master once more, he assembled all his forces, and ensured to himself a renewed majority in the elections should his Kartell be finally defeated, since in the Palace he no longer commanded any support. To conquer the Reichstag and the Sovereign, to draw the one to himself by means of the other: this was a spur to his fighting instinct. After an estrangement of a decade and longer, the old enemy Windhorst actually now re-entered Bismarck's house. The Catholic enumerated his conditions for procuring Bismarck a majority in the Centre Party.

The Emperor could not bear Windhorst: hence the outcry over this interview suited him well. He ignored the

Chancellor's proposed visit for the next day, announced himself (by a messenger who never arrived) at Bismarck's official quarters, appeared after his morning ride, towards nine o'clock, in Herbert's room, and sent for his father. Bismarck, who even at the best of times was a bad sleeper and lay late, could not but regard a visit at this hour in the light of a surprise-attack, and met him with ostentatious astonishment and his gruffest manner. As the Emperor, in his agitation, remained standing nearly all the time, Bismarck had to stand too; and so, for this half-hour, they looked one another straight in the face.

Bismarck: "I have to report to Your Majesty that Windhorst has thrown off his reserve, and has been to my house."

The Emperor: "And you naturally showed him the door!" (At these ominous words Herbert left the room.)

Bismarck: "I naturally received him as I . . . am bound to do with every representative holding his social position."

The Emperor: "You ought to have consulted me beforehand!"

Bismarck: "In my own house I must be permitted to receive any one I choose, especially official visitors."

The Emperor: "You got Bleichröder to send Windhorst. Of course—Jews and Jesuits always stick together."

Bismarck: "I am much honoured by Your Majesty's precise information regarding incidents of my private life. It is quite correct, except that the choice of intermediary was Windhorst's, not mine—but that does not signify. In the new situation prevailing in the Reichstag, I was obliged to make myself acquainted with the plan of campaign adopted by the leader of the strongest party, and therefore was glad that he consented to parley with me. I know now that his conditions are unacceptable. If you make this a reproach to me, Your Majesty might as well forbid your Chief of Staff in war time to make reconnaissances of the enemy. I can by no means submit to such control in matters of detail, and my personal intercourse at my own house."

The Emperor: "Not even if your Sovereign commands you?"

Bismarck: "Not even then, Your Majesty!"

Up to this the conflict—of a few minutes' duration— had swelled to its climax with deep-drawn breaths; the old man's resentment, the young man's agitation, coming finally to a head when the master and sovereign commanded, the functionary and subject declined to obey. This was the point at which the officer, not only on board ship, draws his sword upon the rebellious subordinate and is ready to run him through, no matter whether he is right or wrong in his defiance.

As the Emperor was fully convinced that his functionary was wrong, his military feeling now demanded that after Bismarck's last words, he should leave the house either with or without an adieu. Whether from fear or respect, he did not do so; but changed the subject, and this time as always uncertain in action, took back the imperious word of command. Not because he was unconstitutionally inclined; only because the blue lightning from those bushy-browed eyes had struck him, did he suddenly add after a pause: "It . . . is not a question of a command, but of a desire. It surely cannot be your intention to stir up the people in the way to-day's newspapers point to!"

Bismarck, conscious of victory: "That is precisely my intention. Such confusion shall prevail in the country, such a hullabaloo, that not a human being shall know what the

Emperor is at with his policy!" By this obstreperous piece
of nonsense the old man lost his advantage, and gave the
Emperor a facile retort:

"On the contrary! My policy shall lie open plain and
clear before the eyes of my subjects. I desire no conflict
with the Reichstag. The Army Bills must be cut down, so
that they are safe to pass. I have asked Falkenstein to
make sure of the most we can possibly obtain by negotiations." What a blunder, to blurt out to the Leader of the
House how a General was negotiating with the Reichstag!
Thus affronted, Bismarck was emboldened again to tender
his resignation; but this time, he intended that the Emperor
should bear the responsibility:

"I have remained in Your Majesty's service only because
I promised my old master to do so. If Your Majesty desires it, I shall willingly go."

For the second time the Emperor flinched. Why did he
not grasp the nettle on this morning of agitation? Was he
still afraid? As his nature precluded him from venturing
an open attack, he tried a side issue: "I—never get any
verbal reports now from my Ministers. I have been told
that you had forbidden it. Your Serene Highness must
have resorted, in that case, to dog-eared old regulations, long
since forgotten. I must request you to abrogate them without delay."

Bismarck declared that the regulations of the year 1852
were indispensable, took his stand upon old times, and said:
"No Premier can remain responsible if the monarch makes
decisions on the advice of all and sundry." Again the Emperor had opposed him; but again without firmly demanding
obedience, somewhat embarrassed still—still under the spell.
For the second time the question who was to be master lay

undecided between them. Bismarck was determined to be dismissed rather than, after all that had passed between them, let his adversary be relieved of him on the plea of tender consideration for his "health." But what was he to do, in that event, to indemnify himself for all this injustice? Was he not perhaps seeing him for the last time to-day? How was this young man to be humiliated? Ingratitude and disloyalty must be avenged!

And suddenly he referred to the Tsar, again advised against the proposed visit, and took, as if to confirm his warning, some papers from a locked portfolio. In these, the Ambassador in London had recently reported some expressions let fall by the Tsar about the Emperor, which had reached the Court of England. The old man had lately perused the pages with satisfaction, showing his son the unpleasing remarks, and assuredly telling his wife of them as well, for she had longer than he been filled with distrust of the Emperor. Now he selected one, probably the worst, of these reports, and held it in his hand, turning over the sheets with slow, tantalizing fingers. The Emperor, always anxious about his personal effect, and especially when English opinion was involved, felt that there were things rustling in the Chancellor's hands which he was not acquainted with, and was not to be allowed to learn. He said impatiently: "Well, can't you read it out?"

Bismarck feigned consternation: "I could not possibly bring myself to do that. To hear such words could not but wound Your Majesty."

Then the Emperor grabbed at the papers: in silent ecstasy Bismarck saw them wrested from him. The Emperor read. For the first time—perhaps for the last—he read some truths about himself. He read that the Tsar had said of him, among other things: *"Il est fou. C'est un garçon mal élevé et de mauvaise foi."*

Yet again, he did not fly into a rage; he seemed disconcerted. Before his eyes, as he read, he had seen the Tsar and his Court, his English grandmother and her son; his own mother, all his adversaries, knew of these insulting words about him; and there stood the man who had tempted him with the mysterious documents—Bismarck had dared to let his sovereign read such abominations! The Emperor's vanity had never been before, and was never to be again, so severely wounded. He quivered. Silently the adversary observed him.

He turned to go. Could he still give his hand to the old man? Again a half-measure: he took his helmet in his right hand, so that only two fingers were left free; these he offered to Bismarck. Bismarck escorted him to the halldoor steps. Then the Emperor bethought him of his usual tactics—just as under the eyes of the servants he was stepping into his carriage, he leaped from the step again, and before these witnesses shook the Chancellor cordially by the hand.

At the Palace he told Waldersee the story, and Waldersee left nothing unsaid that could fill the measure of his wrath. The Emperor was glad to be egged on; summed up, as if to justify himself, the troubles in the realm, and concluded: "How's that for a 'Great Chancellor'? What *are* his merits?" Now Waldersee dared all, and advised instant action; as he was leaving, the Emperor said reflectively, somewhat cast down: "I think it will soon be in train." Then he pulled himself together and cried, as he was fond of doing: "Good sport!" He might have been shouting to his beaters: "Got him! *I'll* bring down the octogenarian!"

7

As if for yet another warning, a railway train next night deposited in Berlin Count Schuvalov, arriving from Petersburg. The Ambassador was charged with the renewal of the Russian agreements with Germany. The fate of the realm hung on this understanding. Within the next three days it would be decided.

The Emperor, doubly enraged by the recently perused iniquities of the Tsar, would have done anything to revenge himself on him as well as on the ruthless intermediary. Were there no intriguers at hand to provide him with a pretext? Waldersee, ever resourceful, pulled one out of his pocket at the psychological moment: reports from the German Consul at Kiev, in a state of alarm over movements of Russian troops—a hundred sheets all fastened together, the oldest several months old. Of these reports, Bismarck had shortly before sent some to the Staff, others to the Emperor. Waldersee, who had been on friendly terms with the powerful and dangerous Privy Councillor von Holstein ever since the latter had been working against Bismarck, procured the whole series from him, showed them to the Emperor, exaggerated the affront, saying that this was a deliberate withholding of important information—then added: "There has been repeated offence in this direction; it is one of the reasons why the Chancellor cannot leave his post. He has too often . . ." the pause to be filled in with "deceived."

The Emperor's face lit up. He could fell the old man with this document—here was his revenge for the London despatch. He seized a sheet of paper, and without any superscription indited an open letter, to go with the documents to the Foreign Office, be seen in all the bureaux—

such papers being there opened in the ordinary course of
business.

> These reports leave no doubt whatever that the Russians are
> in full strategic disposition for war—and I must very much deplore
> that I have received so few of the papers. You could have long
> since made me aware of the terrible impending danger! It is high
> time to warn the Austrians, and take counter-precautions. . . . W.

It is clear that excitement over his imminent emancipation was working up his fears and his aggressiveness to its
measure. His hate for Bismarck sought imposing historic
justification, his revenge was to be dramatic—war was to
be at the door, and the old man was never to have noticed
it. The realm in danger? Old consular reports, the par-
ticulars of which had long been made known to the Staff by
its spies, were to represent a disclosure of impending war!
To impart this in an open letter to the Chancellor, so that his
officials should read it before he did, grin, and learn to
venerate the youthful monarch—what a momentous day for
William the Second!

For to-day—he knows it, he alone of all the millions—
to-day Bismarck shall fall. Vainly had he yesterday sent
General Hahnke to demand withdrawal of the ill-omened old
regulations. "That is impossible," Bismarck had said. "If
the Emperor wishes to quash the orders, he will have also
to terminate the existing Presidency of the State-Ministry.
I have no objection to that."

"Surely some middle course can be found?" Hahnke
had gently answered. But when that ironic refusal was reported to the Emperor, his patience (so he afterwards
averred) gave way altogether: "My old Hohenzollern family
pride was in arms. Now it was a question of compelling the

old hothead's obedience, or parting once for all. Now it was simply 'Emperor or Chancellor on top?' "

In reality it was the "Russian war threat" which had thus inflamed him. . . . Now he took heart of grace; that very day he sent the General for the second time—it was the 17th March, in the morning. The General entered the Chancellor's room, summoned up all his martial intrepidity, and spoke by the book:

"His Majesty insists on the withdrawal of the order in question. Following the report given by me of our yesterday's interview, His Majesty can now only await Your Serene Highness's immediate resignation. Your Serene Highness will be good enough to be at the Palace at two o'clock, to hand over your office."

How long a pause was then made by Bismarck has not been recorded. . . . Very quietly he said at last: "I am not well enough to go to the Palace. I will write."

When, an hour later, the Emperor drove past the Grand Staff, he said to Waldersee on getting out of the carriage: "The business is in train. Hahnke has been to the Chancellor; his answer is not the order, but his resignation." Then he entered the room in which the Staff was to-day to consider the setting of tactical problems. He was quit of his old man of the sea, the King's uniform was everywhere around him, only leal and obedient men were to be seen. Here he would shine!

And in fact he rose after the Chief of Staff had made his report, and imparted his own solution of the principal problem, which differed from the official one.

Unfortunately [reports Waldersee] his performance made a very poor impression. Every one of the numerous audience felt the erroneousness and crudity of his opinions; so it was very regrettable that the Emperor, over-estimating his knowledge as he did, should have so exposed himself. . . . I answered not a word (W. 2, 119).

As no one answered, he could return to the Palace in high good humour. Still nothing from the Chancellor? And on the pretext that he feared Bismarck "might take steps which would disturb our Foreign policy," he sent to him that evening for the third time—this time Lucanus, the dry, cool Chief of his Civil Cabinet.

Bismarck had just risen from table. Since the morning, much had happened to him and through him. While the Emperor, as a theorist, was imparting to his Staff his remarkable solutions of military problems, Bismarck, as a practical man, had been trying to get the said problems out of the way. He had received Count Schuvalov, who had declared himself fully empowered to renew the Russian counter-insurance, and whose discomposure was marked on learning that by next day his old friend would no longer be Chancellor. Then Bismarck had expounded the situation to his Ministers, and he records with sardonic appreciation their chill passivity—not one of them had suggested a general resignation of the Cabinet, though that was the obvious course.

And now the slender Lucanus stood before the giant. Much more hesitant than the General had been in the morning, he blurted it out at last, without preamble: "His Majesty sends me to inquire why the farewell visit requested by him this morning has not yet been paid?"

Bismarck, as quietly as before: "The Emperor, as you know, can dismiss me at any moment; it could not be my intention to remain against his desire. I stand ready to append my counter-signature without delay to a straightforward dismissal. But on the other hand, I do not propose to absolve the Emperor from the responsibility for my retirement—but rather to give full publicity to its true source. After twenty-eight years in office, which have not been without their influence in Prussia and the Empire, I require time to justify myself in the eyes of posterity, as well as at a farewell visit."

Lucanus had the civilian's courage; he dared all, and disputed the Chancellor's right to give publicity to such matters. What reply Bismarck may then have given him the Chancellor does not record, and Lucanus had every reason to bury it in oblivion; his coolness, writes Bismarck, gave way to a sense of mortification in the course of this interview.

While Bismarck, that evening, was drafting his document, Eulenburg, for years an intimate of Bismarck's household, was sitting with the Emperor: "They were hours of acute suspense." Dinner with a Duke. Then the Emperor: "Well, that's enough. Now we'll have some music—you shall sing. . . . We'll clear our heads, and think of other things." Whereupon Eulenburg sang some of his ballads, chosen by the Emperor, the pages turned by him.

He was wholly absorbed, thoroughly enjoying himself. His remarkably adaptable temperament did not desert him in these anxious hours. Only for a few minutes was the music interrupted by the burning political question—the Emperor, called out to hear Hahnke's answer, sat down again at once by the piano, and said softly: "The resignation is all right." Upon this, we went on singing (E. 238).

What dominated him that day was the mortal fear of the old man's compelling him to a high-handed dismissal before the nation; no wonder he drowned his perturbation in music.

But the veteran made him wait half a day longer before, "pale and agitated," he had the paper in his hands at last. Six sheets, attributing to the Emperor alone the entire responsibility for his retirement: not till long afterwards made known to the nation. Instantly the Emperor wrote, as though it might still fall through, the word "Accepted" on the document.

Thereupon he forbade publication of this statement, and promulgated his own, which (in two handwritings) spoke of Bismarck's precious health, of the hope that his wisdom and energy might still be available in the future, and of the conviction "that further attempts to induce you to rescind your offer of retirement would have no prospect of success." Thus did he falsify to the world the actual causes, ascribed all the desire, and all the responsibility, for this final step to the mighty man dismissed, and sought by the title of Duke, by appointment to be Major-General, even by the offer of a donation (that is to say, hush-money) to soften the effect of a decision which he had not the courage to take upon himself. Strange figures! as Bismarck's drawing-room door opened, and to him and his old friend Kardorff there entered, with bland expressions and courteous bows, Hahnke again and Lucanus again—yesterday grave-diggers, to-day bearers of condolences, for each had in his hand a biggish blue envelope. But Bismarck suppressed all malicious innuendoes, and received the Imperial script with due reverence.

When, next day, the Emperor announced the Chancellor's retirement to his Generals, and made no concealment of his satisfaction, not one of them was shocked except the old fellow combatant. On the steps, at his departure, Moltke stood still a moment; the nonagenarian lips, usually compressed, were opened now to say: "This is a bad business. The young monarch is going to set us a good many problems."

Meanwhile the Emperor held forth to the people, and that in the manner of a patriotic ballad, ever welcome to their ears. Despatch to a Grand Duke: "I feel as sad at heart as if I had lost my grandfather over again. But we must submit to God's will, even though it destroy us. The duty of officer of the watch upon the ship of State has now fallen to me. Our course is the old course. Full steam ahead!" The German soul was very cleverly appealed to here. It learnt that all this was Destiny; and with its weakness for tragedy, and at the same time for the strong man in command, it obediently perceived the youthful ruler at the wheel, and there by God's decree; nor was anyone startled to find the Emperor declaring himself openly to be his own Chancellor.

And indeed the general effect was much slighter than the Emperor had had reason to fear. The Prussian House of Representatives received the announcement of its Premier's retirement, after twenty-eight years of office, in unbroken silence. The Liberal sheets welcomed the removal of an "insurmountable obstacle. . . . The nation will soon reckon the 18th of March, 1890, among the days to be thankfully remembered." Among the high officials reigned a sense of emancipation; of one, Hohenlohe records that he was "cock-a-hoop (*froh wie ein Schneekönig*) to be able to speak out at last. This agreeable sensation is predominant here."

Even in diplomatic circles, it was only abroad, not in Berlin, that they grasped what had happened to Europe. "Yesterday" (the 18th) "there were amateur theatricals at the Saxon Envoy's" (so the Austrian Ambassador wrote home); "and I could not get over my amazement at noticing that one scarcely found a single group discussing the great event of the day. People were much more interested in each other's impressions of the evening's entertainment." This Austrian could not forsee that on that evening amateur theatricals were, in sober fact, inaugurated at Berlin; but he had a sufficiently ironical sense of the historic to send to Vienna, some days later, a visiting-card which Bismarck had left at his farewell visit, with the words "Imperial Chancellor" crossed out in pencil.

The Emperor exulted; his people had understood him. To ensure their peace of mind still further, he tried to get Herbert to remain in office.

He appealed to their old friendship, which had long decayed; he even sent again to Herbert's father, asking him to persuade his son. But the intermediary received for answer only Piccolomini's saying: "My son is of age." Woe to Herbert, if he *had* remained! Bismarck had constantly striven to assure the office to his son; but now, with battle joined, honour prevailed over security. However, he permitted his son to remain a week longer so as to save the Russian treaty, against which Bismarck's enemies had instantly conspired. When Herbert reported to the Emperor that Schuvalov declined to renew the agreement with Bismarck's successor, the Emperor wrote in the margin: "Why?" That one word revealed his total failure to realize Bismarck's authority in Europe, if likewise all the naïveté with which a youthful monarch believed that he could accomplish everything by means of good intentions. "Why?" That is the word with which, after thirty years had gone by, he still was to express, in full assurance of his own goodwill, his wonder at a ruthless world.

But, astonished and uneasy, he did not fail to realize the importance of the treaty; he too for that reason wanted to retain Herbert, in order to guard against any impression of a change in foreign policy. And now he fell into a sudden state of nervous apprehension; he caused the Russian Count to be awakened in the middle of the night, with a request to come to him at eight o'clock next morning. Schuvalov was startled; he thought the Tsar must have been murdered. In the morning the Emperor assured him: "Nothing is changed by the Prince's retirement; I am entirely in favour of the treaty. Please settle it with Herbert, and assure the Tsar of my constant friendship." When the Tsar received these words by wire some hours later, he called a council of the Ministry; inquiries flew to and fro, there was another debate at Petersburg—the treaty seemed a settled thing.

But in the meantime the Epigoni rushed upon the master's abandoned masterpiece, eager to destroy it as quickly as might be.

Caprivi, the new Chancellor, a General unversed in politics, was appealed to by the darkly foreboding old man—their interview took place in Bismarck's garden. "Bismarck," so Caprivi relates, "asked me if I did not propose to renew the secret treaty of 1887. My answer was: 'A man like you can keep five balls in the air at once, but other people do well to restrict themselves to one or two.'" No further confidences took place; for Caprivi, invited to lunch daily with Bismarck until the latter removed from Berlin, went only once; "for I had been witness to censures of the Emperor, and that from feminine lips, which it was entirely unfitting that I should listen to a second time" (*v.* Eckardt, *Caprivis Kampf,* 59).

And why always Bismarck? Meanwhile Caprivi had

got advice from other authorities; above all from Privy Councillor von Holstein, best judge of all foreign matters, whose opinion was against the renewal. "It offers nothing tangible; but if it comes out, we shall be accounted double-faced fellows." The Tsar was not, by the Treaty, cut off from France; while on the other hand, if the secret were betrayed in London or Vienna, it might break up the Triple Alliance and throw Germany into the arms of Russia once for all. Neither to Holstein nor to the younger Kiderlen-Wächter, whose conclusions were the same—neither to their recipient Caprivi, nor to *his* recipient the Emperor, instructed by the new Chancellor in these adverse arguments, did it occur that Bismarck had kept the treaty a secret from Vienna, not from a bad conscience (which was not in his line) but by the Tsar's desire; nor did it strike any of them, either, that convenants are based on interests, and will not be broken because one of the parties seeks pacific insurances in other quarters as well.

It was something else which influenced the Baron von Holstein to his decisive vote. "Thus," he wrote to a confidant, "we are dependent on Russia's discretion, and Russia might formulate conditions for our further intercourse. The first would be: 'I will do business with my old friend B. and with no one else.' Do you grasp the situation now? Hence this hectic zeal!"

Hence Holstein's and his creatures' zeal! Now, when the crisis sharply separated friend and foe before Bismarck's eyes, all those who had forsaken him could not but tremble at the thought of his return. The dwarfs, with hasty hands, were already stopping up the cave of their habitation lest the bear should again break in upon them. In these days, when the Foreign Office watched the question:

"With or without Russia" trembling in the balance, and every man was straining at the collar, even a Registrar could have his importance. When Herbert, still Secretary of State, wanted to remove the whole of the negotiations to St. Petersburg so as to sequester them from the rancours of Berlin, he ordered the papers for the German Ambassador to be taken out of the secret archives.

"Those papers?" said the old Registrar. "They were taken away by the Baron von Holstein."

Too late. Holstein, going behind his chief, had taken the papers himself, and handed them over to the new Chancellor. And Herbert fell upon the old official with all his brutality: "How dared you produce secret papers without the permission of the Secretary of State?" Whereupon there ensued "a most violent scene, in which Holstein became involved." To this eldest of his confidants, whose secret defection Herbert had long divined, he cried angrily before witnesses: "You seem to think me dead and done for rather prematurely!" (Eckardt, *Caprivi,* 51).

Next day Herbert too resigned: the conflict was abandoned.

The Emperor alone decided the problem at last, according to his own discretion—and with it, for the first time, a vital question for Germany. The new Chancellor, unversed in politics, would never in his first weeks of office have made a Cabinet question out of a decision in which he himself must have taken practical advice. Why then did the Emperor change his mind?

The Russians were even ready to renew the agreement, hitherto valid for three years, for a period of six; thus preparing the ground, as they made clear, for a permanent alliance. This signified no less than an insurance against the war on two fronts. The Emperor had grasped that, and therefore desired the renewal, despite his private grudge against the Tsar. But now, with the malefic obstruction at last removed from the prospect, the path lay open, new faces encircled the ruler, every one had something to say against Bismarck—now, for the first time counselled by a man who was his own discovery and therefore bound to be of value, stuffed-up with plausible arguments about loyalty to allies, and at the same time assailed at his weakest point, his timidity . . . now he was his own man, and now he followed Caprivi's advice the more willingly, because Caprivi offered such a contrast to the failing attributed to Bismarck.

"Tranquilly, unambiguously, and openly let us proceed, without any diplomatic gambles." This phrase of Caprivi's the Emperor drank in eagerly; yes, they would be plain and German, not like the old fox—that consorted well with the God-fearing attitude he loved to display, and it was uttered by a simple soldier, who knew nothing of the arts of the pen. The good Caprivi, indeed, had frankly declared his incapacity when he abandoned the idea of diplomatic ball-play; he was but dimly aware that Holstein, the deciding voice, was not concerned for the Empire, but only for himself, when he advised against a policy which might bring Bismarck back. And if the Emperor *had* been informed of this by Caprivi, the same motive might well have operated with the monarch also as an admonition against renewal.

As if to make clear to all the world what course the Emperor had but now been counselled to avoid, he appeared, at a visit of his Uncle Edward's on the 21st, for the first time in his life as an Englishman at the festive board. Appointed Admiral of the British Fleet, he, in his brand-new uniform, raised his glass and drank to the old comrade-ship-in-arms at Waterloo, hoping that "the English Fleet would co-operate with the German Army in keeping the peace." And once again Moltke's close lips opened for the startled words: "It is to be hoped this speech won't be reported in the Press" (Ho. 463).

Now it was vain for Schuvalov to reveal his consternation, to offer renewed conversations, even to remind the Chancellor of his recently pledged word. Vain for the German Ambassador to warn them that "Russia may seek elsewhere the support she has failed to find with us." Precisely because the Parisian movement towards Russia had been discouraged in Berlin, it must now be the more carefully guarded against. . . . No use! The Emperor had made up his mind.

Three months thereafter, in the June of 1890, the Tsar, isolated by the German withdrawal from the treaty, took the first step towards an alliance with the French Republic, which had hitherto been repugnant to his absolutist ideas; and the Russian Prime Minister soon afterwards said to the German Ambassador: "With our treaty fell the last barrier between Russia and France."

In this fashion, from ignorance of Europe, from the confessed incapacity of his chief official of state, above all from an intrigue against Bismarck—wholly, then, as a result of the premature dismissal of the master-statesman, was demolished the treaty with which his state-craft had bound up the security of the Empire. With prophetic insight Bismarck wrote somewhat later, twenty years before the World-War, of the simultaneous events: "I could not but regard this as a caprice of destiny, and history may have to call it a fatality."

He who decided all was the Emperor. When in those

days he received the Chancellor's farewell visit and asked after his health, on which account he was supposed to have let him go, Bismarck said quietly: "That is good, Your Majesty." Whereupon the Empress gave him a bunch of roses. He with his own hand laid three roses on the old Emperor William's grave. When he was leaving Berlin, the crowd broke through the barriers, on to the station-platform. There stood the Ministers and their new Premier. The crowd had expected to see the Emperor. Neither he nor his brother, nor any of the Federal Princes, put in an appearance. The only Royalty present was Prince Max von Baden.

In the waiting-room, among flowers, there had been placed by hands unspecified a globe, wreathed round with crape.

BOOK II

POWER

". . . Could great men thunder
As Jove himself does, Jove would ne'er be quiet,
For every pelting, petty officer
Would use his heaven for thunder; nothing but thunder."

Measure for Measure, Act II, sc. 2.

CHAPTER IV

CABALS

A TALL, well-grown man issues from the old-fashioned door of the Foreign Office. The hall-porter reverentially wishes the Herr Baron good-evening, for this man is in authority, always the last to leave the office—it is past nine o'clock again to-day. Upon the steps he turns up his collar, presses his hat down lower, thrusts his hands into the capacious pockets of his cloak, and without once looking round departs, keeping close to the wall as if to avoid encounters. His firm step, his robust form—he is only fifty-five—are not in keeping with such careful muffling-up; it is evident that he is not guarding against the cold, but against his fellow-beings; and anyone who should succeed in casting a lantern-ray upon his features would be surprised to encounter, from above the aquiline nose, a distrustful furtive scrutiny, with a hint in it of puzzled melancholy; and would see a countenance, grey as the eyes and the spade-beard, from which all colour has been drained by the air of close rooms. Nor would any-one imagine that to-day, as every day, he has a revolver in his pocket.

In spite of his age he has frequently of late resorted to a shooting-gallery, though he is not a soldier and has long given up the chase, so is interested neither in weapons nor in sportsmanship. His chosen gallery is a small unfashionable one, for there he can practise pistol-shooting incognito. . . . Perhaps, when on leave, he is fond of strange wild places? Or explores the underworld? Quiet little watering-places in August, the smallest of parties at Borckhardt's in Berlin—these are his recreations; never does he go to Court or great entertainments, scarcely to any other tea-table than that of one clever woman in whom he has confidence. It is merely with an eye to all his social and official compeers that he proves his skill at firearms.

For distrust is the fundamental principle of the Baron von Holstein's being—a misanthropy and wariness amounting to malignity, from which no one is exempt. True, destiny has thrice struck at and wounded him.

At his ancestral home in the Mark he, as a boy, beheld his father perish in a blazing barn. Later, in some unrevealed experience, the young man's vitality was "sapped by terrible suffering." He who records this, a keen-sighted observer, perceived in Holstein's nature

a womanish trend, which caused him to avoid everything that might lead to conflict, fuss or sensation. To conceal this, he wrapped himself in an apparent inaccessibility which was not in accordance with his true characters. Holstein, so two of his oldest colleagues have told me, was never to be found when decisions likely to be productive of troublesome consequences were in question. Similarly, he had not the courage of his opinions when thoughts had to take shape in deeds. . . . His self-confidence always seemed forced (Eckardt, *Caprivis Kampf*).

But though, according to this and many more outspoken indications from those who knew him best, he had certain perversions to conceal—even Hammann dwells upon his morbid tendencies—such effeminate uncertainty of temperament accounts only partly for his conduct in general. He was still a young secretary at the Paris Embassy when the Princess Hohenlohe, as her son writes, was often conscious of being watched by him on leaving the Palace, and was warned of his espionage; indeed, even earlier than this, Bismarck had caused him to be kept under observation at the Petersburg Embassy, and by that very means had become aware of his peculiar, subterranean talents.

So, later on, he seemed to Bismarck the fitting instrument for the surveillance of his second chief at Paris, Count Arnim, who was Bismarck's enemy; and confidential reports upon his chief were openly asked for and received from this secretary.

But after Holstein had thus furtively paved the way in Paris for Arnim's terrible fall, Bismarck obliged him, during the legal proceedings, to give evidence on these activities. The stain clung to him, and was partly responsible for his embitterment. "The Bismarcks branded me on the forehead like a galley-slave, and thus got a hold on me."

By these dark methods Bismarck held Baron Holstein in the hollow of his hand, but so did Baron Holstein hold him; for it was odious to the Chancellor to keep him in the Foreign Office. He called him the man with the hyena-eyes, and vainly pressed upon him the position of Under-Secretary of State, so as to get rid of him in that way— the enigmatic Councillor declined any sort of promotion. "A troublesome passenger," said Bismarck afterwards, "but if one had tried to remove him from the coach, there was the risk of his beginning to blab in foreign parts." Indeed, Eulenburg professed to know on good authority that Holstein had seriously made a proposal to Bismarck of having the Crown Prince Frederick poisoned, and explained Holstein's frightful hatred for Bismarck by his having been told that the Chancellor had betrayed this proposal to his circle (E. 2, 383).

Though Bismarck, like himself, was caught in these terrible toils, that circumstance could avail Holstein but little against the All-Powerful. But the fiercer their mutual hatred burned (inflamed as it was by Holstein's now almost indispensable expertness in all questions of foreign policy), the more ardently did Holstein watch for any indications of a change, and scented the morn when, daily posted in all gossip as he was, he heard of Prince William's earliest differences with the Chancellor. Was the hour of deliverance to dawn at last? It was about this time that he withdrew from Herbert and allied himself with Waldersee, supplying him, by his insight into all important matters, with material for the instigation of the Emperor; and so, in the event, he bore a large share in the responsibility for Bismarck's dismissal. The scene in the Secret Archives, whence he had spirited away the Russian papers from his whilom friend Herbert's keeping, was only the decisive victory in his campaign of 1888–90.

And now there he sat, practically the sole executor of Bismarck's testament, for when Herbert left there was no one in the Wilhelmstrasse who possessed Holstein's knowledge of affairs. His passion for politics could now take a straighter course, and the more because he remained —and he alone in that quarter—wholly devoid of extraneous ambition, despising rank, titles, decorations, refusing the post of Secretary of State that he might more surely retain the power attached to it. From his greatest weakness, dread of responsibility, he derived, in this form of indirect authority, his greatest strength.

Here was no ironical renunciator, bent on aiding the Fatherland in times of danger by unselfish counsels: here was a man impassioned for the *métier,* a supreme artist of the diplomatic chess-board, who loved the game for its own sake and could not give it up; but who shunned tournaments, because his aim was never to be in the newspapers. For years he avoided the photographic plate like an infectious disease; and while his colleagues courted rumour and the daily Press, the Emperor's favour and the Reichstag's, a dazzling position at Court and in society, or at the very least the eye of history, this one man moved among them, fearing and abhorring all these things. But because of this, he concentrated all his tireless energy upon issuing, from his little room, ciphers and letters which should have preponderant influence in the European capitals, upon keeping Ambassadors, Ministers, and all such puppets dangling at the end of mysterious wires, hidden from the people and the peoples. Thus he would enjoy the diabolical triumphs of an invisible magician.

Hitherto his encyclopædic familiarity with agreements and treaties had been placed at the disposal of a master who used him as a born subordinate; but now he was to grasp the reins, direct the course, himself. There in his den he sat, the secluded wizard; for decades now he had scarcely ever left it, had studied the actual world, those countries other than his own, in nothing but the magic mirror of their Press—and thus, wholly unacquainted with the new men and the new conditions now prevailing there, he wove the costly tissue to the pattern of his own impressions.

These were strangely at fault. He reckoned with numbers but rarely with magnitudes, and in calculating imponderables he was prone to go wrong. Lucidly logical, but devoid of psychological insight, the solitary eccentric played the great European game as on a chess-board; and because none was his equal there, because he was an adept in all paths, all short-cuts, all mysterious byways, all the fine shades of diplomatic hints, *démarches,* and notes, the chiefs of every Embassy feared him and sought his approval. So it had come about that he, a Privy Councillor, not even a Head of Department, corresponded—and that not always privately—with most of the Ambassadors, himself sending them despatches in cipher, which he often withheld from his Chief and from the Archives, thus contriving to keep the Foreign Office informed only of what he wished to be known.

If he was at odds with an Ambassador, he would sometimes instruct the Secretary at that Embassy to come to an understanding with the foreign Power concerned—this over his Chief's head, and again without informing anyone but himself. If any one tried to oppose him and sent a formal official report of his own views, it was usually supplemented by a second communication which the Secretary of State could lay before the Privy Councillor: "directed to the Holstein psychology" (Eck. 2, 239). Hundreds of reports upon the gravest affairs bore, to guard against his jealousy, the superscription: "Private: Baron Holstein," after which they passed into official circulation and thus reached the hands of the Secretary of State.

This singular position could not fail to develop his autocratic tendencies; he exacted obedience and secrecy, and one of his countless despatches to the Ambassador in London —Hatzfeldt, then dangerously ill—begins: "Extremely glad to hear from you again, but why, even if you were ill, you should have left me without your news for so many weeks, is incomprehensible to me." Ambassadors, who never failed to ask and receive access to the Secretary of State at any time, he would keep waiting for days or fail to receive at all; when Alexander Hohenlohe at an interview happened to make use of the expression: "I should advise you," Holstein refused to receive him again, though he was the Chancellor's son and possessed his confidence, until at last the father discovered the reason and set things right.

If the mood took him he would send a long letter, of three closely-written sheets, and in no wise urgent, in cipher to London. Though he could frame brilliantly logical memoranda, such despatches were rather in the nature of soliloquies—slangy, beginning with "Well!" or containing such expressions as, "Monkey-tricks. . . . What is the meaning of this sort of policy. . . . Well, let us see what the difficulties are" (Eck. 2, 213). When he went on leave he would lock up the most important papers, making any further steps impossible before his return, for he left no address when away; in his little house, situated in an unfashionably remote quarter of the city, he was never to be found at home.

As he suffered no contradiction, his circle grew ever narrower, and this enhanced his Olympian aloofness; he became more and more arbitrary, would select for the most important positions such men as from poverty or a doubtful past were everywhere, and in every sense, dependent and therefore the more certain to be submissive; and ultimately disposed of all foreign appointments of any importance, or stopped the appointment of anyone else by his veto. After Bismarck's fall he refused two candidates, removed an able Under-Secretary of State, and only con-

sented to the appointment of Baron Marschall von Biber-
stein because, being a novice in Imperial politics, the Baron
would always be sure to refer to him. "I can't make
Waldersee Chancellor," said the Emperor, "for Holstein
declares he won't stay if I do" (W. 2, 260).

Holstein's passion for dethroning the mighty, for breaking up established groups, was even greater than for king-
making. For years he sought to embroil Bismarck's sons
with one another, and both with their father; then Eulenburg with his two highly placed cousins; ultimately Eulenburg with the Emperor. His distrustfulness amounted to
persecution-mania. "Whenever," writes Hammann, "he
suspected anyone of assailing him in his special sphere of
authority, whenever he was a prey to passive or active apprehensions, whenever his hysterical jealousy took possession of him, he was as a man beside himself." Eulenburg
and Bülow called him the Lynx; and Eulenburg says of
Holstein's distrustfulness that if anyone happened not to
bow to him,

this was enough to institute a persecution of the enemy which never
came to an end. Even a word that somebody might somewhere
have let fall . . . sufficed to establish a lasting enmity. . . . He
never kept a servant long . . . for he was fully convinced that any
one of them would let himself be bribed, would steal from him, or
even murder him. . . . All his energies were concentrated on
politics, and that in the region of intrigue. To be sure [Eulenburg
was bound to continue] intrigue is always at the bottom of all
political activities.

Because this judgment is true of Holstein, though not
of political activity in general, Holstein's operations were
harmful. For all his expert knowledge of affairs, he was
essentially unenlightened; and therefore, penetrating though

he was, his solutions of the three or four fundamental European problems were erroneous. Holstein perceived neither the fragility of the Triple Alliance nor the impending break-up of Austria; he declared everyone a simpleton who considered an entente between England and France to be possible, and everyone crazy who believed in a similar possibility between France and Russia. These had been his theses and his prejudices for three decades; from them resulted, as the various questions arose, all his mistakes in details.

One problem only he judged rightly from the first—and that was the problem of the Emperor. Him he avoided, declining all invitations. "Once and once only," William states, "in the course of many years, did he condescend to dine with me at the Foreign Office"; and then he had to apologize for his morning-coat, for he possessed no evening-dress. Holstein was one of the first to take the Emperor's measure; so early as 1892 he compared him to the Emperor in the second part of *Faust,* and predicted his fall, and even the Republic.

No wonder, for he was the Emperor's very antipodes. William always wanted the appearance of authority, Holstein never; William wanted to shine everywhere, Holstein nowhere; while the one liked to be the cynosure of every eye, unpacked his heart to all and sundry, was never alone, always egotistical and always optimistic, the other kept in the background, was inaccessible to most people, was always alone and always sceptical. William was the most frequently, Holstein the most rarely, photographed German of that period.

And yet they had one notable trait in common. Both wanted to avoid responsibility in all things, to throw the blame for every mistake on other people; both felt unsafe, and never went out unarmed—the Baron never without a revolver, the Emperor never without a policeman.

2

For a period of seven years the foreign policy of the German Empire was conducted by three men whose names were signed to no vital official document. Holstein, Eulenburg, and the Emperor were judicially without responsibility, the two first even morally so, for what servant can help influencing his master? For nine years more they remained in power; not supplanted, but supplemented by a fourth— by Bülow. So that if the German Empire, for the first seven years after Bismarck's fall, was ruled only by irresponsible individuals, these were in time overshadowed by a friend who was their equal in authority. The political fountain-head, during these sixteen years, was Baron Holstein.

His judgment was, from the time of Bismarck's retirement to that of his own—that is from 1890 to 1906—the preponderating one in all important questions of foreign policy. . . . Doubtless his policy would have been paramount, if the Emperor's intervention had not so frequently given State affairs a turn which did not represent Holstein's views.

This statement of Eulenburg's is corroborated in every particular, but especially by the documents, which almost uninterruptedly demonstrate whose voice prevailed in every conference of State. And if Eulenburg seeks to absolve himself of this assignment of responsibility, it is only on the practical side, of which he knew nothing; how great his personal influence was he states in arresting words:

There would have been a certain sense of impotence but for my part of mediator between a hyper-temperamental Emperor, who would fall like lightning from heaven upon the assembly at the Foreign Office, and a brilliant, domineering Privy Councillor of marked pathological tendencies, to say nothing of an Imperial Chancellor who . . . regarded the said part of mediator as a necessary evil.

Eulenburg himself—the brilliant Eulenburg, of marked pathological tendencies—was a necessary evil; for since between the Emperor and Holstein any personal intercourse was, so to speak, impossible, between Eulenburg and the Emperor it was natural; and Holstein's aberrant logic had to be refined upon by Eulenburg's psychological insight before the Emperor, in many instances, could come to any sort of a decision.

Hence, as the new star arose, these two irresolute beings perceived the advisability of a close alliance, for each felt that such an alliance would add an extra advantage to those he already possessed. Eulenburg, almost incessantly at Court and in society, disseminated and enlarged upon the eccentric's ideas, bound them in crushed-green morocco, and set them under people's eyes—became, so to speak, the publisher of Holstein's theories. Holstein regarded his new friend as a Court-minstrel who could lure the Most High with harp-music; Eulenburg his as an alchemist whose potions were indispensable at Court; each considered the other crazy, abnormal, and impossible. Nevertheless each had a certain respect for the entirely different gifts of the other, and when in his company was moved to a kind of compassion—not amounting to affection, but liable to be transformed into hatred at any moment, because both avoided all responsibility and in any given case would try to shift it on the other.

In 1889, indeed, when Eulenburg was still Secretary in Munich, he received the first of Holstein's secret letters —addressed to him, moreover, at Starnberg, "because for your sake I do not wish your present Chief to see my handwriting." By 1891 Holstein was talking about "old pals like ourselves," and saying "for an old bachelor it was a novel task to get up some amusement for your youngsters"; going on to praise his friend's execution of his ideas as masterly. Eulenburg's answers were of the most sentimental:

> With Mussigny's incomparable and never-fading crimson-lake I paint in my heart your name, first known to me some years ago as that of a peculiar, unapproachable personage, never likely to unveil to a young Secretary of Legation, who was more occupied with poetry than with diplomacy. . . . But there is a destiny in all things. . . . I cannot now imagine what my life was like without you (E. 2, 165).

With such siren strains he responded to Holstein's bardic chants, and yet it would be absurd to infer a relation arising from the abnormality of the two men. Eulenburg, in the middle forties, could charm this friend only by his part of intermediary in intrigues; and both the writer of this love-letter and the ten-years-older recipient laughed in their sleeves while giving and taking. Not more than two years later Eulenburg comments: "Directly a situation becomes complicated, Holstein goes quite off his head. The imputation is positively grotesque. . . . I am no Holstein, but an Eulenburg"—regarding this as a superiority in itself, besides which he was poet and Count, Guardsman and musician. In the year 1894 hatred is plainly revealed:

If poor Caprivi (whom they're destroying between them) got hold of this sheet of paper, my friend Holstein's days would be numbered. But as we cannot—I had almost written, alas!—do without him, I shall . . . not show the aforesaid sheet to the good Caprivi. My God, how dramatic! . . . If I were anything but what I am, friend Holstein would fling me overboard.

In such an atmosphere of brooding storm, each hating his accomplice yet unable to sacrifice him, the political decisions of the German Empire were made during those seven leaderless years.

For Eulenburg indefatigably carried out the behests of friend Holstein in his intercourse with friend William, whom he could frequently meet and always write to. In this way, by "inspired" letters from the Count to the Emperor, they began in the year 1892 by bringing down the only man who still preserved his integrity, Count Zedlitz (E. 2, 66). High politics were likewise their province. If Holstein thought it politically undesirable for the Emperor to meet the Tsar at Danzig, Eulenburg had to discover personal reasons for detaining him. If Holstein wanted to incite the Emperor against the Conservatives, he caused Eulenburg to tell him of a letter received from the Conservative leader, which had never really been received at all. If a Russian Prince were expected, Holstein in his room at Berlin drafted the conversation, partly in French, which the Emperor was to have with the visitor, and transcribed it for his friend in Munich so that he might pass it on to Potsdam (E. 2, 76).

But it was not only Holstein who made use of Eulenburg. "Hundreds of letters" poured in on him, urging him to warn or actuate the Emperor; by his choice among these pleas decisions were very much more affected than by the Chancellor's representation. Eulenburg's special gift was for the divination of reactions—in this his value consisted. He bore the guilt of many a perilous decision, in that he had caused important positions to be filled by his incompetent bosom friends; but against this we must set a number of admonitory letters from him, which may be regarded as genuine although submitted by himself, much after date, from the rough drafts, and only occasionally authenticated by the Imperial replies. Thus, at the end of 1891 he writes to the Emperor: "All parties without exception are offended by Your Majesty's phrase: *'regis voluntas suprema lex'*; it was liable to be exploited in a manner most insulting to Your Majesty."

A year later, after the speech:

I shall lead you to days of glory [Eulenburg writes]; Your Majesty's great eloquence and charm of delivery exercise a fascination over your audiences. . . . But on a cool consideration of the content, a different impression emerges—say, under the handling of a German Professor. The days when an Imperial phrase was inviolate, removed from the interpretation of dunderheads, are long gone by—and that precisely because Your Majesty's Imperial phrases are by yourself regarded in a different light, and are given too much, and too frequent, publicity.

Telegraphic reply:

Best thanks for letter, which told me nothing essentially new. Am very wretched, though, and must abstain from work. Condition caused by over-strain and over-exertion. . . . Shall perhaps, when better, have to break away and take a change of air. Therefore all politics, home and foreign, are for the moment quite out of my thoughts, so long as they keep the usual course. Best regards from yours, WILLIAM.

We perceive that he was hurt, evaded the point, boasted of his exertions for the Fatherland, and looked forward to a change of air, from which he had but just returned. Friend Holstein applauded: "For once at any rate it may be said that there was one person who told the truth to William the Second. But I really believe that there was only one." This is doubly false. Two or three more were to arrive who should venture so far, and that without the protection of friendship; but Eulenburg, the declared favourite, to whom at that time everything was permitted told the truth far too rarely, concealed his apprehensions, and will be the more severely judged by history because he often saw aright, and kept silence about dangers which he perceived more clearly than any one else did.

However, he had early known the Emperor: we must not forget that personal affection made him leniently inclined. In 1890 Waldersee could still describe him as a devotee of the Emperor, of whom he took an idealistic view; by 1892 he perceived in Eulenburg "a transformation; his view is much modified, and he sees with apprehension the downward trend of affairs." But when he was implored to speak the truth to his Imperial friend, he burst into tears: "Ah no! I can't tell him anything unpleasant— I really can't!" (W. 2, 374). When at that time he witnessed the Emperor's performance as Field-Marshal in the manœuvres, his head swam

at the thought of the frightful confusion which would arise from any change in the Staff. . . . It brings back that fear of megalomania, which I combat incessantly. Here is scope for its development, and the young Emperor is daily exposed to it. Conscious of standing at the head of the most powerful army on earth, with the qualities of a gallant commander in the field, and crowned "by the Grace of God": this is perilous indeed (E. 284).

So clearly did he see the danger—and held his peace.

He continued to hold his peace when soon afterwards he noted down for his own perusal the more generalized truth:

Unity of command is lacking, because His Majesty has no unity in himself. The Maison Militaire has been pompously inaugurated with Plessen at its head, who talks of nothing but gun-fire. . . . I can tell no one what I really feel, because there is no harmony in any quarter—and because it is impossible to attain that harmony. When one remembers such a master-spirit as the old Emperor was, how everyone put a shoulder to *his* wheel, which was that of the coach of State. . . . And now! Everyone snapping at everyone else, hitting at everyone else, hating everyone else, lying about everyone else, betraying everyone else. More frequently than ever before I feel as if I were living in a madhouse. Insane narrowness, insane controversies, insane arrogance. Bedlam—Bedlam—Bedlam! (E. 2, 108).

The newly designed Court shooting-dress being not to his taste, he complains:

But why, besides all the rest, brown boots should be supposed to go with silver spurs is an enigma to me. . . . When the Emperor pays me a visit, imagine having to prance about in my old Lieben-berg got-up like that—laying papers before him, in my own quiet room with clinking heels; and as a climax, singing to my piano in high brown boots with silver spurs!! . . . I will *not* be dressed like the Imperial "household." I am something other than that (E. 2, 111).

And yet, despite just perceptions, partly the fruit of common-sense, partly of wounded artistic sensibility, he never would leave this circle but rather consolidated his position in it with every passing year, for he held that "*l'amitié d'un grand homme est un bienfait des dieux.*"

Soon the Emperor offered to "drink brotherhood" with him —that is, as from master to servant, for the sovereign said *"Du,"* but Eulenburg continued to write to him in the third person, and most deferentially; indeed, he was so entirely the courtier that even in letters to intimate friends he would write of the Emperor as He and Him, and in reporting the Imperial conversation would use a capital for *"Ich"* and *"Mein"* even in his rough drafts.

He charmed the Emperor, because there was nothing he could not do. After he had excelled in sport and song, shown himself a perfect host, led the conversation at table "so that the meal was spiced with gaiety, without being uproarious," there would ensue "a discussion between me and the Emperor of very important political questions, which from their confidential nature were, morally speaking, an extra added to all other responsibilities." Or after lunch he would be left alone in the *coupé*

with the beloved Emperor, whereupon a flood of objurgations broke over my head. . . . I could only catch his dear hand and press it, saying that Prussia was still powerful enough to have suffered no real damage. My emotion stemmed his anger; he felt at once that I understood him entirely, and that assuaged his grief.

If we add to this the Berlin jokes, whereby according to his own retrospect he generally played upon the Emperor's moods, and "on dark days talked like Ristori and had a similar success" (E. 2, 381), we shall have an epitome of all the unmanly elements, of the combined sentimentality and theatricalism which were necessary for the Emperor's subjugation.

In such forcing-houses as this false sentiments encroach upon the heart; overbearingness and ambition transform

themselves into sense of duty in those who cherish them;
master and servant come really to believe that they are
victims in the cause of the Fatherland. When at the end
of 1896 Eulenburg had reason to fear, from attacks in the
Press, that there was a desire to remove him from his
Viennese appointment, he writes—not defending himself,
but with suppliant duplicity, to Bülow: "Dear Bernhard,
. . . Would the poor Emperor could be spared from having
to sacrifice me! It would cause him great suffering. I feel
distinctly that he cares for me more than ever." Or in
lengthy communings with this same man, whom he had
selected for Secretary of State, there are no such words as:
"Soon it will be yours; then you will have the authority
you have so long waited for"—but: "Apart from this,
dearest fellow, that you really mustn't give up your work
altogether, your health is infinitely important for the Emperor, the country, and the Government."

The Sovereign's favourite was courted by all. He was
still only an unimportant Ambassador in Oldenburg when
Marschall, who was shortly to become his superior in the
service, that is, Secretary of State, wrote "begging you to
aid me by word and deed, and when necessary, by unsparing
criticism." True, Marschall knew that his Ambassador in
Oldenburg might be Secretary of State at any moment;
but Eulenburg knew quite as well why he fended off this
promotion—he feared that the Imperial friendship "might
be spoilt by the perpetual meetings and discussions" (Ho.
497). Why assume responsibility when one could enjoy
authority without having to countersign? And why, in the
comfortable present, take upon one's elegant shoulders a
portion of the grim German future? No—we fend off, we
resign ourself:

The poor Emperor is getting on everybody's nerves; but it cannot be helped. When a marriage turns out badly, the couple can separate. But as between King and People that is not so easily accomplished, the unhappy union must go on.

Beyond his two or three intimates, no one had any idea that such swift realization had come to a man who perpetually flaunted his favoured position, and who therefore must have been looked upon as either very petty or very perfidious if he were to be regarded as seeing so clearly and yet holding his peace. So far as the Emperor was concerned, Eulenburg was neither petty nor perfidious; only weak and vain, only infatuated, and best portrayed by Bismarck.

Something of a Prussian Cagliostro. . . . A mystic, a romantic rhetorician . . . particularly dangerous for the dramatic temperament of our Emperor. In that high personage's presence he assumes adoring attitudes, which I believe to be perfectly sincere. The Emperor has only to look up, and he is sure to find those eyes fixed worshippingly upon him.

That he deserted Bismarck, despite his long intimacy in the household, is not, in him, so very blameworthy. He was the Emperor's, not the Chancellor's, affinity; for he felt, with his abysmal knowledge of himself, that he was "instinctively and profoundly repelled by forceful personalities. On the stage they are indispensable, in history they delight me; but in personal intercourse they are unpleasant —indeed unendurable." If, after this, he depicts his abandonment of Bismarck as a conflict between two friendships, there is none the less some truth in it; "for the Emperor was the weaker one in the decisive hour, despite his royal authority, and I could not bring myself to fail him in his unswerving conviction that my loyalty would be

his buttress in that time of trial. I stuck to his colours—
and that was to be my disaster." Bitterly, in his old age,
did he add the concluding words, for not till long afterwards
was his lifelong friendship to be betrayed.

3

The man who "signed" for four of these years was a
General; the only wonder is that this military State, during
its half-century of existence, should have been officially
governed by a uniform for so short a space of time.

Waldersee had fallen. Vainly did he try to stifle his
ambition for the Chancellorship by perpetual asseverations
in his diary that he would not for the world have been
Chancellor. The Emperor had been clever enough to say
gracefully: "You are too good for that"; and made him
Chief of Staff when old Moltke, warned by Bismarck's
fate, retired of his own accord. But Holstein and Eulenburg had otherwise ordained. Waldersee seemed dangerous, for he too was clever and intriguing, while what they
wanted was a harmless novice; hence they made a pretext
of his piety, which Eulenburg's mysticism had made unfashionable at that time, and represented to the Emperor
that Stöcker was working in the Protestant interest and
Waldersee in Stöcker's. Thus both fell into disfavour.
Waldersee ended by venturing on an unfavourable criticism
at the manœuvres, woke from his dream of impartiality to
find himself in command at Altona, was thenceforth an important eye-witness of events, and, a decade later, withdrew
from the world-stage amid unmerited ridicule.

Caprivi was much better. Compared with Waldersee
he seems like the Old-Prussian General, duteous and
genuine, brave and austere as the old Emperor had been

—a contrast to the place-seeking, wire-pulling, intriguing, swaggering type of the new era. For a young man of narrow means the Guards was even in the 'sixties too expensive a regiment; if he managed, from the time he was Captain, to keep out of debt on his pay, not to have to give up his horses, lead a secluded existence, deny himself all domesticity, he was entitled to boast of the achievement in his grey hairs; but in a life so puritanical such an one could have seen nothing of the world of which he might suddenly be called upon to rule a portion. To command and to obey —these were Caprivi's fundamental principles; and even as Imperial Chancellor he obeyed no less meekly than as General—that is to say, he obeyed his Supreme War-Lord.

Only in his obedience did he accept the position; he regarded himself as ordered to the Wilhelmstrasse as he might have been ordered to the conquest of a South-Sea island, and said in the early days to Bismarck:

If in battle, at the head of my Tenth Division, I receive a command which causes me to fear that in its execution by my men both the battle and myself will be lost, and if the expression of my honest doubts has no effect, there is nothing for me but to execute the order and go under. What's the odds? Another man done in—that's all!

So he leaped into the breach, with his bullet-head like a seal's, his clear bright eyes, and curt quiet movements; and there he stayed until he was thrust out from behind; then he went quietly and wrote no memoirs. He was without pretensions. "I feel as if I were groping in a dark room. . . . The great man overshadows me completely."

For all his genuineness, however, he could be guilty of enormities. Bismarck has nothing against him but "the wicked destruction of splendid old trees in the Chancery-garden"—unique in Berlin—which the General had had cut down so as to get more light in his room. People with such paucity of imagination are certainly incapable of "Keeping five balls in the air at once," and are likely to let go a Treaty of State whose very essence and operation belong to the realm of spirit. Caprivi was too good an officer to be apt, in his old age, for politics. Nevertheless in the cardinal question of England, he, the commonsense layman, displayed more insight than the specialists who succeeded him.

With such a naval policy [he said] they enfeeble our defensive power on land, and will end by bringing us into conflict with England, our only natural ally. . . . For Germany, now and in the immediate future, the only naval question is how small our Fleet can be—not how big.

His interest was concentrated on land-defences: he aimed at larger cadres, but in compensation at a two-years' service. This was so original and daring that when he first propounded his views, one of the Staff replied with: "If the Emperor hears of it, he will send for the police and have you arrested." All the dangers of the uniform in the wrong place are revealed by this pleasantry. But while in everything else he was biddable, the General's courage was stimulated by his desire for more striking-power: he challenged the Reichstag, and did succeed in obtaining his cadres by a small majority. In this conflict of 1893 he was self-reliant, equal to his task, and thereby displeased his masters. But when he proceeded to advocate more reasonable social measures, and that in opposition to the secret conclave, these worthies made up their minds to destroy him.

Nothing was easier: they awaited the next occasion of displeasure, and then set to. October 1894: The Emperor receives Caprivi's adversaries from the Eastern Elbe district, who are demanding forcible measures against the Socialists. Caprivi begs to be allowed to resign, the Emperor assures him of his entire confidence, catches him by his sword-belt: "You have promised to let yourself be shot for me. You must remain." Whereupon Holstein, in his room, dictates an article to a journalist sworn to his service, which points out the contrast between Caprivi on the one side and the Emperor and Botho Eulenburg, Prussian Prime Minister, on the other, and exults in Caprivi's victory over them both on the Socialist question. Everything that Holstein has foreseen in due course follows: Eulenburg (*i.e.,* Eulenburg the Great) shows the Emperor the article at a shooting-party; the Emperor sends Lucanus to say that the Chancellor must repudiate it—he refuses, having in no wise inspired it. Follows dismissal, a few days after that touching appeal to his loyalty. Two hours later Caprivi is saying: "Now I am frolicsome and free! I am off to Switzerland. Do everything you can to restrain my Press from attacks on the Emperor."

Such assassinations, perpetrated by poisoned arrows from the background, and resulting in the highest positions of State being relegated to untried men, were at that time as likely as not to be brought off in the idyllic surroundings of a royal shoot. Eulenburg's pen, as apt as his heart for the things of intrigue, wherein according to his own testimony all politics essentially consist, can depict such scenes with mastery. After his cousin Botho too had asked, during lunch in the Liebenberg forest, to be allowed to resign,

the Emperor came to me with that peculiar pale, pinched look of his. I asked him whether the shoot was to go on, and went with him

to his station. It was grey weather; everything looked dismal. . . .
I have seldom seen him so upset. . . . "Whom can you suggest?
I have no idea whom I can call upon—don't you know of anyone?"

When I spoke to the Grand Duke of Baden about the possibility
of a change, my friend replied by suggesting Hohenlohe as a stop-
gap while we looked out for someone else, as we should have to do.
. . . People like variety, Hohenlohe is something new, and at any
rate no one can find fault with him, so far as that is ever conceivable
in Prussia.

"I will write to Hohenlohe as soon as I have spoken to Caprivi,"
said the Emperor. We talked of this throughout the drive, and of
course only in French, on account of the beaters who were standing
behind us. The sows that came running up to be shot, naturally
bolted.

Scene: The Most High, annoyed by the shoot being
spoilt, upset because these troublesome Ministers will
keep on asking to resign, and that at lunch. The Favourite,
too astute to take the responsibility of advice, produces an
uncle who has thought of another uncle, not perhaps exactly
the right man, but a grey-haired stop-gap, a curiosity as it
were, who will do for a change. Behind them, capable keep-
ers, the only men about the place who know their job, in
silent wrath because His Majesty is missing the best game,
and jabbering French while he misses it. But even the
Favourite, a minor poet, and therefore prone to generaliza-
tions, can see the irony in this rescue of the sows through
Caprivi's downfall, and does not notice how he spoils it all
by the implication that the terrified game had no dearer desire than to die for their sovereign.

4

A few days later Eulenburg beheld himself and his confederates portrayed as poisoners in *Kladderadatsch*. For

months the comic journal had been showing up the two friends, and with them Herr von Kiderlen-Wächter.

This blunt junior, with his bulldog face—which he lived up to by an eternal fat cigar and an ostentatious outspokenness—was an astute Suabian, Holstein's equal in political ardour, Eulenburg's in knowledge of the world, and greatly the superior of both in pluck. He was the normal one of the trio, a great lover of women, wine, and Havanas—a connoisseur indeed in the two last; in education, humour, and literary style a *Korpsstudent,* brutal yet not vicious, but above all a fighter, differing from his two friends in being unafraid of responsibility, resolute—in a word, a man.

As he could neither sing nor do conjuring-tricks, his attraction for the Emperor was his humour, which in the two printed volumes of his private letters cannot be said to overstep at any point the limits indicated above; and thanks to this, Kiderlen was permitted to accompany him, from 1888 to 1897, upon his Norwegian cruises. While in the course of these ten summers he made fun in his private letters of the Emperor and the party in general, he was likewise inditing, under the master's eye, a series of travel-letters for three newspapers. "The Emperor always insists on my reading them aloud to him, then he contributes his own ideas, and copies go off to the Empress." Besides these Byzantinisms, which cramped his native intelligence, he made great play with the Emperor by dogmatic criticism of the deposed Bismarck, who in his day had discovered Kiderlen, and of whose early recognition the latter had been wont to boast.

The rôle of "Nature's gentleman," for which he had cast himself, the rough outer husk which he so easily assumed without possessing any sweetness of kernel, made him as great an object of interest to false democrats as the wise true-

hearted woman whom, although she was not very much his
social inferior, he hesitated for twenty years to marry. His
want of deference and tact was looked upon as forthright-
ness; and if, when in festive mood, he talked about "Court-
parasites and a pack of Court-women," why! that was just
the "hare-brained youngster," and simultaneously the new
Bismarck—for he aped his elder even in handwriting. In
reality Kiderlen was neither hare-brained nor rough; he had
no trace either of Bismarck's enigmatic character or of his
high competence; but he *had* political dexterity, and being
more of a worldling, he could make better use of it than Holstein in his cell could make of his. Holstein indeed could
get on with him better, in practical affairs, than Eulenburg
could; for Eulenburg only put up with him as the Emperor's
protégé, but was secretly repelled in every sensitive nerve
by Kiderlen's mere proximity.

For months Holstein, Eulenburg, and Kiderlen vainly
sought to detect the dangerous jester who made fun of them
in fables and verses, depicting them wittily and with uncanny knowledge, in *Kladderadatsch,* as Friend Oyster,
Count Troubadour, and Cock-sparrow. As each new number appeared, they would meet for consultation with Secretary Marschall in Holstein's room; if one was absent, the
others would wire him the day's attack. They tried to
suborn the editors; and when the text became more critical,
wholly abandoning fantasy and humour, they despatched a
General to the publisher of the journal, commissioned to
threaten him with military legal proceedings, since he had
been a lieutenant of the line, "discharged with the right to
wear uniform!" But the publisher was not impressed, and
threatened *them* with such darts "as kill in a few seconds."
Then a little Rhenish newspaper charged the three gentle-

men under their real names with inspiring virulent articles which, as Bismarck's enemies, they launched in Bismarck's Press, in order to widen the breach between him and the Emperor—and more feverishly than ever were the trio haunted by the question: "Who is behind all this?"

Their natures reacted variously. Eulenburg smiled and took no sort of action, secretly resolving, however, to separate himself from his two compromising friends. Kiderlen challenged the editor and wounded him; but Holstein strode furiously up and down his room, accusing the most utterly impossible people—the Secretary of State (his Chief), who must be trying to get rid in this way of the dual régime; then Herbert Bismarck, who was covering his tracks by the Rhenish article; then Count Henckel, because he had money in a paper which joined hands in the work—ultimately calling out that perfectly guileless gentleman, who refused his challenge. But Holstein, who was thirsting for blood, made Eulenburg put pressure on the Emperor to command Henckel to fight, whereupon Eulenburg feared "that Holstein will hate the Emperor now, if His Majesty does not admit the case against Henckel; and a Holstein-hate for the Emperor would lead to very serious consequences." As a matter of fact, Holstein never did forgive the Emperor for vetoing the duel.

Meanwhile, as in a farce, the miscreant was sitting in the next room. He was, as they learnt long afterwards, one of Holstein's functionaries.

From their conduct in this affair we can confidently predict how these three diplomats will behave in any serious political crisis.

Still greater was the sensation spread far and wide abroad in the same year of 1894 as the result of a scandal at Court. For two years all ranks in Court society, from the Empress downwards, had been receiving anonymous letters in the same handwriting: telling of intrigues, cabals, instigations, and enclosing pornographic pictures in which the heads had been cut out and replaced by photographic ones. All these missives, like *Kladderadatsch,* were so well-informed about personalities that they could only come from the Emperor's immediate environment. Though the charges were exaggerated, they were in most instances founded on fact, so that the whole Court trembled at every fresh revelation; and there were more than two hundred. The most exalted personages were accused of the most heinous misdemeanours—illicit love-affairs, fraud, calumny; the Empress Frederick said maliciously: "One half of the Court is writing letters against the other half." As the Baron von Schrader was especially attacked, suspicion fell upon his antagonistic colleague, one Herr von Kotze, for both were Masters of the Ceremonies. The convivial Kotze was a universal favourite, much liked by the Emperor, who would often thee-and-thou him, and thus he was the envy of his superiors in general. So now they discovered the clues they were set on discovering, and further—the damning proof: two sheets of blotting-paper in his office, which when held before a looking-glass displayed the very remarkable and evidently disguised handwriting of the letters in question.

With this blotting-paper they convinced the Emperor. Confronted with such documentary evidence, he instantly fixed upon the guilty person; and it was the work of a few moments to ordain the ruin of a well-tried friend and functionary, who had never been reproached with anything worse than frivolity and love of pleasure, armorial bearings, and decorations. He did not take into consideration the conviviality of the accused and the austerity of the accuser, ignored the latter's possible motives, ignored no less the fact that Kotze too had received these letters; he consulted no graphologist upon the blotting-paper, nor did he even try the obvious experiment of at once, and secretly, sequestering Kotze and then seeing if the letters continued to come; least of all did it occur to him to give the accused an opportunity of speaking, or invite the opinion of some trusted person—not one of these things did he do. In a quarter of an hour the man was repudiated. Returning in the best of spirits from his mother's country house, Kotze no sooner entered the Palace than he found himself arrested: "In the King's Name." Since as Master of Horse he came under military jurisdiction, they took him, an hour later, in a Court carriage, and in uniform, to the Military Prison.

Inquiry by the Military authorities. No evidence. Writing materials forbidden, his wife to have access to him only in the presence of an officer. Nevertheless, in a few days more letters were received at Court. *Now* a graphologist was consulted. The new letters, he pronounced, were from the writer of the old ones, but these had not come from the person who had used the blotting-paper. A week went by before the Adjutant-General released the Master of the Ceremonies, no evidence having been obtained. What did the Emperor do? Did he send for his old friend now? No— he washed his hands of the whole thing. When the scandal, carried far beyond the boundaries of the Court by his order of arrest, began to take effect upon the public, he declared: "I have nothing to do with this business. The investigation is now being conducted by the Judge Advocate of the Corps." Followed hostilities between the Kotze and Schrader parties and families, a constant stream of aristocratic witnesses, a whirlwind of threats, of insults; for nine months this went on. At last, shortly before Easter, came full acquittal.

"What will the Emperor do now?" asked all the world. Receive the acquitted in full Court? Give higher rank, and fuller confidence, to a servant so horribly and so mistakenly assailed? By a title and decorations proclaim to all the world that to err is human, to be rash is possible, but that a king can make kingly amends? He took counsel with Kotze's successor and adversary—what is to be done in such a situation? An innocent man cleared, a dead man resuscitated: very troublesome. Receive him? Out of the question. But some sort of token of favour! A breast-pin? A snuff-box? Have we got it at last? We have, your Majesty!

Next day, on behalf of His Majesty, an Easter-egg composed of flowers was delivered at Herr von Kotze's abode. He never saw his sovereign again. But his enemy—the Baron von Schrader—him he killed in a duel. Nevertheless his life and his happiness, his reputation and his family's privileges were gone, his name was brought into dishonour— from Siberia to Cape Town "Kotze" was synonymous with wanton calumny. And in this affair likewise, the real offender sat, unsuspected, in the next room.

According to Waldersee, it was a near relative of the Emperor's.

5

The Court of William the Second, with its cold glitter —which we propose to ignore, though of its sycophants we shall have something to say—was not the favourite abiding-place of its master. The excitement of bedizenments and banquets quickly palled; splendour repeated itself *ad nauseam;* the craving for publicity was only to be satisfied by the streets, by perpetual goings and comings, by entries on a much larger scale and with much more resounding effects than at first. None the less, everything had to be kept up to the mark in Haroun-al-Raschid style, for the visits of foreign potentates who were to be dazzled by the power and glory of the German Empire, as symbolized by the Weisser Saal. Not only was gala dress supplied for six hundred Court lackeys, but so many were kept, in view of the great banquets, that none officiated on more than 139 and many on only 81 days of the year. The Grooms of the Chambers were on duty from 150 to 70 days in the year; the rest of the time they—mostly young men in the middle twenties—lounged away idly in Berlin.

The table appointments of the Palace were worth something between one and two millions (Z. 52). Once, when a touring automobile was out of order and the Count responsible represented the heavy expenses incident on taking reserve cars, the Emperor said angrily: "It doesn't matter what my wishes cost. I require everything to be up to the mark. You are answerable to me."

Reischach, who had superintended in the old Emperor's time, states that the royal stables under William the First had been regarded as a luxury—only their Majesties, the Mistress of the Robes, the Palace- and Court-ladies having carriages. Under William the Second,

we had to turn out something like two hundred teams every day, and these for the Mistress of the Robes, the wives of Court officials and the Ladies of Honour, the Adjutants-General and Aides-de-camp, the Heads of Cabinets, the Lord High Steward, the Masters of the Household, the Chamberlains on duty, the Prince's tutor, the two physicians, and the Grooms of the stables, besides horses for the Household. . . . Most of these went out twice every day, and frequently three and four times. In the Royal Stables we had our hands full nearly the whole year round in Berlin, Potsdam, and the New Palace, and if a journey was ahead of us, we were often kept at it in three different parts of the monarchy at once.

And if two Adjutants-General left Potsdam on duty, taking the train to Berlin, his calculation is that even so twenty carriages would be requisitioned that day for the pair of them. As the allowance paid by the people to their monarch, and modestly termed the Civil List, mounted higher and higher by reason of the manifold demands for extra grants, the Emperor, who could economize for himself, was able to lay by four millions after only two years of his royal services (W. 2, 157).

The Court-Marshals had the heaviest task of all. "The Emperor did not like to be asked many questions, but could be very ungracious if one had neglected to consult him about this or that. One scarcely dared to put more than two or three questions, and had to be very careful to choose the right moment for those" (Z. 52). The proud Augustus Eulenburg, a Master of the Household, aged seventy, had often to go out to Potsdam in the evening and spend the night there, so that he might, in the morning, meet his sovereign on the return from his ride, walk with him along the eighty paces to his room, and there and thus bring forward the most essential questions, although the Emperor was never for two hours in the day engaged in serious work. This arbitrariness increased:

If at night in the smoking-room [so Zedlitz relates] some cigarette-ash chanced to fall upon the carpet under the Emperor's eye, it was: "Of course; just like my Court-Marshals! Instead of taking care of my things, they do more to spoil them than anyone else!" And shaking his fist in my face, he continued: "But I'll soon teach you what's what!" Although such attacks from the Emperor were by no means uncommon . . . this incident offended me very deeply. I felt immediately that, just because it did, I should find it difficult to take any notice of it; the Emperor always did these things as it were between jest and earnest, sensible people being supposed to see that after all it was only his fun. . . . That was precisely what gave the Emperor such power over those who surrounded him; everyone dreaded the inconsiderateness he could show. And of course he always had the jeerers on his side.

Afterwards, the Court-Marshal did declare himself to have been offended. The Emperor: "I haven't the least idea what you're talking about." Explanation. "Ah, *now* I know what you mean." Further representation by the Court-Marshal that junior officers were present, while he was forty-four years of age. The Emperor: "But you don't look a day over twenty-eight. You mustn't be so thin-skinned!" Then, with a nod: "Come, it's all right!"

This admirable narrative of a just reproof is followed by one sentence which sums up the whole. Zedlitz concludes with: "Whereupon I bowed, and withdrew." The offender, king though he be, is for once called to account; he at first remembers nothing about it, then makes an irrelevant and ambiguous remark upon the youthful appearance of the complainant, advises him to acquire a thicker and more accommodating skin, and finishes with a nod and an affirmation resembling that of the Deity after his day's work of creation: "He saw that it was good.". . . Before him stands a Silesian Count of ancient lineage, not a stranger but a part of his daily surroundings. No matter; the monarch is nowise abashed, for he knows how such rare reproofs must always end—in a silent bow.

How could it have been otherwise, when we consider the anxieties and terrors which undermined the vitality of these functionaries? Here is the programme of an ecclesiastical ceremonial at Metz:

Their Majesties were invited by the Bishop graciously to proceed to the chairs placed, in the Cathedral, on the right of the altar in the choir. On His Majesty's left the Legate, on Her Majesty's right the Lord-Lieutenant, were to take their places. It had as well been verbally agreed that both the Legate's and the Lord-Lieutenant's seats were to be somewhat behind, and a step lower. But completely disregarding this arrangement, the Legate, instead of taking his place on the left of Their Majesties, seated himself obliquely opposite, under a sumptuous baldachin, on a chair which overtopped those of the Royalties (Z. 35).

The indignation at this was universal: such invectives were heard as in the Middle Ages would have given rise to many years of war. But what had the Legate at Metz to do, from his exalted seat? Had he to confer upon the monarch the anointed Crown? Or preach him a sermon? Nothing of the kind. "Thence he proceeded to confer the blessing," which, if placed a step lower than those who were to receive it, he could not, technically speaking, have properly done.

Happier than at Court was the Emperor at the chase. True, his shooting-estate, Rominten, one of the finest forests, belonged to the State, not to the Crown; but its 100,000 acres were transformed by the Imperial desire from a primeval forest with lakes and rivers into a sort of sportsman's chess-board—for every shoot was on the drive principle, his enjoyment consisting rather in the numbers easily despatched than in the more arduous outwitting of individual victims.

An army of foresters attended on bicycles, in carts, on horse, and on foot, so that actually every . . . point was under the keenest observation from first to last. . . . Besides this, most of the preserves were lavishly provided with carriage-roads, observation-posts, and shelters . . . so much so that I often could not avoid a sense of regret at seeing so magnificent a forest turned into an artificial shooting-demesne (Z. 39).

Even Eulenburg, so frequently present, says that

the shoots were horrible. This massacre of unfortunate creatures, utterly unable to escape from their fate of destruction, is no kingly recreation. Strangely enough, no one at Court has any sort of sense that it adds nothing to the glory of a sovereign to cause these hapless wild creatures to be driven into an immense enclosure, in the centre of which the noble sportsmen are posted, pouring their shots upon the panting desperate brutes, as they hurl themselves perpetually against the farthest hedges, and this never stops till all are dead or else dragging mortally wounded on the ground, until at the end of the day they are put out of their agony.

As numbers were the sole aim, and the game was driven up to the gun's mouth, the Emperor, in three December days with Prince Donnersmarck, could proclaim his one thousand six hundred and seventy-fifth head; and in his forty-third year cause to be inscribed in golden letters on a block of granite: "Here His Majesty William II brought down His Most High's fifty thousandth animal, a white cock-pheasant." For the rest, the exalted sportsman sometimes had to turn his attention to the game when he least expected it, would be summoned from his royal labours by the cry of "A Stag!" and never knew that Tirpitz, when submitting papers, had arranged with the Head Forester to omit such

signals during his conference (T. 138). It was really necessary, when questions of State had to be brought to Rominten
for decision, and the only train to Berlin be caught, so as to
speak next day in the Reichstag.

But happiest of all was the Emperor on his yacht. Safe
from the submission of papers, surrounded by a little group
of boon-companions, sheltered from every conceivable onslaught, far from wife and family, in a patriarchal little domain where he could keep an eye on everything, even the
kitchen, look after everything himself—absolute monarch
of all he surveyed, no democratic cheeseparing to be feared,
on Sundays even acting parson; inaccessible, and yet able at
any moment to flash his wishes along the wire to the world at
large: thus blissful was his life in Greek bays and Norwegian fjords. With the latest news, conveyed to him tele-
graphically by the Foreign Office, he would dally so long
that his tantalized companions got their friends to wire them
the same information; and then the over-trumping of each
other's tricks between the initiated on board was like that of
a parcel of schoolboys on a country walk.

It was a kind of perpetual floating casino, and the tone
was to match. In the mornings,

it amused him to make members of his suite, including the oldest
Adjutants-General, do open-air exercises and gymnastics on deck,
and while they were bending their knees or squatting, he would
take the opportunity of giving them such a push that they sprawled
all over the place (E. 2, 110).

The old boys professed to be greatly delighted by this attention,
but clenched their fists in their pockets, and afterwards abused the
Emperor like fish-wives.

The mental recreations during these weeks of idle companionship are best described by Kiderlen:

As Chief Companions of the Yacht were designated: Count Waldersee as Punch-maker, von Hahnke as Chief Trencherman and Head-Conductor in E-sharp, Count Goerz as handy-man in all emergencies and member of the choir, Count Wedell as expert in Eti-Piquet-questions, Count Eulenburg as bard and ballad-maker; Dr. Leuthold, Aesculapian to the First Class. Von Senden was Navigating Officer under both tropics, but especially that of Cancer

—and so forth. Then he describes how Count Goerz had to go through his repertory of animal-imitations every evening.

The evenings were partly musical, partly devoted to conjuring-tricks by Hülsen; sometimes we had to get something else. I have already done the Dwarf, and turned out the light to the Emperor's vast delectation. In an improvised sing-song I did the Siamese Twins with G; we were connected by an enormous sausage.

The company's ages ranged from thirty-five to sixty.

As he could never be alone, the Emperor spent the evenings, when guests were not present, with the Empress. Remembrances of his early youth, hatred for his mother, had made him apprehensive beforehand of feminine influences, and even in the beginning "he kicked against the pricks of marriage" (E. 89). Before long, too, he was irritated by his wife's piety—in and near Berlin she had forty-two churches built in ten years, which on a rough calculation is one every three months—and he was bored by the limitations of her Ladies of Honour. In these surroundings he could even be reticent, for liberty's sake; and though he probably never indulged in dissipations, he would break away—so Zedlitz relates from his seven years' experience—

as often as he can; is always in the highest spirits the instant he departs. and best enjoys his life at a distance from family re-

straints. On his every return I noticed the depressing effect it had
on him. He always wants to get away, but his consort does her
utmost to prevent him. . . . This clinging affection is womanly
and touching enough, but I was often inclined to think it ill-advised,
for running after others always makes us wearisome to them.
. . . His extreme restlessness, the perpetual need of something to
look forward to, arises from the Emperor's dissatisfaction with the
limitations of his family circle. His temper, always somewhat
gloomy in the New Palace and at Potsdam, undergoes the most
agreeable transformation from the moment any plan is in progress,
for instance a journey, and most noticeably when stimulated by
male society and the prospect of a complete change.

What went on behind closed doors in this conjugal relation of a gifted, highly nervous man with a sweet-natured
narrow-minded, devout country-girl was revealed to few,
and by fewer still reported; compassion for the hapless consort of an hysterical autocrat disarmed all criticism. She saw
through many an insincerity in the Emperor's sycophants;
but when once she was complaining of the faked reports
from the Kadinen Estate, and Count Eulenburg (the elder)
begged her to let the Emperor hear the truth for once, she
would only repeat: "Unfortunately I can't do anything; he
would say 'Go away; you don't understand these things' "
(Z. 74). From two dialogues at which the Court-Marshal
was present—from two momentary states of mind—we can
reconstruct many years of matrimonial tedium, wherein the
wife is by far the most to be pitied. Two days before his
birthday the Emperor once countermanded a dinner to
thirty-four Princes, on account of the illness of one of his
sons. The Empress: "But, William, surely you won't do
that!" The Emperor roughly pushed her away: "I decide
these things—not you!"

Shortly before that, on one of the few quiet winter

evenings at the New Palace—no guests, only two Ladies of Honour and four gentlemen being present—the Empress sewing, he reading despatches or newspaper-cuttings, occasionally aloud, the others turning over illustrated journals at the big table, till close on eleven o'clock: "The Emperor had been reading to himself practically the whole evening, when suddenly he said to the Empress: 'Do you intend to stop here all night?'

" 'No, William; but I didn't like to disturb you, as you were so busy reading all the evening.'

" 'Well, what else can I do, when this place is so frightfully boring!' " (Z. 94).

A conjugal dialogue which no dramatist could surpass.

Reverse of the medal for his subjects: A speech at Schleswig:

"Her Majesty—the shining jewel always at my side! The embodiment of all the virtues proper to a German Princess, it is she whom I have to thank for being able to fulfil my exacting duties."

Commemoration Day of the Borussia Students; Imperial Speech:

Never before, in the whole recorded history of the German Universities, has any one of them been honoured thus. At beautiful Bonn, the Empress, the first Princess of the land, encircled by her illustrious ladies, is present at a Students' festival. . . . I hope and believe that all you young Borussians, on whom Her Majesty has smiled to-day, will feel that their whole lives are henceforth ennobled.

6

General Head-quarters: thus, immediately after his accession, did the Emperor rechristen the old-time Maison

Militaire, and this martial style might seem to point to mobilization; but it was no more than the rodomontade perpetually inspired by his duality, for he prized but scantly the counsels of his aides-de-camp. The desire for security against external danger sprang rather from that sense of dangers within the realm which kept him in constant fear of popular revolts throughout his reign of thirty years; this was, again, the reason why he trusted no class, no party— none but his paladins. Officer of the Bodyguard: this, and the Bodyguard as a whole, were ideas which in his mind regained their most literal meaning; he even established a Night Bodyguard for his own person. His Guards were, each and all, the men who in the hour of danger were to shield him with their own bodies; and no such danger could ever confront him on the battlefield, where modern commanders of troops do not appear in person—it could come only from the heart of his realm, from the Red Volcano in its midst.

So the motives urging William the Second to reliance on the Army were twofold; hence we should expect to find him shining in that sphere, where interest and ambition joined hands. In a hundred speeches he revealed himself, and amazed the nation.

As in 1861, so now—division and distrust prevails among the people. Our German Empire rests upon a single steadfast cornerstone—the Army. . . . If it should ever again come to pass that the City of Berlin revolts against its monarch, the Guards will avenge with their bayonets the disobedience of a people to its King!

At first he went in for reforming everything—General Staff, manœuvres, uniforms; he wanted younger Generals;

he personally interfered in every quarter, they were each and all bewildered. This lasted a year. Then came the un-expected: the group he most distinguished, his own special group, began to compare the Old-Prussian tradition with the New-German fashion, and got uneasy. So early as the May of 1890 Waldersee, as Chief of Staff, confesses:

It is very painful to me to be told that the Emperor is visibly losing ground within the Army. The disaffection has been gradual, but is now decidedly more widespread. The causes? Marked preference shown for the Navy, as also for the Guards, and very little interest in the Line. . . . Considerably less courtesy to highly placed officers than his grandfather was wont to display. An artless love of playing at soldiers, unmistakably evinced by the incessant alerts, for no reason whatever. . . . Contempt for the judgment of experienced men. Frequent favouritism towards in-dividuals, attributable only to personal sentiments, and on the other hand excessive severity towards others. . . . Indiscreet comments to officers upon their superiors in rank. Finally, the inclination to make himself popular at the expense of the Army. . . . I write this down, because it is over and over again con-veyed to me from the most widely different quarters and by the men who are best capable of judging. . . . The senior officers are not left long enough in their positions nowadays. . . . A very evil result of this is the sense of insecurity it awakes in them, and the consequent lack of pleasure in their work. That affair of the critique [on the manœuvres] is widely known in the Army, and has made bad blood there. . . . The Emperor . . . is severely blamed; they say, "What will be the end of it, if there's no authority that counts!" If *I* hear of such grievances they must be genuine; for as I am supposed to be a particular friend of the Emperor's, most people are very cautious with me (W. 2, 126).

This is the first dark saying we are given to reflect upon —it comes from the principal soldier in the Army. Some months later, during the Imperial Manœuvres of 1890, he resumes in still gloomier tone:

Last year, even, it went off better. Now there is greater certainty of touch, but along with it, over-estimation of his own capabilities. . . . The Emperor is extraordinarily restless, tearing about in every direction, going much too far forward in the fighting-line, interfering with the Generals' leadership, giving innumerable, frequently self-contradictory orders, and barely listening to his advisers. He always wants to win, and so takes an unfavourable decision by the umpire in very bad part. *I* should know this, having once ignored that desire. . . . His disposition of troops was decidedly bad; even the night before, it was clear that he must lose the battle, and there was marked satisfaction at this among their Highnesses and the suite. . . . If he insisted on taking the command in war, not merely as a matter of form like his father and grandfather, there would be a disaster.

The day after the critique the Emperor sent privately to ask Waldersee if he would care to take the Stuttgart Command. Moltke held that the Chief of Staff could not be dismissed "without injury to paramount interests." Three months afterwards Waldersee *was* dismissed, but quite graciously—the Emperor saying: "The Chief of Staff will be little more than a kind of amanuensis under me, and for that I require a more junior officer."

To make up for his failure in the manœuvres he turned his attention to tactical work, again without success. What was to be done, to prevent his being present at the critique? "It was adroitly conveyed to him that there were measles at Head-quarters. If he *had* been present, Schlieffen [the new Chief of Staff] would probably have been obliged to send in his resignation" (W. 2, 234).

To avert a third discomfiture next year—that is, in March 1893—

his aide-de-camp made confidential enquiries of Count Schlieffen as to his solution of the problem set, and worked upon this basis with the Emperor. Thus at the critique, the monarch could confidently uphold the Chief's views, and let it be perceived that he himself had hit upon precisely the right solution (W. 2, 286).

Count Schlieffen, having got off once by measles and next by a vicarious breach of confidence, was now to be confounded by a new plan of campaign for the war on two fronts, drawn up by the Emperor.

The Emperor's idea is a simultaneous offensive against France, and in this view he has depleted the Eastern forces by something between two and three divisions. We are to attack their fortresses, and there is every prospect of a sanguinary repulse. Whereas we had a really good chance if, as I wished, we let them advance . . . and then cut them to pieces, as we could have done. . . . But Schlieffen will have to choose between his appointment and preventing the Emperor from carrying out his crude ideas (W. 2, 318).

This particular war-game turned into deadly earnest—twenty years later the Emperor's scheme helped the French to win the Battle of the Marne.

Here is Eulenburg's opinion in the same year of the Military Cabinet:

The idea that an aide-de-camp is sacrosanct, the symbol of perfection in a human being, is one that I simply cannot get into my head. . . . Such men as these—and with them Senden, partly out of his mind, and Plessen! . . . It's really a blessing, after all, that in this witches' kettle, not to say mad-house, there should be something to laugh at (E. 2, 248).

Admiral von Senden-Bibran, once, through his own fault, severely snubbed in England, had imbibed a furious hatred for everything English, and tried to instil this into the Emperor "with mulish stubbornness, and a malignity and pettiness that years seemed only to increase." Adjutant-General von Plessen's insight may be judged by a later dialogue with the chief naval authority, to whom he said: "Now that England's at war, Germany must proceed against her."

"But we have no ships, Your Excellency!"

"That doesn't matter. Get a single division landed—and we're rid of England."

More protests from the Admiral.

"Well, if that won't do, we and Russia can march against Egypt and India!" (Eck. 2, 44).

Everything had to be militarized, including the Ministers. At a dinner in the beginning of 1889 the Emperor, in expansive mood, announced various promotions—told Gossler, the Minister of Education, that he was now a Major and von Scholz, Finance Minister, that he was a Lieutenant. The latter took it as a joke, but three days later read with pure amazement the printed announcement that Sergeant von Scholz was now Lieutenant. It was only six months after William's accession, but already the *Germania* was in ironical mood. "Hard luck! The Chief of the Prussian Ministry of Finance is fifty-five years old, and up to the present has had to be satisfied with the modest rank of sergeant. But now he has climbed so high as a Second Lieutenancy."

Not that such promotions by any means enhanced the Ministers' prestige in their sovereign's eyes, for at heart he held all officers of the Reserve to be a little ridiculous; such popinjays were not regarded as belonging to the *élite* of humanity. All the same, as military attachés they were privileged to disport themselves in the diplomatic sphere;

indeed, their activities in foreign capitals quickly wrung this confidential minute from Eulenburg:

They are permitted to send letters and reports direct to the Emperor, who takes every word they say for gospel. He thinks ever so much more of these communications than of reports from any one of his Ambassadors who does not happen to have been at some time an officer on the active list. . . . These gentry, cavalry-captains or majors, are solemnly preparing themselves to step into an Ambassadorship one of these days. . . . Over and over again I can trace the influence of the military group, which represents a permanent camarilla, but is not recognized as such by the militarized German State. For if anyone lets fall a remark about military intrigues, up gets some General or another, twists his moustache, and says: "I, General So-and-so, herewith declare that any such expression as 'Aide-de-camp Politics' is a foul slander" (E. 2, 245).

That this protest against a dual régime should come from Eulenburg enhances its piquancy. The favourite, jealous of all other favourites, informs posterity of a camarilla which at the worst was merely running counter to another one.

Such were the influences shaping the Emperor's home-policy.

"I know only two political parties—that which is for me, and that which is against me!" The motto of an absolute ruler. These words, spoken at the age of thirty, at a time when good intentions were at their highest and infatuation was at its lowest, introduce the theme which for three decades he was to vary by alienation from all parties in turn. The Reichstag and the Prussian Diet (*Landtag*) were to him assemblies of ignorant headstrong persons whose political hues he could barely distinguish. When differences arose, his one idea was to send home for his Guards and let *them* take the recalcitrants in hand; from a *coup d'état,* which was openly urged on him, he was deterred only by the uncertainty of the issue.

His inmost feeling was made manifest in the year 1897, when he said to Baron von Stumm, in the hope that his words would go further: "If the Reichstag doesn't vote me my ships, there'll be such a row as there's never been before!" If everything had been "his"—ships, soldiers, subjects—this arbitrariness might have been in order. At first it was only in confidence that he revealed his heartfelt contempt. To the Tsar in 1895: "Both parties are about ripe for being hanged in batches." And on an official document in 1899: "Just what I've been preaching daily for years to those mutton-heads in the Reichstag!" On the visit to Ballin's ship in the Kiel Week he kept all the male guests standing, and talked the whole time with ladies only, because he had seen with disgust on the list of those present the names of Bassermann and Stresemann, two members of the Reichstag who had never attacked him. So profound was William the Second's disdain for the representatives of his subjects.

His early ambition of conciliating the Socialists had been buried in oblivion after the first attempt. Caprivi's fall and Bismarck's were caused by directly opposite reasons —Caprivi's because he was not in favour of emergency mea-sures against Labour, Bismarck's because he was. Now it was clear to the Emperor that "the men" were not to be won over, that the class and the Party were identical, and so the class also became in his eyes the enemy of the State. Force alone could prevail. As the Socialist Press grew more and more critical, Plessen was soon saying to the Emperor: "We must turn on the guns at once—that will put a stop to it."

This simple policy the Emperor repudiated with the trenchant reply: "Rubbish! I'll have you call out *every* blighter that insults me!"

Count Mirbach, in the House of Lords, moved a proposal for a new franchise; Köller wanted a State prosecution of those Socialists who refused to stand when the Emperor's health was drunk; the Die-Hard Press was for association of the German Princes in a New Federation whose aim should be the abolition of universal suffrage. At the same time, on Sedan Day in 1895, the Emperor described the Socialists as "a gang of men unworthy to bear the name of Germans," and appealed to the sword against the "treasonable rabble"; "we must get rid of these elements once for all." This speech was followed by other incitements to civil war.

All the more closely, one might suppose, he would now have attached the loyal Right. Were not the Conservatives his Triarians? They were the Agrarian Party. When in 1894 they defeated the Commercial Treaty with Russia, and in 1899 the Rhine-Elbe Canal Bill, on both of which the Emperor was keen, he became more rabid against them than even against the Socialists—the latter he had feared from the first, but the former he had regarded as a buttress against the enemy. Now his very Bodyguard was tottering, for the Guards and the Agrarians were of kindred blood. If the most ancient nobility was refractory, where was the Royal Authority? A wholly Frederician conception of affairs—only, just a hundred years too late.

First he appealed to tradition:

With a very heavy heart I have been obliged to recognize that by those who stand nearest to Me among the nobility My best in-

tentions are misunderstood, and in a sense defied; nay, the word
"Opposition" has actually sounded in My ears. An "Opposition"
by the Prussian nobility is a thing in its very nature inconceivable.
As the ivy clings to the trunk of the gnarled oak-tree, decks it
with its foliage, and protects it when the tempest rages round its
head, so does the Prussian nobility adhere to My House.

But the ivy, which never yet protected a single oak in a
tempest, but has strangled many a one which it appeared
to beautify, twined still more stiflingly about the gnarled
orator: "If the nobility" (it was written) "are henceforth
to venture on no opposition whatever, they will have—so
far as their relation to Parliament is concerned—to renounce
either their rank or their mandates, even in the House of
Lords."

The Emperor was beside himself—proscribed the
Kreuzzeitung at Court, deprived Count Limburg-Stirum,
who had shown that it was the duty of the Lords to expos-
tulate with the Crown, of the rank of Ambassador, and wired
to one Dönhoff who by voting for the Russian Treaty had
broken his pledge to the Party: "Bravo! Done like a true
patrician!" In the second skirmish he forbade a dozen
"Canal-Rebels" to appear at Court, and according to Jagemann, forms were actually printed and the names filled in.
"So-and-so is for the present banished from Court by reason of opposition not only to My policy but My Person." At
the same time he suspended from office two Presidents and
sixteen *Landrats,* but rescinded all these measures when
alarmed by the increasing outcry.

While these things were going on the Emperor's friends
stood by, apprehensively noting symptoms which they
judged to be alarming; nor has anyone—if his rough drafts
did not undergo subsequent retouching—analysed more skil-

fully than Eulenburg the causation and the inherent perils of the new régime.

The King of Prussia [he wrote to Holstein] is empowered by the Constitution to rule autocratically. Does William the Second commit indiscretions? Does he promulgate decrees which overstep the limits of his rightful authority? . . . This is not the point at issue—which is, that Germany and Prussia will no longer suffer the Emperor to assert his private will and pleasure. It is melancholy to say it, but the establishment of the German Empire—that is to say, the transfusion of Liberal South-German blood into Prussian veins, the amalgamation of the ruling States-man with the slumbering Barbarossa—has been the ruin of the Old-Prussian monarchy. An autocratic sovereign, be his rights what they may, is no longer conceivable by a progressive educated people. Only those monarchs will be tolerated who accept the parliamentary forms of government. . . . If the Emperor is now assuming autocratic authority, he is well within his rights—the only question being: Who is going to win at that game? I fear that nothing but a successful war will give the Emperor the neces-sary prestige for that. . . . Another form it might take is that of Imperialism—logical, this, for the autocratic Emperor. But it would mean, if not for him for his successor, the end of the mon-archy. . . . That His Majesty is by his very nature impelled to this attempt at restoring the system annihilated by the much-belauded amalgamation is, of course, elementary.

Here the origin and outcome of the autocratic régime are set forth with admirable perspicacity; and only one thing spoils our relish for such unerring insight. It is that its pos-sessor, the Emperor's bosom friend, imparted his views, not to him, but always to his affinity, Holstein. Who for his part was ready with a cynically prophetic rejoinder; he answered in a semi-official style, usually foreign to his private corre-spondence:

I do not conceal from myself that H.M. is living on his royal capital, and that what he is heedlessly squandering now will one day be sorely needed by his son—nay, in a few years probably by himself. One of the gravest portents of the imminent extinction of German Imperial sentiment is the fact that even *your* intelligence refuses to contemplate the issues for which the present erratic régime is too surely preparing the ground.

Thus, after six years of the Emperor's rule, did those nearest him anticipate events, tip one another the wink—and hold their tongues.

7

The Russian wire was cut. A year after the ending of the Germano-Russian agreement, the Tsar—on his visit to the French fleet—had stood during the playing of the detested Marseillaise; in 1892 followed the military convention. At last, after twenty years of isolation, France had the allies she longed for. It was not till some time afterwards that Holstein disclosed the real reason for his veto on the Russian treaty—fear of Bismarck's return. "It would have been dangerous to let Prince Bismarck into the secret of such a transaction." These words sum up his character: the man was such an intriguer, so perfidious in every decision he made, that he believed everyone —believed even Bismarck—to be capable of imperilling the Empire by betrayal of a treaty for the sake of personal revenge! Because Bismarck like himself could hate, he thought that the Bismarcks can feel as the Holsteins feel.

Not more than a month after his dismissal Bismarck, in his newspaper, wrote in favour of Russia as against Austria's schemes in the Balkans, and said emphatically that it was "not Germany's business to further Austria's Balkan ambitions." The Emperor, on the other hand, said to his Generals: "Russia wants to occupy Bulgaria, and is claiming our neutrality. But my word is pledged to the Emperor of Austria, and I have told the Tsar that I cannot leave Austria in the lurch."

This was his article of faith. The friendship with Austria, which was ultimately to be the ruin of Germany, was—in so far as the Emperor was concerned—inspired by the feudal House of Hapsburg, and would never have been manifested by him to a confederation such as Switzerland, in which the eight States would have been united not under a monarchy but a republic. As he despised republics, and could not regard a "shadow-king" as the Most High's equal—as he took his stand upon the supremacy of the "Monarch-by-the-Grace-of-God," his friendly feeling for the Hapsburg and the Sultan was less a political sentiment than a dynastic emotion, which kept him in permanent alliance with these two Imperial rulers, and with them only. Nothing in William the Second was more genuine than this disastrous idea of "fraternal loyalty," but only in so far as it attached the Emperor to a sovereign whom he reckoned as his equal; not at all because that sovereign ruled a partly German people. And so, as between Vienna and Petersburg, the Emperor's conscience was never at rest; this was why the son of that Tsar who had outraged him, and whom he had abandoned in defiance of Bismarck, was for twenty years solicitously courted—simply because he was an autocrat in the old style, a Tsar, an Emperor like himself. An Alliance of the Three Emperors, such as had been concluded in 1884, would have been for William the only really congenial arrangement. But as to republics! They were his natural enemies—they stirred the discontented among his people to emulation. Thus in the Tsar's alliance with France he saw more danger to the Throne than to the Empire. Accordingly he more than once spoke to the Tsar, and never more plainly than in a letter at the end of 1895, of the increasing danger to the monarchical idea in general which was implicit in alliances with republics:

The perpetual presence of Princes, Grand-Dukes, Statesmen, Generals in full-dress at reviews of the troops, public funerals, dinners, race-meetings, cheek-by-jowl with the President of the Republic or in his immediate environment, causes these Republicans to imagine that they are quite respectable people with whom royalties can consort and sympathize. But what would be the result of this sort of thing at home, in our own countries? Republicans are by nature revolutionary, logically to be regarded as people who will one day have to be shot or hanged. They say to those of our subjects who are still loyally inclined: "Oh, we are not such very dangerous folk—you have only to go to France, and you'll see Royalists like yourselves walking about with revolutionaries. Why shouldn't it be the same with us?"

Don't forget that Jaurès—not by his personal guilt—now sits on the throne of the hereditary King of France and his Queen, both of whom the revolutionaries beheaded. The blood of Their Majesties still imbrues the land. Think—has it ever been prosperous or peaceful since then? Did it not stride from war to war in its great days, till it had drenched all Europe and Russia with blood, and in the end drawn down the Commune for the second time upon itself? Take my word for it, Nicky—the curse of God lies heavy on that nation! A sacred duty is imposed by Heaven on us Christian Kings and Emperors—to uphold the doctrine of the Divine Right of Kings.

Then he goes on to tell of a Russian General who in Paris had recently replied to the question: "Would Russia break the German Army to pieces?" with "No; we should go under; but what matter? Then we should get the Republic!" ... "That, my dear Nicky, is what I fear for you."

Seldom did the Emperor so coherently, so lucidly, pursue a train of thought. That was because therein lay his article of faith. Why Their Majesties were deposed and beheaded he did not know, any more than he knew why the Russian General had so unmistakably found *veritatem in vino*. He did not foresee by what fateful devious ways his words were to come true for that same Tsar, when twenty years should have passed—still less that he himself would have to pay so terrible a reckoning. His vision was of public funerals and race-meetings, dignitaries in full dress, and whey-faced black-hearted bourgeois rubbing elbows with hereditary Emperors, and pluming themselves on being respectable. He was living in the world of 120 years ago, more like a descendant of the Bourbons than the descendant of Voltaire's friend; he regarded Jaurès in the Chamber of Deputies as Jaurès on the throne, and at the bottom of his heart considered all those people who desired to be something more than subjects as only fit to be shot down—except that hanging them would be more suitable.

That was why the Emperor continually hankered after Petersburg, from which he had turned away at the time of Bismarck's fall; but the consciousness—never avowed—of remorse for an act of folly was complicated by fear and distrust, and so the path of return was thorny with perpetual entanglements of purpose. For four-and-twenty years the Emperor's Russian policy was symbolic of his vacillating temperament. In the beginning of 1891, "his anxiety about Russia is plainly to be seen. With others, as with himself, he regards a sensational development as always on the cards. . . . One day he thinks that everything looks promising for peace; the next, that war is staring us in the face. . . . This will lead to our utter undoing" (W. 2, 204). Two years later, he was so incensed by the strengthening of the Dual Alliance, which he himself had made possible, that Caprivi was instructed to breathe fire and flame against Russia, whereupon Schuvalov, utterly distraught, remarked: "For eight years I have been working towards the amelioration of Russo-German relations. Now my work is destroyed."

The death of Alexander—whose contemptuous allusion to him, wrested from Bismarck's willing hand, he certainly had not been invited to forget—brought to the throne in the person of the weak muddle-headed Nicholas a man whom the Emperor could dominate, and whom (especially in letters) he played with as a cat with a mouse. These letters form his only continuous correspondence in the course of twenty years. Nicky and Willy (as they called each other), totally dissimilar both in virtues and failings, exhibit in their friendship as it were one of those tortuous relationships between a man and a woman, wherein she, mostly absent and living among his enemies, will nevertheless in moments of weakness inspired by fear, yield to the man's desire—only to avenge herself (and soon) when courage is renewed by absence, with malignities and infidelities—and this with good excuse, since he too, once they are apart, is no less treacherous to her.

By preference with England. But in this most ticklish of relations, it was the Emperor who played the woman's part. With imperishable hatred and imperishable desire he reviled and wooed the powerful Briton, His German

Majesty forever emulative of the British model—studying it from afar as it were through opera-glasses, and when detected assuming an air of pure indifference and perfect self-reliance; brusquely rejecting long-awaited advances as may a beauty, tardily invited to the dance, reject her would-be partner—because she wants to see him on his knees to her, because she seeks not love but triumph. All this because, do what he will, he never can forget that in the past this man and this man's family have been insulting to him— and he belongs to the family!

Vanity, so wounded in those youthful German-English days; ambition, vulnerable to his mother's rankling shafts; mistrust, forever brooding on the possibility of these people's secret derision—these people whose calm power he admires, whose wise action he jealously appreciates, whose blood it is at once his pride and his misgiving to feel within his veins . . . such intimations of inferiority, of which at any price he fain would purge himself, and which, all through his life, even in his dreams could put him out of conceit with his power—it is to appease these emotions that he resolves to build his Fleet, to be the Sea-Lord of a great Sea-Power, for only so can he cry quits with the Island-Kingdom, with the Mistress of the Seas.

His mother's influence was in the wrong direction. "Just imagine!" he said to Waldersee at the end of 1888, "my mother is going to England, and has sent me word by the Home Secretary that she won't see me before she goes, because I have disgraced the memory of my father" (W. 2, 19). The tension was so great that at the end of 1890, before the unveiling of a monument to the Emperor Frederick in England, neither the old Queen nor her daughter sent any intimation to the Emperor, who read of it in the newspapers and despatched an adjutant to lay a wreath upon the first memorial erected to his father.

She has no religion [was his next complaint]. She is encouraging my sister in Athens to change her profession of faith—not that I should care if she turned Jewess! I gave her a handsome jointure and several castles, and much thanks I get for it. Lately she has even threatened me, and prophesied that my "autocratic behaviour" would inevitably be my ruin!

When at that time she wished to visit the prematurely confined Empress, the Emperor would not permit her even to enter the house, but led her straight back to her carriage (W. 2, 167).

Just then, in the early nineties, English opinion was still unanimously Germanophil, still strongly influenced by the tradition of Waterloo and the policy of Disraeli, who had always been in favour of Germany as against Russia. There was as yet no talk of German competition; Bismarck's legacy, embodied in his approach to Salisbury, still "lay on the table." It was reserved, then, for William the Second's dynastic sentiments to bring about the estrangement of two countries which had fewer reasons for antagonism than any other pair of nations.

The Prince of Wales, who was about twenty years older than his nephew, was as different from him as the plate is from the impression—everything in him was white where in the other it was black, and vice versa. The one seems to come out of a play by Sardou, the other out of Ibsen's *Wild Duck*. Prince William's youth had been empty of gallantries; Prince Edward's age was even still prolific in them; the virtue and emotionalism of the Emperor presented a sharp contrast to the Prince's notorious libertinism, and to the easy-going irony which took its toll of everything. The one always wanted to dazzle, the other never—rather did his royal station bore him; and while the nephew's fantastic imagination craved for the return of the Middle Ages, the uncle asked for nothing better than Merry Old England. Neither nerves nor susceptibilities worried this man; a great respect for his own mother made it the more difficult for him to understand the nephew's hatred for *his*— indeed, this Prince of Wales had even expunged from his heart that impatience which had embittered the existence of his brother-in-law Frederick, and had taken refuge in pleasure from the humiliations of inactivity. For all that, he was not only shrewder and more experienced, but in a certain sense more energetic, than his restless nephew.

These contradictions of temperament could have found no worse intermediary than Victoria. It was a distorted picture of his nephew which she painted for her brother, before they really knew each other; and she and Edward were so attached that till the day of her death they wrote to one another every week (Reischach, 155).

But even in his youth the Prince had included his mother's brother in his hatred for herself—at first, no doubt, simply because he *was* her brother. Even then he gave away his English uncle to the Tsar, which is the more surprising because that Tsar was by no means friendly to Prince William, and on the other hand was Edward's brother-in-law, and might retail it all to him. When his uncle was a guest at Potsdam in 1884, Prince William boasted of his antagonism in a letter to the Tsar:

The visit seems to be bearing fruit under the fostering hands of my mother and grandmother. But these English people happen

to have forgotten my existence . . . and I swear to you that everything I can do for you and your country, shall be done. But it
will be a long time first.

A year later:

I don't in the least look forward to enjoying the Prince of
Wales's visit—forgive me, he's your brother-in-law, after all!—
for with his intriguing disposition he will certainly try to play some
political game with the ladies. May Allah consign him to perdition, as the Turk says. . . . It's to be hoped that the Mahdi will
drive all these English into the Nile! (Lee, 480).

Scarcely had he come to the throne when he made his
uncle feel that *he* was only a Prince. At his first visit to
Vienna, in September 1888, the young Emperor, knowing
that Edward had announced himself for the same time,
laid down as a condition that he must be received alone,
even refusing Edward's offer to be present in Prussian
uniform at the Vienna railway-station. He obliged him
to leave Vienna for a week and go to Hungary—and never
reflected that this uncle would ere long succeed his ageing
mother, and would revenge himself as a King can; nor yet
did it occur to him that no man of honour, though but a
private individual, can ever in his life forget such a humiliation. Who can wonder then that the uncle, before his
nephew's visit to London, demanded a letter of apology,
that this was a very half-hearted acknowledgment of error,
and that but for Salisbury's urgent intervention the
Emperor would never have been invited at all?

This first visit likewise—by the wise old Queen invested
with all the glitter which was sure to gratify her grandson
—was complicated by mishaps behind the scenes. Edward,
only recently appointed Admiral of the British Fleet, could

not enjoy seeing his nephew promoted to the same rank at thirty, and it must have been with silent derision that he observed him presume upon his honours as if he had really earned them. For the Emperor lost no time in advising the Queen to station twelve units in the Mediterranean, instead of five; and told Edward, at the parade of the Fleet, that *his* was going to be much more modern in equipment (Lee, 656).

And yet his jealousy drew the Emperor towards this country as toward none other; there was no foreign state which he visited so often, for Norway in his estimation meant no more than a few harbours. For the next five years—that is, from 1890 to 1895—he went to England every summer to take part in his uncle's regattas, though he liked Edward as little as Edward liked him. During these eighteen midsummer weeks, in the precarious intimacy of life on board, the antipathy of the two men developed into an enmity which was to affect the history of the world.

The nephew would be the Emperor at one moment; at the next, a merry-andrew. His uncle was treated—by Eckardstein's account, who was with him four summers —"partly as a *quantité négligeable,* partly as the victim of his schoolboy pranks, conversational and otherwise."

His uncle, who was unused to this kind of thing and disliked it, gave the Emperor's friends his frankly ironic opinion:

I can't precisely make out my nephew's Colonial game. I can understand a man wanting to buy diamonds when he hasn't got any, but if he can't afford the big ones, it is more practical to chuck a hopeless game. The Emperor's interest in ships is all very well, but when one sees him taking a hand in everything with that paralysed arm of his, as he's doing just now on deck, one can't help being afraid he'll do himself some damage (E. 2, 81).

Whether Eulenburg was prudent enough to keep this to himself, or mischievous enough to repeat it, certain it is that these poisoned shafts did sooner or later reach the Emperor and implant in his heart such wounds as never ceased to rankle. With every year his reception grew cooler; the Prince called his guest "the boss of Cowes," and said: "The Regatta used to be my favourite relaxation; but since the Emperor has been in command here, it's nothing but a nuisance. Most likely I shan't come at all next year" (Eck. 1, 207).

He had his trials, assuredly. In August 1893 a sudden coolness with France over the Far Eastern question seemed to point to war with England—couriers came from London to the Queen, the Emperor too had to be informed. During dinner with Edward the Premier's private secretary arrived with letters and reports: France, relying on her Russian friends, was aiming at an expansion of territory in Farther India. "When the Emperor had read the despatches he burst out laughing, clapped his uncle on the back, and cried: 'Well, now you can go to India and show whether you're any good as a soldier!'" (Eck. 1, 208). Whereupon he returned to the "Hohenzollern."

There he summoned Eulenburg to his cabin—and completely broke down. "I really never had seen him so lose his self-command. . . . Following on the visit of the French fleet to Cronstadt, it was the second shock resulting from the non-renewal of the Russian Treaty." The Emperor said:

"England's Fleet is weaker than the French and Russian ones together. Our little one would be no use at all. Our Army isn't strong enough yet to fight on two fronts. That's why the French have chosen their moment so cunningly! Our prestige is at an end, if we can take no leading part. World-power—without that, a nation cuts a deplorable figure! What *are* we to do?" Eulenburg and two other intimates soothed him, but when they were leaving, he still looked wretched, white and nervous, biting his lips. . . . He felt himself suddenly driven into a corner, as it were, with his Big Navy talk, and politically speaking put in his place—which for one's poor dear vanity is always a tough morsel (E. 2, 83).

There was a yacht-race next morning, and the Emperor was exclusively interested in the steering and manning of his boat. Edward breakfasted and lunched on board, remaining there from ten o'clock to four, when reassuring news from London relieved the tension. He never heard anything of his nephew's collapse, which was well, politically speaking; though from the human point of view it would have been better that he should know of it, thus (as we today) explaining the Emperor's bluster as the bluff put up against his nervousness and sense of impotence. But as it was, his uncle regarded him as first impertinent and then indifferent; and as the nephew never asked what had been arranged in London, the impressions of the dinner and the breakfast and lunch next day were all that Edward had to judge by.

In the same week, the yachts were becalmed in a race round the Isle of Wight. As the Emperor was expected to dinner that night by the Queen, Edward tried to induce his nephew to abandon the race and so get back in time. Answer by flag-signal: "Race must be fought out, no matter when we finish." When, after ten o'clock, he was announced to his aged, punctilious, dignified grandmother, he had offended her more keenly than any kind of note begging her not to expect him could have done; and had again exacerbated his uncle, to whose respect for his mother such remissness had hitherto been unthinkable.

In the summer of 1895 England was isolated. The Liberal Cabinet was dissolved, Lord Salisbury returned to power, and with him Chamberlain; friends were looked for, Germany first of all. In July Salisbury mooted the break-up of Turkey; Hatzfeldt was electrified by the magnitude of the scheme. What Bismarck had striven for through a decade—the delimitation of the Austrian and Russian spheres in the Balkans—was at length made possible; the Russian coolness with Germany might now evaporate, the Dual Alliance would lose its *point d'appui*— while England, at long last, would automatically join the Triple Alliance.

But the name of Salisbury was enough to awaken Holstein's distrust, because Bismarck had highly esteemed him. Even private letters from the Ambassador failed to convince him—here again he judged others by the light of his own duplicity, saw England as insidiously aiming at the destruction of the Triple Alliance and bringing the Balkans down on their heads. "England," he summed up, "is not yet ripe for an alliance; we can wait." He even refused the Ambassador permission to go any further. This point of view was suggested to the Emperor in the usual way; it corresponded only too well with his own feeling. He repeated it, word for word, to Rothenhahn, and added a heightening touch: "Anyhow we are in the agreeable position of being able to watch and wait, since no one in Europe can do anything without us." . . . And now, again on the way to England, he was requested to palter with Lord Salisbury.

Lord Salisbury did not arrive at Cowes at the appointed

time, nor until an hour later, excusing himself by *force majeure,* a defect in the engine, no other boat available— all demonstrable reasons. But the Emperor, whom no sense of dignity protected from a suspicion of his not being regarded with sufficient deference, was offended, lost his temper, not only declined the proposal but derided the Turkish scheme, so that the interview came to an end "in very considerable agitation." Invited to a second, in which the Emperor evidently wished to efface the impression, Salisbury never appeared, wrote his excuses; and "the result," says Eckardstein, "was a deep-seated, lasting coolness between the Emperor and Salisbury. . . . The latter, years afterwards, repeatedly said to me, referring to the disastrous interview: 'The Emperor seemed quite to forget that I am not the King of Prussia's Minister, but the Prime Minister of the Queen of England.' " But Holstein, who had desired the issue, though not in that brusque form, ascribed the affair to a passing mood of the Emperor's—the same in which a few months later he despatched the Kruger telegram.

Personal jealousies were the driving or counteracting forces in these political doings. The nephew, at this precise juncture, got himself snubbed by his uncle because he wanted to take control of the Regatta; and revenged himself by entering for the Queen's Cup and withdrawing his yacht at the last moment, so that his uncle had to cover the course alone. Then he offended him again by telling him that he had never been a soldier. Is it astonishing that in such moods, which were reflected in the suites, each should hear what the other said of him? "He is an old peacock," said William. But Edward said more wittily:

"He is the most brilliant failure in history."

8

At Bismarck's writing-table sat a man as slight and short as the Chancellor was stalwart, as elegant as he was negligent—punctilious, worn, and usually with bent head where Bismarck's would have been combatively lifted; but the finely domed skull, the quiet well-weighed speech, were testimony to the old diplomat's abilities. He ate about half as much as did Bismarck, who thoroughly enjoyed his food. But at one point this Prince oddly repeated the other —for at seventy-five he took over the task of which Bismarck had been relieved, at seventy-five, on the pretext of his advanced age.

"I have made up my mind to keep calm, and let things rip. Otherwise I should have to send in my resignation at least once a week" (W. 2, 365). Why, indeed, should this accommodating old man have perturbed himself? Of the blood-royal, uncle to the Emperor, his new place conferring no added distinction on him, long since becalmed upon the ocean of ambition, or stirred, if stirred at all, only by brief gusts of curiosity, he had to be asked twice before he would accept, and even then his wife had vainly besought both Emperor and Empress to let him off. Holstein had suggested him because he was "safe"— the Grand-Duke of Baden being ostensibly the discoverer, so that Eulenburg might mention him during that scene at the shoot. "I have no one else," said the Emperor.

Prince Chlodwig signed for six years. Dominated by Holstein, who found him easier to drive than the strait-laced soldier who had preceded him, he was counselled by his extremely able son Alexander, one of the last real Princes of the epoch. But Alexander was a decadent, no adept in the diplomatic sphere, Holstein was profoundly experienced and indefatigable; the Prince was high-minded and a man of the world, the Baron tortuous and an intriguer, the terror of all in the Foreign Office and the Legations— and so once more and yet more irresistibly, he was master in the Wilhelmstrasse.

The silent battle of each against nearly all the others went steadily on. Holstein hated the Emperor, the Emperor loved Eulenburg, Eulenburg was beginning to hate Holstein, Hohenlohe no longer hated or loved anyone, distrusted all three, and no more proposed to edge anyone out than to be edged out himself. In the background an untried blood-horse was pawing the soil, eager for the moment when he should be let loose for his gallop. . . . Of the trio's methods of government, take this as an example.

The Emperor, who since his angry retreat from London had repeatedly threatened the English Military Attaché and had had reason to regret it, underwent a sudden change of mood at the end of the same year, 1895, and said to Colonel Swaine: "You might have forced the Dardanelles all right; I would have seen to it that Austria and Italy joined hands with you" (E. 2, 182). Holstein, instantly informed of this remark through Eulenburg, rightly divined with what celerity it would travel from Berlin via London to Petersburg, and there cause unpleasantness; for this same Emperor of theirs had always assigned Constantinople to Russia's tender mercies.

So this one dangerous remark was taken by Holstein as the signal for a little campaign. "It cannot go on like this," he wrote to Eulenburg, now Ambassador in Vienna. "To-day I warn you again. Take care that history does not in time regard you as the Black Knight who was at the

Imperial wanderer's side when he turned into the wrong path!" This moving prophecy was followed by a comment —only too well justified—from the hidden ruler on the ostensible one:

> The Emperor his own Imperial Chancellor—regrettable in any circumstances, but in these! An impulsive and, unfortunately, wholly superficial-minded monarch, who has no conception of public right, political precedent, diplomatic history, or the manipulation of individuals!

And Holstein directed his fire towards Rome, as well as Vienna—bombarded Bülow too, Ambassador in Rome, with his letters; suggested that Eulenburg should work on old Hohenlohe (who was shortly expected on a visit in Vienna) to write the Emperor a letter, and while repudiating all responsibility for intervention, enclosed a sketch for this letter. From Berlin he prompted Bülow in Rome to wire to Eulenburg at Vienna in French cipher, and himself wired at great length to Vienna, commenting on his own letters to both capitals.

When this attempt failed, Holstein altered his course. In the spring of 1896 he took the field himself against Hohenlohe, Eulenburg, and the Emperor. His courage was thriving in its background, his pace getting twice as fast, his megalomania coming to a head. In this period of most affectionate correspondence, he was calling his friend Eulenburg, in private, the "man with the cold eyes of a snake," and having it announced in the Press, simply to injure him, that he had been selected for Chancellor. He tried to establish with Hohenlohe "a system of intimidation of the Emperor," which the Chancellor would have nothing to do with (Al. 318); he sent in a fresh resignation every few weeks, not neglecting to clear out his desk on every such occasion; launched vitriolic articles against the Chancellor, repudiated their origin in a letter to Eulenburg, which he did not sign; burnt papers, withdrew from Kiderlen, whom he had but lately designated as the only possible Secretary of State; and in his strenuous ferocity made only one mistake, which by itself is enough to disqualify him as a diplomat—he trusted to Eulenburg's secrecy.

Eulenburg, however, revenged himself in knightly fashion. When Holstein wrote to him: "I expect that a crisis, if it comes, will come very speedily, so as to profit by the Emperor's present agitation and give him no time to quiet down again," Eulenburg took this confidential letter, sent it as it was to the Emperor, and added: "Holstein's concluding remark is very amusing. One would think that I struck terror into every heart when I appear upon the scene. . . . But from afar I can only implore Your Majesty to take no hasty steps." By this treachery he made the Emperor privy to Holstein's intrigues, while demonstrating his own innocence. Terribly was he to rue it, ten years later.

Meanwhile they stuck together, smilingly detesting one another. Holstein: "I can say of you that you've been a true comrade to me in all sorts of weather." Eulenburg: "Your concluding words touch me profoundly . . . they breathe a spirit of friendship which—perhaps I *do* deserve a little, but for which, all the same, I most truly thank you." A week later, in his diary: "Holstein's proper place is that vacant box in the stable which is reserved for biters and kickers" (E. 2, 204).

They sulked and made it up alternately like two women.

In the beginning of 1897 Holstein was sulking. He was hostile to Count Goluchowski, the new Austrian Foreign Minister, because this wealthy brilliant Pole, married to a Princess Murat, had snubbed the obscure Baron Holstein twenty years ago, when they were both secretaries in Paris. Now he scolded his friend for his good understanding with this Minister, whereupon Eulenburg in two ingenuously disingenuous letters threatened to retire.

> When I am found fault with, my susceptible artistic temperament gets the upper hand. I flounder and do worse than before. So it will be very easy for you to scare me away. . . . But I am so intimate with you, have so much personal affection for you, that I could not long be angry with you. . . . Still, I do take my stand on this—that I simply cannot exist officially if I do not possess your confidence and recognition, and that of the Office as a whole. . . . My artistic temperament gets hold of me—and I am repelled by everything else, and flee from it. I am laying bare my very self to you. If you want to keep me—you must bear with me!

By such convulsive tremors, working in two neurasthenics, was the foreign policy of the German Empire tossed and torn in those distracted years.

9

In the course of five years' visits the Emperor had roused English feeling against Germany; by his conduct towards his uncle he had offended the Court, by that towards Salisbury the Cabinet; by his prattle he had annoyed society, by his menaces the Press, by his indiscretions the man in the street, who read of them in the papers. The situation in the Transvaal, where England was about to come to grips, stirred the Emperor to definite threats—in October 1895 he overwhelmed Colonel Swaine in Berlin with reproaches:

England has as good as threatened her old friend, the German Emperor, with war—and this on account of a few square miles of territory, all niggers and palm-trees! Your attitude positively forces me to go in with the Dual Alliance. England must make up her mind whether she's for or against the Triple Alliance.

This singular method of offering an alliance (wherein the threat to join the opposite party was pure bluff) Hohenlohe hastened to transform by wire into something so very much milder as to be almost its contrary (A. 11, 5). But Swaine's report was privately printed for the members of the Cabinet, and not for them alone, we may be sure. The Chancellor of the Exchequer described it as "the most significant document that has ever been sent us from Berlin."

None the less Holstein suffered the Emperor, until near Christmas-time, to solicit England to join the Triple Alliance—the monarch again brandishing the bright sword: "Otherwise you might easily find the Continent closed against you one of these days!" London made no reply, and this was what Holstein wanted—to put the English in the wrong, on no account join forces with them at such a time, show them they weren't wanted! These labyrinthine paths to an uncertain end, congenial to his cankered temperament, were quite the reverse across the water. But a few hours after Marschall, by Holstein's desire, had on the last day of the year threatened the new English Ambassador Lascelles as the Emperor had lately been threatening Swaine, there came from Africa a kind of justification. Jameson, an English doctor, with the connivance of Cecil Rhodes and the Johannesburg agitators, had raided the Boer Republic of the Transvaal from Cape Town.

That was a Happy New Year for Holstein—Albion caught out at last! Now he could act. Telegraphic orders

to the Consul in Pretoria, to requisition crews from the
German ship "Seeadler." Telegraphic inquiry to the Ambassador in Paris: "Will France look calmly on at these
confiscations by England?" Plan of a continental understanding (*Holstein's Memoranda*). Telegraphic orders to
the Ambassador in London: "Should Your Excellency
be of opinion that this violation of national rights is approved [by the Government] you will ask for your pass-
ports." London lost no time—as Holstein must have
foreseen—in repudiating any connection with the raid;
nevertheless Hatzfeldt was obliged to send in his drastic
memorandum. Then the news reached Europe of President
Kruger's victory over the meddlesome adventurers. Hatzfeldt, that night, withdrew his memorandum, which chanced
to be still unopened; nevertheless the withdrawal had an
unfavourable effect in London.

Still happier was the Emperor: here was the ill-wind
and it was blowing *him* good! Now for the championship
of the weak, now for the German Flag in the Transvaal,
now for Europe against England! On January 2nd he
wired to the Tsar: "Never will I suffer the English to
oppress the Transvaal"; and three days later said to the
French Ambassador: "At that moment the English Fleet
was not in readiness. . . . If all the European States
had joined hands with us, we might have done something
worth doing" (A. 15, 407).

On January 3rd he called a conference at the Imperial
Chancery. There were present the Emperor, Hohenlohe,
Marschall, Admirals Hollmann and Knorr. The Emperor,
highly excited, opened the proceedings: "Now is our
moment. Germany can obtain the Protectorate of the
Transvaal." The means thereto: mobilization of the

Marine Light Infantry; troops for the Transvaal, a landing in Delagoa Bay; under this pressure, a conference for the neutralization of the Transvaal; at the conference, cry raised against England; issue—position of most-favoured-nation for Germany, hitherto England's prerogative. Both statesmen dismayed; Hohenlohe saying quietly: "That means war with England." The Emperor flashed out the answer: "Yes, but only on land."

So he had not reckoned with the most certain and immediate consequence—that England would forcibly resist the landing of German troops overseas, would seize German transports; his dream was of victory without war. Nor did he perceive the moral and political impossibility of impartially intervening in favour of the Boers, and at the same time mobilizing. Despite the forcible counter-arguments of his Ministers, he persistently refused to be convinced; though at first he yielded, he still insisted on despatching an officer to clear up the situation, and was evidently bent on taking some sensational step against England. Warnings only made him more acrimonious; it was "an excessively animated and even dramatic conference." As no resolution satisfied him, and everybody was at his wits' end, the Emperor broke off the conference with the command to Marschall: "Ask Holstein."

Holstein, as ever, was sitting in his room; he refused to come over at Marschall's behest (for he never would meet the Emperor if he could help it), and referred Marschall to the Colonial Director, Kayser. Why did Holstein keep out of this affair? His aloofness from other men and from the Emperor was only one reason, and not the deciding one. He had before him the Secretary of State, in urgent quest of a solution which might in some way pacify the Emperor, robbed of his triumph as he was; he had listened to a rapid, half-whispered summary of the Imperial plans, and felt the gravity of a moment in which the ruler of an Empire was so offhandedly deciding its future. And out of his fortress was *he* to come, to take his place at that table, and in the Emperor's very ear—or else in a protocol, which he feared more than he feared the devil—relieve Chancellor and Secretary of the responsibility which for twenty years he had avoided? Undertake to pacify the Emperor, whom he himself had set ablaze? Never! One asks one's self, indeed, if, given Holstein's nature, this may not be the explanation—that he wanted the Emperor to expose himself, having long desired to clip the wings of that solitary rival?

Meanwhile the Colonial Director had thought of a way out: "Congratulate Kruger." Marschall breathed again —the sedative for the Emperor was found! The Director wrote, not omitting to append his initials; Marschall returned to the conference, proudly presented the idea as his own, with the argument that it was necessary to consider public feeling—then read the draft of the telegram aloud:

I send you my sincere congratulations on having, without any appeal to friendly Powers, succeeded through the energy of your own people in opposing the armed raiders who have invaded your territory as disturbers of the peace, in restoring tranquillity, and in upholding the dignity of your Government in the face of alien aggression.

All was well—except that the Emperor, after his own flourish of trumpets, listened rather grumpily to this mild performance and said: "There ought to be something about their independence." Instantly "the dignity of your Government" was keyed up to "the independence of your country." Nobody pointed out that this independence had been definitely restricted by the 1884 conventions; it struck nobody that the faintest reference to the fact that the raid was a defiance of the English Government, which had yesterday repudiated it, would destroy the point of the whole thing. Marschall appended his signature, Hohenlohe avoided that ceremony, the Emperor countersigned, the draft was immediately despatched, and the conference came to an end.

No sooner had it done so than two men did their best to arrest events. The worthy Admiral von Knorr, who was hard of hearing, only now had a chance to read the telegram; he instantly perceived the danger, and implored the Emperor not to send it. And now, worked upon by vigorous predictions of the effect in England, he did actually yield, and again consulted Hohenlohe, only to learn that the message was already on the wires.

In the very same hour Marschall visited Holstein—their rooms were close together, like a faithful old married pair's—showed him and Baron Mumm, who happened to be there, the telegraphic fruit of their deliberations; but now it was Holstein who was dismayed and urgently advised that it be suppressed. "You don't *know* what the Emperor would have done but for this!" cried Marschall, and described the first proposals. "So you see it was the very least we were obliged to concede him."

The effect was unprecedented. Never had the Emperor so stirred his people's soul as with these words, put in his mouth by a mere Director, and reluctantly signed as a feeble compromise. The nation applauded as with one voice. In London, it is true, German dock-labourers were bludgeoned, from offices and hotels Germans were dismissed by hundreds, the German clubs were closed. "It is difficult to speak calmly of this telegram," wrote the *Morning Post*. "The fitting retort would be the ordering of our Mediterranean Fleet to the North Sea. England will not forget it, and her foreign policy will in future be strongly influenced by the remembrance." Hatzfeldt, who had to bear the brunt in London, wanted to resign, "because of the incomprehensible insanity which has come over the Wilhelmstrasse" (Eck. 1, 278). The Emperor, by his own account, received threatening and abusive letters from members of English Society.

The Prince of Wales was petrified. Doubtless he would fain have said to this nephew what had been said to another nephew in Shakespeare's *Henry VI*:[1] "With silence, nephew, be thou politic." The immediate consequences were: a minatory retort by Chamberlain to this "inadmissible intermeddling with a foreign Power's affairs"; five days after the telegram, establishment of a flying squadron in the North Sea; some weeks later, non-renewal of the Mediterranean Treaty, whereupon dissatisfaction with Germany was freely expressed in Vienna and Rome.

Some days after the telegram the Emperor wrote a letter of apology to his grandmother, assuring her that he had only desired "to express his indignation with the rabble who had acted in opposition to the peaceful intentions and instructions of Her Most Gracious Majesty. . . . I challenge any gentleman to point out to me wherein this was in any sense offensive to England." No reply.

The Germans in the City [wrote the Ambassador to Holstein, after many another week had gone by] can hardly get any English-

---

[1] These words are spoken by the dying Edmund Mortimer, Earl of March, to his nephew Richard Plantagenet, Duke of York (*Henry VI*, Part I, act ii, scene 5).—Translator's Note.

men to do business with them. In the fashionable Clubs, for instance the Turf, the bitterness is beyond measure. . . . If the Government likewise had lost its head, or had desired war on any grounds whatever, public opinion would have been unanimously in its favour. [Salisbury he said] was prepared for its coming either to a rupture with us, or . . . the breaking-up of the Triple Alliance in a measurable space of time. . . . More serious is the evident desire to draw nearer to France.

But the gravest effects of the telegram consisted neither in the applause of the one nation nor in the outcry of the other; but in the clever misuse made of it by naval circles in Germany. It was Tirpitz who gave the Kruger Telegram the credit of having, more than anything else, "shown the nation the necessity of the battle-fleet."

10

Your Serene Highness is most respectfully requested to be good enough again to furnish a memorandum of the amount of your quarter's salary, increased on January 1st, for the eleven days from the date of your retirement from the Imperial Service up to the last day of March.

Caprivi. Imperial Chancellor.

This was, according to Bismarck, the only document upon which he ever beheld his successor's signature. He was never consulted, he was visited only for non-political purposes. At first everyone was glad to be rid of him; and Hohenlohe in the summer of 1890 noticed, as a new thing, "that, individually speaking, everyone seems bigger —feels more of a personage. While in the past, under the dominating influence of Prince Bismarck, individuals felt crushed and oppressed, they have now swelled out like sponges that have been put in water." Still prettier is

the image that the Emperor, in his Memoirs, either invented
or quoted—it was in those days just as if one had rolled away
a block of granite in a field, and found vermin swarming
underneath.

Nevertheless, the old man in the eight years of his
banishment gave him much more trouble than in the days
of their official differences; and Eulenburg in no way exaggerated when he wrote to his friend: "I don't regard the
change to a Republic as a negligible prospect. If Bismarck
were now only fifty, it would perhaps be carried out after
the Cromwellian model." The few who knew him intimately
declare that, despite his royalist convictions, it was only his
age which, after all that had happened, deterred him from
open revolt.

It did not deter him from opposition. A month after
his dismissal he began in the *Hamburger Nachrichten,* as
also in speeches designed for consumption abroad, to promulgate such criticism as found—at any rate in foreign parts
—a more attentive audience than the Imperial utterances
could command. "Every Prussian," he declared, "has the
right to express his opinions freely, but God help him if
he does!" With savage cynicism he must have felt how the
weapon forged by himself against the people was now turned
upon himself, who was but one of them—just like that other,
by which he had conferred upon the monarch the right to
strike, and had been himself struck down. For whichever
way he turned, it seemed that someone was against him.

To the Germans, fonder of being told about heroes than
about the hearts of men, the re-emergence of the old champion was at first distressing. They would have liked to
picture him in the golden autumn of his life as happy between grandchildren and municipal addresses, but above

all as cordially reconciled to his loved Emperor. And so there was many an eager hand solicitous to smooth things down for the nation, and at the same time pacify the monarch's wrath. To Eulenburg, whose nature made it easy for him to be on "cordial terms with both sides," it occurred, after a year of this, that the Emperor might offer the Prince the Palace of Bellevue as a habitation, if he should become a member of the Reichstag. "If he refuses, he will accentuate the contrast between them; if he accepts, he would be, as the Emperor's guest, rather frowned upon by public opinion, should he make himself disagreeable." To this courtly logic Holstein's sleepless distrust responded: "The offer of Bellevue would be looked upon as a proof of uneasiness, and would make the enemy still more insolent." This pair of psychologists failed to see that Bismarck might never become a member of the Reichstag, but would have plenty of plausible reasons for refusing the offer of the Palace.

But Holstein's mortal apprehension of Bismarck's return was reawakened, and in long letters he conjured his friend—this was at the end of 1890—as follows: "The Emperor *is* actually talking about Bellevue—for God's sake come! Or write!" And Eulenburg did hasten to extinguish the flame he had himself kindled, by retailing Holstein's arguments in no less lengthy letters to the Emperor, and warning him that "experiments of so dangerous a kind might lead to catastrophe, if the country were disaffected. . . . On the other hand, to pile arms before Bismarck would mean a most frightful fiasco for the monarchy."

And yet his uneasy conscience could not get quit of the problem—intriguer that he was, who had betrayed his earlier patron to his newer one; and Eulenburg's second idea, imparted to his friend after the first had been abandoned, is simply and solely grotesque:

> When the Emperor next comes to Kiel, Prince Bismarck might be on the platform at Friedrichsruh for three minutes or so, and the Emperor might shake hands with him. . . . No compromise . . . an article in the *Hamburger Nachrichten* soon afterwards . . . but they would have shaken hands. Simultaneously there should be a demonstrative recognition of Caprivi's services. . . . The offer of Bellevue I should have considered inadvisable only if the Emperor were to be a guest there—that would have looked like undue influence.

Delicious—the way this courtier consigns his own idea to oblivion in a paraphrase, conceiving the situation of a host who should take no notice of his guest; but then reverts to the dear old method of the railway-station—three minutes or so; and in spirit peruses, next morning, the official despatch and simultaneously the account of the presentation of a ribbon to Caprivi, who is to receive the Order as a souvenir-medal on the platform at Friedrichsruh!

The Emperor had ears for nothing but what the Olympian gods might have to say to him about Bismarck's dismissal. The Tsar, *he* must know of it! He gave the Emperor his hand, when he heard the tale: *"Le Prince avec toute sa grandeur n'était après tout rien d'autre que ton employé ou fonctionnaire. Le moment où il refusait d'agir selon tes ordres, il fallait le renvoyer."*

The half-gods had a harder row to hoe. What was one to do when one was, like Waldersee, Commander of the Forces in Altona; or, like Kiderlen, Envoy in Hamburg? Call on the veteran, or cut him? Kiderlen's visit to the Prince who had discovered him a few years ago, lasted thirty minutes, and he complained that he was not offered bite or sup—for only in the article of appetite had he any claim to be nicknamed the New Bismarck. Waldersee, who had first inquired of Eulenburg whether he might, should, or must, received as marching-orders: "Visit him, but don't breathe a word of politics where a coachman or a servant can hear it, to say nothing of a member of the family"—who would be sure to see that such a betrayal of the Emperor got into the newspapers. And the General, who had once enjoyed Bismarck's confidence, very cautiously doled out his visits, professed loud admiration, but took care that his Press denied any close intercourse between them, so that the old man remarked: "I always feel, at his visits, that he is or should be taking note whether it's time to order a suitable wreath."

In the third year of the boycott a concentrated effort was made.

At the beginning of June, 1892, the Emperor sent Waldersee to tell the veteran that he would be ready for a reconciliation, but "the first step must, in all the circumstances, be made by the Prince. He must, in the most unmistakable fashion, and in writing, approach me directly with a petition or the expression of a desire to be permitted to resume personal intercourse with me." In answer to this message the old man told the intermediary: "I have been kicked out, and therefore cannot possibly beg to be readmitted, but must await an invitation." When the agent was gone, he doubtless exclaimed, behind closed doors: "The laugh's on my side!"

When he thus repulsed the Emperor, he had just heard of a minute to all the German Legations, directed against his utterances in the Press, wherein a distinction was made between the Prince Bismarck of the past and of the present —the implication being that the existing one was to be regarded as either feeble-minded or disaffected. Immediately afterwards Berlin was panic-stricken over a projected journey—the Prince was about to attend the wedding of his eldest son, and had announced himself to the old Emperor in Vienna through his personal friend the Ambassador, one Prince Reuss, requesting an audience. Upon this Holstein composed a minute to the Ambassador, which was applauded by Kiderlen and signed by Caprivi. The Ambassador was to take no part in the wedding ceremonies, was to show the greatest possible reserve at the visit, was to communicate this to the Foreign Minister in Vienna, was to prevent the audience with the Emperor. When the Ambassador in Vienna urgently pointed out the danger of all this, they wired back that he was the personal representative of the German Emperor and must not "show weakness" by any sort of cordiality. Simultaneously, a letter from the Emperor William to Francis Joseph:

Bismarck is to be in Vienna at the end of this month . . . in order to arrange for systematic ovations by his admirers. . . . You also know that one of his masterpieces was the secret treaty *à double fonds* with Russia, concluded behind your back, and abrogated by Me. Ever since he retired, the Prince has waged war in the most perfidious manner against Me, Caprivi, and My Ministers. . . . All his craftiness and cunning are directed towards making it appear that I am the one who makes the advances. The climax of his programme in this affair is the idea of an audience with you. I would therefore beg of you not to increase the difficulties in this country by receiving that disobedient subject, before he has approached me with his *peccavi*.

This letter belongs to the most terrible documents of a decadent epoch. The malignity with which the creator of the Empire is slandered by its ruler, with which the inheritor of the work of genius accuses its maker to a third party, so that he may not be the loser in the game—this tone taken by the master against the subject, the snarling tone of a weak man who has tried to lay low a mighty one, and hears him breathing still . . . all this, after a magnificent achievement, after a generation of inestimable services to the House of Hohenzollern, written by one Emperor to another—what an epoch, wherein such words must be inscribed on paper bearing the Imperial Crown, before a nation can be roused to wrath!

For the public excitement was unparalleled, at this affront to the most popular of Germans. Even on his way to Vienna half Berlin awaited him at the railway-station; and when the Prince, standing at the window, answered the demands for a speech with: "Is it for me to speak? My duty is silence!" a voice was heard to exclaim: "If you are silent, the stones will speak!"—a cry so stirring and so daring as perhaps had never before broken from a crowd in Prussia.

In Vienna—closed doors. The man who, even as an insignificant Junker of Hinter Pommern, carried in his heart and on his brow a conscious sense of power, before he had given any proofs of it—the man who for a generation had been then accustomed to awaken fear or reverence—this man, this Bismarck with his seventy-seven years upon him, now for the first time in his life encounters an embarrassed "not at home," "away in the country," "unfortunately prevented from coming to the wedding breakfast". . . while the Ambassador, not man enough to leave home from one day to another, has gone to bed in a panic and given himself out to be ill. And now at last the old heart pulses young again, the doughty champion scents the fight. He has an open enemy to meet once more, and he begins his last of epochs with the one thought: Vengeance! And very actual shall be its first expression—he gives the editor of the *Neue Freie Presse* an interview, so that next day Berlin and Europe are reading these words:

Naturally Austria has known how to profit by the weakness and inefficiency of our negotiators in the matter of the Commercial Treaty. This result may be ascribed to the fact that in our country such men have come to the front as I was careful to relegate to their native obscurity, precisely because they would be sure to change and upset the whole course of affairs. . . . Most assuredly I am now absolved from any personal obligations whatever towards the dominating personalities of the moment, as well as towards my successor. Every bridge between us is broken down. . . . In Berlin there is neither personal authority nor confidence. The Russian wire is cut—we are estranged.

In this way did the interview proceed.

The Berlin Government was beside itself. The bomb had exploded; Emperor and Ministers were unanimous for once in deciding on energetic measures of defence. The Government organ declared that Bismarck's utterances were offensive both to Royalist feeling and the respect due to the Emperor. His exposition of certain incidents was so evidently erroneous

that all who have an intimate knowledge of them cannot but perceive with apprehension that the Prince's memory has begun to fail him completely. . . . And so the men to whom has been entrusted the honourable task of carrying on Prince Bismarck's work are confronted with the duty of protecting their efforts above all against him whose achievement they are called upon to uphold.

Two days later, Bismarck's rejoinder in his Hamburg paper. He wished to protect himself against the responsibility implied in the statement that "his work" was now being carried on.

In Berlin they were all of a tremble. Was the old man always to have the last word? A five-hour Ministerial conference; resolution—the minutes regarding the Prince to be made public. Oh, not the Emperor's letter—no one knew anything about that; but the minute to Prince Reuss, soon to be dubbed by Bismarck the "Urias-Letter," that in which he was deprived of intercourse with the German functionaries in Vienna. After five hours of discussion the Ministers had resolved to make *that* public! They, who were called upon to understand the sentiments of foreign peoples, to make alliances and friendships in the highest interests of the Empire—these broken-winded, beribboned, gold-laced Knights of the Order of Cowardice and Calumny knew so little of the hearts of their own people that they thought to injure their bugbear, and instead were to make him first the fetish, and then—what he had never been till now—the darling of the nation.

The nation rose as one man. In every region, every class, there was rejoicing when they read in Bismarck's organ, as his answer, that in the Foreign Office Archives of no matter what Great Power there would scarce be found a parallel to this communication. Not only his return from Vienna, but the whole summer through, was the occasion for such tributes as the Germans had never offered their Chancellor in the days of his glory. Bands of pilgrims marched to Friedrichsruh. Be sure that Bismarck himself was the first to perceive the marvellous revulsion in his favour—he spoke of it at a torchlight procession in Munich:

In the past my energies were all directed towards arousing
Royalist sentiment in the public. In the official world I was belauded, but the public would fain have stoned me. Now the public
acclaims me, while in other circles I am timidly avoided. I believe
this is called the irony of fate.

More exultantly still did he shape to his purpose this
ultimate, perhaps this most indelible, of his experiences, when
he said at a birthday-procession in Kissingen:

For years I fought the Reichstag tooth and nail; but I perceive that that institution was debilitated in that very battle with
William the First and myself. . . . I was eager to strengthen the
Crown as against the Parliament—possibly I went too far in that
direction. . . . We need the fresh air of public criticism. When
the people's representatives become powerless, the mere instrument
of a more exalted will, we are bound ere long—if things go on as
they are—to revert to absolutism unconcealed.

Wide was the circuit, stern the experience, which led Bismarck to avowals such as these. His Royalist creed had
made him for a lifetime the foe of democracy; his enmity towards his fourth and last King made him, in his old age, half
a democrat himself. His party waxed commensurately—
now for the first time it comprised Greater Germany. The
Emperor had literally made a present of him to the common
enemy.

The Emperor had lost the Great Game.

11

And yet he was resolved to win it, were it only in appearance. Was there to be a man in his German territories who
could steal hearts from him, a rival *not* by the Grace of God,
a foe of such calibre as to ensure, if he wanted it, the ever-

dreaded revolt? What could be done? An illness arrived in the nick of time.

For weeks, in the autumn of 1893, the Bismarck irreconcilables had kept from the Emperor all knowledge of the old man's dangerous attack of pneumonia, lest a reconciliation should take place before he died. But when he did hear of it, the Emperor forgot principles, forgot defiance, took that first step which he had demanded of the Prince, and telegraphed:

. . . In the desire that your recovery may be really complete, I beg Your Serene Highness to change your winter-quarters from the somewhat unfavourable climate of Varzin and Friedrichsruh for one of My palaces in Central Germany. I will, after consultation with My Court-Marshal, designate the particular Palace to Your S.H.

Snub indirect:

With the profoundest acknowledgment of Your Majesty's most gracious interest . . . but feel that my recovery will be best assisted by the domestic surroundings long familiar to me.

Despite this ominous repulse the Emperor would not give up; for it may safely be said that nothing in those years of the nineties caused him such uneasiness as the existence of three men—Bebel, Edward, and Bismarck. In them he saw the only dangers—to the security of his Throne, his Empire, and his popularity.

In the same winter of 1894, at a conferring of honours, Herbert Bismarck made his first reappearance at the Palace; and after dinner

his friends arranged that he should be in the Emperor's immediate proximity. But the Emperor did not speak to him, which caused

great indignation in the Bismarck-party. . . . It had been hoped
to engineer a *rapprochement*, and so make an end of Caprivi (Ho.
509).

Thus from the sphere of Court-politics emerged a pretext
for another attempt, for it could be represented to the Emperor that his neglect of the son was an affront which made it
advisable to approach the father once again.

The Emperor bit his lips, swallowed his rancour, and sent
a second message—this time that personal invitation which
Bismarck had demanded. Soon after the Honours dinner an
aide-de-camp arrived at Friedrichsruh with a bottle of old
Steinberger-Cabinet, together with an autograph letter, congratulating the Prince on his restoration to health and inviting him next week to the Birthday. As Bismarck wished to
avoid the ceremonial banquet, the 26th was arranged for;
but he did not allow the opportunity for another lunge at
his foe to escape him. He invited the Emperor's most
notorious opponent, Maximilian Harden, to his house—
knowing that Harden would talk about it, and desiring that
he should—and poured him out a glass of the wine with the
remark: "You wish the Emperor as well as I do myself."
Then he set off for Berlin.

. . . The Wilhelmstrasse echoed with the panic-stricken
shriek: "The lion is coming!" Deadly terror ruled the distracted scene; and as the disaster staved off for four years
was now to be an actuality in four short days, the principal
actors had time only for cipher-telegrams. Holstein, Kiderlen, Marschall, all wired to Eulenburg long screeds, letters
came flying after—he must prevent the worst, that terrible
return to power. Caprivi owned that he had not been informed, "made a resigned complaint"; his adversaries ex-

ulted, Hohenlohe predicted that this would injure the monarchy—finally, on the last day, Holstein dived under, spluttering as he went: "If Bismarck gets in again, either himself or his creatures, there'll be such slaughter as not one of us all will escape!"

Still more ill at ease was the Emperor. Ought not the old man to have said *peccavi?* Was he not the enemy of the Empire? Nevertheless, William's love of theatrical display was so strong that even out of this defeat he had to make a spectacle. But to show the world that there came on a visit next day merely "a Major-General with the rank of Field-Marshal," everything was to be on military lines, the suite in uniform with epaulettes and high boots. He himself—admirably described on this occasion by the younger Moltke (M., p. 166)—ran from pillar to post, his nerves on edge, went up the wrong staircase, left questions of ceremony unanswered, wandered restlessly for a full hour through the rooms assigned to the Prince, which were still in the hands of the housemaids, disarranged the flower-vases—then went striding out to the Guard of Honour, wanted to know if each individual composing it was in his place—all indications of an embarrassment and anxiety for which we well may pity him. Truly, on this forenoon, the Emperor expiated all that he had done to the old man two years ago.

While the Headquarters Staff were taking their places in the ante-room, and someone found an album with pictures from the play *Der Neue Herr*—which some malicious fairy might seem to have wished that Bismarck's eye should light upon to-day and here, and which Moltke hastily suppressed —the Emperor was pacing up and down in his own room next door, for he intended to be alone when he received the Prince. Was he then so uncertain of himself? Did he, never weary of feeling all eyes upon him, seek in this moment of capitulation to avoid the dozen or so of lookers-on who might observe a paling of the cheek, a quivering of the lip, and make a story out of it?

But what is this? A message from the railway-station: the Prince has just arrived, and his son is with him. Another little lunge from the veteran—the Firm of Bismarck is to be received, or none of them. "The Household was much exercised about the proper treatment of this *fait accompli.*" The Imperial solitary is disturbed in his pacing to and fro— he is found to be memorizing his speech. The Emperor, disconcerted, ordains that Count Herbert shall remain in the ante-room, shall not enter his room with the Prince.

But hark! the Linden is alive with cheering. The prisoner of state is fully escorted, well shut-in, both before and behind the carriage; beside him sits Prince Henry. The roaring swells to the skies, the carriage is in sight, everyone rushes to the window to see the Prince alight and cross the threshold. Only the Emperor stands, alone, behind the closed door of his room; he dares not trust himself at the window yet, he scarcely trusts his own ears, for when till now in his thirty-five years of life has he heard his peoples' Hurrah! without the delight of feeling: "It is all for me?" When long ago the cheers were for his fathers, he was there too— a little Prince at first, and then a tall one. But to-day—to-day he feels quite out of it. His people, his own Court, are all agog to see the only man in his Empire whom he has not been able to get the better of; and he, the sovereign, who alone among the millions has the Grace of God upon his forehead—*he* stands and drinks the bitter cup of this great jubilation, head bent low within his room, like one who would transcend as though with antennae the few yards that divide him from the window. In these few minutes only one thought upholds him: "At three o'clock *I* shall get it!"

When Bismarck, in the uniform of the Cuirassiers, enters the ante-room on Prince Henry's arm, he is taller by a head than his escort. Presentations—a little incident. "Colonel von Kessel." "Kessel? You've grown smaller since the old days." In truth, they all seem to him to have grown much smaller; but this he does not say.

Dead stop. A lackey takes his cloak and gloves. Dead stop, a longer one. "Will Your Serene Highness go in to His Majesty now?" A silent bow. The folding-doors divide. "The Emperor, who was standing in the middle of the room, came quickly towards him with outstretched hand, which the Prince, with a deep bow, caught in both of his. Then the Emperor bent forward and kissed him on both cheeks. The doors closed again; the two were alone."

Was it a Judas-kiss? By no means. It was only a stage-kiss.

Outside the crowd was shouting and cheering; *Deutschland, Deutschland* was sung. After the lapse of ten minutes the Emperor sent for the Princes; then followed lunch, alone with the Emperor, Empress, and Henry.

Three o'clock. The Emperor rides out with his suite— this is a game at which two can play. And how well he knew his subjects! They seemed to have gone mad—through Linden and Tiergarten there surged on foot and on wheels a thankful people, cutting across the escort and shouting its admiration, its reverence—nay, its love—to the Emperor *in excelsis*. "Three cheers for the beloved Kaiser! The noble-hearted Kaiser! Our generous Kaiser!" The merest ritual of the occasion, the commonplaces of the gilt-edged manuals —platitudes of the heart strewn at the feet of their liege lord—the crown conferred by peoples on the sovereign crowned by Heaven. And the Emperor drinks it all in, he cannot have enough of it, he rides till dark has fallen—rides till six o'clock.

Then a quiet dinner in the Prince's rooms with Herbert and the suite—no ceremony, splendid wines; the old man "in his low voice" telling anecdotes of the Empress Augusta, and how his black dog Tyras once nearly flew at the Grand-Duke of Weimar. Everyone laughs; they bandy good stories from the great days of Germany, until for the second time the Bismarck family announces itself in uncourtly fashion—during the *rôti* they are told that Count Bill is outside. The Emperor wants to call the dishes back for him—but Bill is gone, is followed, finally arrives with the coffee; so that in the end the old man sits for half an hour at any rate between his two sons, in the Palace of the Hohenzollerns. Nay, on this day of victory he does what he has never done before —he smokes (perhaps for the joke of "smoking the calumet of peace") a cigarette with his Emperor.

There he sits, close on eighty, plagued with an intolerable high collar, lying back heavily in an armchair, absurdly unlike himself with his flimsy cigarette; and gazes, stimulated by the wine, around the room with eyes that frequently are somewhat dimmed—the look is that of Faust, the thoughts are those of Mephistopheles. Three feet away sits the slim Emperor in Hussar uniform, pulling at his moustache with nervous fingers, laughing a great deal, somewhat schoolboyishly. And he over there—yes, that is Moltke, but not a bit like his mighty uncle. And that's Kessel, is it?— Kessel who has grown so much smaller; the lanky fellow is Plessen. "All of them scoundrels!" reflects the veteran. It's a mercy that Herbert and Bill are here to purify the air*!*

Is it really only four years ago? Have they not ruined more than twenty years can build again? Oh yes, the Emperor is full of good intentions—after all, it's his House and his Heritage; how should he *not* have good intentions? Only he doesn't know how things are done; and to-day, when he has talked about nothing but horses, the weather, and uniforms—to-day he could have got more good out of a few hours than out of years of other people.

The carriages are announced; return to the station with the Emperor; Bismarck sitting on his right. Departure. The Emperor, relieved: "Well! Now they can put up triumphal arches to him—I shall always beat him by a length!"

The visit had lasted eight hours, the enmity eight years. To-day was a short armistice. The veteran has four good years before him still. The end is not yet.

12

"Jupiter Ammon! Germany is groaning under the weight of Bismarck's dæmonic personality . . . overshadowing everything or else lighting up the country with flame which is not that of the sun. Impossible—whether in or out of office!" By this striking picture, Eulenburg consoles himself for the old wizard's ascendancy.

The Emperor was groaning too. He did not perceive the one way by which he could have attached the Prince— by confidential questions, by asking for practical advice, which no one in the world was better able to give him. But that way was closed to him, for so he would have owned to the superiority which was oppressing him. Accordingly he did the exact reverse, was persistently unpolitical, and on his return visit in February produced for the Prince's inspection two Grenadiers, one in the old, the other in the new, active service equipment, and on this occasion actually did ask his advice. "Which does Your Serene Highness think the more practical?" The most infuriating thing he could have done—and Bismarck went on with his criticisms.

The veteran's eightieth birthday fell next year. A ceremonial visit, with troops, to Friedrichsruh. Grand entry of the Emperor on horseback, for this enabled him to speak to Bismarck as from on high. A golden sword of honour as "Germany's Tribute." Instead of a speech of thanks the ironical response: "My military position towards Your Majesty forbids me to enlarge upon my feelings. I thank Your Majesty." What he really felt in that pseudo-historical moment, he described next day: "While the Emperor, in his cuirass, reined in his tall horse and addressed me, I could not take my eyes off a drop of rain which was slowly running down his glittering armour."

When on a later visit and in a larger circle, Bismarck was speaking of the third Napoleon and his constitutional theories, and stressed the importance of the Guards, on whose protection he had counselled Napoleon to rely in all contingencies, the Emperor, who was sitting at some distance from the old man's armchair, interrupted by asking across the table: "Who was in command of the Parisian Bodyguard at that time?" Bismarck, always easily put out by an irrelevant question, answered: "That has nothing to do with it. Napoleon could rely on them in any circumstances. It doesn't matter who was in command. I remember . . ." And he went on with his story (M. 203).

The Emperor could never forgive him such lessons before witnesses.

With growing apprehension the octogenarian looked on at events in general. In Hamburg he said to Ballin, when going over a new Transatlantic liner: "I am rather over-whelmed, as you see. Yes, it is a new epoch—a new world all round." If he failed to perceive the full significance of this expanding "new world," he did see very clearly its danger for Germany. His premonitions grew darker and darker; he said to Radowitz: "I see how my work will be undone by unskilful and shortsighted people" (W. 2, 357).

It was under the influence of such forebodings that in October, 1896, during a crisis, he read some violent attacks in the Liberal Press on his having failed to come to an understanding with Russia in the past. This was not to be borne, and he caused an article to appear:

Until the year 1890 both Empires were in complete agreement on the point that if one of them were attacked the other should preserve a benevolent neutrality. This understanding was not renewed after the retirement of Prince Bismarck. . . . It was Count Caprivi who declined to continue the mutual insurance, when Russia was ready to do so. . . . Thence ensued the Marseillaise incident at Kronstadt, and the first approximation between the absolutist Russian Empire and the French Republic—in our opinion wholly the result of the ill-advised Caprivi-policy.

He knew what a storm would be raised by this disclosure, and in his eighty-second year was fain to let it loose. Holstein shook in his shoes—did Bismarck want to expose them to universal obloquy?—and got an article into the *Reichsanzeiger* about "violation of the most sacred secrets of State, and destruction of all confidence in German good faith among the Great Powers." A tactical error—for it was nothing less than confession of an intrigue which had never really existed. Vienna had long known all; and now Germany was ringing from end to end with the question: "Why was your successor so stupid?"

But the Emperor! Was this the return for his magnanimity? Did the old man propose to live for ever? "It was with difficulty that the Emperor was restrained from rash proceedings." He wrote to the Tsar: "I imagine that this last outbreak of Prince Bismarck's, and the disgraceful way he treats me in his Press . . . will cause the more clear-sighted to perceive at last that I had good reasons for removing from office this insubordinate base-minded man." After a swearing-in of recruits he actually spoke to a few hundred lieutenants of his overwhelming anxieties, and finished with an allusion to "highly placed personages," and "high treason against Me and My country."

What a rage he was in, and how well he might be! On the centenary of the old Emperor's birth Bismarck was punished by not being notified; and the Emperor made his own presence at a wedding conditional on the withdrawal of an invitation sent to Herbert Bismarck. But it was no good—as by some magic lure he was drawn, and knew he was, perpetually towards the insubordinate old man whom he could neither get the better of nor win unto himself; he simply was not able to let him be. With every year that added to his patriarchal age the figure grew more legendary—till at last, it seemed, the people would believe only what Bismarck answered for. The Fleet! If *he* would praise the infant Fleet, would tell the people it was necessary! One word from the veteran would mean a hundred votes for the Navy Bill. Let us then conquer ourselves in the service of the Fatherland—let us call the newest ship by his name: that cannot fail to flatter him!

Accordingly, in the summer of 1897, an invitation to the launching of the ironclad cruiser *Bismarck*. Declined on the plea of old age. Letter from Tirpitz, asking for an interview. Returned unopened with a note to the effect that the Prince could accept no letter without knowing from whom it came. A second letter. Tirpitz permitted to come. He finds the family at table; the Prince stands up, and remains standing until the guest has taken his place. Marked coolness. After the meal—the ladies gone—pipes, the chaise-longue. Then—as Tirpitz relates—Bismarck, without a preliminary word or hint, gives him an annihilating look and says: "I am no tom-cat, to send out sparks when I'm stroked."

A frightful moment—the Admiral ought to take up his despatch-case and go; but he finds a soft answer, and produces his papers and statistics. "I know we want more ships," snarls the veteran, "but not battleships." To all arguments he retorts angrily, unpropitiously. Then in the open carriage, driving through the rain, with bottles of beer to right and left of him, he speaks so unsparingly of the Emperor that Tirpitz begs, as an officer, to be allowed to intercede for him. "Tell the Emperor I want nothing but to be left alone, and die in peace. My work is done; I have no future, and no hope." The Princess had died the year before.

A quarter of this was quite as much as the Emperor could endure to listen to. Nevertheless he visited the Prince for the fourth time at the end of 1897. It was their last meeting (T. 93).

The old man was seated in his invalid-chair at the door of his house, when the Emperor arrived with his attendant gentlemen; the visitors had to pass one by one before the host, and so again at their departure. When Lucanus, who had brought him his dismissal seven years ago, approached in his procession and held out his hand,

a remarkable little scene took place which made a strong impression on us all. The Prince sat like a statue, not a muscle moving, gazing into vacancy, while before him writhed Lucanus—until at last he understood and took himself out of the way.

But at dinner, with strangers on either side, Bismarck revived under the influence of champagne. He looked at the Emperor sitting so close to him, in radiant health, not yet forty—and he himself so fabulously old! He felt that he might never see him again. Forgive him? Never! But what signified hatred, when his restless brain was fevered by the thought of all that he had achieved and was to leave imperilled? For eight years of so critical an European epoch they had not exchanged one political idea; in the four years of their renewed intercourse the Emperor had never asked him a single question—and what questions there were to be answered! So the old man flung away his pride—pride be hanged for once in his life!—the grave was before him, the Empire behind him; and Bismarck began, entirely of his own accord, to talk politics.

But if the Emperor rejoiced in the veteran's attempt to regain some influence, it was only because it gave him an opportunity of showing the table that He was Master and the other merely an old *radoteur*. He left him unanswered, and asked conundrums.

"What is the difference between a mother-in-law and a cigar?" The Prince, confounded, listened for a while; then he began again—this time alluding to Germany's position towards France. Again the Emperor heard him not; he asked another conundrum. The company sat speechless. "Every time Bismarck touched on politics, the Emperor abstracted his attention." Moltke whispered to Tirpitz: "This is horrible." "We all felt it as wanting in respect to such a man."

And Bismarck thought: "Very well! If the Emperor is

determined to know nothing and learn nothing, he shall listen to a warning as from a dying man—but it shall be spoken as casually as if we were sitting again at Biarritz, those thirty years ago to-day, and Napoleon was to be gently threatened, at table, with Prussia." And suddenly, "on some pretext or other, he came out with a remark which penetrated us all with its prophetic pregnancy:

" 'Your Majesty! So long as you have these officers around you, there is no doubt that you may do exactly as you please. But if ever that should not be so, it will be quite another matter.' "

"The apparent nonchalance," writes Tirpitz, "with which he brought this out, as if it meant nothing in particular, was a proof of great presence of mind—the master-spirit stood revealed in it." The Emperor seemed scarcely to have heard. At any rate, if he did grasp its import, he chose to ignore this last exhortation from his dying foe.

Six months later he was standing beside his coffin. For this visit to Friedrichsruh the Court functionaries had allowed twenty-eight minutes, including prayer and display of emotion. There stood the Emperor, and he was thinking:

"Where is your everlasting, harassing criticism now? You're lying in that box, but I am standing here with my funeral-wreath, in the full bloom of health, the undisputed master. Jealousy and revenge—they were the only reasons why for these eight years you strove to irritate my people. And what was the meaning of your last threatening speech that day at dinner, in the room close by? Is not my Empire flourishing? Are not my subjects happy? Every year the royal might grows stronger, and more unafraid. Europe fears the greatest army in the world. Go to your grave! The victory is mine."

CHAPTER V

BÜLOW

1   1898–1908

WITH every year the power of the alchemist increased. Holstein from his den could call to office or hurl from it those whom he had elected or condemned; and by this choice of high officials he shaped the international policy of the Empire to the pattern he had from the first resolved that it should take. This Privy Councillor's predominance is the clue to German foreign policy throughout the next ten years.

That this was not black magic, truly, yet that dark influences did control the game, it would seem that a few men realized even then. The historian, who cares nothing for piquant revelations but much for the practical consequences of certain personal peculiarities, will be content with the revelation afforded by two passages which, in two volumes of memoirs, resemble arresting black asterisks among a series of brilliant pictures. "No Imperial Chancellor," writes Eulenburg, "could have dispensed with Holstein. Even Bülow could not let him down—to be sure, there were particular reasons for that; because the noose Holstein had put round his neck was not to be got rid of, with the best will in the world" (E. 2, 385). And again Waldersee: he "would have supposed that Bülow would instantly have shelved Holstein, but the bottom-truth is that Holstein has a hold on the Emperor. The 'why' is more than I should care to entrust to this sheet of paper" (W. 3, 171). In the thousand printed pages of his most secret diary there is no other such implication—or rather the editor has replaced many passages by asterisks, so that in these also Waldersee may have set down for himself what posterity is not permitted to learn.

And yet Holstein was in no sense intimate with the two men who were most to influence the next decade; the Emperor he never would see, Bülow he never knew well until he was nearly sixty. We must therefore postulate a certain kind of knowledge stowed away in Holstein's intriguing brain, and used for the putting-on of pressure in government affairs; for although Holstein was deeply engaged in money-matters, there seems to have been no question of money between these three oddly linked men.

For years Holstein had striven to prevent Bülow's emergence. The new favourite had long been made known to the Emperor by the old one, and it was years since Bülow had ecstatically succumbed, in the course of many visits, to the Emperor's fascination; but Holstein would suffer only small fry as his superiors, was quite content with Marschall and Hohenlohe as the drivers of his chariot, and it was only to please Eulenburg, whom he could not do without, that he consented to some slight contact with Bülow. But Eulenburg, whose effeminate nature always craved for a masculine one to admire, and who now was driven to regard the Emperor as little more than the object of a maternal kind of compassion, beheld in Bülow the man of his heart, and was resolved to lead him on to that authority which his own timidity had never allowed him to accept.

They had discovered one another in Paris when neither was much more than thirty, and this friendship was in fact the most fruitful one that either ever had. Eulenburg was attracted to the Emperor chiefly by his power, possibly too out of sympathetic friendship; to Holstein, from first to last, only by the deliberate calculation that it was better to intrigue with him than against him—the former was ten years his junior and inferior to him in every respect; the latter ten years his senior and immensely more adept in politics. Bülow was of his own rank and training, but in contradistinction to his other friends was the only one of his elective affinities in whom he could find (as he instantly did) the born statesman; and so Eulenburg, who always did well for his friends, never thought of any one but Bülow for the Chancellorship. To Eulenburg Bülow owed his whole career—which, when all is said, remains the only statesmanlike one of William the Second's reign.

Bülow indeed combined nearly all the discrepant qualities which were divided between Holstein and Eulenburg. He united Holstein's knowledge of affairs with Eulenburg's psychological insight, Holstein's capacity for work with Eulenburg's dexterity; and while as a politician he was no less acute than Holstein, he rivalled Eulenburg in his aptitude for giving the right courtly aspect to his permutations. He was the first since Bismarck's day to possess political talent along with that readiness to assume responsibility which for the other two had been their lifelong bugbear. As he was less sophisticated than either, more optimistic, and more human-hearted too, he was immune from Eulenburg's cloying sentimentality and Holstein's goblin malice. His brilliant talents, none of which seemed typically German— rather for the most part Latin—made him appear like some fabulous many-coloured bird in the drab Prussian aviary, and the more because even his weaknesses were un-

Prussian. Unsystematic and unprejudiced, always making new friends, nobody's enemy, captivating but entirely without effeminacy, rather indeed something of a graceful cynic, he was like a highly polished ball that rolls upon the level, meeting with no obstacles and reflecting in its glassy surface a bright picture of the world around—in miniature, it is true, and just a little distorted. Above all he knew how to captivate the man on whom he depended. Though he thought no better of the Emperor than Holstein did, he courted him in the Eulenburg fashion; but having none of Eulenburg's genuine affection for him, was able to flatter him far more grotesquely, and gradually encircled him with an artful trellis-work of flowery language through which he, himself unseen, could peer continually, reading the master's mood upon his features. Between Holstein's aloofness and Eulenburg's fervours, neither of which was always effective with the Emperor, Bülow soon sailed before the wind—his cunning adulation eagerly lapped up by its guileless object. If Eulenburg had long been the subordinate-familiar, Bülow was the familiar-subordinate, who put forth no claims to the master's fidelity, who could be paid by the gift of authority; while the friend of his youth wanted nothing, and therefore ventured now and then to assume the tiresome aspect of a mentor.

Was it any wonder, then, that the discovery soon outshone the discoverer—that the Emperor found Bülow's temperate glow so congenial that ere long he somewhat forsook the Eulenburg hothouse? From this arose the first catastrophes.

Bülow was indeed the equal of his friend in adaptability; but he knew that he was playing a part, while Eulenburg had long lost sight of the distinction between the natural

and the artificial. Even in their letters, Bülow's false sentiment is visibly false; Eulenburg's, on the contrary, is genuine
for all its spuriousness. When after ten years of friendship
they reached the *Du* stage in 1893, Bülow "made a night of
it" on paper:

Listen—outwardly unlike in so many ways, we are inwardly
each other's true affinity. Not only because we have so many
memories both sweet and sad in common, but because in the depths
of our souls, we think and feel alike, and in the daily round are
one another's complement. Our spirits, like two sisters, crossed the
mysterious bourne of being; only we were given differing raiment
and variously hued pinions. If the Heavenly Powers conferred on
you the magic gift of bewildering and brilliant talents, *I* can nevertheless . . . from the storehouse where so gradually I have heaped
up treasure, furnish many a commodity that will assist you—drawn
into the political arena as you have been, against your will but for
the good of our Emperor and Country—to enrich the temple which
with lighter but surer hand than mine you now are building up.
You are perhaps more Germano-Hellenic, like the Second Part
of *Faust*, *I* more Prusso-Latin; you more knightly, I more soldierly.
. . . But if your head touches the stars, your feet are firmly
planted on this good round earth of ours; and if I am rooted in
the soil, I can at least look upward to the star-sown empyrean.
. . . You with your infinite delicacy of feeling, a beautiful falcon
in a forest filled with foxes, bristling swine, and cackling geese.
. . . How glorious was that Saturday night of ours! Never, so
long as I live, will it fade from memory. Past and present, visible
and invisible—all combined to create such a mood as belongs only
to moments of consecration. . . . May the Everlasting Might
which guides your steps uphold you always, my Philip!

Eulenburg had inhaled the fumes of this kind of incense
for a lifetime, without suffocating; but Bülow swung such
censors only on high-days and holidays. He could speak

the Bayreuth jargon as fluently as five other European languages—almost without thinking, yet never at a loss for a word; and despite this languishing nocturne, he certainly was at this time genuinely attached to his friend. The truth is that he was as sound as a bell; he could drink with the Agrarians, do battle with the Socialists, everywhere concealing his inmost self, whereas Eulenburg wore his like a buttonhole on all occasions; and he managed to turn all his acquirements to such good account that experts in every sort were sceptically inclined to regard him as a lexicon wherein great erudition was set off by a stupendous power of memory.

And now, while Bülow was making ready with Eulenburg's help to climb into the balloon for his ascent with the Emperor, Holstein was tugging at the rope from below and using all his force to wind it round the boulders of his cavern. He had now to contend with a pair of allies who were much too wary to do anything towards disabling him. "If Holstein knew how we trust one another, he'd smash up the whole game" (E. 2, 226); and earnestly did Philip instruct Bernhard in Holstein's hatred for the Emperor. Such confidences were responded to by Bülow with sovereign skill; he too was always writing for posterity, and took good care not to put dangerous reflections on paper.

Not only do I admire Holstein's intensity and power, but he has made me fond of him. Though many would not understand this, *you* will not mistake me. I love that tragic nature of his. I would never abandon him—I should like to help him. But for us there is a great difficulty in the fact that Holstein flies off at such a tangent whenever he thinks his system is threatened, or even likely to be obstructed. . . . In high quarters, or even against yourself, there is little he would not be ready for, if he did not believe His Majesty and you to be his indispensable allies against his own confederates and his numerous gang of enemies. . . . Holstein must feel sure of us—that is a cardinal necessity.

Under these specious phrases—which might fall into the hands of some spy though the Embassy-bag were never so carefully padlocked—the cautious Bülow, in his letters to his dearest friend, disguised his fear of the crafty Holstein whose teeth they were to draw before they could begin in earnest. Dreading some personal treachery from Holstein, who in his eyes was neither tragic nor lovable, he took from Eulenburg's Thesaurus the turns of phrase that would be most effective, and not forgetting the potential illicit reader, gained by that very precaution the sympathy of his correspondent who, for all his flowers of speech, made no mistake about his meaning.

Meanwhile, Eulenburg was pleading his cause before the sovereign, as did the fabled Princess that of her heart's elected. "Anyone who is blind to Bernhard's knowledge and capacity in political affairs," he wrote as early as 1892 to the Emperor, "is simply an envious fellow. . . . I am glad that Your Majesty has an eye for talent, and in the decisive moment will attribute the portentous disapproval on the said fellow's countenance to its true motive." In this way he began by removing his friend from the obscurity of Bucharest to the wider sphere of Rome. In the year 1895: "Bernhard is the most valuable functionary Your Majesty possesses—the predestined Imperial Chancellor of the future"; whereupon at the end of 1895, the Emperor (E. 2, 225) proclaimed as his incontrovertible decision:

"Bülow is to be my Bismarck!"

2

But once again the Emperor had forgotten Holstein. He did succeed in surmounting that obstacle, but by a means entirely unknown to himself.

In the beginning of 1897, a year after the Kruger Telegram, a new danger emerged from one of those negligible quarters of the globe where the European Powers find pretexts for their mutual jealousies. Crete revolted against the Turks, and was supported by Greece. On this the Emperor, in defiance of his Ministers, officially informed the foreign diplomats that Crete must be shown her place. The Great Powers were to blockade the Piraeus on the Turks' behalf. Hohenlohe was powerless, Holstein infuriated; Marschall tried to quell at least the uproar at home by promising the Reichstag a debate on the Cretan question. Thereupon the Emperor, feeling himself disavowed, wired from no one knew where in a white-hot rage:

This should not have been thought of without My express commands. The decisive step towards the settlement of this question had been taken by Me, directly and personally, and it is I alone who have to give an explanation to the Reichstag. . . . On My return to Berlin the Reichstag will be summoned to the Palace, and will be fully instructed with reference to My previously promulgated Imperial communication, on the attitude of My Government towards the Cretan question (A. 12, 348).

It might be supposed that at these words from Caesar, Chancellor and Secretary of State would instantly beat a retreat. But not at all. They only got Holstein to wire for help to Eulenburg: "You must be aware of these disturbing events—disturbing on account of the excitable strain in the Emperor's telegram. The few who have seen it are one and all equally uneasy" (E. 2, 216). Eulenburg tried, like an old doctor who had seen other purple-clad lunatics at large, to tone down the impression: "I too think the telegram in question excitable, but . . . the excitement is not of an alarming nature, either psychologically or otherwise"—the whole thing being, he declared, merely the result of the Emperor's defective education in these matters. A few days later, the latter made the famous speech in which he described his late grandfather as the creator of the Empire, any others concerned being no more than his hodmen.

At this time the Empire was plunged in gloom about the strained relations with Vienna, which were at bottom an outcome of Holstein's hatred for Goluchowski; then came the rejection of the first Bigger Navy Bill; then State-Secretary Marschall's libel action against his detractors, which the Emperor disapproved of—everything was at sixes and sevens. In only one respect were the Foreign Office and the Emperor completely in accord—each thought and said that the other was crazy. "The existence of Baron von Holstein, who is a rare fool, is not sufficient camouflage for a dummy Foreign Secretary, either for me or anyone else," the Emperor said in confidence at this time (E. 2, 231). What Holstein was simultaneously thinking about the Emperor, Eulenburg reported to his friend in Rome: "Unfortunately I must tell you that the relations between H.M. and the Office are very nearly impossible: this, because that Office quite frankly considers H.M. to be mad!!" (March 1897).

But Eulenburg was showing his good sense in two respects: publicly defending the Emperor, and privately warning him. "It is not unlikely that Your Majesty's personal intervention may prevent the machine from working. I must repeat that harmony between Your Majesty and the

Office is a very urgent necessity." After this letter he spoke to the Emperor, and in May 1897 was sent by him to arrange for an armistice in the Wilhelmstrasse.

It was late at night; all the confederates were sitting in Holstein's room. Hohenlohe was resolved to go if the Emperor sacrificed Marschall; they were considering how to muzzle His Majesty. While Eulenburg was addressing the party, there arrived,

smelling of wine, and spluttering, Kiderlen from a drinking-bout. . . . Holstein said the Emperor would have to submit blindly, and dismiss Lucanus. His Majesty would have to be treated as the child or the fool he was. . . . Alexander Hohenlohe agreed; and Kiderlen, the skunk, spat poison along with the saliva from his dribbling jaws—disgusting! The Emperor was to choose between complete submission, and the Chancellor's *belle sortie.* . . . I have seldom had a deeper sense of loyal love for my good noblehearted sovereign, who towered like another Siegfried before my inward vision! It was only by tremendous self-control that I repressed such words as would have made an irreparable breach between me and the dragon-brood around me (E. 2, 233).

At such moments Eulenburg's loyalty to the Emperor is wholly to be believed in; and if we delete the Siegfried and the other superlatives, which mean nothing in him, his behaviour did him credit as a friend, if not as a man of affairs; for he knew that Holstein would be estranged once more, and Bülow's emergence imperilled.

And then the whole thing ended in broad farce.

As thus: Marschall wanted a decoration for a Privy Councillor, who had been falsely accused of the authorship of that article in *Kladderadatsch,* and so had fallen into disfavour. The moment Holstein heard of this, he put two and two together and felt he had the clue to the mystery—it was

Marschall who had got up those attacks! In the twinkling
of an eye, Marschall's champion was transmogrified into his
deadly enemy. Here, in his own room, brooded treachery!
There was only one thing to be done—join hands with the
friends whom he so profoundly distrusted. That night he
invited Eulenburg to dine with him at Borckhardt's, and inquired in his note what wine the guest would prefer, for it
was to be a very special occasion.

At dinner he told Eulenburg all—as this latter lost no
time in telling Bülow.

> He was in a state of quivering agitation. . . . All his powers
> of hatred were suddenly and catastrophically directed against
> Marschall. Simultaneously there emerged a tender, wellnigh im-
> passioned affection for me and you. Yes! and as suddenly he was
> whole-heartedly on our side in his view of the situation—Emperor,
> public opinion here, Foreign Office, and all. The revulsion has this
> much to recommend it—that, if the cup is not to pass from you,
> if you are to be summoned to power, you will find Holstein in a
> totally different frame of mind and will be able to work with
> him. . . . His view is that we must stake all on keeping you on
> with Hohenlohe, and making you Chancellor when he retires. . . .
> You see, whatever happens now, Holstein won't move a finger
> against you and me . . . . I am very much impressed by this
> surprising turn of affairs. I am inclined to regard it as a Divine
> dispensation which will smoothe the way admirably for your ap-
> pointment, inevitable in any event. . . . I am yours, dear fellow,
> in anxious sympathy.

After God had so unmistakably revealed himself between
a decoration, a comic paper, a bottle of Chambertin, and the
persecution-mania of a Privy Councillor; and the mightily
relieved king-maker had floated over the Alps a missive of
congratulation to his friend, wherein the joy of seeing the
way clear at last was transformed into a cup that might not

pass from him and was proffered with anxious sympathy—
the whole affair turned out to be a mare's nest. The candi-
date for an Order was not that enemy at all. Holstein made
up his quarrel with Marschall, but now he had gone too far
to draw back. The Emperor was not to be appeased—Marschall had to go.

Enter Bülow.

3

The honeymoon lasted a very long time. "Bernhard—
glorious chap!!" wrote the Emperor in his tempestuous fashion at the end of 1897 (E. 2, 240). "He has done splendidly, and I adore him! . . . What a joy it is to have to
do with a man who is devoted to one, body and soul, and
wants to understand one too, and *can* understand one!" In
the summer of 1898:

From the moment Bernhard arrived everything went right;
everything was in his hands. The Privy Councillors are quite out
of it. Who ever talks about Holstein nowadays? . . . Since
Bülow took the reins, one positively doesn't even know the name of
any one of his councillors.

More interesting is the anti-strophe. Bülow, in August
1897:

His Majesty as a personality is charming, touching, irresistible,
adorable; as a ruler, by reason of his temperament, his lack of
discrimination and sometimes even of common judgment, his tendency to let his desires prevail over calm and sober reflection . . .
he will stand in the very greatest danger if he is not surrounded
by prudent and, more especially, loyal and trustworthy servants.
Upon this it will depend whether his reign is to form a glorious or
a melancholy page in our history. With his individuality either
is possible.

So instantly did Bülow's intelligence perceive the power of influence upon this erratic monarch. But after they had defined their positions with "glorious chap" and "very greatest danger," Bülow reverted at once to his cautious calculations, and wrote his friend only such letters as could be shown at the Palace. At the beginning of 1898:

I hang my heart more and more every day upon the Emperor. He is so remarkable! Together with the Great King and the Great Elector he is far and away the most remarkable Hohenzollern that has ever existed. He combines in a manner that I have never before seen the most sound and original intelligence with the shrewdest good sense. He possesses an imagination which can soar on eagle-wings above all trivialities, and with it the soberest perception of the possible and the attainable; and—what energy into the bargain! What a memory! What swiftness and sureness of comprehension!

One might think the man had taken leave of his senses. But to be familiar with his style is to perceive the sublimity of his cynicism. Bülow could dash off these rhapsodies by the page, whenever he felt inclined; and they were of course intended to be shown by his friend to the Emperor. He could have given no clearer proof of his swift assessment of the Imperial endowments than his conviction that William's vanity would swallow such coarse fare as these preposterous parallels. Other intelligences, more remote from this atmosphere, were confounded. Ballin said:

It can't possibly last long; the Emperor is much too clever not to see that Bülow is perpetually humbugging him. But Waldersee, who had known him longer, comments on this: I was of a different opinion; the Emperor can never have too much of that kind of thing (W. 3, 176).

Bülow almost openly defended his technique. "After all, I could not begin by annoying the Emperor with contradictions—I had first of all to consolidate my position." But that is the point—a little contradiction in the first week might certainly have annoyed the Emperor, but might also have made him more tractable. Bülow, who never liked saying No, was not very likely to begin by saying it to his sovereign; but, trusting to his master's volatility, he did eventually do pretty well as he thought best, and only seldom forgot what sparks may be struck out of a neurotic autocrat. On such occasions, indeed, he did encounter

an annihilating look, which sooner or later would be followed by an outburst in which his Majesty would brusquely express opinions that brooked no discussion of any kind. The moment this look and tone were seen and heard, a devout silence would fall upon the master-spirit before him, who in his own good time would discreetly put in a word (Z. 37).

Zedlitz, for years a subtle observer of Bülow's behaviour at Court, in another passage deplores the fact that he too would never say anything but smooth words to the Emperor:

If he had even once shown the least reserve, or let it be seen that he was, as he actually *was*, independent of his position, he might have done great things, for personally speaking no one could have replaced him with the Emperor. Unfortunately that was not in his nature.

Thus his influence, instead of being productive, tended rather towards placating and restraining the Emperor. The State Papers are full of instances. Take an interview with the Tsar on board the "Hohenzollern." The Emperor: "I wish you would assume, from now on, the title of Admiral of the Pacific. I shall call myself Admiral of the Atlantic." Nicholas, either alarmed or embarrassed, shook his head. Bülow, sitting by, turned hot and cold. What was to be done? Something, and at once! In a second or two he had pulled himself together, and smilingly said: "That title would be peculiarly appropriate to Your Majesty, since Your Majesty is a declared lover of peace: hence Pacific!" The Emperor several times recurred to the subject, and on his departure signalled: "The Admiral of the Atlantic salutes the Admiral of the Pacific." Nicholas merely answered: "Bon voyage!" Then Bülow begged the captain to order all the officers and crew to hold their tongues about the signal. But the Russians told the story—every word of it.

Bülow's great achievement was to restore, after the seven years of chaos, as much tranquillity to the Foreign Office and its policy as the Emperor would permit of.

No more explosive despatches [writes Eulenburg, well satisfied]. No frantic letters from Holstein. . . . I am possessed by the feeling that after terrible storms I have at last steered the ship we may call "the Emperor's Reign" into at least a tolerably safe harbourage. If I honestly ask myself whether the vessel would have reached this haven after these nine years without my help, I am bound to answer No.

Eulenburg is entirely justified in this view; but still more in the uneasiness which, none the less, still haunts him when he reflects on the destiny of his Imperial friend.

It always makes me uncomfortable [he writes to Bülow in the beginning of 1899] when I think that you are our dear good master's last card. No other can—and still less will—do all for him that you are doing . . . the affection of a loyal servant, which has taken in you the form of a father's love for an unruly child.

During these early years of office Bülow's intimacy with Eulenburg was still so close that the latter sent him a kind of journal of an Imperial trip; and Bülow answered: "I say, write, and do nothing political without thinking of you." But Bülow did not long hold aloof from Holstein; he managed to get over that wish of Eulenburg's by giving the impression that at the Foreign Office he alone was master.

The motto of the main group [he wrote to his friend immediately after his appearance there] may now be said to be "A bad conscience makes us afraid." Holstein is elegiac ("For twenty years I have felt like a father to you"), Kiderlen reminds me of an earwig. . . . Of course the group has not yet abandoned all hope of their ideal future: Hatzfeldt Imperial Chancellor, Kiderlen Secretary of State; in the background the muzzled Emperor (E. 2, 240).

Eulenburg knew better, but he held his peace. He knew why Bülow could not hold aloof from Holstein; and while the Emperor was exultantly saying "Who ever talks about Holstein now?" the initiates were all talking about him— except Bülow, who was for ever talking *with* him.

4

Three times in the next few years the English sought an alliance with Germany; three times the decision lay with the Emperor, who dominated foreign affairs precisely as Bismarck had before him—nothing was done without his approval, and this was never a mere formality.

Chamberlain took the first step.

It is an attempt at political organization of the civilized world. It is the dazzling scheme of an English merchant, whose modest imagination embraces both hemispheres. . . . Heretofore . . .

Europe had been the vantage-ground for political ambitions and manœuvres. If Great Britain . . . joined hands with Germany, America might throw in her lot with them; and thus a World-Group would have been formed, against which no other Power would venture to measure itself. . . . The scheme was a practicable one (Fischer, *Holsteins Grosses Nein*).

Two years after the Kruger Telegram, in the March of 1898, Chamberlain made the first advance to the German Ambassador, Hatzfeldt (A. 14, 197).

Isolation is a thing of the past, he said; England is about to take far-reaching decisions, and inclines towards Germany. "This would have been equivalent to England's joining the Triple Alliance, and could have been consolidated by arrangement for which our conditions were to be formulated." They were requested to decide without delay.

What was now within reach had been the dream of Bismarck—that England should be obliged, by continental developments, to seek German support. Prophetic indeed were Bismarck's words in that instruction to Hatzfeldt of January 1888:

The question here is not that of greater striking-power in the event of war, but of precluding war. Neither France nor Russia will break the peace if they are officially informed that, should they do so, they will have England against them from the first. . . . If it were now established that England was protected against French aggression by a German, and Germany by an English, alliance, I should regard peace as ensured for so long as such an alliance subsisted. I believe that the effect would be alleviating and tranquillizing throughout the whole of Europe. . . . In my judgment, England gains nothing by carrying her policy of isolation so far that every continental Power, for example Germany, is obliged to make arrangements for safeguarding its future without regard to England.

Nothing but pressure from England was wanting to make Bismarck's authoritative opinion successful in obtaining this last and most valid guarantee of peace—a few more years in office and he would have won England over. Now, three months before his death, the ripe fruit fell to those who had presumptuously wrested the Empire from his mighty grasp. And they refused it.

For Holstein was against the alliance. Bismarck had declared that it was nonsense to suppose the Russo-English antagonism would last for ever; hence Holstein was bound to declare that a collision between them was "in the nature of things," that this made a Franco-English alliance an impossibility, and that the desirable part for Germany was "that of umpire." And now was Germany to "pull the African chestnut out of the fire for England?" Never! It was all English devilry, "delirium and bluff"; they wanted to estrange Germany from Russia. So in this matter also he attributed his own perfidy to others, vindicating thus his own political propensities.

Bülow would not have submitted these arguments of Holstein's to the Emperor, if he had not been well aware of his morbidity about England; and the Emperor was indeed delighted: "So they've come off their high horse, have they? No grabbing at them though—let them wait!" He wrote:

The proposition arises from their uneasiness about the results of our Naval measures. By the beginning of the next century we shall be in control of an ironclad armada which, in combination with others, may be an actual danger to England. Hence the design either to constrain us to an alliance, or, as with Holland in the past, to annihilate us before we are strong enough to resist. If England were in good faith, the agreement would be an excellent one for our future, and we should be assured of colossal commercial advantages.

The refusal, couched in the form of a postponement, was attributable, therefore, to the Emperor's disbelief in the honesty of English intentions—that is to say, it was the psychological fruit of his unhappy youth and the vexatious domestic experiences of his manhood. The secondary motive was his wish for the Fleet, that instrument and symbol of jealousy, which could only be obtained from the Reichstag in the event of friction with England, never if he were in alliance with her. On the ground that Germany needed the assent of both parties in the English Parliament, and was even less sure of that to-day than she had been two years ago, Bülow procrastinated over the negotiations; and when London offered the desired debate in Parliament, he declined on the pretext that it would alarm Russia.

Meanwhile the Emperor seized his pen and in May 1898, all unsuspecting, wrote to the Tsar—having suddenly conceived the idea of obtaining preferential treatment from him on the ground of his personal feeling against England. Taking as his starting-point their inherited friendship, he confided to him that England had twice approached him with an offer of alliance, had been coolly dismissed, but nevertheless had repeated her offer for a limited period, and with enormous advantages for Germany.

Before I give my answer I wish to let you know, my valued friend and cousin; for I feel that it is, so to speak, a matter of life and death. . . . Now I beseech you . . . to tell me what you can and will offer me, if I refuse, before I . . . give my answer. Your proposals must be clear and frank and free from mental reservations, so that I can consider them in my heart and lay them before God, as I am bound to do, since the blessing of peace for my country and the world is at stake. . . . By this letter, dearest Nicholas, I show you that I put my entire faith in your absolute secrecy—not a word to anyone. . . . The next generation is in our hands!

The solemnity of this fatuously astute letter is best perceived in the apostrophe to "Nicholas," whom in all other circumstances he called "Nicky." Let it be further said that this production, which tells with vast exaggeration of prodigious offers, and implies that a decision, which had in fact been made, still hangs in the balance, was eleven years afterwards to be demanded back by the Emperor from the official archives (A. 14, 250). Equally astute, but less solemn, was the rebuff which arrived in a few days from Petersburg. In this the recipient—merely Willy—is overtrumped with the information that England shortly before had made hitherto unprecedented offers to Russia, thus seeking indirectly to disturb her friendly relations with Germany. Therefore Nicky can neither advise nor respond.

The Emperor was incessantly haunted by the thought of all this. Between his longing to refuse the offered hand, that he might build a fleet himself, and the uncertainty whether this great alliance were not forever lost to him, the conflict of conscience raged within this weakling who would fain have been a Hercules, and drove him to attacks upon England, boastings against England, that so he might in some sort indemnify himself. Angry remarks to the English Ambassador about Salisbury were reported to London. Then, when his grandmother refused the Emperor's offer of a visit on her eightieth birthday, he poured out all his mortification in a letter to the aged Queen.

Your Minister has treated us as if we were Portugal, Chili, or Patagonia . . . and all on account of a ridiculous island [Samoa] which can't be worth a pin to England compared with the thousands of square miles she annexes right and left every year without encountering any protest (May 1899).

The Queen had frequently in the last ten years taken her grandson's part against her son—her strong dynastic feeling constraining her. But now even she had had enough; and she answered:

Dear William. . . . I must tell you frankly that your letter has very much astonished me. The tone in which you write of Lord Salisbury I can only ascribe to a passing nervous irritation. . . . I doubt if one monarch has ever before written in such a tone to another, and this to your grandmother regarding her Prime Minister! I would never dream of such a thing; I never even disparaged Prince Bismarck, though I knew what a bitter enemy of England he was. . . . Your visit to Osborne, not to Cowes, I will take as my birthday-visit, since I could not receive you on the day itself. Your loving grandmother, V.R.I. (A. 14, 620).

Except in the last adjective she was telling him the unvarnished truth. But he was glad to be allowed again to visit England after four years' absence, for since the Kruger Telegram the English Press had taken a threatening tone about visits from the Emperor, which in its turn reacted upon the German Press. It was all the more plucky of Chamberlain, in Germany the best-hated of men, to bring forward his proposal. Now the Emperor entered his "Meteor" for the regatta, as of old; was the absent victor, and Edward in the evening made the speech of ceremony on the hero of the day. The next morning a telegram from the Emperor was opened in the Royal Yacht Club. It was one dire insult: "Your handicaps are simply appalling."

Instantly the English temper veered round.

He really drives one to despair, said Edward to Eckardstein. Here am I taking the greatest trouble to rehabilitate the Emperor after all those incidents . . . and the first thing he does is to throw mud at us. . . . You know the effect such remarks will have, our people being so sensitive, and so proud of their fair play in sporting matters! (Eck. 2, 29).

And then, when the Court functionaries were making arrangements for the visit, Edward expressed a desire not to see Admiral von Senden, who had offended him the year before, in the Emperor's suite. "I'll take whom I choose!" said the Emperor, and took von Senden.

Such were the mutual tempers when in the autumn England welcomed, after some years' absence, the Emperor, the Empress, and Bülow.

5

In November 1899 the Press took the tone that public opinion in both countries was still so excited that any official reference to politics would be unwise; and so the reports dwelt only on the facts that the two monarchs had kissed one another on both cheeks, and that the Emperor had shot one hundred and seventy-eight pheasants, three hundred and twenty-eight rabbits, and one partridge. Even the solitary partridge, figuring among the record slaughterings of the royal shoots, was liable to be regarded as the attempt of some anglophobe to reveal the nakedness of the land to German readers. England, harassed by the Boer War, was seeking a friend; Chamberlain and his group adhered to Germany, and tried yet again to attach her before resorting to the alternative. In two long interviews he expounded the situation to the Emperor, other members of the Cabinet did likewise; the Chancellor too was interpellated—finally Bülow expressed the desire that Chamberlain would make a public speech on the subject of their mutual interests.

"Hence," wrote Chamberlain, "my speech of yesterday, which I hope will satisfy Bülow."

The day after the Emperor's departure the Englishman had publicly spoken at Leicester of the new scheme.

> That far-seeing statesman [Disraeli] long ago desired that we should not remain isolated on the Continent; and I think the most natural alliance is that between us and the German Empire. . . . A concert—an alliance, if you will—anyhow, an understanding between these two great nations would in actual fact be an assurance of world-peace. . . . Thus a new Triplice between the Teutonic and the two great branches of the Anglo-Saxon races would be a still more momentous factor in the future of the world.

Frantic was the answering cry. The bloodhound of the Transvaal is upon us, he would fain tear the Triplice to tatters, would fain exploit German friendship in Paris—all inspired by Holstein, who fed the Press. Though he was warned by Hatzfeldt and other well-informed persons in England, Holstein's opinion was:

> I am opposed to this friendship-agitation . . . and am the more distrustful because the threatened understanding between Russia and France is mere English delirium. A reasonable arrangement with England will, in my judgment, be attainable only if the sense of urgency becomes much more general there than it is at present.

Bülow knew better. "Feeling in England," he wrote after his return, "is much less anti-German than ours is anti-English." Even Court circles, he said, were impressed by the grand conception of a World-Alliance of the Three Empires; for now, fighting simultaneously in Egypt, the Transvaal, and China, England needed a powerful ally. But Bülow was no less dependent on Holstein than on public opinion, which was in great part shaped by the latter. He did not dare, as Chamberlain was doing now, and as Bismarck had done in the sixties, to modernize national opinion by teaching it to envisage unfamiliar groupings; and he answered the speech he had himself requested the Englishman to make by a rebuff in the Reichstag, deferential in its tone towards France and Russia.

> Our policy is purely German. Whether and when, how and where, we may be constrained to safeguard our position in the world . . . to abandon the reserve we have hitherto practised, depends upon the course of events . . . and that no individual Power can determine.

But to determine that course was precisely what the statesman was there for; the "permutation" of which all Europe was talking should have been dared in Germany, and dared with a fearless hand. What use for Bülow afterwards to cause England to be informed that his speech had not meant what it said, that he had been obliged, in making it, to think of the agitation in Germany and of the Navy Bill?

> I will not [wrote Chamberlain privately] express myself on the way in which Bülow has let me down. Anyhow I must abandon all further negotiations in the matter of the alliance. . . . It really grieves me very much indeed . . . but for myself I grieve a good deal too. Everything was going well; even Lord Salisbury was quite amicably inclined again, and of one mind with us with reference to the future relations of England with Germany. But alas! once more it was not to be (Eck. 2, 125).

To let the sands twice run out—that was the Emperor's revenge! But already he was trying once more to satisfy his will-to-power, and making use of the recent dalliance and England's necessity to instigate the Russians against the English. At the New Year of 1900 he expressed to the

Russian Ambassador his admiration at the rehearsal for mobilization on the Afghan frontier.

The Emperor saw in this the confirmation of his own opinion that only Russia could lay low the power of England. This theme led him on to declare warmly that if ever our august sovereign should decide to lead his armies against India, he himself, the Emperor, would guarantee that there should be no trouble in Europe—*he* would stand guard over our frontiers.

After this communication, which the Ambassador made public by the Emperor's explicit permission, from Petersburg to Paris and the other capitals the question ran whether London should not be called upon to conclude her war—in other words, whether continental pressure should not be exercised, even at the risk of a World-War.

But when in the beginning of March the Ambassador approached the Emperor in this sense, William drew back with the remark that he must first make inquiries in London. For in the meantime he had likewise betrayed Russia to England, had warned Edward in letters of February: "I want a strong, unhampered England. It is eminently necessary for the peace of Europe. Be on the look-out" (Lee, *King Edward*, 768). At the same time he was condoling with him in frequent despatches, and with vast exaggeration, over the English casualties. He wrote with unconcealed satisfaction of the "Black Week," and said "Your losses, as they are made known, little by little, are quite appalling and find every sympathy with our Army" (Lee, 755). The impartial reflections on the military situation which he added to one of these letters were not to be generally known for many years, but even that was years too soon.

But not even yet was the alliance entirely a thing of the

past. In London three Germans were working for it; and although the sagacious, but old and somewhat failing, Count Hatzfeldt spared Holstein's and the Emperor's nerves in his despatches, he *did* emphasize—as did the fearless Baron von Eckardstein, who moved more freely in society, and was *persona grata* with Chamberlain and the Prince of Wales—the magnitude of the opportunity. Then the affair was taken in hand by Count Wolff-Metternich. He, for ten years Ambassador after Hatzfeldt's death, reopened the question, first in the form of an alliance, later in that of a permanent entente; and further kept up a fire of despatches, some of historical importance, against the Naval Policy of the Centre Party in Berlin—until the Emperor silenced this warning voice as he did all others.

The death of Queen Victoria in 1901 brought about a reconciliation between the Emperor and England. His arriving in time to find her still alive, and then remaining on to be present at the funeral and the ceremonies of accession, had its effect upon English sentiment—that is to say, upon the whole nation. "Thank you, Kaiser," said an isolated voice in the street, when he was received by a silent crowd. The dying Queen did not recognize him; with the poignant irony which belongs to death-beds, she called him Frederick, taking him for his father. Relations between the nephew and uncle were more amicable, in the intimacy of emotion; for the first time for years they talked confidentially. The Emperor, at the moment in an anti-Russian humour, seemed more approachable than before; and for the third time in the course of three years Chamberlain expounded his desires.

The period of splendid isolation, he said at this time, is over for England. Our desire is to discuss all questions of international policy, especially those of Morocco and the Far East, with one or other of the great national groups. It is true that there are voices in the Cabinet in favour of joining the Dual Alliance; the rest of us are on the German side (Eck. 2, 236).

But the Emperor was no sooner home again than his mood veered round. The Big-Fleet party got at him— for the third time he decreed a reserved treatment of the question, and seized the earliest opportunity to give his uncle, the new King, some advice and criticism. This was in April, when he designated Edward's Ministers as "unmitigated noodles."

What would your Emperor say [remarked the King to Eckardstein] if I allowed myself to call *his* Ministers such names! For years I have believed, and believe even now, that we are natural allies; together we could act as the world's police and keep the peace indefinitely. Undoubtedly Germany needs colonies and a wider sphere of influence, and she can have them both. . . . But these perpetual buckjumps of the Emperor's are more than anyone can put up with. That's why some of my Ministers have lost all faith in him, and in Bülow too. I have always tried to restore their confidence. But everything comes to an end at last (Eck. 2, 298).

Shortly after this, a prominent champion of the alliance, Baron Alfred de Rothschild, wrote:

No one here is any longer taken in by Bülow's fine empty phrases . . . for that matter, your Government doesn't even yet seem to know what it wants. . . . Chamberlain, who has been dining with me to-night, has utterly lost heart; he won't have anything more to do with Berlin. "If they're so short-sighted," he says, "that they can't see it's a question of a new international constellation, *I* can't help them" (June 1902).

And so it came to pass that the same Chamberlain who had ignored all previous friction, now angrily repudiated attacks in the German Press on the undoubted brutalities of his troops in the Transvaal, and made a speech comparing the behaviour of his soldiers with that of other European armies, including the Germans in the war of 1870. Whereupon a fresh storm arose in Germany. Bülow, though warned by the well-informed in London, could not resist the temptation of going with the stream instead of stemming it; and answered in the Reichstag that Germany would suffer no criticism of her soldiers. "Whoever attempts it will find he is biting on iron!" The deafening applause which greeted this speech was paid for by the final breaking-off of negotiations. Chamberlain complained: "Bülow let me down before, two years ago—now I've had enough of it. There can be no further talk of coalition." Three months after, in February (1903), he began conversations with Cambon, which two years later led to the Entente Cordiale.

6

In Berlin there is now more widespread apprehension . . . that one of these days we may fall between two stools. Unfortunately the Emperor *has* made love to all the Powers in turn, and of course they all know he has. Moreover he is terribly imprudent in his utterances—when he wants to stand well with England he says the most impossible things about Russia, and vice versa; then each tells the other what he said. . . . He is convinced of his own infallibility and astuteness; when anything goes wrong, others get all the blame. Sad to say, he is not a bit more conscientious about work, rather the reverse (W. 2, 368).

A year later, when Bülow took charge, Waldersee followed up these political forebodings with others of a military kind.

People are taken in by the frequent violent speeches. . . . Our opponents are still of opinion that we may fall upon them any

day, and as yet have no idea that it is we who are in the position
of dreading attack from *them* at any moment. One of the most
unfortunate ideas is that of protecting our long Eastern frontier
by fortresses. . . . An offensive is the only thing there, and our
having abandoned all idea of that is disturbing indeed. What would
the Field-Marshal of immortal memory say if he could hear of it!
. . . Unfortunately very powerful influences are at work in that
direction; the immense sums made by Iron Industry over steel-clad
turrets, gun-carriages, armour-plates, etc., induces the magnates
to encourage the Emperor's fancy for that kind of thing. The
Emperor met with no opposition when he depleted the Eastern army
in favour of the Western (W. 2, 401).

As a matter of fact, the Emperor did not in the least
believe there would be any conflict with Russia. Ever since
Nicholas had been Tsar he had danced attendance on him.
He had talked himself into a hate for the yellow races, all
on account of Russia; in 1895 he sent the Tsar his painting:
"Peoples of Europe, guard your most precious possessions!"; but at the same period received the very yellow Li-
Hung-Chang with marked consideration, and told him that
China and Germany were natural allies. In the aforesaid
painting the mild Buddha was transmogrified into an idol
presiding over a bloody holocaust, Russia and Germany
standing sentinel over the apostles of the true Gospel in the
Far East. "I designed this drawing in Christmas-Week,
under the glitter of the Christmas-tree candles," he wrote to
the Tsar in Eulenburgian style, after he had ordered this
chocolate-box cover from a Court-painter. Soon the representatives of Germany in Tokio were complaining that such
pictures, fluttering all over the globe as they quickly would
be, would put an end to friendly feeling in Japan. Besides,
the universal question was how those Christian sentinels accorded with the Sultan's amity and the three hundred million

Mohammedans, whom the Emperor had, in Damascus, described as his friends when hanging a miracle-working lamp over Saladin's tomb.

When after a Japanese victory in China it was thought well to call upon the conqueror to hold her hand, the Emperor took a personal stand against Japan. No sooner had the slogan of the Yellow Peril sounded in his ears than his heated imagination beheld yellow armies and navies overrunning Europe; Russia was the only Power who could tackle these. This idea of keeping the Tsar busy in the Far East, so as to disembarrass Germany's eastern frontier, had become a foible of the Emperor's, and was later on to facilitate and expedite the outbreak of the Japanese War. So long ago as the April of 1895 he had promised the Tsar to cover his rear if he took the field in Asia, and this without the knowledge of the Foreign Office. When in process of time he sent him the painting, and heard from his Ambassador that it had given pleasure and was to be carefully framed, the Emperor wrote in the margin of the despatch: "So it works! That is very gratifying." None of his utterances is more pathetic than this. Here he does definitely show as a dreamer who was incapable of seeing things as they were. One Emperor sends another a politically suggestive painting; the recipient is embarrassed, his Ministers laugh, cascades of bon-mots ripple round the drawing. What do they do? "Very beautiful," they say, and get the thing framed. This most guarded of acknowledgments is enough to irradiate the monarch—*qualis artifex!*—and he is so guileless as to indite, for all his representatives to read: "So it works!"

It worked by making the Empire completely dependent on the Tsar's dubious authority in Court and realm; it worked by implicating Germany in the moral responsibility for the Russo-Japanese War, to which she had encouraged Russia; it worked by estrangement of the anglophile Japan. "We had staked all upon a card which was not even in our hand" (Brandenburg, *Von Bismarck zum Weltkrieg*).

In the next few years there were trumped-up meetings with the Tsar; in 1897, "one has been brought about by hook or by crook. As before, he is dancing attendance on his exalted cousin—nay, one might use a harsher expression. . . . Truly it is only to be explained by the fear of war" (W. 2, 374). In the year 1898 he sent the Tsar another picture by the same Court-painter Knackfuss, representing Germany's fraternization with Russia; at this, Bülow ventured only to look a little aghast. With a persistency which no Prussian interest urged on him, the Emperor pursued his correspondence with the Tsar at this time (it lasted altogether twenty years) and awaited his answers like a suppliant at Court. "This morning came at last an anxiously awaited letter from the Tsar. There was great delight and excitement about it. These letters are always long expected, and never come soon enough. Often the joyful anticipation of such a letter will last for months" (Z. 101).

When in the beginning of 1904 Russia declared war, it was with difficulty that the Emperor was kept neutral; he allowed the Tsar to coal at Kiao Chao, and when Japan protested he was furious and made threatening references to England. About that time he wrote down his political programme—August 1904—as a marginal note to a despatch, which was to go to all his representatives.

For the instruction of all my diplomatic functionaries! . . . This will be the decisive battle between the two religions of Christianity and Buddhism, between Western civilization and Eastern semi-civilization. It will be the battle which I prophetically delineated in my painting, wherein all Europe, acting as the United States of Europe, was to assemble under German leadership and defend, as we are bound to do, our most precious possessions. . . . It is instinct which implants in Japanese bosoms the same feeling towards us which Caesar had towards Casca, and Wallenstein towards Butler! . . . Therefore our sympathies are rightly Russia's! Therefore it is of the most vital importance that the Baltic Fleet—when it is ready and trained—should sail to reconquer the mastery of the sea and wrest it from Japan. . . . The future of Russia, and indirectly of Europe, is at stake! I know well that we shall one day have to fight to the death with Japan, and I am making my preparations to that end! The Russians . . . later on, will assuredly aid us in repulsing Japan; but it would be better if they could give them a sound thrashing now.

In this document all the elements of his being are fused into a unique amalgam which is the authentic William—the fervour of the Crusader, the lawlessness of the pirate, the rant of the star-actor in a Grand Historical Melodrama, the craving for hegemony, the infatuation of the deluded, while as a finishing-touch the Germans are twice likened to classic murderers. Nor was his steadfast faith at all shaken by the issue of this bout between the religions, for he said to the recruits: "We must not conclude from the Japanese victories that Buddha is the superior of our Master, Christ."

Behind all this lay political calculations. Would not Russia be at his disposal in any event? If she won the war, Germany would have counselled and supported her; if she lost it, she would be weak enough to be forced into an alliance. This last idea was elaborated by Holstein, and in October 1904 was laid before the Chancellor with the argument that the combined pressure of Russia and Germany would oblige France likewise to join in! Two Empires— so Holstein's ingenuity reasoned—which had allied themselves only for the purpose of sooner or later crushing a third, were assuredly neither to be separated nor individually won over; but together they would be ready to appear upon the third party's platform as expiators of their error by reversing the original aim of their alliance. Thus Holstein's scheme provided for an alliance which was, after a year and a half, to be a substitute for, and improvement upon, that which the same intelligence had rejected in the shape of the counter-insurance. According to this scheme, the Emperor was to make a "defensive and offensive alliance with the Tsar for the preservation of European peace"—with which humbug, indeed, the majority of alliances were preluded in the Europe of the past. In the event of an attack upon either of the two Empires, each party undertook to assist the other with all its available forces; the arrangement was to become valid, a year of grace intervening, from the time when the Japanese concluded peace. The Tsar was to inform France and propose her adhesion.

No one knows anything about it [wrote the Emperor to the Tsar] not even my Foreign Office; the work was done by Bülow and myself alone. The point is this: If you and I stand shoulder to shoulder, the principal result will be that France must frankly and formally join us, by the mere fulfilment of her obligations to Russia; and this is of the greatest importance to us, especially in consideration of her fine harbours and her useful Fleet, which would then be completely at our disposal.

Then he proceeded to designate the heads of the Republic with which the Tsar was allied as "Clemenceau and all the rest of the ragtag and bobtail." That was the reason why they must first be of one mind between themselves, for as those Frenchmen "are neither Kings nor Emperors, I cannot put them on the same footing in a confidential matter like this as I can you, my cousin and friend."

If in this letter we substitute "Trust" for "Countries" and suppose it to be written by the heir of a coal-magnate to his principal rival in business, and sent without consulting anyone whatever, it is clear that no general manager could retain his position in that colliery. Bülow indeed *had* read the original paper, but not the letter; instead, it was read by the ragtag and bobtail in Paris, which was neither King nor Emperor, but merely intelligent and hostile. Before long came the answer from the Tsar which anyone might have expected—he would be obliged to begin by showing such a proposal to his Paris *"compagnon."* As this was impossible, Holstein's masterpiece vanished into the Secret Archives.

7

Six months later it was resurrected in a form which Holstein, on another occasion, called "Operetta-Politics." The Emperor had devised a scene, the like of which he never in the whole course of his existence had the bliss of figuring in again. Russia was finally defeated in the naval battle near Tsushima in May 1905. "Kings are easily caught in the depths of such doldrums," thought the Emperor, and arranged for a secret meeting of their yachts in Finnish waters. He started without delay, had the contents of the pigeon-holed document wired to him the day before the rendezvous, copied them with his own exalted hand, altered them at a critical point, and prayed—in the absence of Bülow—to the Lord "that He may lead me and guide me according to His will, for I am but the instrument of His hand, and will do what He gives me to do, however arduous the task."

Next day, on board the "Polar Star" in the Bay of Björkö, he was embracing Nicholas, who undoubtedly must have been glad, in his then situation, to sink upon the heart of a friend. As soon as they were alone, they established the fact that "France had flatly refused to dance to our tune, and evidently had no intention of ever fighting in the cause of the two Empires." Then the talk turned on England, and they outdid one another in reviling her. The Tsar—so the Emperor quickly informed Bülow (A. 19, f. 458)—described King Edward, in English, as the greatest mischief-maker and the most disingenuous and dangerous intriguer in the world; whereupon he gave the Emperor his English word of honour that never in his life would he combine against him with England. Followed a junketing on the "Hohenzollern," which lasted till broad daylight.

On awaking next forenoon the first step was yet another interview with God, who, before the Emperor began to haul in his dear friend, was consulted after the manner of the Moravian Brethren and caused him to open at the pregnant text: "He shall reward every man according to his works." The work being now certified as pleasing to God, the Emperor stepped, full of joyful anticipation, into his boat "with the treaty in his pocket." Another embrace, this time on the rope-ladder, and then "an excellent lunch in the saloon." ("An historic lunch," thought the Emperor.) As the Tsar spoke sceptically of the French, the Emperor ventured to express a suspicion that Edward had possibly made another of those "little arrangements" which were a foible of his, behind Russia's back with her ally.

The Tsar hung down his head very dejectedly, and said: "That is too bad. What shall I do in this disagreeable situation?" I felt then that the moment had come! As his ally, without informing or consulting the Tsar, had taken a free hand in policy, *he* was of course at liberty to do the same. "How would it be if *we* were to make a little arrangement, too? . . . Germany had begun to be quite good friends with the Gauls, and now all obstacles are removed."

"Oh yes, to be sure. I remember well, but I forgot the contents of it. What a pity I haven't got it here."

"I possess a copy, which by an extraordinary chance I happen to have in my pocket." The Tsar caught me by the hand and drew me out of the saloon into what used to be his father's cabin, then he shut all the doors himself. "Show it to me, please"—and his dreamy eyes lit up. I drew the envelope from my pocket, unfolded the paper on Alexander's own writing-table, right in front of the Empress-Mother's photograph . . . and laid it before the Tsar. He read it once, twice, thrice. I sent up a fervent prayer to the good God that He would be with us in this moment, and guide the young monarch aright.

There was a dead calm; only the gentlest murmur from the sea, and the sun shone bright and clear into the pleasant cabin, while right before my eyes lay the "Hohenzollern" in her dazzling whiteness, and the Imperial Standard fluttering high in the morning-breeze. And I could read there, on its sable cross, the words *"Gott mit Uns"*; and as I read, the Tsar's voice said beside me: "That is quite excellent. I quite agree!" . . . My heart beat so hard that I could hear it; but I pulled myself together and said, quite casually as it were: "Should you like to sign it? It would be a very nice souvenir of our interview!"

He ran over the pages again. Then he said "Yes, I will." I flung back the cover of the ink-bottle, handed him the pen, and he wrote, with a firm hand, "Nicholas," and gave the pen to me. I signed my name under his; and when I stood up he folded me in his arms, much moved, and said: "I thank God, and I thank you. It will be of most beneficent consequences for my country and yours." . . . Bright tears stood in my eyes—and indeed, my brow and spine were quite wet with perspiration—and I thought: "Frederick William III and Queen Louise and Grandpapa and Nicholas I—

they surely have been near us in this hour? They have been looking down on us, at any rate, and joy has filled all their hearts!"

When I drew the Tsar's attention to the fact that it would be well to have counter-signatures, as is the custom with such documents, he quite agreed and we instantly sent for Tschirchky to come over and Admiral Birilow to come down. . . . We gave them both a résumé of the treaty, and the old sailor mutely caught my hand and kissed it reverentially. And so the morning of July 24, 1905, at Björkö is a turning-point in the history of Europe, and a great relief for my beloved Fatherland, which will at last be emancipated from the Gallic-Russo strangle-grip.

This letter, filling seven sheets, is one of his most pellucid revelations of character—more natural, more guileless, than the Directions to his Diplomatists. Here we have a vivid, starkly veracious narrative of a successful exploit, written to an intimate, without a trace of the "Kaiser-pose": a tale that might be told at a cavalry-mess by a twenty-three-year-old subaltern, and nothing is really astonishing about it except that the teller is a forty-three-year-old monarch. Here is the inspiring consciousness of good intentions and clever management, the sense of having acted for the highest good of his country; here that arsenal of jesuitical pretexts and provisos whereby he so easily excuses the psychic pressure he has exercised; here the omnipresence of God—all taking the place, for him, of Constitutional Right, Secretary of State, and diplomatic insight. We are in presence of a believing Christian who, after a night of jollification, devoutly turns up a text and reads good omens on the Imperial Standard fluttering in the morning-breeze, putting his trust in these and in the signature of a defeated, deserted monarch, trapped in the cabin of his yacht, while from high heaven above look down their ancestors, allied of old as these to-day, and no less mutually treacherous, we may be sure. His tears of joy are as authentic as the ruthlessness with which he constrains the helpless weakling to betrayal of his allies; the oriental dodge of the counter-signatures is as natural to him as the historic thrill at the sight of the antique writing-table; the murmur of the sea is as actual as the luncheon, the cold sweat of suspense as the kiss of friendship.

Only one thing is amazingly unconvincing, and that the thing for which he was notorious the world over—his sense of drama. His introduction of the subject of the treaty, his description, twice touched in, of the perfect nonchalance and ease with which he took the decisive steps—all this gives a picture of such clumsiness as must have made Bülow, the adept recipient, feel himself indeed a master as he read. If we did not already know it from a hundred posturings and rantings, the artless chicanery of this letter would be enough to reveal all the dilettantism of the man who was so perpetually represented as a consummate actor. It was nothing but amateur theatricals on board the "Polar Star," very much as on that July evening on board the "Hohenzollern"; the level of the Siamese Twins was not exceeded; and if to-day, when both Emperors have made their exits, this scene were represented on the boards of a theatre, the simplest soul in the audience would reject it as incredible.

And that was what history did with it. Bülow at once discovered that the Emperor had materially impaired the value of the treaty by his independent clause, arranging for support "in Europe" only. He consulted Holstein, and they agreed that he should base his request to be allowed to resign on this clause—one of the cleverest moves ever made by this expert in human nature, for in the existing mood of benignity he was certain of risking nothing whatever, but rather consolidating his position and gaining to some extent

the upper hand of his sovereign. It pierced the Emperor to
the very heart. His refusal (A. 19, f. 496) has not its equal
in the length and breadth of William the Second's correspondence.

First comes a boast of his achievement. "If Bismarck
had succeeded in this . . . he would have been beside himself with joy, and would have made all the nations acclaim
him." Then began reproaches and lamentations for Bülow.

To be treated like this by my best and most intimate of friends
. . . it has dealt me such a terrible blow that I feel quite broken,
and cannot but fear I may have a serious nervous attack. . . .
No—you shall not do this, for both our sakes! We are elected by
God, we were made for each other. . . . You yourself are worth
a hundred thousand times more to me and the Fatherland than
all the treaties in the world. . . . To please you, and because the
Fatherland seemed to demand it of me, I consented as it were to
ride (with my disabled arm too!) a horse I knew nothing about,
and if it has brought me within an inch of my life, *you* are accountable! . . . And now, because I'm in this quandary, you, for whom
I did the whole thing, want to let me down like this!! No, Bülow—
I have not deserved it of you! . . . Why, it should be a disavowal
of your whole policy, and I should be a laughing-stock for the rest
of my life. But I should never survive it! . . . Telegraph "All
right" as soon as you get this, and then I shall know you're not
going. For the day after I receive your resignation, the Emperor
will no longer exist! Think of my poor wife and children!

Only once again are we to see the Emperor in a like
state of collapse—in November 1908; but Eulenburg and
other intimates describe this nervous breakdown as typical,
when external events unexpectedly overwhelmed him. Then
all the bluster perpetually and obstinately imposed upon a
body and a will which were unequal to the burden, would
evaporate, revealing all, and more than all, the underlying
weakness—it was as though an inflated balloon should strike

and burst, the gas escaping in the twinkling of an eye, and then should sink and lie, a little flaccid wisp, upon the ground. These are the moments in which the observer is constrained to sympathy—a man of habitual pretensions loses grip upon himself; the theatrical hero casts his skin, and emerges as a pitiable being, frightened, trembling, yet even while he trembles asserting himself, claiming his rights, throwing all the responsibility upon his friends, who are shamefully leaving him in the lurch.

So that instead of Bülow being brought down by the treaty, Bülow stayed, and the treaty lapsed. For what was bound to happen in the next act? The Tsar, when he got home, was drastically called over the coals. Lamsdorf, "in the greatest agitation," showed Witte the document, pointed out that Russia would have to defend Germany, if Germany had to fight France, though for fifteen years they had been vowed to do that for France against Germany. "These details," said Lamsdorf with blighting irony, "no doubt escaped His Majesty in the flood of the Emperor William's eloquence"; and forthwith he delivered up the secret of the cabin to Paris, whence it took flight to London, so that Edward was soon acquainted with his nephew's schemes, designed to league the Continent against him. How agonizing for Nicky! After the nuptial embraces in view of the ocean, the ancestors, and the flags—what a come-down to have to write to the Emperor and say that unfortunately he "had not had his papers at hand," and must first consult France: should she refuse, the treaty would become invalid in the event of France going to war with Germany. That meant: "It was a summer-morning dream, and my Ministers have waked me with the words: 'The Dual Alliance is the Dual Alliance.'"

Thus was the hero of Björkö twice robbed of his laurels. The consequences of his adventure were increased distrust in France, who sent a General to keep an eye on the Tsar; revulsion of feeling among Germanophiles in Petersburg, who considered it a piece of foul play; reinforcement of the anti-German group, who moreover attributed the lost campaign to the Emperor's advice—even Witte, long inclined towards Germany, seceded; and early in the following year the most formidable of her adversaries took the reins— Isvolski.

The Emperor's false sympathy on the "Polar Star" turned to envenomed hatred (A. 19, 528):

Enclosed I send you yet another precious production from the schoolboy ideologue who sits upon the throne of Russia. The latest phase of the Russo-Gallic alliance . . . makes it clear that Paris will always have a *contre-coup* to let fly whenever the two Emperors attempt to approach one another, and that the Tsarlet will always, on the plea of their immemorial alliance, go in off the deep end. That he should get out of it by talking about "my" Triple-Alliance-Idea, as if *I* were to get any particular advantage out of it, is really something a little more than childish innocence! And all this served up under the snivelling mask of eternal heartfelt friendship!

How well the last phrase described himself, he quite failed to perceive.

William the Second regarded the Sea-Scene at Björkö as his masterpiece: long after his fall, long after 1918, he starred it in a rejected dedication of his Memoirs to General Suchomlinov—a dedication which is interesting for other reasons as well.[1]

---

[1] This document, hitherto unknown, is given at the end of this book as a specimen of his handwriting.

It runs:

The treaty concluded by the Tsar Nicholas II and myself at Björkö laid the foundations for a pacific and amicable coalition between Russia and Germany, which both monarchs had at heart. Its effect was destroyed by Russian diplomacy (Sasanov, Isvolski), by the Russian High Command, and her most prominent Parliamentarians and politicians. The World-War, so greatly desired by them, falsified their hopes, made havoc of their plans, and cost the Tsar as well as myself our thrones.

The terrible consequences of the onslaught on Germany both for Russia and the world at large enforce the lesson that the future welfare of both countries depends upon such loyal co-operation as was theirs a hundred years ago—that is, when once both monarchies have been restored.

Best thanks for sending me your Memoirs.

William, I.R.

Doorn, 1. viii, 1924.

8

La Conférence serait, Dieu aidant, d'un heureux présage pour le siècle qui va s'ouvrir. Elle rassemblerait dans un puissant faisceau les efforts de tous les Etats qui cherchent sans sermon à faire triompher la grande conception de la Paix Universelle sur les éléments de trouble et de discorde. Elle cimenterait en même temps leur accord par une consécration solidaire des principes d'équité et des droits sur lesquels reposent la sécurité des Etats et le bien-être des Peuples.[1]

This peroration to the famous Peace-Manifesto wherein the Tsar, in August 1898, convoked the world to the First

---

[1] "The Conference would, under God, be of most happy augury for the new century. It would unite in powerful co-operation all the Powers now unobtrusively engaged in the attempt to make the vast conception of Universal Peace prevail over the elements of unrest and discord; and at the same time would cement their accord by hallowing and consolidating those principles of equity and justice whereon repose the security of States and the welfare of nations."

Hague Conference upon disarmament, was answered by the Emperor in these words: "Can we picture a monarch, a Supreme War-Lord, disbanding his illustrious historic regiments, consigning their glorious flags to arsenals and museums, and thus delivering his cities over as a prey to anarchists and democrats?"

Yet these two spheres of thought were less remote from one another than they seem. The Tsar's humanitarian impulse happened to be, at that time, in accordance with the views of those surrounding him, who otherwise would have put a spoke in his wheel; but the Emperor was timorous at heart, despite his trenchant rejoinder. Behind their glittering phrases both monarchs were uneasy. At the Conference it was soon made manifest that genuine Pacifists there were none, except the United States. The time was not ripe. Europe, for her awakening, needed the stench of ten million corpses.

But from the very first day no one was more explosive and cynical than William the Second in his opposition to the ideas with which, at the end of the old century, it was sought to formulate the political conceptions of the new one. Even now he was less afraid of alliances outside the Empire than of the insurrection of the Reds within it; he could listen more tranquilly to the ocean roaring round the coasts of Germany than to the subterranean growlings in the interior. Hence his allusion to anarchists and democrats, certain to destroy his cities if his soldiers were withdrawn. The troops, the troops! The mailed fist to protect him, the big guns that with a turn of the wrist could be swung round to shoot inward instead of outward, the bullets that would spatter, if need were, upon the heads of his mutinous subjects! When during the Tramways-Strike of 1900 riots broke out on Dönhoffsplatz in Berlin, he wired to Head-quarters: "I trust that at least five hundred will be snuffed out by the time the troops return to barracks" (Z. 75).

This fear of his subjects, which never left him, was here as elsewhere one with the desire to make clear to all resolute Germans—in other words, to the greater part of the nation —that their Supreme War-Lord could and would show his teeth. Prussian drill, and his un-Prussian pusillanimity, combined to make the Emperor too derisive of the pacifist ideal. That the other Powers should have interpreted this as martial ardour was an inevitable misapprehension, since they knew nothing of the reverse of the medal.

In Germany itself the few psychologists who had strayed into Court circles could detect his uneasiness in the very violence of his comments, written and otherwise. "Sheer imbecility! Bedlam!" he wrote on a statement of the Russian Minister's; and on the proposal that all the Powers should refrain from calling more than a certain percentage of their peoples to arms: "If he suggests that to me, I'll box his ears!"

He sent to the Conference as his expert adviser a belli-cose Professor, despite a caution from Prince Münster, who accompanied him; and directly the heart of the matter, the Court of Arbitration, was approached, there was no holding him at all. Here the Emperor was undoubtedly at one with national sentiment. Half Germany was laughing, and Hol-stein for once expressed what all were feeling when he too pronounced against "such a ludicrous institution" (A. 15, 189)—suitable for little nations, not for great ones, since "the State has no higher purpose than the protection of its interests. These, however, for Great Powers, are not neces-sarily identical with the preservation of peace." And Bülow quoted Holstein by the page in his communications to the Emperor—who wrote, beside Russia's announcement that she would always be ready to submit to arbitration: "I never will!" And beside the word Peace-Bureau:

O *herrjeh!* Manageress, Frau von Suttner! . . . The East-Prussian Frontier is sealed with a chain of fortresses and quick-firing guns, and behind that is infantry with Maxims. . . . I take a part in this Conference-comedy, but I keep my dagger in my belt for the dancing afterwards! (A. 15, 196).

He did not stand alone. In this instance his diplomats' reports, which all said the same things, were written not for his eye only, but for the hearts of the people. By his word "Comedy" the Emperor gave the signal for recalcitrancy to his representatives at the Conference. When at The Hague, on the motion of the United States, there was an attempt to declare private property on the high seas to be inviolable, and the Emperor wrote "No" in the margin, Bülow forwarded this word as "His Majesty's Orders" with the comment: "The question is . . . accordingly decided in the negative."

That fighting-men should be in opposition at the Peace Conference was a matter-of-course. The British Admiral Fisher was no better than the German Colonel von Schwarzhoff—both were sent there to make trouble. The former said: "Might is right"; the latter wrote: "Thanks to our remarkably skilled leaders . . . the Russian Disarmament Proposals have been finally negatived today." But in London the Premier, Lord Salisbury, was contending, as a declared Pacifist, with his military group; in Berlin, the Chancellor and the Cabinet were militarized. In this way the ultimate result was that Germany was in conflict with almost all the other Powers—the grouping of the World-War was adumbrated in the deliberations over the World Peace.

For instance, Münster wrote (A. 15, 285): "Nearly all the delegates have worked themselves into a state of enthusiasm over the arbitration-proposals which is incomprehensible to me; they will, to win us over, agree to yet further concessions, merely to get the Court going"; and so he advised a formal assent. But Holstein would not, and even succeeded in procuring "a chilling reception" for the American delegates who came in person to Berlin to persuade the Emperor and Chancellor. So the German refusal stood alone, after (as the report states) "the arbitration-proposals had found eager support." And how elated was Berlin! The Emperor laughed, and wrote on the report: "Because none of them can mobilize as quickly as we can! And that's why we were to be handicapped!"

The Germans, in fact, so upset the apple-cart that Bülow proudly stated (A. 15, 302):

Scarcely more than the name is left . . . by reason of the clause inserted on Germany's demand, whereby compulsory arbitration is debarred in all instances where the vital interests or the honour of a State are affected. . . . The idea of arbitration is in every respect unattractive. Through Your Majesty's firm and decisive attitude it has, however, been possible to persuade the remaining States to abandon all that was of importance in the idea.

In like fashion, nineteen hundred years ago, had the Tetrarch made his report to Caesar upon the suppression of the dangers threatening to arise from the new Galilean teaching. These leaders of Europe, brought into contact with a spiritual ideal, passed by on the other side, and thought with *démarches* and protests, clauses and annotations, to gut a vast conception, to parody an apostolic gesture by the antics of a clown. The danger past, a reflective epilogue is supplied by the Emperor: "To think of the immensities that dreamy youth was playing with, in that silly prank of his!" But soon he reverts to his old part of the soldier trusting in his God, and retrieves with it his native speech, for he concludes: "In practice I, at any rate, will henceforth rely and call upon God and my bright sword alone! And damn their resolutions!" (A. 15, 306).

9

For executing this intention he found, within a year, an appropriate opportunity in China. The Boxer Riots had supplied European rapacity with a pretext for a crusade against the heathen, whereby a yellow port or two might sample the ennobling influences of Western civilization. "Then I may count on you for China?" said the Emperor to Waldersee. In the summer of 1900 he was undergoing one of his recurrent phases of extreme excitability (W. 2, 448). The Partition of China was then a novel idea.

It was not for some days afterwards that he heard of the assassination of his Ambassador at Pekin. That the death of this "gentle Mortimer" was eminently opportune, he soon made manifest by the frantic haste—more headlong even than usual—with which he arranged for a punitive expedition. *Weltpolitik*—that was the watchword; and where more easily acted upon? And in a periphrase sufficiently astounding for its style alone, the Emperor just then exclaimed, at a launching: "The ocean is indispensable to Germany, but the ocean makes its own demand, which is that on it, and on the other side of it, no great decision shall be taken without the German Emperor." So in all haste an expeditionary force, and an iron-clad squadron into the bargain, were ordered to China.

Honestly speaking [wrote Moltke, who was in the Emperor's suite at this time], it is pure greed—we want to cut our slice out of the Chinese cake. We want to get money, make railways, set mines going. . . . We're not an atom better than the English in the Transvaal (M. 243).

The political question offered greater difficulties, for as the Emperor was at Wilhelmshöhe, the Chancellor on his Russian estate, the Secretary of State at Norderney, the Under-Secretary of State at Berchtesgaden, Holstein, who reigned alone in Berlin, was unable to restrain his sovereign from taking his own measures, and failed to convince him of the danger of provoking England. While he, against his will, was obliged to receive Waldersee—his whilom enemy, then his friend, and then once more his enemy—in order to give him political instructions before he sailed, Bülow was enraptured with the new Commander of the Forces. He saw his only rival for the Chancellorship disappear across the ocean—for Hohenlohe was eighty, and about to retire for good and all.

Great days for the Emperor—State-drives and speeches, flags, cannons, and the drums of war were in prospect, and no need to diminish the Home Forces. And then Peace played another trick on him, or tried to do so. On the evening before the festivities of departure came the tidings that the allied troops had taken Pekin, and that the Imperial Court of China had fled.

Naturally [writes Waldersee] this was at first a great disappointment to the Emperor. He had got it firmly fixed in his head that his Ambassadors and all their *personnel* had been assassinated long ago; the Allied advance on Pekin, till now regarded as impracticable on account of the rainy season, was, directly on my arrival, to begin under my supreme command, and mine would be the glory of capturing Pekin. That dream was over; the Ambassadors were alive, there had been practically no rainy season . . . and Pekin had been taken without much sacrifice of life (W. 3, 6).

What! Was the great idea to be ruined by petty side-issues such as retarded rains and assassinations? No—there could be no going-back in this! The very next day the Emperor addressed the Marines on parade:

You must know, my men, that you are about to meet a crafty, well-armed, cruel foe! Meet him, and beat him! Give no quarter! Take no prisoners! Kill him, when he falls into your hands! Even as, a thousand years ago, the Huns under their King Attila made such a name for themselves as still resounds in terror through legend and fable, so may the name of German resound through Chinese history a thousand years from now, and may you so conduct yourselves that no Chinaman will ever again so much as dare to look crooked at a German!

The mounting excitement in each successive speech of the Emperor's could hardly be ascribed to the murder of the Ambassador, of which he had known for three weeks, because he had laid his plans for the raid before he heard of it. Moltke sufficiently accounts for that. Anyhow, Eulenburg, whether he knew of this speech or only foresaw it, had in the meantime secretly summoned the journalists and given them, in his own cabin, a quite different Imperial oration to take down. But one of them "slipped through the official fingers, and *he* snapped up a bit of the speech— before long, it was all made public."

Its effect endured for twenty years. Nothing made it easier for Germany's enemies, even in peace, to demonstrate that the Germans were barbarians at heart than did this speech of the Emperor's; and when in the World-War nation after nation was led to believe that in the middle of

Europe sixty million Huns had their habitation, and worshipped the new Attila as their sovereign, it was not only the right instincts of the German people that were misapprehended, but also the wrong instincts of the Emperor. And so, after the lapse of a thousand years, that reckless, dæmonic, savage robber-chieftain among kings was insulted by being likened to William the Second. In the dual fallacy of this parallel lies the explanation of the dual misunderstanding, all over the world, of Germany. A great and peaceable people, conscious of its subjection to a boastful little monarch, was obliged to pay for the claptrap of its vainglorious sovereign, who only degraded them with the title of Huns that he might ape an Attila.

He began by aping hegemony. The troops of all Europe under a German Field-Marshal—that was his dream; and when the Tsar, urgently consulted about Waldersee, wired his acquiescence, the Emperor proclaimed to London that his friend the Tsar had offered the supreme command to Waldersee. Whereupon the Tsar said to the German Ambassador that it was "only out of fraternal feeling for the Emperor" that he did not disavow this representation; while Salisbury "could not understand why the Emperor was so set upon a German General having the supreme command, since it always implied great risks for any Power which undertook it" (Eck. 2, 187). Bülow and the Office were superseded; the Emperor wanted "to direct the whole business as a purely military affair—from the saddle, as it were," wrote Eulenburg, imploring Bülow for help (E. 2, 258).

Waldersee on his departure was given (as he states himself) the marshal's baton, a saloon-carriage to Naples; then the very best cabin on the boat, together with two hundred bottles of champagne, fifty bottles of spirits, and two bodyguards, on whom the Emperor impressed these commands: "If the Field-Marshal ventures too near the fighting-line, your duty is to hold him back—if necessary, to catch hold of his bridle!" Then the Emperor urged the commander of the forces to be sure to squeeze out a big indemnity, for he needed money for his Fleet. Scarcely had the "World-Marshal" vanished to the accompaniment of plaudits from German railway-platforms and laughter from the rest of Europe, than the Tsar despatched a collective Note to the Powers, bidding them withdraw their troops to the coast, for all danger to Europeans was at an end. The poor Emperor reviled this as such "want of consideration, such a complete misapprehension of the circumstances, and such a lack of even superficial judgment as are positively devastating."

When Waldersee set foot in China six weeks later, he could still hold a grand parade, uninterrupted by the rains. The foe was either beaten or extinct, no quarter was given, no prisoners were taken—all the Emperor's behests were strictly carried out.

Meanwhile the effects abroad had had their counter-effects at home, and German princes and German Parliamentarians revolted at last. The Emperor, they declared, had undertaken the campaign without asking the Reichstag for the wherewithal. In these circumstances the hoary Hohenlohe preferred to make his final exit; and Bülow, the new Chancellor, was clever enough to imitate Bismarck's speech of 1866, and save the situation by demanding an indemnity—this time, it is true, without a victory behind him. In his fear that something might still be on the cards, he wired to Eulenburg:

As you long ago foresaw, the danger of a coalition between the German Princes and the Reichstag against H.M. is immediate. . . . Find some pretext for writing to the Emperor, or better still, wire him at once, advising some caution in his speeches until the Chinese question is settled in the Reichstag (E. 2, 258).

Whereupon Eulenburg did warn the Emperor in this sense, and the Emperor retorted that he would say what he liked. . . .

By such arts had minister and friends to restrain their sovereign's eloquence, so as to bring about a belated harmony between the results of his brilliant ideas and the opinions of the legislature.

10

When Tirpitz said that the Kruger Telegram had awakened the nation to the necessity for a Fleet, he was mistaking a symptom for a great event. For twenty years the animosity between Germany and England, which was almost entirely dynastic, had led to a steady increase of armaments in both countries, and this in its turn to increased animosity. In the European competition born of the distrust of every individual Power for all the others, the German Fleet-building was, psychologically speaking, the most negligible factor; for if the two monarchs in question had not been personally jealous of one another, the German Paladins would never have had to don the tarpaulin over the cuirass.

Bismarck, who was the last to call a halt before embarking on the battle-fleet and world-power, protested to his dying day against a policy whereby Germany was risking her security in Europe for dubious acquisitions in Africa and Asia. If in this he was blind to the new potentialities in the merchant-service, he saw clearly enough the dangers attendant on a battle-fleet, and never would listen to the contention that Germany needed such a fleet to protect her Colonial possessions. Had not he, relying solely on continental power, obtained the first German colony from England without possessing a single ship? Moreover he knew that France and Russia, which had never been first-rate naval powers, were none the less classed with England as great powers; and he derided the further argument that Germany had come "too late" for her share in the undeveloped continents, which as a matter of fact had been passing from hand to hand for centuries.

Throughout a decade Bismarck had striven in vain for what his successors were offered in the year of his death; and when they thrice refused the alliance with England, it was the Emperor's antagonism for England which thrice turned the scale. He could not get over his grudge—he was unchangingly hostile; and this was because he did perceive her to be a higher type of the modern State, yet refused to acknowledge it. Nothing excited him like English attacks on himself—they flattered him by making him feel a martyr. He had the deck-house of the "Hohenzollern" hung with English caricatures, and always insisted on seeing hostile English articles, such as were kept from him if of German origin. Thus he was for ever reopening the wounds which, dealt in his youth, had never been quite skinned over. Just as Prince William, when a young officer, had tried to avenge himself for his mother's slights by a brilliant display of regimental leadership, so now this most indelible and painful of his experiences was a perpetual goad impelling him to a similar display in his uncle's country. From

his childhood onward to the days of the race of naval armaments—from 1872 to 1912—one long chain of resentments
had been forged in William the Second's heart, disastrous
alike for him and for the German people.

When England, deeply offended, frowned on him after
the Kruger Telegram, he asked for the first large loan—
three hundred million marks—and negotiated on his own
responsibility with the Vulcan Shipyard Company. Even
then, in January 1896, Waldersee wrote: "The Emperor
seems to have gone quite off his head with excitement about
the Big Navy Bill." Hohenlohe would have nothing to
do with it; he said that "so far as one can see, it is a
practical impossibility—still-born, in fact" (E. 2, 213);
while Eulenburg made it a principle, as he says, never to
mix himself up in any warlike matters. The sagacious and
very popular Admiral Hollmann was obliged to retire. But
in the Emperor's suite was still that Admiral von Senden-
Bibran, hostile to England for personal reasons, whose
political insight is best revealed in his answer to a friendly
caution: "What business is it of England's? I suppose
we may build as we please!" To his unremitting pressure,
daily brought to bear upon those who surrounded the Emperor, Eulenburg attributes very great influence.

The incidental music most congenial to the Imperial
ears was supplied by the *Flottenverein,* which worked up
general enthusiasm in every possible quarter, and was
already adumbrating an expansion of the "Great German
Federation"; "Firstly, the existing little German Empire
along with Luxemburg; secondly, Holland and Belgium;
thirdly, the German part of Switzerland; fourthly, the
Austrian Empire." These things were mooted not only
in German beer-houses and newspapers, but in the Palais

Bourbon at Paris. But so long as the politicians held aloof, and only fighting-men and the bourgeoisie prattled—so long as the Emperor was without a Grand Vizier—the whole thing was, in Hohenlohe's words, still-born. What was needed was a Court-Admiral with Waldersee's intelligence and malleability.

Then Tirpitz came on the scene. The Emperor always had a good eye for the sort of men he wanted; in this instance he certainly fished out the most talented officer in his Navy. Even in the Army Tirpitz scarcely had his match in energy, sagacity, and courage. Here was a man who, unlike all those hitherto surrounding the Emperor, disdained to flatter him, knew what he wanted, and was prey to no corroding vice—a specialist, who combined a genuine passion for his calling with the profoundest knowledge of it. Tirpitz had only one failing—he told lies. At Court he was called the Story-Teller.

He had to lie—the German battle-fleet had to be built, if the diplomats were ever to come to an understanding with England. To this end he invented two slogans: Emergency-Fleet and Danger-Period. Such a fleet would deter England from creating the "emergency"; and Germany had only a few years of the Danger-Period to get through, during which her building would be objectionable to England and therefore dangerous to herself. These slogans were in everyone's mouth, and only the sceptics said among themselves that England would surely keep pace with Germany, and the "Period" be everlasting. Tirpitz himself believed not a word of it all; he was a sailor, and as such what he really wanted was a fleet strong enough to challenge England, in, say, twenty years' time.

To gain this end in the face of all opposition he was

forced to lie. If, like the British Admiral Fisher, he had—
even in the most secret of sessions—thumped the table and
shouted that Germany intended to annihilate England and
supplant her in the empire of the world; if he had played
the rabid sea-dog, the buccaneer, the pusillanimous Emperor
would soon have had no use for him. It was only by diplomacy that he could prevail against the diplomats. Tirpitz did not follow in their devious tracks to keep himself in
power, as all others did, but to realize in the face of opposition a scheme in which he thoroughly believed. A fervent
German and a fervent fighting-man, he pinned his faith to
his own phrases about "the German people nearing the
zenith of maturity," or "the military spirit of Prussia, on
which the national existence and the national welfare was
founded in the past, and must be founded in the future."

To everyone acquainted with the temper, history, and
position of England, Tirpitz's idea could only appear
absurd, since the strongest naval power could not possibly
allow the strongest military power to build an approxi-
mately equal fleet without endangering her own existence.
Without a fleet, Germany could get on with England—
with a fleet, it was out of the question. Hence England
offered the alliance at a time when, as Tirpitz writes,
Germany could not be sure "whether the bid for real sea-
power ought to be risked, or whether the whole undertaking ought to remain a demonstration on a point of principle." Tirpitz won the Emperor's support for the battle-
fleet in a couple of conversations, was appointed Secretary
of State in the summer of 1897, obtained Hohenlohe's assent
to his first Navy Bill in September, and when Bülow took
over the Chancellorship in November, confronted him with
nothing less than a *fait accompli*. Bülow would have had

to be an expert to discern the future of fleet-building in the aspect it then presented.

For from the very first it was necessary for Tirpitz to lie. Only seven ships of the line were asked for, but in this skeleton proposal there lay wellnigh imperceptibly provision for thirty-eight; and in the later estimates the new leviathans figured as smaller types. At the time these deceptions were known to a few initiates, not to the people's representatives. Nevertheless Tirpitz had great difficulty in restraining the Emperor from premature bragging. When in the autumn of 1899 the second Navy Bill struck the first note of *Weltpolitik,* he tried in vain to prevent an Imperial speech at a launching. The Emperor was incapable of quiet, long drawn-out achievement; he must always create a sensation, and that at once; so instead of (like the Japanese, for instance) unobtrusively building up sea-power, he delivered that resounding oration, with its rallying-cry: "Stern necessity demands a mighty German Fleet!" When Tirpitz, after this, wanted to keep back his as yet incomplete new estimate until the Reichstag assembled, the Emperor urged him on. It was not in every instance that Tirpitz yielded; he was not much afraid of disfavour, holding that in his position "a state of slight disfavour" was the most desirable one. According to Ballin, "he was far from congenial to the Emperor, who only put up with him because he had the same ideas in policy."

It was in vain that the Emperor was advised to "guard our fleet as a precious, indispensable secret, and let the English hear and see as little as might be about it." Beside these words of Bernstorff's he merely wrote: "Out of the question!" Doing the exact reverse, he once more revealed the deep-lying motive. "The Fleet alone gives me the prestige I require in England," he said in 1904, and made up his mind to show Edward his new glories without delay. When at last, for the first time in many years, the latter came to Germany, the Emperor on his yacht at Kiel was in a tremendous state of excitement.

He personally superintended the smallest details in the decoration of the "Hohenzollern." An immense awning was stretched over the promenade-deck, there were marvellous arrangements of flowers, little fountains and waterfalls tinkled and splashed refreshingly in every direction. A dinner for one hundred and eight persons, and a tea-party for two hundred and twenty, were given in honour of the King. The Emperor took all these matters so seriously that he was fully dressed three-quarters of an hour before the festivities were to begin, walking restlessly up and down the deck, and scarcely able to endure the waiting (Z. 78).

But at last he could parade the entire German fleet before King Edward. That was his moment: now he could impress the detested uncle who had said, five years ago: "Let him play with his Fleet." But unfortunately he impressed him too deeply. For the King soon forgot flowers and tea-party, waterfalls even; but not the strength and the modernity of the ships he had been shown. Perturbed and reflective, he went back to his island. Two months later, the Press and the House of Commons began the campaign against German fleet-building—the Navy Scare—and this time the statesmen gave the signal. Lord Fisher proposed to do with this German Fleet as of yore with the Danish; the King promised Delcassé English ships against Germany; Mr. Arthur Lee, the Civil Lord of the Admiralty, envisaged a surprise attack and for the first time in fifty years sent a squadron to the Baltic; there was open speculation as to the possibility of landing one hundred thousand English in Schleswig. The ball had been set rolling—henceforth there was to be no stopping it.

All this the nephew regarded as his uncle's malignity. After supper he once said to a small circle of nine: "The King is setting the whole Press on me, out of personal spite—paying them with English money. He is a fiend! No one would believe what a fiend he is!" (Z. 153). His favourite confidant was the Tsar; to him he described Edward as the arch-intriguer, the wrecker, and wrote in August 1905:

> I have ordered my fleet to dog the British, and as soon as they cast anchor to lie alongside, give them a dinner and make them drunk, so as to worm out as quickly as we can what this [their North-Sea Cruise] may signify; and then they are to make off at once. . . . Don't tell anyone, for the secret must be well kept. Ta-ta! I've really finished now. Willy.

When shortly after this, his uncle passed through Germany without letting him know, and the Emperor—in October 1905—caused inquiry to be made if "he wants to pick a quarrel with me, that he traverses my realm without giving me any sort of notice," the Ambassador did say in reply that the King was displeased by the way the Emperor was calumniating him all over Europe, and so could not have made any attempt to see him (Z. 32). At this time everyone abroad had ceased to take seriously anything that the Emperor said. The Master of the Household, just then, asked the English Ambassador why he was so definitely cool to them all nowadays, and was answered in a tone of some amusement: "If I had reported to London all that your Most High has said to me of late, we should have had war not once, but twenty times" (Z. 33).

The Emperor was happy. When the next estimate had secured six more armoured cruisers, he said:

I've taken in the Reichstag properly with the new Bill! They hadn't an idea of the consequences when they let it through, for *this* Bill lays down that I am to be granted anything I choose to ask for. . . . Now I've shot them sitting, and no power on earth can prevent me from getting the very utmost that can be got out of them. The dogs shall pay till they're blue in the face! (Z. 159).

11

Of the many Prussian provocations which between 1890 and 1906 led to the encirclement of Germany, there was one—and an important one—for which the Emperor was not responsible. In the year 1904 he laid stress, first to King Edward and then to his own advisers, upon his *désintéressement* in Morocco. He realized from the first the danger of any intervention in that French quasi-colony, and for weeks, even to the last moment, was opposed to the landing in Tangier. Ardently desirous of reconciling France, he had never at any time taken a menacing tone towards Paris, and would much rather have spared her than humiliated her in Africa. The responsibility is Bülow's, who wanted to "do in" Delcassé by this coup; with him were Holstein, who branded any compliance as "another Olmütz or Fashoda," and Herr von Kühlmann, the chargé d'affaires in Tangier, who suggested the Emperor's visit. Nothing in the Morocco imbroglio was done by the Emperor's desire; it will not, therefore, be treated of here. But why, we may ask ourselves, did this autocrat ever allow himself to be driven into that great error?

Here we see him under a new light. When his desire for a demonstration was opposed by his ministers, his nervous craving would instantly increase—speeches, despatches, interviews, invitations given and accepted, journeys, were defiantly and hastily projected, just to show his henchmen that such was the royal will and pleasure! Eulenburg and Bülow alone could put the brake on the Imperial motor. The easier method with him was to substitute one activity for another, since to be doing, continually and visibly, was his insatiable demand; and after all it was much the same to him whether he wired to Kruger about the Protectorate, or only to congratulate him. On the other hand, it may be said that until 1909 it never was really necessary to urge him to action.

At this particular time—between 1904 and 1905—the Emperor was in one of the phases of depression which followed and preceded those of extreme excitement; and it was precisely then that his diplomats were trying in every way to humiliate France. At the end of the year 1903, so prolific in boastful speeches, he underwent an operation for a polypus in the throat. Had he inherited the disease which had killed his father, and of which his mother too had lately died? The question obsessed him; a strain of melancholy seemed to take possession of his tormented mind, and was a blessed relief to his over-wrought nervous system. In such moods we shrink from noise and blusterings; we perceive more clearly the problems inherent in prolonged negotiations, the questionable advantage of perpetual leaps in the dark. So early as the New Year of 1904 he forbade the despatch of a German ship to Morocco; and a year later, it was only by Bülow's argument that France would represent any other course as weakness that he was induced —even then with difficulty—to consent to the landing in Tangier. Indeed, he made at Bremen, immediately before his departure, one of his best speeches, which stands alone among hundreds.

When I came to the throne, after my grandfather's mighty reign, I swore in my military oath that so far as in me lay I would put aside bayonets and cannons, yet keep them always burnished and in good repair, so that jealousy and rivalry from without should never call us away from the completion of our garden and our stately House within. My study of history led me to take counsel with myself, and inwardly to vow that never would I strive for a vain empire of the world. For what was the end of all the great so-called World-Empires? Alexander, Napoleon, all the mighty conquerors—had they not waded through blood, and left behind them subjugated peoples who cast off the yoke as quickly as might be, and brought those vaunted Empires to decay? The world-dominion of my dream consists above all in this—that the new-made German Empire should everywhere be regarded with the most absolute confidence, should enjoy the reputation of a tranquil, fair-dealing, pacific neighbour; and that if ever, in the future, history should tell of German world-dominion or a Hohenzollern hegemony, neither of these things should have been founded on conquests by the sword, but on the mutual confidence of nations animated by a similar ambition. . . . Her material frontiers round about her— and the frontiers of her spirit nowhere to be traced!

But suddenly, after these finely conceived phrases, he broke out into:

The fleet is launched, and in building. . . . Its spirit is the same as that which inspired Prussian officers at Hohenfriedberg, Königgrätz, and Sedan; and with every German warship that leaves the docks another guarantee of peace on earth is launched upon the waters. . . . The duty of our German youth . . . is to hold fast to the conviction that our Lord God would never have so striven for our German Fatherland if He had not meant great things for us. We are the salt of the earth, but we must make ourselves worthy so to be. . . . Then only shall it be written of the

German people as you may read upon the helmets of my First Regiment of Guards: *"Semper talis!"* Then . . . we shall stand, our hand upon our sword-knot, and our shield upright before us on the soil, and say: *"Tamen!* Come what will!"

Arresting antithesis! The incessant challenger sets forth to speak the things of peace to the whole world eight days before, for the first time in all his life, he is unwilling to challenge—and, self-suggested, there arises to his inward eye a mystic Empire of the Spirit and the Prince of Peace, and he is orator enough to clothe his vision instantly in the fine symbol of the garden. He who for a lifetime had been ever for appearances, never for the truth of things, undergoes a profound revulsion of feeling—for the space of three minutes William the Second shows as a prince inspired by a wise and generous ideal; and, for sure, in those three minutes he was glad at heart. But then he looks around him; there they are—the uniforms, the scintillating Orders, the stiff backs, drilled poses, fierce moustaches; and confronted by the rigid system, his uneasiness takes refuge in bluster, his uncertainty of the effect he may have made in a resolve to make a more sensational one—and out they foam again, the names of battles, armoured cruisers launched and building, blazoned helmets, and the German God in the machine, who is to prove his loyal solicitude for German interests, since "we are the salt of the earth." Sword-knot and shield and "Let them all come!" Before he knows it himself, the Emperor who began *andante* is strutting to the quick-step of Up and At'em.

Under the heights of Tangier, prostrated by a stormy passage and the thought of Spanish anarchists, he wanted to turn tail an hour before the landing; and only one suggestion availed to overcome his reluctance—that of "derring-do" and "an historic entry." Even when the dripping Kühlmann presented himself, the Emperor was still reiterating: "I won't go ashore!" At last, when his aides-de-camp had made a trial trip, he did pluck up courage; but though Bülow had wired, ordering "a horse warranted steady," the appointed steed was so uncourtly as to put an end to his composure once for all. The whole grotesque imposture of Colonial protectorates is laid bare when we see the monarch of one country, who desires to take another country down a peg in its prestige, paying an operatic call on a black Sultan's uncle, and guaranteeing that potentate in his full rights of sovereignty in order to diminish the influence of a rival.

The artificers of this set-piece were in high feather, for as Delcassé in Paris saw in the display the provocation he was meant to see, his colleagues fastened eagerly upon this pretext to get rid of his autocratic rule, and by their submissive attitude awakened the drowsy Eumenides of France. "Prestige," that blazon upon Satan's scutcheon, was shrieked from every journal, every throat, in Paris. "We have been humiliated by the Germans"—the conciliatory mood of France, perceptible even in school-books, was a thing of the past; armaments duly increased, and at the Conference on the Morocco Question the Entente became at last an actuality. "Our policy"—so Brandenburg pronounces—"was a petty one, dictated partly by uneasiness, partly by greed and considerations of prestige. Once more, great perdurable things were forgotten in trivialities."

And here, in Algeciras, where England first threw in her lot with France, while Cambon was coming to an understanding with Grey over Belgium—here the naval rivalry was at the heart of all. In sundry estimates for what was called the renovation of the Fleet, Tirpitz disclosed his secret scheme for German eyes—but, unfortunately, English eyes as well—to take stock of. No more mystery now; so many ships to be built up to 1917-20; and England, thus threatened, could not but be alert to build in defence. When Bülow tried to slow down, it was too late.

He is to be excused, and not only by the layman's ignorance. No sooner was he appointed than the scheme confronted him; and ten years later, at the height of his power, he opposed it. "If in our naval competition we laid more stress on defence, the principal reason for tension between us and England would be removed, and possibly it would also be better for our own security." Thus actuated, he recommended submarines and coast-defences; and in August 1908 wrote to the Emperor: "A young tree has to be protected from the storms which might uproot it. If our fleet-building progresses at this rate, it is unlikely that the royal couple will visit us." He wrote likewise about the risk of a war on three fronts. Still graver were Metternich's warnings from London—if Germany declined some arrangement about the fleet, the danger of war with England would be sensibly increased.

But what good was the defensive to the Emperor? Resolute not to attack, he yet longed to stand "in glittering armour" before his blood-relations; and while Tirpitz went on building battleships, the Emperor's faint heart beat high and he contemned all cautionary talk of the increasing sensation created by the Pan-German spectacular drama, as with every ship it mounted higher till at last the very bourgeoisie were in a flutter. What! Germany be told how many ships she might graciously be allowed to build?

Did England pay for them, then? This talk about unending competition in armaments?

It is all nonsense; England is exaggerating on purpose [wrote the Emperor]. We are legislating for forty ships of the line in 1918-20. Tirpitz and I have decided that this number will be entirely adequate, and the Reichstag has passed the estimates. . . . Neither he nor I have the faintest shadow of an intention of . . . over-stepping this programme for ships of the line. . . . A big estimate in 1912 or later is not in our views, and exists only in the imagination of Britain, which has gone stark staring mad. . . . From 1920 onwards we shall be in a position to make our own terms with them.

These are such asseverations as frail ladies make—only this one adventure, and then we will for evermore be good!

But the majestic figures were too small for Tirpitz, and soon it was known in high quarters that he had fresh schemes up his sleeve. "A show-estimate," so Admiral von Pohl, the Admiral commanding in the War, sums up; "a show-fleet, a prestige-policy, was what Tirpitz chiefly wanted; so the small cruisers and the torpedo-boats have fallen below standard in size and armament." And so it was vain indeed for the Emperor, in February 1908, to assure Mr. Arthur Lee in a personal letter that his intentions were wholly pacific; it only created a scene in the English House of Commons. Lee got into trouble, for the King expressed displeasure at the exchange of letters between a monarch and a subject; Lord Roberts declared that a German invasion was in sight; and Metternich, assailed by the Press, persistently and emphatically declared that it was England's bounden duty to preserve her supremacy at sea. "Well, they will just have to get accustomed to our Fleet," was the

Emperor's reply, "and from time to time we must assure them that it's not for use against *them*."

About this time, in the summer of 1908, two intelligent Jews put their heads together, and tried without false sentiment or any sentiment at all to do what two influential business men might to settle the affair. Ballin and Cassel —independent-minded intimates of their respective monarchs; the Englishman more of a *grand seigneur*, the German of a self-made man; Cassel enjoying the freedom of a land which not long since had entrusted the government of the State to a Jew; Ballin contending with the thraldom of another, where he had to be for ever on his guard against racial insults. Cassel in a part he well knew how to play, Ballin in the painful position of him who has to deal with something unfamiliar and embarrassing.

Cassel: "It is our anxiety about Germany's growing Fleet which urges us to the Entente. We shall have to ask Germany, once for all, when she intends to cease building."

Ballin: "The question would of itself mean war."

This blustering answer had been arranged beforehand with the Emperor. Bülow said the same thing in a circular letter—and then it occurred to these two gentlemen that what would suit them was what they had refused eight or ten years ago. "The simplest solution is an alliance with us," wrote the Emperor. "Then all our troubles would be over. For the English to think we will attack them is delirious nonsense! We should never be such idiots. That would be *harakiri* pure and simple."

When Metternich, thus emboldened, frankly declared in July 1908 that the English Ministers were all for peace and only wanted a reciprocal diminution in the Navy Estimates, the Emperor was infuriated and wrote in the margin: "A veiled threat! We will suffer no dictation! Ambassador has exceeded his instructions!" Further:

It must be made clear to him that an arrangement with England at the expense of the fleet is no desire of mine. It is a piece of boundless impudence, a mortal insult to the German people and their Emperor; it must be imperatively and finally discountenanced. . . . The Law will be carried out to the last fraction; whether Britain likes it or not is nothing to us. If they want war, let them begin it—we are not afraid! . . . I must beg that the Ambassador will henceforth take no notice whatever of this kind of vapouring!

Thus the Emperor, having "properly taken in the Reichstag so that the dogs would have to pay," assumed the post of an evangelist not only before the world at large but even in the privacy of marginalia: "for this is the fulfilling of the Law." Bülow, who sent only a very emasculated version of this reproof to the Ambassador, did advise a reserved attitude towards England, taking his stand on "Emperor's Orders." And now came the critical moment. Bülow, without being exactly a lion, nevertheless took refuge in his lair when the King of England arrived on his visit, though the King brought Hardinge with him, and arranged that Lloyd George should be in Berlin at the same time, to discuss (despite all menaces) the question of the Fleet once more. Lloyd George needed some arrangement, in order that he might put through his Land Bill without being held up by the fleet-building trouble—otherwise the Cabinet foresaw angry debates. And so the English came. They wanted to compose all differences; they came with the best egotistic intentions.

At Friedrichshof, in that August of 1908, the King said not a word to his nephew on the subject; but Hardinge, after dinner, went straight to the point. In the course of the conversation he said: "Would it not be possible for both countries to make a mutual arrangement for limitation of armaments?"

The Emperor: "Only in accordance with our requirements."

Hardinge: "An agreement is conceivable whereby both might cease to build, or build at a slower rate."

The Emperor: "That is a question affecting national honour and dignity. We should prefer to fight!"

Whereupon Hardinge flushed as red as the ribbon of the Order of the Eagle (first-class) which he was later to receive.

The Englishmen went home, feeling that there was nothing more to be done; but the Emperor wrote a jubilant report to Bülow, and received for answer yet another cautionary letter, saying that the danger of war was increased by this failure to come to an understanding, and that a war with England might have disastrous consequences for Germany. The Emperor only reiterated his opinion that every English proposal for a limitation of armaments was a hostile act.

This was the moment for Bülow to resign. September 1908: how was it that his amazing intuition—one of his finest faculties—did not enable him to foresee what would happen two months later, and unpropitiously for him? Had he gone then, it would have been as a warning prophet.

At the end of the year the question again became acute. Metternich had written, disputing the Tirpitz theory of rivalry and English jealousy with an energy rarely shown in ambassadorial communications to the Emperor, who was their reader-in-chief. He said that "the cardinal question in our relations with England is the growth of our Fleet. This may not be very agreeable in the hearing, but I see no purpose in concealing the truth, nor could I reconcile it with my duty to do so." He warned Germany against believing that either increased taxation or fear would drive the English people into her arms; on the contrary, they would redouble their precautions. Tirpitz answered that they would soon be short of money, and would then cease to build. Immediately afterwards Lloyd George's Land Bill was passed, and building still went on. Then Bülow put the incisive question to Tirpitz: "Can the German nation fearlessly survey the prospect of an attack from England?"

The Admiral was silent for the space of a fortnight. Then he wrote to say No, and advised acceleration in fleet-building, which would frighten England off. Bülow retorted that that was no answer; Germany's best course was defence of the coast, and at the very utmost three battle-ships a year. Tirpitz threatened to resign, in that event— he could well risk it, being the Emperor's mouthpiece. Bülow, who had proffered his resignation on account of a couple of words in the Björkö Treaty, could not now venture on a similar step, for here lay the Emperor's vulnerable point. Even Brandenburg sums up with: "The Emperor's personal feeling that Germany would be humiliated by such an admission . . . was the decisive factor."

Between an importunate Admiral, a Cassandra-like Ambassador, a too soft-spoken Chancellor, and complete liberty to decide the vital question by his casting-vote, the Emperor could do no other than obey his own profoundest instincts and emotions. They were those of his wounded adolescent pride.

12

I am fully conscious that the Kings of Prussia could not have achieved their historical triumphs if they had not had such a people as ours behind them, by their officers and soldiers, their officials in all classes, disciplined to such a pitch of excellence as scarcely any other people has attained.

Despite the disfigurement of this phrase by the word "disciplined," the subject is at any rate honoured with the title of "people." It is the Birthday-speech of 1901. Two months later, a young man at Bremen threw a fragment of iron at the Emperor, which scratched him slightly in the face. Followed investigation—the perpetrator was pronounced to be quite irresponsible for his actions. Nevertheless it made a deep impression; there was great dejection, presentiment of the ever-dreaded revolt. A fortnight later the next speech said:

My Alexander-Regiment is called upon to act to some extent as a body-guard both by day and by night—to be ready, if occasion arises, to fight to the death for the King and his household. And if the City of Berlin should ever again as in the year 1848 revolt against its sovereign, then, Grenadiers, you will be called upon to drive those insolent and unruly subjects in couples before you with your bayonets.

In the following year *Vorwärts* began a series of revelations about "Krupp in Capri," wherein his long-known degenerate tendencies were reported in detail. Krupp, as it happened, was then with the Emperor for the Kiel Week; and people wondered whether he would bring an action. He killed himself. The Emperor said at the funeral:

I repudiate these attacks on him . . . a German of the Germans . . . his honour so assailed. Who were the men that made this infamous attack upon our friend? Men who till then had been looked upon as Germans, but who are henceforth unworthy of that name; and these men come from the German working-classes, who owe so infinite a debt of gratitude to Krupp.

Though the working-classes were not of the same opinion, it was contrived to get up a reverential response, which they afterwards publicly repudiated. Krupp's widow, however, abandoned her action, the Attorney-General having stopped the proceedings.

At the next elections the Socialists lost several seats, but in those following regained them twice over and entered the Reichstag as the strongest party, numbering one hundred and ten. What were the Emperor's reflections on this? In January 1908 there really were disturbances in the capital. The Emperor summoned a guard of one hundred and fifty to the Palace, and blustered to his aides-de-camp: "If I had known of this disorder on Sunday, I would have called out the Alexander-Regiment and cleared the streets myself!" Whereupon a courtier told some terrified novices: "He doesn't really mean it; the Emperor talks like that, but nothing ever comes of it" (Z. 187). Again, when thirty wounded were reported, the Emperor said: "I am very well satisfied with the conduct of the police. But next time they must strike, not with the flat, but the edge of the sword!" (Z. 185).

From these two utterances we can forecast the Emperor's behaviour in a revolution. Ferocious commands, but no foot set outside the Palace, which is filled with armed guards; the desire and the behest for more blood in the streets (by no means any in the Palace)—so that he might at any rate dye the end of his reign in blood, though he had at its beginning shrunk from anything of the kind. But if the body-guard had revolted . . . ?

Even the Federal Princes were looked upon by him as little more than a bigger body-guard. "For I must be obeyed," as he had said in his juvenile letter to Bismarck about setting a precedent for the uncles. In reality a *fronde* was gradually forming against him, impalpable, but every bit as strong as that of the Socialists. It was the oldest of these Princes who first realized the danger inherent in the Emperor's personality. So early as the December of 1888, he of Lippe-Detmold said, with all the discretion proper to a miniature-monarch:

> The Emperor has wellnigh despotic tendencies, yet with them very Liberal ones, an amazing power of memory, and swift apprehension. So it is better not to make any unconsidered observations in his presence, for they stick and may have unforeseen results, given his tendency to rash decisions.

When in the year 1891 he wrote in the Golden Book of Münster *"Regis voluntas lex,"* the earliest murmur arose— the only debatable question being whether this challenging phrase referred to himself or to the two crazy Bavarian kings. Soon afterwards, on a question of fleet-building, he wired, not in cipher, to Eulenburg his Ambassador: "Don't be put out by the clamour of the idiotic Bavarian loyalists, who never fail to make fools of themselves. . . . How often have I laughed over the incredible folly of the good Bavarians!" The horrified Eulenburg most respectfully begged him to send any future messages of the kind in cipher.

The Federal Army, which was under the Emperor's command, was bound to be a source of jealousy. The excellent King of Württemberg, who resembled the Emperor only in name, had expressed himself so angrily at some manœuvres in the autumn of 1894 about the command in Stuttgart that the Emperor left in a hurry. Much the same thing happened in Bavaria; and when in consequence of the perpetual cropping-up of the question of German primacy a German Consul, receiving Prince Henry in Moscow, spoke of the "King and his retinue," the Bavarian heir-apparent said for all the world to hear at the Moscow banquet that the German Federal Princes were no vassals.

It was thus that the "old uncles" interpreted obedience.

The smallest state had the biggest grievance. When in the summer of 1908 the new Count-Regent of Lippe-Detmold claimed the title of Serene Highness and the military royal salute for his family, the Emperor sent a curt refusal. To a courteous "petition and representation," the euphemism in which he clothed his complaint against the High Command, the Regent received the following reply: "Your letter received. Orders of the High Command are given with my approval. . . . To the Regent, as Regent, I have nothing more to say. Except that the tone in which you have thought fit to address me, I now forbid once for all."

Then the least of Regents in the country uprose against the greatest, and was so manful as to enter a protest in the shape of a circular letter to all the German Princes. In each of the twenty capitals the excitement was much greater than the Princes' common sense of dignity allowed them to make public; every one of them was horrified—this impertinent tone might be used to any of the Kings to-morrow! Followed a protest in the little *Landtag,* a debate in the *Bundesrat,* a judgment in the Imperial courts. The Emperor had as good as refused recognition to the Regency in the person of the Prince's son, had forbidden the swearing-in of recruits. Intervention of Court Jurists, who circumstantially demonstrated that right was wrong, till the case went hopelessly against them; and the Emperor was for the first time in his life, though it were but by German Princes, forced to give in.

13

His nervous temperament had long been the theme of private discussion, and after his abdication was publicly analysed by psychologists. Now that we have reached the middle of his life, and of our delineation, we propose to enlarge upon this subject. In the year 1919, patriotic Germans sought to prove that the Emperor was mentally deranged, in the hope of convincing the enemy that he was innocent of responsibility for the war. That effort was superfluous, for with this eminently unheroic monarch there could never have been any question of set purpose, but only of how far his recklessness had involved him. Not until now has the discussion of his nervous condition been to the point. As a private individual, William the Second would not be declared legally irresponsible in any court of law, by a physician who knew his business. It is true that such gifted and complex natures as his are never normal—they are always on the dividing-line; but while it may please the psychiatrist to write him down as a case of neurosis, the psychologist will be particularly careful to avoid this "flight into illness," and will seek to account for him simply and naturally as the inevitable product of heredity and environment, unmodified by controlling and counteracting influences.

The only questionings of his normality which have any importance are those of early date. Waldersee wrote, when the Emperor was thirty-two; "It is said that many people, and especially doctors, are quite openly debating whether— possibly in connection with the ear-trouble—there may not be some very gradual process of mental derangement" (W. 2, 228). When he was thirty-seven:

Since the Scandinavian trip, the old affliction in the ear has set in again, and depresses him badly. His nerves have repeatedly broken down since this reappeared. . . If any political disappointment were now to occur, which is always on the cards, it would mean a complete collapse (W. 2, 374).

In his forty-fourth year his physician Leuthold reports: "We must have recourse to a stay in one of the spas, under a strict régime." But Eulenburg, warning Bülow, writes as follows:

I want to give you a hint of the gradual alteration in the mental and physical condition of our dear sovereign. . . . It is difficult to convey the idea, but you will understand the bearing of my letter. . . . I may add that the crisis would certainly not— as so many fear (or hope)—take the form of mental derangement; but that of nervous prostration.

Now, when so sagacious and intimate a companion— one of more than twelve years' standing—apprehends nothing worse than nervous prostration, it is clear that the crucial pathological question is: How will the Emperor react to the greatest crisis of all? Neither at the beginning nor the end of the war was he even for a moment mentally deranged. After all that has befallen him, he is now a vigorous, hale and unaltered man, of close on seventy.

The gifts of high-strung natures are his, beyond a doubt.

Two of those who knew and judged him best, and long were near him though not actually of his Court, maintain to this day that his talents are exceptional. Certainly he did, from the English side, derive a measure of intellect and talent which for a century had been rare indeed among the Hohenzollerns; but otherwise the inherited attributes were ill assorted, for there was not a trace in him of his two genuinely noble grandfathers, while from his parents he took only their weaknesses. Frederick's affectation and vanity, Victoria's ambition and self-will, were blended into the uneasy self-consciousness of a slightly deformed man who was forever in the public eye. All his tendencies towards Caesarism were born of his anomalous resolve to seem case-hardened, though it is true that they became more spontaneous as his authority increased.

The vivacity of his unstable temperament supplied his quick brain with those happy thoughts which struck everyone by their raciness and aptness. They have something of the born demagogue's pregnancy. "The trident of Neptune belongs by right to German fists"—that is unforgettable. At the opening of a Polytechnic: "Mathematics and physical science have shown mankind how we may force the door of God's stupendous workshop." At the inauguration of a Naval College: "I think of your work not only as a means of accumulating knowledge, but also as a literal interpretation of the words Duty and Energy. . . . Character comes first here." Or they would take the shape of such charming things as this, in a birthday-letter to his grandmother:

How incredible it must seem to you that the tiny weeny little brat you so often had in your arms, and dear Grandpapa swung about in his napkin, has now reached the forties, just the half of your prosperous successful life. . . . It is to be hoped you are not ill-pleased with your queer and impetuous colleague (Lee, 740).

With what a delicately ironic smile the Queen must have read these words, irresistible despite the incessant conflicts!

Delighting as he did in the part of munificent caliph, he would bestow orders and titles with a delicate appreciation of the fine shades possible in certain instances, which enchanted many besides the recipients. To arrange for a performance of old Menzel's concerto for the flute at Sans Souci; to send the victorious flag as a birthday-present to the nonegenarian Moltke's house—these were very attractive little inspirations. And there were political ones as well. When Carnot was assassinated, the Emperor amnestied two French officers, imprisoned for espionage, and sent them home as a token of his sympathy for the country. He was opposed to duelling, and obliged his officers to discourage that evil practice; in the year 1907 he even attempted to mitigate the penalties for *lèse-majesté*.

When reason and instinct could occasionally play their part so well, and that in the face of contrary advice, why not oftener? His gifts and perceptions might have made this monarch a valuable one, if they had not been perpetually thwarted by wilfulnesses and resentments, misgivings and affectations. No one has better analysed these dangerous tendencies than Waldersee, who as Chief of Staff has to say of him at thirty—that is in the summer of 1890:

The Emperor has no steadiness of purpose in any department, and does not really know what he would be at. He is easily influenced by anyone with a spark of intelligence, and goes off at the most disconcerting tangents. He has only one motive in everything he does—popularity-hunting. Concern for his personal safety has something to do with this; but, besides, he gets more conceited every day. I thought the Emperor Frederick a very vain man, giving to dressing up and showing-off, but he was nothing to the present monarch. He positively hunts for ovations, and nothing delights him like a frantically cheering mob. As he is very much taken up with the idea of his own capabilities, which unfortunately is a good deal of a delusion, he will swallow any amount of flattery. He likes to play the Mæcenas, and squanders money quite recklessly. All this has developed so quickly that I go from amazement to amazement. He can be most fascinating, and wins hearts wherever he goes—and doesn't stay (W. 2, 137).

His most conspicuous traits, then, were already in evidence at thirty—vivacity, vanity, arbitrariness, instability, charm, extravagance. Everything that was repellent in his behaviour can be explained by the nervous self-assertion to which his infirmity impelled him from his earliest years. "He could not bear to be looked straight in the eyes" (Al. 359); cultivated a loud shrill laugh, while in society his voice took on a disagreeable stridency. Though he was always trying to conciliate the French, he had himself painted for the Paris Embassy as a Garde du Corps in a black cuirass and the royal purple, with a Field-Marshal's baton in his hand, so that Waldersee said the verdict of twenty years hence would be that if he had done great deeds it was an admirable picture, and if he had not it was simply laughable. But Gallifet, standing before it, said to the Ambassador: "Pour vous dire la vérité, ce portrait-là, c'est une déclaration de guerre!" (Eck. 1, 240).

The effect of this pose on international peace was first perceptible in Russia, where in the early days the Emperor's utterances were taken seriously by politicians. Waldersee writes in 1892:

It is a fact that Russia is increasing her armaments, because there it is believed that we are aggressively inclined. Unfortunately there can be little doubt that . . . our Emperor is to blame for this. He has repeatedly given expression to most incautious anti-Russian views—for example, how he would like to give the Russians a beating. . . . I do not doubt that these remarks have been still more frequently made in the family circle, and of course have gone further. . . . My conviction is that all these sayings are the outcome of uneasiness, just as a child will scream to keep up its courage. . . . But as our monarch would not on any account have this suspected, he gets more and more obstinate and violent about trifles, and talks himself into the idea that he is a very mettlesome person (W. 230).

Pusillanimity and vanity united to foster that spirit of absolutism which like a cataract flooded every channel of the administration. So early as 1891 Waldersee writes: "No one may say a word to him; he gives forth his own views with absolute confidence, and apparently means to permit of no opposition." About that time the Emperor said in public: "There is only one ruler in this country, and that is myself." Two years later he had come to saying: "I intend to put through this Army Bill, cost what it may. . . . I'll see that drivelling Reichstag damned, if it opposes me" (W. 2, 274). He had much the same view of the rights belonging to the Federal States—in the year 1895 he gave orders to the independent Free Town of Hamburg as to where, and with what escort, it should receive him as its guest. Four years more, and he went a good deal further.

How graciously condescending! [he wrote on a despatch from Petersburg]. Nicholas must have talked something like this to Frederick William IV. But I'm a damned different proposition. Heels together, if you please, Herr Muraviev, and stand to attention, when you address the German Emperor! (A. 14, 554).

But even that was not the climax. "The Emperor is more autocratic than ever," writes Zedlitz in 1906. When he came home from a pleasure-trip to Palestine, he ordered Berlin to be hung with flags for his re-entry as if it were from a victorious war. A medal struck for the consecration of the newly built church at Wittenberg had to bear his image instead of Martin Luther's. When his physician was commiserating him for his "little cough," the Emperor suddenly drew himself up, looked sternly at the doctor, and said: "A great cough! I am great in everything!" (Z. 174). He was only half serious, but the jest reveals more than he intended. A proposal from the Ministry of State to amnesty prisoners on the birth of his first grandson was returned with the comment: "It is for the Ministry to wait until the Sovereign conveys his wishes." When Wissmann came home from Africa, and in beginning his verbal report made use of the chivalrous phrase: "For my speedy success I have principally to thank the ability of my officers," the Emperor interrupted him. "They are *My* officers"—and left him dumbfounded.

But in these modern days of half-gods, whence shall a monarch procure the emblems of divinity? It might please Alexander to proclaim himself the son of Jupiter, but Napoleon said that the very fishwives would laugh in his face if he made such pretensions. In a word, how shall an Emperor turn himself into a Field-Marshal? He began by a hasty promotion of his two foremost men (one of them after a failure in the manœuvres) to be Generals-Commanding with the rank of Field-Marshal, which Moltke had not been granted after either Königgrätz or Sedan. When he promoted himself to Adjutant-General at the Centenary Celebrations, he gave out that William the First had ap-

peared to him in a dream and appointed him to that rank
(Jagemann, *Aus 75 Jahren*); thus accounting by a mystic
apparition for a senseless promotion, that he might bedizen
himself with a particular stripe of gold lace. Then in
May 1900 he assumed the Field-Marshal's badge, after having issued orders that the two most senior Generals were to
beg him to do so. But he imagined that with the rank he
had automatically acquired the discernment of a Field-
Marshal, for he was soon saying at the manœuvres: "I
don't require a General Staff; I can do very well by myself
with my aides-de-camp." This led to interference in the
conduct of the manœuvres. "Schlieffen's aides were beside
themselves, but they had to submit and listen patiently when
the Emperor found fault with the General Staff before a
large gathering" (W. 3, 225).

Another form of this absolutism was the rudeness to
friends, guests, and intimates which Zedlitz observed year
after year. The Emperor tweaks an old Major's ear, and
gives him a staggering slap on the back. On the way to
the shooting-butts he greets the War Minister and the Chief
of the Military Cabinet with the words: "You old donkeys
think you know better because you're older than I am!"
(Z. 68). Even ladies—the Princess Fürstenberg at
Donaueschingen, the Princess Leiningen at the Strassburg
Viceregal Palace—were "beckoned up for His Majesty to
take in to dinner. The Grand Duke Vladimir got such a
thwack on the back with the Marshal's baton that it resounded again. Of course it was supposed to be in fun"
(Z. 69).

At a Silesian shoot in the autumn of 1904 he held Colonel
von B. down in the snow for a long time,

and then covered him all over with snow to the great amusement of the onlookers—just as one schoolboy will bully a weaker one. The whole shooting-party and hundreds of beaters were watching. Count Roger Scherr-Dobran had a still more unpleasant experience. I may remind my readers that he is a Prussian Chamberlain, a member of the Upper House, has two sons officers in the Hussars of the Body-Guard, is fifty-three years old, and as a great landed proprietor is much looked-up to in Silesia. The moment he saw him the Emperor said, very loudly: "What, you old swine, have you been asked here too?" The bystanders, including the ladies, could hear this apostrophe quite distinctly. The Count was naturally most indignant, and said so to those of his acquaintances who were near him (Z. 91)

—instead of there and then putting the Emperor in his place before them all.

Or he would play the autocratic head of the family, and tell "very amusingly" how the Grand-Duke of Weimar had come, officially announced, on the night before his wedding to say that he could not get married next day, for his future bride had insulted him. Whereupon the Emperor: "When I . . . the German Emperor . . . come to your wedding . . . you can't come saying, the evening before, that you won't get married. You have sworn me fealty in your military oath, and I command you to be married to-morrow." After this misinterpretation of the oath he proceeded to persuade the bride, but waited in her ante-room while she dressed so as to conduct her himself to the carriage, lest she should give them the slip (Z. 113). From the hell of this marriage, which both parties were desirous to avoid at the very last moment, the lady was released, after two years of it, by her death.

The Emperor's view of art-patronage was likewise autocratic, and has been much derided; but is now the less to be emphasized because it was the only department where his follies did no real damage. Art and Literature were in fact more invigorated than otherwise by their conflict with the sovereign. On this subject, moreover, he presented us with some of his most priceless sayings—for instance, the critical remark to Tschudi about Leistikow: "I know the Grunewald —I'm a sportsman myself." The only German who will live both in the history of Art and of William the Second's Court —Menzel—owed his Black Eagle Order to an accidental choice of subject rather than to his mastery. But the naïve follies uttered, ordered, unveiled, and installed by the Emperor in the domain of art pale into nothingness before the disastrous results of his absolutism in the political department.

His love of absolutism and his faith in the Divine Right of Kings were separate though similar sentiments. The former was born of his physical disability, the latter of his profound belief—the absolutism was temperamental, the belief fundamental, and therefore more genuine. When he wired to the Tsar in 1905: "We have clasped hands and sworn before God, and He has given ear to our vow. So I hope that the treaty will have a good effect," he was honestly impressed by the solemn sense of a covenant between two God-appointed sovereigns; and we are merely looking at the ludicrous reverse of the medal when next year we find him declaring that "the thought of a consequential aide-de-camp of our colleague, the wood-cutter Fallières, cheek-by-jowl with you, is tremendously amusing."

Before the inauguration of the North Sea Canal, the Lloyd and Hamburg-America interests were in rivalry about the royal ship—Ballin wishing to have at any rate some of the Princes as guests on his vessel. "That is impossible," said the Emperor; "such gentlemen cannot be brought into contact with other persons—they must keep together" (W. 2, 343). He really believed this, ridiculous as it is. It was the same feeling which made him sceptical—forebodingly sceptical—about Shakespeare's Richard II, the only monarch whose destiny his own was closely to resemble; and this too caused him to circulate an English article upon the King's superiority over Parliament with the comment: "May My Ministers keep in mind old Homer's saying: 'One master, one King!' and take earnest note of the conclusion of this article." And again this conviction led to the following —on a diplomatic despatch which said that no one could see far into the future, he wrote: "That gift has been known to exist! In sovereigns often, in statesmen seldom, in diplomatists almost never."

Upon this theme of ancestry he played variations for thirty years, deducing his own greatness from the long line of his forbears. The Siegesallee in the Tiergarten testifies to this; but its marbles had to suffer the proximity of Kant and Bach behind their insulted royal backs. Though the Emperor, in his earliest speeches, was addicted to invoking Frederick the Great, he soon perceived that there were certain contradictions between the world of that time and his own, and hastily fell back upon his nearest ancestors. Thus he tried to turn the noble and unpretentious image of his grandfather which was cherished by the nation into that of the great conquering Emperor, and spoke of capable advisers "who had had the honour of being permitted to carry out his ideas, but were merely the henchmen of his exalted will." An article in which Bismarck was described as the founder of the Empire came back with the delicious comment: "Grandpapa was that!"   (Hammann, *Um den Kaiser,* 80).

God, he said in a letter to Hollmann about his Christian faith, sometimes reveals Himself in great natures: "Hammurabi, Moses, Abraham, Homer, Charlemagne, Luther, Shakespeare, Goethe, Kant, the Emperor William the Great"; and to this schoolboy list he added in complete good faith, the commentary: "How often my grandfather expressly said that he was only an instrument in the Hand of God!" He was evidently determined to canonize his grandfather, for (as he said in a speech), "if that sublime ruler had lived in the Middle Ages, he would have been sainted, and pilgrims would have come from far and wide to adore his relics." Even his poor father, who as Crown Prince had never gained a victory, and to whom as Emperor no time was given in which to prove his quality, had to be framed in gold.

When the rosy dawn of the German Empire filled the skies, it was his to realize, as a full-ripened man, the dreams of his adolescence. Wielding the German sword, the son wrested the Imperial Crown of Germany from the field of slaughter, and conferred it on his sire. He struck the decisive blow—we owe it to him that the Emperor's armour was forged of such impenetrable steel.

Nay—indirectly, through God-given Princes, even the subject masses could be numbered among the elect, as in this boast, which he always deprecated from any other nation: "And so the Creator has ever kept this nation in His sight— the nation elected by him to bestow the gift of peace at last upon the world. . . . That God should choose a Prussian— that must mean great things!"

Here is the logical origin of the German God.

14

His nervous temperament was not so obviously revealed in these quasi-intellectual aspects of him as in the sexual sphere. The whole domain of the will was out of equilibrium; one asks one's self what were the latent causes?

The only serious testimony to an inordinate degree of sexuality in the Emperor is Bismarck's; but neither he nor other informants, far removed from the category of Court scandalmongers, imply that it extended beyond his conjugal relations, which began at so early a stage of his manhood. Herbert Bismarck, indeed, did say in the first few years after his accession that they "would have to find a mistress for the Emperor, and that might make it easier to govern the country" (E. 247). In the mess of the First Regiment of Guards,

it was forbidden to talk bawdy in the Emperor's presence; but with the Hussars of the Bodyguard this order was relaxed, and the young ruler, who was always ready for a joke, was as much delighted by this diversion as a child by a new trumpet. He blew it incessantly, and will probably go on blowing it for the rest of his life—and yet it means nothing, really, in him (E. 220).

That these words come from Eulenburg adds greatly to their significance. The Emperor, despite his ever increasing absolutism, despite his temperament, his love of change, and his indifference towards his consort, never showed any desire to take a mistress; but again and again chose effeminate-natured men as his friends. There can be only one explanation of the undoubted fact that this deficiency never took any active form of perversity; and once more, we find it in the old subjective trouble—he could not bear to be suspected of any weakness. Now Eulenburg's group, though they were mostly family-men, were none of them entirely normal; if the Emperor were not akin to them, why did he surround himself with such types? His craving to seem energetic and virile protected him from any erotic accentuation of the womanish, capricious, loquacious nature which could be enthusiastic about rings, bracelets, Orders, and jewellery of every kind; and subconsciously he revolted against the very same weakness in himself by which Eulenburg had enchanted him in his twenties. In the bawdy of the messes he could drown the unacknowledged sensibility which might have made him lead a life resembling that of his friends in its refinement, but would certainly not have added any virility to his decisions. William the Second, incessantly eluding his deficiencies, incessantly bent on being first and foremost the Prussian officer, fought down all his inherent dissimilarities, because he longed to be a wholly typical male.

But with so unstable a nature as his, he could not be that. Hinzpeter, who had trained him and had considered him a girlish sort of boy, made shrewdly cynical remarks about him behind his back: "It is not at all necessary to let the Emperor carry out an idea; the thing is always to have some excitement for him. Unless he has some novelty in prospect, he gets apathetic" (W. 2, 174). His uncertain moods influenced his attitude towards functionaries, other monarchs, and the people. Take his relation to Windhorst. In March 1890: "If Windhorst comes near the Palace, I'll have him arrested." In December: a long talk with Windhorst at the Imperial Chancellor's, who had been told to invite him. In January 1891, when Windhorst had an accident: "Would it be going too far if I let an aide-de-camp enquire for him?" Immediately afterwards, reading the list for the next Court ball: "Why isn't Windhorst's name here?" (W. 2, 184).

These shifting moods injured himself more than any-one else, because at first men of all parties believed in him, and afterwards all felt that they had been taken in. He was a fervent Lutheran, yet would say smooth things to Bishops about the Pope, and behaved to him with such deference as no Protestant monarch had ever shown before. Or in the end of 1889, when he could still adorn his speeches with the idealisms of youth:

It will take me all my life, no matter how long it may be, to repay the devotion you have just shown me. Often I wonder if I am worthy of my task, and then it is always like a tonic . . . to hear that you have confidence in me.

Who that heard could feel aught but "What a faithful servant of the State!" Three days later, on no pretext what-ever:

It will come to this in Berlin—that the Social-Democrats will be in the majority; and they will at once proceed to plunder the citizens. It is nothing to me. I shall have loop-holes cut in the Palace walls, and we'll see how much plundering will take place!

Thus the effect of the earlier speech was destroyed.

The disastrous political results of this instability were manifold and evident. That was why the choice between Russia and England never got made, for according to his mood he alternately betrayed each to the other. To take only one example, let us recall the Emperor's telegram to the Tsar in August 1905: "The arch mischief-maker of Europe is again at work in London. Delcassé's revelations . . . point to a projected war against our two pacific na-tions. They are positive bandits!" Nine months later: "I really hope that the exchange of ideas between Uncle Bertie and myself, which turned exclusively on the maintenance of international peace, may be of service to you and your great Empire."

Other symptoms of this unbalanced nervous condition were his favourite occupations—journeys and speeches. The perpetual journeys—symbol of a heart in flight from itself and from tranquillity—were early, but in vain, opposed by his physicians; the speeches too, which often took place four times a day, were an outlet for his febrile nervous energy. The moment when, at the festive table, everyone stood up and gazed at him with eager eyes, when literally all were hanging on his lips—the silence, the sense of universal absorption in his every utterance, the idea that next morning all the capitals in the world would be conning the words that now fell from him: he could no more do without this than without the constant succession of entries and processions, receptions at city-gates and guild-halls, full-dress and maids-of-honour, falling of veils from statues, glidings of vessels from slips, tuckets and marches-past, hurrahs and flags, flowers and the grand farewell at the railway-station. In the year 1894 there were one hundred and ninety-nine goings and comings; in seventeen years five hundred and seventy-seven public speeches were delivered, which means a Kaiser speech every eleven days.

Another aspect of the womanish element in him was his love of baubles. His favourite toy was the Army—new devices, chin-straps, belts, changes of uniform succeeded one another incessantly through twenty years. The Conservative *Schlesische Zeitung* reckoned, in 1903, thirty alterations in the course of fifteen years, not counting badges, and said that at the utmost five had been of any real utility. About this time the Emperor introduced a new regulation for gun-drill, after endless pains had been spent on getting rid of the so-called gun-exercise in order to give the infantry more time for things that were of greater importance. "I might," sums up Waldersee, "describe the attitude of the Army as one of resignation. We often ask each other: 'What's the object of *that?*'" (W. 3, 192). But the most explicit outburst over these frivolities comes from the chief soldier in the Army, the younger Moltke, in the year 1905:

Next Sunday we have another great Flag-Nailing in the Museum. We are still of opinion that victory in a life-and-death combat is won by a bit of coloured bunting. . . . I tremble, looking on at all this humbug, in which the real thing . . . is completely forgotten. People are bedizened with straps of gold lace as badges of their prowess, and all it does is to hinder them in the use of their weapons; everything is done to excite ambition, nothing to inculcate a sense of duty: uniforms get more conspicuous every day, instead of being designed for invisibility in the field; drill is nothing but a theatrical entertainment. "Decoration": that is the order of the day; and behind all this gimcrackery grins the Gorgon-head of War, hanging over us like a thunder-cloud. And no going back upon this road—it gets worse and worse every year! (M. 337).

Reading so grave an indictment by the most responsible of his Generals, we take refuge in the thought that Henry V, in the moment of pressing danger, cast aside all his frivolities and became a soldier and a king. Perhaps, we reflect, these are no more than the results of having nothing particular to do, as we behold the Emperor frequently change his dress twelve times a day, attend a performance of the *Flying Dutchman* in naval uniform, unveil the hunting-groups in the Tiergarten in the Court hunting-dress, have his bathroom fitted with a vent like those used in the Navy, and send his Chamberlain all the way to Petersburg to show the Tsar how to fasten the cuirass of the regiment of cuirassiers which had been lent him.

But how did it go when things turned serious? When at the end of 1904 Russia, disastrously defeated, was gnashing her teeth, the Emperor wrote to the Tsar: "Here's luck in the big game!" But what his own heart felt when war came threateningly close is revealed in a comment by Zedlitz, of March 1909:

Just now the Emperor's whole interest is concentrated on a more or less necessary mobilization. Unfortunately quite irrelevant matters hold the stage, such as a greave on his helmet, a special contrivance for fastening the chin-straps, double seams on the trousers, a perpetual overhauling of his wardrobe with Daddy Schulz [his Chamberlain]—on these subjects the Emperor will hold forth for hours at a time.

Just as in the Army he was all for show—for drill and uniform—so it was as an actor that he everywhere surveyed the scene in which he was to play. Here lies his affinity with Eulenburg; but one is inclined to think the Emperor's theatricalism more genuine, because he was so much more naïve. It led him into similar absurdities, as for instance when Moltke died at the age of ninety-one, forgotten by the Emperor, though tardily pensioned. It was little more than a memory which died with him; but the Emperor, who lived in a perpetual stream of telegrams, since his moods and behests were not to be subjected to the limitations of time and space, in this one said no word of sympathy for the survivors, recalled no traits of the great soldier, dying with so many years upon him—no, all he was concerned with was: "What does a sovereign say on the death of his oldest General?" And he declaimed over the wires: "Am wellnigh stunned! Returning in all haste. Have lost an army; cannot realize it!" And on the way to that secret rendezvous at Björkö, did he not wire to the Tsar: "Not a soul has the slightest idea!

All my guests think we're bound for Gothland. . . . Have important news for you. My guests' faces will be worth seeing when they suddenly behold your yacht. Tableau! What sort of dress for our meeting? Willy."

The actor's power of sinking his own personality in that of the character presented was to this extent the Emperor's —that he could be a different person to everyone: as imperial with the Tsar as he was democratic with Cecil Rhodes, American with Roosevelt, French with Saint-Saëns and Massenet. Almost everyone was enchanted with him at first; Gordon Bennett, who met him at Kiel and instantly detested him, may be said to have been wellnigh unique. If he hit the right nail on the head when he described journalists as snippet-snappers, he might himself be called a journalist; for, says Zedlitz,

he was very clever and quick at getting a superficial notion of any subject (for instance, a new theory of the Origin of Being), and was able to talk about it as if it was his own discovery, or as if he was a professor of astronomy and had spent years and years in an observatory. Even the most renowned experts were taken in, and would praise his acquirements, his astonishing capacity for work, and his phenomenal powers of apprehension (Z. 211).

These histrionic tendencies were still more evident in the sermons for which life on board afforded him an opportunity —though he occasionally took the pulpit on land as well, as at Wernigerode in 1906. Among the yacht-sermons is one delivered at Heligoland, when the first ships had started for the Far East. He preached on a text from Exodus (xvii, 9):

Why do the heathen Amalekites so furiously rage together in the Far East? Because their aim is, by force and cunning, by fire and sword, to prevent the penetration of their land by European trade and the European spirit. And once more has gone forth the Divine Command: "Choose us out men, and go out, fight with Amalek." . . . But to us who must stay at home, constrained by other sacred duties—to us it is said: Hear ye not the behest of God, which bids ye: "Go up upon the mountains! Lift up your hands to Heaven!" Mighty are the prayers of the righteous. . . . Ours shall be not only a great fighting-force, but we will have our praying-force as well—our great, our holy force of suppliants. . . . And will not our soldiers be strengthened, be inspired, when they think: "Thousands, nay millions, bear us in their prayerful hearts at home!" The King of all Kings cries: "Forward, volunteers! Who will be the Empire's suppliant?" O, that we may say this morning: "The King hath called us, and all of us, all of us are come!" Let not one of you be missing! He who can pray is a man indeed!

This performance, which should arouse professional envy in the breast of every Salvation Army captain, belongs to the inception of the Operetta-War, and rings most villainously false. Not for spiritual things did the Germans go to China, but for sordid things—for gold, not good; it was not God who sent the troops, but a sensation-loving sovereign; and not sacred duties but the protest of the Powers kept the others back. Millions were there indeed; only they were laughing, not praying. But he, in his bombastic ardour, must needs make Heaven to the pattern of himself and his conception of a king—from God's mouth must issue the Prussian slogan: "Forward, Volunteers!" It was this militarized theocracy which not long afterwards made him, at the Hamburg banquet, cry in a voice that pealed along the glittering table to the jewelled, scandalized assembly: "Eyes front! Heads up! Look to the skies! O, bend your knees before the Great Ally who never yet forsook the Germans!"

Of his theatricality were born his affections. **These** were not only the majestic moods which were for ever at the disposal of photographers, ranging from portentous gravity to gentle seriousness, and from a kindly smile to a defiant scowl; there were other poses, no less indicative of character. After a male choir competition he told the principal German conductors not only how the choir ought to have sung, but also that nearly every piece had been set too high, and "should have been, in most instances, half or three-quarters or even a fifth of a tone lower"—which a musician, even if he agreed with it, would certainly never have so expressed. Or again, when he was not yet thirty, Moltke (who was twelve years older) being announced by his new rank of Major, the Emperor looked up—and affecting the prematurely aged ruler, worn by his sublime reflections and anxieties, exclaimed: "Good God! Are you a Major already? We're getting old. When I think that I first knew you as a young pup of a subaltern!" (M. 148).

The third and the most marked manifestation of neuroticism was his poltroonery—a flagrant contradiction of the Attila pose. It was the hard-shelled Conservative President of the Chamber, the old Junker von Köller, who said to Hohenlohe: "God preserve us from war, while this Emperor is on the throne! He would lose his nerve; he is a coward at heart" (Al. 338). The Hohenlohes, father and son, were much struck by this remark from such lips at so early a stage; later, every one was to know the truth. No one can be blamed for possessing such a temperament, only it is disturbing in the Supreme War Lord of the most militant of nations. Again the disastrous concatenation—a crippled man, more unfitted (as his tutor declares) to be an officer than any other in the country, yet condemned to that profession unless he was prepared to follow the tradition of his family by renouncing the Crown, since in Prussia an incurably civilian temper was a more cogent reason for that renunciation than an incurable cancer; and thus, through life, forced to affect a courageous spirit of which Nature had deprived him in the hour of his birth! Here lies the tragic element in the life of William the Second, with all its immediate effects upon the nation.

For just because he never dared acknowledge even to himself this timidity of the weakling, and concealed both from his nearest and the world at large the inward trouble of his soul, there was born of his inherently defensive nature a semblance of aggressiveness. That was why he so continually seemed to hurl defiance at other nations, when all the time he dreaded war far more than his less boisterous colleagues; and that was why, at home, the self-same man alarmed the bourgeois by his perpetual fulminations against the Red Terror within the Empire.

Hence only Junkers might enter the Guards, and only these might enjoy quick promotion—an arrangement which embittered the line-officers; hence "in his fear of anarchists, he thought of having an armoured turret built in the proximity of the Palace, which should command the Spree and all its bridges"; but at the same period, February 1891, declared in a speech to the Brandenburg *Landtag* that he would lead Germany to days of glory (W. 2, 233). Hence too, whenever he suffered from colic, he would fear poison; Zedlitz tells of three such occasions: "I have been poisoned, beyond a doubt! There must have been something in the food!" (Z. 134). His dread of illness was so great that when the Empress was nursing one of the Princes through inflammation of the lungs, he never would come near her except in the open air, and utterly refused to visit his son, though there could be no possible danger of infection (Z. 109). His nervousness about people with whom it was scarcely possible for him to avoid some intercourse was shown with regard to General von Bissing. The General was dismissed as a result of one of his Army Orders, but not, as an aide-de-camp had advised, confined to barracks. "Bissing is such a hot-headed fellow. If I had put him under arrest, he would very likely have shot himself" (Z. 182). Did the Emperor really mean "himself"?

The war was to put it all to the test.

15

Some very matter-of-fact traits controlled the more neurotic ones. Of the romanticism which so many attributed to him there is hardly a trace. In his ceremonial gestures the Emperor was as little romantic as any other kind of actor— he rehearsed, he studied, every one of them. Mantles and Orders, pages and Court-Marshals, Frederician uniforms and piqueurs—everything was organized; an eternal boy had got up the entertainment, there were the puppets at the end of their wires, and all was for his pleasure. The whole thing was pageantry; he had no illusions about it. The fastest motor-car, the swiftest aeroplane, were much more fascinating to him than the purple of the royal mantle and the servants' powdered heads which were *de rigueur* for his banquets. The romanticism of Ludwig of Bavaria had not one of these features. The true romantic seeks solitude; this Emperor feared it, fled it. Ludwig, all alone in his gilded nautilus-boat, would row to his grotto—William fared forth in his steam-yacht with a score of boon companions. He did not want, like Ludwig, to ride forth from his gates as a knight—

he wanted to ride in at them; and the gold helmet, worn by both, meant totally different things to each.

The Knights-Hospitallers' Ceremonial [writes Zedlitz] was very stately and magnificent, if one could have got over the touch of mummery about it, something essentially insincere. . . . That may be, however, because it had been rehearsed about four times, for an hour and a half each time, in the Emperor's presence (Z. 154).

For such diversions he was indefatigable; not so for affairs of government. All the memoirs and statements agree about the Emperor's increasing indolence. In 1889 Hinzpeter writes of him at thirty as if he were still under tuition: "I have talked to the Emperor about the Labour question in the hope of inciting him to work at it, for he has never learnt to work." And next year Waldersee:

All who have to do with him are worried about his complete loss of interest in any sort of work. Distractions, amusements, fiddle-faddlings with the Army, and especially the Navy, journeys or shooting-parties—these come first with him; so that in fact he has hardly any time left for work. He reads little . . . scarcely ever even writes, except marginal notes on reports and despatches, and approves most highly the official interviews which take the shortest time. It is really scandalous how the Court gazettes deceive the public about the Emperor's industry—according to them, he is hard at work from morning till night.

In the spring of 1894, when he was at Abbazia, negotiations were going on with England about the pact and with the Vatican about Italy, in addition to Reichstag business; and Eulenburg, who was deputy there for all the Ministers, writes as follows:

Every moment fresh despatches come in, which I have to attend to; then I have to return to the Emperor, and there is always some change of dress to be made. In the mornings, lounge-suit; for lunch, black morning-coat; then if we're going on board, yachting-dress, if to tennis, tennis-dress . . . so that I often dictate despatches while I'm washing my hands. Afterwards I have to submit papers; and everything that had been balanced to a nicety at one's own deliberate walking-pace has to be taken at a breakneck gallop with the Emperor. . . . He listens to all my political counsels because I play tennis with him, and between rallies and in breathing-times have a good-humoured Imperial ear at my disposal —ready to yield in uncongenial matters because he is in high spirits. *Ludere pro patria et imperatore!* It's a mad world! (E. 2, 111).

Between April and December, 1901, the King of Prussia did not see any one of his Ministers except Bülow, Gossler, and Podbielski (W. 3, 175). The tutor of the royal children complained that, though he was daily in the Emperor's company, he never could get a serious talk with him about their education; and when on the "Hohenzollern" a sermon was delivered on a text from Psalm xc: "Yet is their strength but labour and sorrow," Moltke wrote: "How true *that* is, we all feel in our enforced idleness. All, unfortunately, except One."

Again, at another period, January 1910, this is the picture Zedlitz gives of the Emperor's day.

The worst of it is that he is getting more and more out of the habit of doing anything of the slightest importance. He gets up late, breakfasts at nine . . . always with three hot courses; it is only with great difficulty—and then very much against his will—that one can pin him down to business for a couple of hours, and those he usually spends in giving his own views to his advisers. Then comes luncheon at one; he drives out at two, then tea, then a sleep, and before the evening-meal at eight he will go through some signing of papers. As a result of the afternoon-sleep, which often lasts three hours, the Emperor sits up regularly every night till twelve or one o'clock, and then his favourite company is a set who listen reverentially to anything he chooses to talk about. So that his life is in fact one continuous idleness. And compare this with what the gazettes say of him! . . . Nine months' travelling; only the winter-months at home. Where is the time for quiet reflection and serious work in this perpetual good-fellowship? (Z. 212, 230).

When Lyncker at about this time took over the Military Cabinet, the Emperor said to him in a pathetically pleading tone: "But, dear Lyncker, you won't bring me nothing but musty papers, will you? Now and again some funny little story or another!" This is a shocking example of his aversion from anything practical, for the speaker was a man of fifty, who still was called the young Emperor.

But he was practical enough about money-matters—not only for personal gain, as in the sale of the painted pottery made on his Kadinen estates. Wealth, as such, impressed him deeply; his unromantic spirit respected this modern form of power—riches, no matter how acquired, were a sufficient attraction. Despite a sensible regulation in the year 1890 or thereabouts that the promotion of officers was not to be dependent on their financial circumstances, his own social intercourse was confined to the rich regiments which could outdo one another in the splendour of their "Kaiser-dinners"; and he added greatly to the officers' expenses by the constant changes in coats, tunics, top-boots, gold-lace, sword-belts, and the like. For example, in 1894 he ordered all officers to procure the new sash; in 1895 he reverted to the old type, in 1896 devised a third, while in 1897 there was a fourth variant.

From the thrice-augmented Civil List he saved all he could for himself, and in the year 1918 this had reached the sum of eighteen million marks. In the quarterly estimates, which amounted to over five millions, there figured as the Emperor's "Privy Purse Expenses" 440,000 marks; as "Current Donations" for the institutions 4,188 marks; for individuals 3,000 marks, among them items such as from ten to five marks quarterly for the children of court-servants and for superannuated gardeners. The sovereign who dispensed these gratuities possessed seventy-three palaces and country-estates.

Never before had the representative of an old royal house been so indiscriminate in accepting the hospitality of the rich. Not only was he the guest at Kiel and in Norway of dollar-kings, but he actually had Marienburg redecorated for the reception of a twenty-six-year old son of Vanderbilt's. When he invited the Berlin Town-Councillors to a beer-party, he would send round a subscription-list for the Fleet, which none of them could avoid signing. In those circles, a title was not so much conferred as sold.

But he had a good eye for business abroad as well. In October 1904 he wrote to the Tsar: "This reminds me of my former suggestion that you should not forget to give orders likewise for new ships of the line, so as to have some ready when the war is over. . . . My private firms will be glad to receive instructions." And three months later, after condoling with him over the Port Arthur affair, continued: "Now . . . I trust you won't forget to remind your functionaries of our great firms at Stettin, Kiel, etc. I am sure they will supply you with splendid types of battleships. I hope you will kindly accept the pair of vases from our Royal Manufactory as a Christmas gift." This certainly does credit to his patriotism, and no less certainly to his vigilant eye for business.

Intercourse with the sovereign was made very difficult
for his servants by the fact that they never knew how they
stood with him—his humour might change at any moment.
The highest officials had to be as careful as those of Louis
XIV. A certain glint in the eye would be the precursor
of a sudden outbreak of nervous agitation—at which times
Tirpitz, for example, "would let everything slide for the
moment. A tête-à-tête interview was the only hope, for
if a third person were present, his real opinion would be
affected by the craving he always had to show that he was
Emperor. It was this which made the Cabinets so powerful" (T. 135). For as one of the three Chiefs of Cabinets
was nearly always present at the Ministers' interviews, and
was afterwards left alone with the Emperor, he had only "to
watch his opportunity . . . to get his own way." Hülsen,
Müller, and Lucanus thus did what they liked in great questions of policy. Waldersee's is the most memorable remark
on the art of managing the Emperor: "It is very difficult to
restrain him, but mere child's-play to set him going."

What the Emperor himself demanded of those about
him is symbolized by his treatment of his horses.

My first impression [writes Reichach, Chief Master of the
Horse] when I watched the Emperor riding, was that it would be
no easy task to find the right mount for His Majesty, for he demanded a great deal from his horse. Gentle action, no shying or
jibbing, smooth in the gallop—and moreover, steady as a rock at
the march-past of the troops, as well as during the critique at the
manœuvres (often lasting an hour) when the map, spread open on
the horse's neck, would several times be smartly struck. . . . The
greatest problem was how far to exercise the horses beforehand,
so that they should not be too fresh. If the exercise was insufficient, the horse was very liable to be restive; if excessive, the going
would be slack.

Bülow alone possessed all these qualifications. He could both gallop and stand still at the word of command; he never jibbed; he stood like a rock during "the critique"; he was not over-fresh, and yet was never slack. When finally he was for once restive, he was replaced by a steady-going old grey who could only trudge round in a circle, but upon whose long neck the Emperor could hit his maps as hard as he liked.

How well he understood the art of cajoling when he chose, it was Waldersee's lot to experience. What did the Emperor do when he wanted to remove him from the command of the Army because Waldersee had defeated him at the manœuvres? First he suddenly transferred the then Commandant at Altona on some transparent pretext, so as to have the post vacant; then on his birthday gave Waldersee a glittering decoration, "to show everyone what good friends we are." Next he expressed a desire to see such brilliant talents in command of a division; and when Waldersee, on this, begged to be allowed to resign, he explained how important Altona was. Three days later at another interview, it was entirely a question of the great value of his friendship. "I want to show the whole world what it means to be the friend of the German Emperor. Whoever says one word against you shall be demolished!" Finally, "he took my hand with the most affectionate of gestures and pleaded with me: 'You *do* accept, don't you? Your Emperor beseeches you!'" As Waldersee was not to be mollified, and gave utterance to home-truths, he changed his tone and got pathetic: "It is all so saddening—I have had so many other disappointments. My best friends are forsaking me." When Waldersee at last accepted, the Emperor kissed him three times and vowed eternal friendship.

A grim, defiant Waldersee would have been injurious to him—hence decorations, affection, pathos, and three kisses.

But amid all this absolutism, now harsh, now cajoling—what hours of loneliness, embitterment, rancour! What a secret loathing he must have felt for the incessant ceremonial, the frivolities of decade after decade; and how he must have longed to revenge himself on those who smiled through it all!

Often [relates Zedlitz] the Emperor does seem to feel the isolation of his autocratic state, and to realize that his best friends only let him treat them as he does for the sake of their personal advantage. Then he gets gloomy and taciturn. I have noticed that at such times he takes a pleasure in making all about him, even the Empress, believe the exact contrary of what he really thinks and feels, and this about the gravest matters. Indeed, in these moments he seems to find a curious satisfaction in wounding others. This happens to most people, just when they think themselves most secure in his favour; then the blow falls all the more severely, and the Emperor takes a corresponding pleasure in its effect (Z. 110).

These penetrating observations on the Emperor at the end of his forties are testimony to the ever-changing moods of an autocrat whom vanity, cold-heartedness, and perplexity of soul had condemned to a lonely misanthropy, while yet he could not live without society and smiling faces round him. So it was that he became himself one of the pessimists whom he had forbidden to exist in his kingdom.

16

Who were the first to take the measure of this man? Who warned the German people—who the Emperor himself? The answers to these questions will help us to understand how it was that a single individual could prevail against a whole nation.

The nation is not answerable at the outset—those immediately surrounding the Emperor are solely to blame. For if it is certain that among the sixty millions of his people, even including the Socialists, there was no one who fathomed either his nature or his conduct, it is no less certain that among the hundreds of persons who came into closer contact with him there was not one who entirely misread him. What Bismarck and Bülow, what the Hohenlohes, father and son, thought of him—what Eulenburg and Holstein, Waldersee and Moltke, Kiderlen and Tirpitz, Zedlitz and Hammann wrote of him either to each other or for themselves—is clearly shown in the present pages; but these are merely fragments of perception, always cautiously presented, as it were by shrugs and glances. And moreover these twelve observers were profoundly diverse and very variously actuated; each was at enmity with the other, the sole bond of union being that all were in the Emperor's service. Behind these few whose letters or memoirs we possess, stand a hundred others, equally aware, whose written or verbal testimonies have not yet become historical documents.

Again, the verdicts of his enemies one and all are excluded from this study—Richter's and Bebel's, King Edward's and the Tsar's; for political interests at home and abroad may have obscured or exacerbated the judgments of these men. Such observations were swiftly made—they all date from the first years of his reign; and they persisted unchanged to its close. This, and the absence of any noteworthy private evidence to the contrary, seem to indicate that we shall have no further contributions towards our knowledge of William the Second, and that the psychological side of the case is concluded. The following passages, supplementary to those already given here, are chosen only from the most outspoken judgments of those who stood nearest him—his best friend, his principal soldier, and his mother.

Psychologically [writes Eulenburg to Bülow during the Scandinavian trip of 1899], there is not the slightest change. He is the same explosive creature, if not even more violent and unaccountable, from his sense of being more experienced—which in fact he is not in the smallest degree. . . . A powerful man shapes the age to his pattern; a weaker spirit will be ground in the mill. When so markedly egotistic a nature dominates a realm, the consequences can be nothing but catastrophic; and we are heading straight for a period which will decide whether the age or the Emperor is the stronger. I am afraid it will not be he. . . . There is so much I would like to say to him, but I am struck dumb by the Caliph, who a moment before seemed a good Haroun al Raschid mixing with his people.

Waldersee, who had been one of the most intimate friends of the young Prince William, writes so early as 1890:

His extreme vanity soon led him to imagine that he was really among the most remarkable of men. . . . It is now evident that the Socialist movement, instead of being checked, has on the contrary been much invigorated. Even the Emperor feels anxious now; people who know him well say: "Anxious about his personal safety."

In the summer of 1895: "His versatility turns out to be mere superficiality; his private life is narrowly watched, and the general conclusion is that he spends most of his time in amusing himself" (W. 2, 291). Ten years later, when Waldersee was again in full favour, a Field-Marshal and the Emperor's representative at King Edward's Coronation:

Will the Emperor's reign increase the power of the German Empire, or destroy it? Our monarch, so richly gifted, so full of the very best intentions, has undertaken far too much, and has alas! not yet accomplished anything, but merely created such confusion as no one can see the end of. I would swear that among all his counsellors . . . there is not one—not one—who does not survey the future with profound apprehension; and most of the Federal Princes are equally uneasy. [In the summer of 1904:] It is grievous to see how our monarch is paving the way for the Revolution. . . . The forces of destruction grow more brazen every day, and he offends and embitters the great majority of those whose interest it is to uphold the State. . . . Even at forty-four, the Emperor has not yet realized that the cheers of the mob mean very little. On the contrary, they greatly delight and impress him, though for years now the school-children have been put up for these demonstrations. . . . I have quite given up the hope that the Emperor may change his course—only some great reverse will bring that about (W. 2, 205 f.).

His mother said: "Don't for a moment imagine that my son ever does anything from any motive but vanity" (Z. 111). And wrote:

One cannot believe that history will not have to tell of retribution and judgment. . . . But we may have to go through—Heaven knows what! A king bears no charmed life, and every day that dawns may be disastrous. Indeed, that seems almost indicated, and it is terrible to think of the dangers that surround us. But there is a special Providence for children—and scatter-brains! One can only pray that insight, patience, prudence, and foresight may come in time, and that too grievous a price may not have to be paid for wisdom. To me it seems that the monarchy is about to be put to the test, and I tremble lest the issue be a woeful one (Victoria to her friend the Baroness von Schrader in 1893).

That none of these should have undertaken to warn the nation is not surprising. They all belonged either to the nobility or to the governing classes; and moreover, any individual action would have been more disturbing than salutary. And Bismarck, who alone by nature and training was equal to the task, was far too old, at eighty, to give free rein to the revolutionary element which in him contended with the royalist.

Those men who did undertake to speak the truth were one and all of the opposition. It was easy for Bebel and Richter to give tongue in the Reichstag, and if they were interrupted every minute by the President they could always go on again, and never suffered for their audacity. When in 1892 Ludwig Fulda in his *Talisman,* and in 1894 Professor Quidde in his *Caligula,* uttered a warning note, they at once attracted universal attention; and the Emperor was so ill-advised as to deprive Fulda of the Schiller Prize and to threaten Quidde. In their footsteps followed Mittelstädt and Baron von Guhle; Mommsen protested against an attack on the liberty of the German Universities. Count Reventlow wrote in 1906, Doctor Liman in 1913, in tones of fearless admonition; many democratic journalists were unafraid and critical, and August Gaul refused to put spread wings on a drawing of a crouching eagle. But more strenuously than by any other was the truth about the Emperor set forth by Maximilian Harden, who was more than once imprisoned for his writings, and whose criticisms profoundly influenced the middle classes.

Of those near him who saw aright and in general held their peace, and those who saw and did speak from a distance, there were only a very few who, coming into close contact with him, ever spoke out to the Emperor himself. That there are no witnesses to these occasions is only natural; but it makes our credence dependent on our view of the narrator.

There is only one instance of a manly opposition before witnesses—in February 1894, after a dinner at Caprivi's, when the Emperor was trying to put through the Commercial Treaty with Russia and said to his guests, who were the leaders of the Agrarian Party: "I have no desire to go to war with Russia for the sake of a few hundred Junkers. The Tsar would be so offended by a rejection of the Treaty that we should have war in three months at longest. If we have, I shall simply abandon the right bank of the Vistula." Whereupon he was answered by Baron von Levetzow, President of the Reichstag—a quiet taciturn man, who now, before this large gathering, spoke in clear decisive fashion to the Emperor: "The loyalty of the Conservatives is beyond all dispute, even if the Party should, on consideration of the Treaty, deem it their duty to vote against it." The Emperor said no more. But Levetzow described the day on which he had had to say this as the saddest in his life.

In the course of thirty years three men, by their own accounts, spoke out *in camera* to the Emperor. Of these three, Waldersee's story is discounted by his character of "Court-General"; Eulenburg's statements—unsupported and therefore to be taken with a grain of salt—are nevertheless too lifelike to be all invention; and he was frank enough, even if we reject half of what he says, to be credited for telling the truth on some occasions at any rate. The indirect report we have of Hollmann's outspokenness, and still more Moltke's direct narrative of his own protest, are both in full accordance with the Emperor's character, and strike one as undeniably authentic. In all, the most important point is the Emperor's reaction. Ballin, too, was outspoken in trivial matters—at Kiel he procured a farewell audience for Dernburg, and so on; but he did not stand out for the truth in important naval decisions. Mommsen, despite his lamentable colleagues, saved the honour of German science when after an inspection of the Saalburg he, though a guest at the imperial table, made fun of the Emperor's admiration for the Roman Caesars; and Ernest von Mendelssohn in 1905 remonstrated with the Emperor for selling his Russian Bonds, and was punished by never again being invited to Court.

When Waldersee was about to resign the command of the Staff he represents himself as having said to the Emperor: "In these last two years [from 1888 to 1890] the Army has deteriorated. The ideal relations between the Supreme War-Lord and his corps of officers, inherited by Your Majesty, have been disturbed; and the lightning-changes in the higher ranks have been most injurious to discipline." The Emperor seemed startled, and said: "No one has ever spoken to me like this before!" Then he went on trying to persuade the hesitant General not to resign. There was an end to home-truths for that day.

It was a much easier task for Eulenburg, the bosom friend who admired and loved the Emperor. How often he wrote words of wisdom we have already seen. He was really the one person who was allowed to speak frankly to the Emperor. When in August 1897 he warned him against personal intervention in the matter of the Navy Bills, lest the people should come to look upon the whole thing as their sovereign's private pastime, the Emperor's answer was: "Sincerest thanks for your most valuable and interesting letter. . . . I am glad to have your frank opinion, and particularly grateful to you for it—since if *you* wouldn't speak out, who on earth would? . . . So in future I shall hold my jaw, and use it exclusively for eating, drinking, and smoking" (E. 2, 251). He must have been in a very good temper before he could have written of himself in so wholesome a strain of irony—the only instance of this in the Emperor's life.

Two years later—in July 1899—during the Scandinavian trip, there was another publicity scare, this time about an imperial telegram referring to "an inflexible will." Eulenburg—by his own report to Bülow (E. 2, 253)—was admonitory in a dialogue on board. "The Government . . . might be forced to resign in the event of some dangerous situation arising and becoming uncontrollable—and that, as well may happen, in consequence of some incautious proceeding of Your Majesty's. Circumstances might then create a national movement in the direction of abdication or a Royal Commission. A mechanism like the German Empire is a subtle, intricate piece of work—a masterpiece of the kind we put under glass. . . . Careless handling of so precious an object might incense the nation." The Emperor looked very grave, and asked with whom such ideas could originate. Eulenburg avoided giving names, but did say: "Cardinal Hohenlohe, whom Your Majesty revered, said very earnestly to me immediately before his death: 'I know that you are absolutely devoted to the Emperor, and moreover in a position to give him really outspoken advice. Tell him to be very careful! I know for a positive fact that the idea of declaring him to be irresponsible for his actions has been widely discussed, and that very many persons, among them highly placed ones, would be willing to support such a proceeding. You must warn the Emperor!'. . . Very much against his usual custom, the Emperor did not break off this conversation with a joke or some strong language à la Royal Regiment of Guards. No—he was very thoughtful for some time."

Ten days afterwards, on a walk by the fjord at Regen:

Eulenburg: "The head and front of the offending is the serious conflict between Your Majesty's personality and the views of the nation. Your Majesty is undoubtedly modern-minded; you might even be called progressive; but that side of you is invalidated by an excessive public display of energy. By your speeches and telegrams Your Majesty gives the impression of desiring to revive the idea of the absolute monarch. But there is not a single Party in the Empire which will ever again accept that idea."

The Emperor, tartly: "I claim the right of free speech, like any other German. I must say what it is I want, so that reasonable people may know whom they are to follow, and how. If I said nothing, the really 'willing' members of the middle-class would not know what they were supposed to do. . . . *You're* only afraid that I may show the Reichstag who is master!"

Eulenburg: "You know very well you are far too modern-minded, and far too intelligent, not to see that Germany will never again consent to do without a Parliament."

The Emperor: "Then it will have to be a modified form of Parliament—not what we have now."

Eulenburg: "There may be something to be said for that, but even so it would have to keep the established course. And that course becomes impracticable when the majority of the nation is in conflict with its Emperor."

The Emperor: "If that were true, it would come to a Revolution—and one way or another we'll eventually have to face that! Everything points to it; so we may as well accept the challenge."

Eulenburg: ". . . Which the coalition of the European Powers is waiting for, in order to attack us."

The Emperor: "Oh, if they'd only see what I really mean

by my exhortations! But the Germans are too limited and short-sighted for that; they are absorbed in petty squabbles. . . . I, an absolute monarch! Have I ever taken a single step which could be said to infringe the Constitution? How on earth do people get hold of such ideas?"

These significant statements are taken from Eulenburg's long letters to Bülow, and it is true that they are printed from his drafts, which he may have revised in later years. Thus they may have been twice touched up; but they cannot be all invention. They reveal William as more than anything else the man of good conscience who is convinced that he is doing his utmost for his people; but also as the monarch who suffers his best friend to tell him truths, and ponders them. The pity is that by next morning he is in a different mood; and if we can commend the oriental autocrat for not showing any resentment towards the truth-teller, we cannot go so far as to affirm that he is convinced. We are shown in these dialogues, which probably were unparalleled in the Emperor's experience, a monarch full of good intentions, brilliant intelligence, and such incurable superficiality that the truth does not alarm him enough for him to keep it in mind.

What Admiral Hollmann ventured to say is not related by himself, and is therefore the more worthy of our credence. Hence it may be true that at the end of 1903 he said to the Emperor, after the latter had undergone the operation on his throat, that he was surrounded by sycophants. "Your Majesty's whole environment, including some of the Ministers, submits to such treatment as only sycophants will put up with." At first the Emperor listened quietly; then he broke off the interview with the words: "That's enough now" (W. 2, 220).

His most remarkable hour in the Palace of Truth was that imposed on him by the younger Moltke (M. 305 f.) who, on being selected for the position of Chief of Staff, said to himself: "It's now or never!"—and opened the interview by telling the Emperor that he could not accept the post until he had frankly expounded his views. Then he proceeded to criticize the manœuvres, which always concluded by making prisoners of an army of half a million in a few days. "Your Majesty is aware that the forces led by yourself invariably make mincemeat of the enemy, so that the campaign is by way of being decided at a single blow. This kind of war-game, in which the enemy is so to speak delivered over to Your Majesty, is bound to instil most erroneous ideas which would inevitably be disastrous in real warfare. . . . And I regard it as still more unfortunate that this arbitrary treatment of the war-game prevents every one of the officers concerned from taking any real interest in it. . . . But what I most deplore, and am bound to mention to Your Majesty, is that the officers' confidence in their Most Supreme War-Lord is profoundly undermined by this proceeding. The officers say to each other: 'The Emperor is much too shrewd not to see that everything is arranged for him to win, and so he must like it that way.'"

The Emperor: "I had no idea of this—I never dreamed that both sides did not fight on equal terms. I have always been in absolute good faith. Tell Schlieffen that at the next manœuvres he is not to treat me any better than the enemy."

Moltke: "Count Schlieffen says: 'When the Emperor plays, he must win.' . . . Your Majesty ought really not to command at all, but stand above both parties. . . . If the decisions of the Generals commanding are constantly to be affected by Your Majesty's expressions of opinion, their initiative will suffer, they will lose keenness and confidence."

The Emperor: "I have always given the Generals commanding a free hand." (Moltke adduces an instance of interference.) "Oh yes, that was because he wanted to retreat with his division, so that there would have been no fight at all on the day."

Moltke: ". . . The whole Army knows now that Your Majesty simply dictated to a General Commanding what he was to do with his division, and that could add nothing to the General's prestige. . . . But Your Majesty would not be in command of a division in the field."

The Emperor: "I take the command so as to show the Generals how I want things done."

Moltke: "Your Majesty could tell them that at the conference. . . . In that way Your Majesty would not be in view of the troops, and this is of the greatest importance—for the soldier who has seen his Emperor at the manœuvres will never as long as he lives forget it. Your Majesty will graciously forgive me for having expressed myself more freely than Your Majesty is accustomed to."

The Emperor: "Why didn't you tell me this long ago?"

Moltke: "Well, everyone can't come to Your Majesty saying 'I approve or disapprove of this or that.'"

The Emperor: "But you are Adjutant-General, so you can always come." Then he gave Moltke his hand and said: "I thank you." When they had talked over the next steps, he shook hands again, went out into the drawing-room where the guests had long been waiting, and throughout the evening "was very silent and reflective. I hated doing it, but God knows I had to. . . . However, he was just as friendly afterwards."

Result at the next manœuvres, eight months later—the Emperor did not take the command, "though it was a bitter disappointment to him," nor did he interfere, but gave great praise to Moltke. "He never resented it when I frankly opposed him."

Again, three years later, Moltke states that the Emperor had done, and even said, what Moltke had advised; "he was sensible from first to last, and his critique was the best I ever heard him give—everyone was delighted with it."

This shows that manly, practical resolution could impress him. During Moltke's indictment he professed a guileless astonishment, scarcely defending himself at all; then twice shook hands with him, and was silent and reflective for the rest of the evening. But eventually he did as was right, forgetting his vanity for the sake of the cause; and the effect of these home-truths lasted for three years, while Eulenburg as counsellor lived as it were from hand to mouth. Nor was Moltke by any means a fire-eater—he was if anything too much of an intellectual; but he was not the Emperor's friend. That was why he prevailed. Eulenburg sought to influence him by heart-to-heart talks, Bülow by the arts of the courtier, and both were content to take short views; but here was a stranger who must be deferred to, because it would never do to lose him.

If we add to this the statements of Ballin, Metternich, and others, who all thought the Emperor responsive to skilful handling, it is clear that the verdict of history will hold his advisers more responsible than himself, for it was their business to confront him boldly, and turn his timorousness to good account.

But in the last resort it was not the business of some twenty persons only. It was a duty laid upon the nation.

17

And throughout thirty years the flatteries of his subjects—from every class and every circle, in every place and every region, at banquets and burials, on holidays and working-days—were ceaselessly outpoured before this sovereign, and differed only in the degree of their fulsomeness. The sovereign believed them all. "Anyone who can read men's faces—and I think I can. . . ." When he was forty he said that at a banquet in Hanover; and being such a reader of men's faces, he discerned in all of them a genuine devotion. It was like a levee—an interminable levee which went on for thirty years—of Germans defiling before the throne of William the Second, and flattering him by speech or silence so that they might bask in his reflected sunshine.

First came the nobility of the land, outbidding one another in shooting-parties, splendour, and blatant adulation, all for his sovereign pleasure. "When at Rominten Prince Dohna brought word of a good quarry, he would manage to look as if he had come rushing headlong to tell so momentous a piece of news, and was almost breathless with excitement and hurry" (Z. 84). Once he besought the favour of being allowed to put the same sort of bells on his cows that the Emperor's wore at Rominten. When Count Ballestrem delivered the Birthday-speech as President of the Reichstag, he made no admonitory allusion to the Emperor's fresh encroachments—rather he egged him on by saying: "Our Emperor understands the spirit of the age, for has he not said, 'I do not intend to be what is called a constitutional ruler, who reigns but does not govern.' I do not think our Emperor would look kindly on anyone who assigned him that rôle."

The most illustrious were followed by the most immaculate.

When in every sermon [such is the statement of the Court-Marshal] delivered or composed by any Court-Chaplain, and afterwards read by the Emperor, there are never-failing references . . . to the monarch's virtuous way of life, it is only natural that a priggish self-consciousness, not far removed from the most objectionable Pharisaism, should make its appearance. Only those who are acquainted with the private goings-on at Court can really estimate the horrible lip-service paid by these sycophantic chaplains. I have often been absolutely revolted by it (Z. 79).

After one of these "detestably Byzantine sermons," at the opening of the Reichstag in 1907, even Admiral von Müller said that there could be only one opinion as to its unsuitability. Immediately afterwards the Emperor remarked: "I haven't heard so fine a sermon for a long time—it was really excellent" (Z. 179).

Next in the procession of flatterers came the Imperial Chancellor. So early as 1893 Bülow wrote to Eulenburg "I was deeply moved, when I was allowed to kiss his hand and thank him for the graciousness he had shown me." Five years later, he designated him, in a memorial, as *arbiter mundi*. "Bülow is utterly ruining the Emperor," said Ballin. "With his perpetual adulation he is making him overestimate himself beyond all reason" (W. 3, 220).

The Ministers followed in his footsteps. When they were invited to the sovereign's dinner-table, "they would stand in a semicircle before the Emperor, all assuming a more or less military bearing. The Emperor, after his brief welcome, would say a laughing word or two to one or another, now and then asking some question, which would be answered as if on parade. . . . One was reminded of a

Colonel with his non-commissioned officers." When Marschall as Secretary of State presented a report on the Bagdad Railway, which was being constructed by the Deutsche Bank, he called it "Your Most Gracious Majesty's magnificent undertaking." In the year 1904 Waldersee sums up (2, 299): "No matter how severely he condemns persons and political parties, it is all received with compliant smiles and bows. The Ministers are there to obey. What we have is literally a Cabinet-Government, subject to the Emperor's autocratic will. In most instances he simply conveys this to the Ministers through Lucanus."

And hence it was not only their reports to him which dripped with the nectar of *"Allerhöchst"* and *"Alleruntertänigst";* they filled their instructions to their subordinates with these honeyed phrases, because such documents were frequently requisitioned for the Emperor's reading, and he might be angry if there were any shortage of superlatives. In their selection of newspaper-cuttings, which they all, but especially the Foreign Office, had to lay before the Emperor, they took care that he saw nothing unpleasing. Some half-dozen men, on a rough calculation, were supposed to draw the curtains and let in the light; but they opened them only half-way, or a little less, or not at all, and so showed him or withheld from view the events and public temper of the day —always on the principle: "His Majesty requires sunlight."

These cuttings, ranging through decades and prepared in the Home-Ministries, display two or three well-censored political articles, then as many reports of accidents and crimes, then Berlin gossip, then an account of an exhumation, the forgery of a picture, or some new medical discovery; then a description of an Imperial Ceremonial, a Military Tournament, or something else patriotic. The Empress, but not the Emperor, was a regular reader of the *Lokalan-zeiger*—the Emperor would not look at the German newspapers, because in his youth he had come across attacks in *Vorwärts* and *Kladderadatsch*. He confined his newspaper-reading to the *Fürsten-Correspondenz*, which did not belie its title.

Next in the procession came the ambassadors. They would frequently be sent copies of the imperial marginalia, so that from these censorial comments they might learn the master's state of mind; and telegrams would go forth with advice for the drafting of their reports in the imperial sense. Wires flew from Berlin to Rome or Constantinople with the information that a rapturous description of the Emperor's recent visit was looked for by His Majesty. During the Petersburg Revolution of 1905 the Ambassador there waited a week before sending any information whatever, lest the Most High should be alarmed. When a freezing reception in England, such as that in 1899, was got over without any violent unpleasantness, the much-relieved Ambassador reported to Berlin for the imperial eye:

After the numerous expressions of satisfaction, pleasure, indeed delight, which have been imparted to me, I confidently anticipate the best results; and this includes the Royal Family one and all. The personal intercourse with our illustrious sovereign had no less marked an effect on Her Majesty's Ministers. Balfour declared that he had never known a more thrilling experience than that of the hour during which . . . he was under the spell of His Majesty's personality. . . . If His Majesty had appeared in London he would have been assured of the most spontaneous and enthusiastic welcome. Though Press and public were obliged to maintain some reserve, they have in general managed to convey anything but an impression of coolness (A. 10, 422).

When in 1895 there were ambitions for a harbour in China, and the Emperor asked the Ambassador, von Heyking, which one he had in view, the answer was, "I had thought of Amoy." On being asked by Tirpitz why he mentioned a place that he knew nothing about, Heyking replied: "I had to give His Majesty a definite answer." At Washington the Ambassador, Speck von Sternburg, publicly announced that the Emperor's was "not only the most remarkable universal intelligence in the world, but that he was thoroughly modern, and comprehended the spirit of industrialism as well as its technique, while he was equally a master in the plastic arts and music."

Next in the starry procession came the officers, at their head the Generals and Admirals, all with the watchword: Obedience. The Emperor devises "an ideal battleship, impregnably iron-clad, rapid, and armed with torpedo-tubes, which would take the place of the torpedo-boats. . . . The construction of this was attempted. We proceeded in conformity with orders received, and when it was clear that no useful result could possibly be obtained, this production came to be called the Homunculus" (T. 134). After a gala dinner to the Staff the Emperor was told that the older Moltke had been, in reality, no great General—all he had done was to carry out his sovereign's behests. "The remark was meant for the Emperor alone. So who can wonder that he should come to think very little of his Staff!" (W. 2, 208).

At the Imperial Manœuvres, completely contradictory commands to the troops would arrive on an average three times a night. No one dares to point out that this upsets the men, that important dispositions of troops are disturbed, that colossal marches result, and that the commissariat is confronted with great difficulties by reason of the requirements thus created. In the actual encounter modern conditions are ignored, the one aim being to make an imposing display; the staff rides through the firing-line, the artillery follow, and the cavalry attack is as feeble as if they were still armed with flint-locks. Everyone sees this, more or less; but no one dares to say anything—certainly not the Chief, Count Schlieffen.

While no one wants to cut his own throat by venturing on a critical remark, there are on the other hand plenty of highly placed and most aristocratic persons to assure His Majesty that it has all been so interesting, instructive, and generally magnificent. . . . Mute, grave, and expressionless, Count Schlieffen goes about his business of carrying out the Most High's behests. . . . From this absolute silence and implicit connivance . . . it has gradually come to rank imposture. In the parades and marches the squadrons are deftly and unobtrusively strengthened with men who have been kept in readiness unseen. The Emperor thus inevitably acquires the conviction that such an immense force of cavalry will be able to carry out the most colossal demands day after day. In reality, only a few horses are fit, and that only by overworking them, to get through the day's work; the others are changed in the manner indicated above (Z. 97, 42).

But the flatteries of the uniforms went far beyond what mere obedience dictated. At Danzig in the autumn of 1904 General von Mackensen, on being presented to the Emperor at the railway-station, kissed his gloved right hand. Instantly this gallant gesture became the fashion, and in the mess of the Hussars of the Bodyguard a lieutenant, honoured with a behest, kissed the hand of the Most High (Z. 84). An old General, who had been through many wars, publicly celebrated a visit of the Emperor's to Aix with the words: "I have been present on many an historic occasion, but I remember none which excited such great enthusiasm." An officer challenged an editor who had allowed the Emperor's "Sang an Ägir" to be described as the work of a dilettante. When in 1890 the Emperor had given the wrong solution of the Staff's tactical problem, he spoke (by Waldersee's account) "to every officer he met on the promenade in the Tiergarten, trying to gain adherents for his erroneous view. Of course there were some people compassionate enough to agree with him." A military essay presented to the Emperor, on Frederick's defeat at Hochkirch, concluded with "Under Your Majesty's command nothing like this would have happened" (E. 2, 319).

The cities followed on. In every province of the Empire, the railway-stations and town-halls, the barracks and public monuments, were in a state of perpetual decoration, expectant of Their Most Gracious Majesties' arrival; at the Brandenburg Gate, and many another gate, stood the frock-coated Lord Mayors; obelisks and festoons sprang out of the ground in one place to reappear next day in another. In Alsace it had become so much a matter of routine that the holes alongside the pavements for the Venetian masts were left open once for all. The streaming flags, the broad thick garlands of pine-branches, served a double purpose in Alsace, for they concealed from the all-penetrating Hohenzollern eye the flagless houses of the Francophile citizens. The city of Görlitz was not the only one to be deprived of the imperial manœuvres and their benefits to trade, because of a democratic municipality. Hamburg, for a visit of the Emperor's, created an island in the river Alster; and when the cities of Cologne and Crefeld wanted to write their names with a K, and were supported by the opinions of two Professors, the voice of the Most High rang out on a stentorian C, and the tribunal of imperial judgment instantly dismissed the cities' petition on the plea of expense.

The private functionaries followed on. His Dutch-tile

manufactory needed a considerable subvention every year, by reason of its cut prices; but the Emperor was shown the lists of orders, and thus convinced that it did immense business. His Kadinen estate was represented to him as a model of good husbandry. "It's horrible," observed the imperial proprietor, "to see how little the farmers do for their men! Why don't they build them houses, as I do at Kadinen? Then labour would not trend westward as it does"; and he told the English Ambassador that every schoolboy and girl on his estate had saved eight hundred marks "in the course of this last one year." And he was delighted when they told him that he had a cow there which yielded forty litres of milk a day—for "here no one shrinks from pouring more milk into a cow than could by any possibility be milked out of her. . . . Strange," concludes Zedlitz, "that the Emperor must everywhere have someone who deceives him!" (Z. 179).

Friends and intimates duly followed.

The bombast, blatancy, and fulsomeness of this composition [by Lauff] are almost indescribable. The most exalted personages of every way of thinking were disgusted, and said so in private. But of some I have to admit that when His Most High expressed satisfaction with the thing, they instantly abounded in admiration and endorsement of his view. This lightning-change, and above all the shame-faced glance at anyone near by who had heard the directly contrary opinion of a moment earlier, was certainly comic enough in its way (Z. 48).

Eulenburg writes of the Scandinavian trip in 1903:

The contrast between the years and the convulsive merriment of the guests is what I find most painful. These men are without exception persons who have reached high office . . . and they are all utterly worn-out. But they retain sufficient energy to put up a show of gaiety, wit, even talent. . . . It very much disgusts me. I can't stand these Excellencies nowadays—always on bended knee; nor can I stand punning and suchlike from nine o'clock in the morning onwards (E. 2, 303).

The compilers of "Emperor-Books" came next. *The Emperor and Our Boys: What the Emperor's Speeches teach our German Boys* appeared in 1905 with two prefaces. From that by a Court-Chaplain: "There are men whose words are their deeds, and among these we all reckon our Emperor. . . . His words stand for deeds . . . they exhale a profoundly practical knowledge of life." From the editor's preface:

Fervent thanks are due to the Almighty for having given us an Emperor impervious to the wiles of flattery or base servility; one to whom the teacher, conscious of his sacred task and earnest in fulfilment of it, gladly points as an august example. . . . The lofty, one might say the religious, sense of duty and responsibility, the tireless zeal and unremitting diligence, the glad recognition of the services of others, the amazing energy displayed in mastering every kind of subject-matter—all this, combined with the magic spell of an irresistible personality, forms a whole of such arresting authority that no German youth can be unaffected by its ennobling influence.

When a clever Frenchman, the artist Grand-Carteret, realized all this, he resolved to get his caricatures into Germany and wrote an open letter, in which the Emperor was thus made game of:

As Napoleon once was for the whole world, so Your Majesty is now—simply "the Emperor." All is said—you are Caesar. . . . The gaze of Europe is now directed ceaselessly to the banks of the Spree. You are the idol, the Jove of our age. . . . The world rings with your slightest utterance. . . . Utter then, O Your Majesty, the behest which will bestow on caricaturists that emancipation which the world awaits from you!

Being a reader of men's thoughts, he uttered the behest; and the foreigner's book appeared in Germany, while German truth-tellers were expiating their audacity in fortresses and prisons.

Among the artists came next in order the manufacturers of Hohenzollern pieces—imperial portraits, allegories, poems—all of whom deferred to the genius of His Serene Highness in the matters of tone and colouring, the construction either of cathedral or drama—the record in this group being held by the architect of the church built in memory of the Emperor William I. An architect's drawing-mark (two intersecting semicircles) which in the original plan made the cross on the church-spire look as if it were surmounted by a star, and on that account greatly delighted the Emperor, naturally was missing when the building was carried out in stone. The Emperor observed its absence and was much annoyed, for it was precisely the redundance of cross and star together which had fascinated him. Herr Schwechter, who had designed the church, was too servile to explain, so were the clergy; and thus for twenty years a "morning-star" in iron gleamed above the cross.

The men of the middle-class who had business connections with the Court followed on.

However independent they may actually be, they all turn courtiers in the Emperor's presence; and many of them soon get even worse than those who are more inured to the atmosphere. If there is any question of serious displeasure they make as little show of their real convictions as any of the others (Z. 62).

Slaby, a prominent physician, "now, alas! passes all bounds in his flatteries and lip-service." He pointed out to the Emperor how in the end he had always triumphed over his opponents. "Yes, that is true," was what the Emperor answered. "My subjects should always do what I tell them; but they *will* think for themselves, and that's what makes all the trouble" (Z. in the autumn of 1904).

They were all in the procession of flatterers—every one of the independent spirits who never once told the Emperor the truth that they afterwards wrote down for their own satisfaction: Ihne, Harnack, and Delitsch, Helferrich and Krupp, Dörpfeld and Bode, Kopp and Faulhaber, Tschudi and Begas, the younger and sometimes even the elder Rathenau; while the renowned scholar, Deussen, in his speech to the Emperor in 1891 expressed the conviction "that the Emperor will lead us from Goethe to Homer and Sophocles, and from Kant to Plato." Even Lamprecht, Germany's leading historian, doubly answerable for truth, broke out into the following ludicrous dithyrambs so early as 1912, in a peroration of the phenomenon presented by William the Second.

His is a personality of primitive potency, of irresistible authority, for which . . . the whole domain of emotion and experience is perpetually opened anew, as for the soul of a creative artist. . . . Self-reliance, fixity of purpose, ever directed to the loftiest aims—these are the distinguishing marks of the Imperial personality.

But the procession of bent backs and eyes that would not see—what figures hover lightly round it, whose are these airy forms, some with cymbals, some softly beating on the drum, that creep through keyholes, float through windows, hindered by no Master of the Ceremonies? They are the Press of the Emperor and his creatures. In *their* faces he can read, when the raptured procession is over, "the sentiments of the people"—smiling, he can say to the President of the

Upper House: "It's extraordinary! They go wild about me everywhere! Oh, I know very well what is said and thought of me among the people!" And while the newspaper-cuttings drop from his fingers, the eyes that for so long have gazed unwearied on the glitter and the genuflexions close in dreams at last, and once again he sees them pass before him: the Princes and Generals, Chaplains and Professors, Ambassadors and Ministers, manufacturers and architects, Lord Mayors and artists, Cardinals and Jews, intimates and acquaintances—all enraptured, all full-filled with gratitude and praise.

Of one class—one only—he has never read the face in that procession. The working-man did not present himself. He was not qualified to come to Court.

CHAPTER VI

CATASTROPHES

1   1906–1909

THE coils woven of distrust and jealousy which the three rulers of Germany had cast around each other and the Emperor, were inevitably rent asunder at long last. Holstein and Eulenburg, in their widely separated spheres of hermit and courtier, were at once linked and alienated by the bonds of mutual interest and mutual hatred. Each wanted to get the better of the other; and as Holstein never met the Emperor at all, and Eulenburg no longer met him as his only friend, both courted the third party, who possessed high office and responsibility, and hence was always at the sovereign's side. Bülow stood between the pair, and was intent on freeing himself from their shackles.

He had the advantage of both in coolness of head. For while Eulenburg was aglow with a soulful exotic ardour for his friend, and Holstein with the craftsman's passionate absorption in the conflicting interests of European Powers, Bülow was moved by no other motive than to avert the lowering dangers conjured up by his master's temperament for as long as might be. He was more single-minded in the application of his energy and cynicism than were his two overburdened friends.

Bülow, on whom in the summer of 1905 after his greatest mistake—Morocco—the title of Prince had been conferred, could cherish only one personal desire at this zenith of his power. That was to isolate his two rivals from the Foreign Office and the Emperor, thus subduing office and Emperor, and with them the direction of affairs, to his sole influence. To this end, two months after receiving the princely title, he proffered his resignation on the Russian Treaty, and reckoned himself certain of the upper hand after that collapse of the whimpering Emperor. He had formerly supported Holstein in removing Eulenburg, though by almost undiscoverable methods; and now he helped Eulenburg in like manner to pave the way for Holstein's downfall—on neither occasion as initiator or even really as intriguer, but merely obeying his nature as an adventurer who takes the first path Heaven points him to.

But Heaven had ordained that first Eulenburg should be partly undone by Holstein, then Holstein wholly by Eulenburg and Bülow, then Eulenburg wholly by Holstein, then the Emperor partly by Bülow, and finally Bülow for good and all by the Emperor. Of this comedy the German people knew nothing, while their good angel stood mourning over the scene of ruin. The whole piece took three years in performance—from 1906 to 1909—first in strict privacy, then in an all too blazing publicity.

The origins dated far back. The conflict about Goluchowski, whom Holstein's wounded vanity caused him to detest, had completely alienated him from Eulenburg, who as Ambassador in Vienna considered himself to be protecting the Empire against Holstein, and wrote: "On Goluchowski, Frau Schratt, and me the whole Triplice depends at this moment." Holstein, for his part, showed the Austrian Ambassador in Berlin, who was at variance with his chief Goluchowski, the Emperor's hostile marginalia on this latter, so that they might be reported to Vienna. By doing this he committed high treason, being guilty of the communication of secrets of State to a foreign power. In the New Year of 1899 the final letters were exchanged between the whilom friends:

"Greetings and best wishes from the bottom of my heart," were sent by Eulenburg to Holstein in an astute composition which, with the object of re-attaching him and so strengthening his own position, concluded on the equivocal words: "We have put through so many stiff jobs together . . . we have been so to speak roasted and stewed by the same fire! . . . The older one grows, the more one clings to familiar conditions." In his startlingly ironic answer Holstein regretted

that you didn't drive out to Semmering and enjoy yourself there. . . . So we bide our time, and drink each other's health in something or other—tea for choice! I hope that the frost prophesied by Falb will assist you and your family to a more cheerful view of life—in so far as that is not yours at present. With heartfelt greetings, Holstein.

These heartfelt greetings were the last deceptions practised on Eulenburg. It was with such supercilious malignancy that Holstein closed a correspondence of twelve years; the next letter he answered not at all, and was "not at home" to Eulenburg in Berlin. A year later he had, for all that, to see Eulenburg made a prince and thereby established in his position at Vienna; but he did not lose heart and contrived, on the pretext of important matters of State, to induce Bülow to put the first official affront upon his bosom friend. A sharply worded minute of March 1900 to Eulenburg, disapproving his policy, was signed by Bülow; and we can well understand Eulenburg's bitter comment: "That Bülow should lend himself to this dangerous folly is proof of his subjection to Holstein. I am beside myself at the picture thus suddenly disclosed to view!"

But when in the course of the same year Holstein set his creatures writing against the German Ambassador in Vienna, Bülow managed to keep in with Eulenburg, though he was simultaneously sworn to Holstein. For a period he resembled a man who by undiminished tenderness obliges his old mistress to accept his new one, and affects to hear both their complaints with gentle sympathy. "When I think," wrote Eulenburg, "that I never did Holstein anything but good, interceded for him, helped him whenever I could, and suffered a lot on his behalf—and now this enmity, this hatred!" In reality he had feared Holstein, helped him only when it helped himself as well, and never once suffered for him. His deceptiveness was turning, to his own hurt, into self-deception.

If at this time Holstein had the upper hand of Bülow, Bülow on his side had subjugated the Emperor, and while swimming in these somewhat turbid waters likewise played the distant Eulenburg on a long line. "Don't be so easily intimidated," he wrote in March 1902; "don't lose your nerve. . . . I often think of Achilles, whom our sovereign greatly resembles, and of whom Homer says: 'His glory-loving heart knows neither fear nor retreat.' " Bülow's effrontery in offering this fustian to Eulenburg is accentuated by the latter's reply: "I assume that in your Achilles-comparison you were not thinking of the hero's heel."

Meanwhile his friend in Berlin was holding the new Achilles in a net of flattery; he even succeeded in eclipsing their common friend in the Emperor's esteem, and paving the way for his retirement. Without touching on politics, he felt safe in saying in his next letter to Vienna that Eulenburg ought to take more care of himself, "so as to ensure many more years of life in which to utilize your brilliant talents in the way that makes you really happy."

What? Can it be only nine years ago that Bülow, not yet admitted to the Holy of Holies, warbled that flute-like strain about their sister-souls to the new moon—and now his friend is to utilize his brilliant talents outside the temple whose doors he had opened to the writer! Bitter moments, those, for the king-maker, reading such counsels from his creature's hand. But Eulenburg knew how to score the dirge of his so plainly desired resignation for the ears of the Court. His climax swelled:

> The state of my health is lamentable—that is the simple truth. I am completely worn-out by ten years of terribly exacting labour with our dear sovereign. . . . My doctor told me lately that if I didn't follow his advice, in a few years I should be a dead man. If I were to take this step, I might possibly be spared a while to my family.

(Despite his terrible experiences, still in the future, he lived for twenty years after this period.)

In May the bosom friends spoke out at last; and Bülow said: "The Prussian genius is hard and ruthless: subtle natures like yours . . . are not attuned to it." In reality it was not a question either of Prussian ruthlessness or a subtle nature, but of a sapient Chancellor who watched his neurasthenic sovereign like a family-physician. Eulenburg, who had known all about the case for fifteen years, is wellnigh touching when after this plain speaking he writes to Friend Bernhard, not yet quite worn-out by toil: "I will not be a burden on your friendship, and indeed I am no longer fit to endure the everlasting see-saw between dark moods and suspicions, friendliness and fine phrases." Only the Emperor's friendship and a lucky turn of events could have bridged the gulf; but now he felt

that in the light of my resolve, high office, politics, society . . . are losing hold on me, and yielding place to my music, my tranquil Liebenberg, the restoration to my family—all like words from heaven in my ears. To how few does God grant such a rebirth— the possibility of return to one's true individuality!

Nowhere does Eulenburg so strongly move us to sympathy as here, when he seems to resign himself. All our compassion is his; after those fifteen troubled years we heartily wish him a serene old age with his music and his verses, refraining from any inquiry as to their quality. And still more when in the summer he lays down his offices of State; and breaks out, to Bülow, in a disavowal of all bitterness, "for at my beloved Emperor's side I see the only possible man—and round your head there floats and waves the mysterious veil of your appointed destiny. May God immerse it in the flowing river of his bounty!"

True, that round Bülow's head there floated, not at all mysteriously, only the zephyrs of party-feeling and the ventilating breezes of the Press; nor would a veil immersed in rivers of God's bounty do much waving—but if everything else were in order, if the favourite had really been wise enough to withdraw in good time to art and oblivion, our respect and sympathy would have followed him to his retreat. But it was all histrionic—a courtier and a favourite he could not voluntarily cease to be; and that was to prove his destruction. In truly prophetic words Eulenburg wrote to Bülow about this time, five whole years before his catastrophe, in such imploring agony as only he can give expression to who has a baneful secret to conceal:

I know I can rely on you this once more. . . . That the Prussian country-gentry and my friends will anyhow empty yet another bucketful of poison and filth on the head of a broken, dying man I have no doubt whatever. . . . Your friendly succour will not fail me in that hour—I know you too well to question that.

Words of foreboding, words of supplication—instinct with anguished doubt of that friendly succour.

2

But Holstein the Destroyer was not long to enjoy the half-accomplished ruin of the king-maker. Eulenburg's intimacy with the Emperor was a guarantee for his continued favour, even though—possibly because—he no longer held high office; while Holstein's aloofness threatened him with complete extinction when once he should retire from affairs. And now at last the storm was gathering round his head also.

Morocco—that had been Holstein's great idea; and when with Bülow's help he had forced the Emperor to make the landing in Tangier, he had felt himself to be master of Europe. True, he by no means desired war—which might have destroyed, and at the best would have interrupted, his machinations; he merely wanted to uphold German prestige; that is to say, he reiterated the catch-word of "national honour," which in his view would have suffered by a reasonable discussion of Colonial questions. But abroad it was inevitably believed that Germany was picking a quarrel with France, at the moment when Russia's hands were full in Asia; and when the diplomats arrived in April with inquiries as to the aim of the imperial landing and oration, Holstein and Bülow gave instructions to "play the Sphinx." To humiliate the French—that was the aim; Bülow, with this end in view, went so far as to suppress an offer from Paris for an amicable discussion of all Colonial questions at the Conference, for the Emperor's pacific inclinations made him uneasy.

In his den sat Holstein, watching over his potions. He had influence enough as Privy Councillor to insist upon a deliberation with the military and naval authorities, in the hope of gaining their suffrage; and while the Secretary of State was speaking against Holstein, Bülow sat in obligatory silence. When, in the spring of 1904, Delcassé said to Prince Lichnowsky that a pacific understanding about Morocco was desirable for France, and summed up the entire problem in the phrase: *"Lâchez l'Autriche, et nous lâcherons la Russie,"* Holstein was so incensed by Lichnowsky's despatch that he caused it to disappear—at any rate it is not to be found among the documents. Holstein regarded anything done in opposition to him, or even apart from him, as reprehensible.

About this time Bülow at last began to withdraw from him. As Bülow's friendship with Eulenburg still subsisted at that date, it is as certain that Eulenburg was hand-in-glove with him as that Eulenburg's influence against the common enemy Holstein was used to the utmost. Bülow himself, after his seven years of predominance in affairs, had no more use for Holstein; and being prone to quotations from *Faust,* may now have said to himself of the one-time indispensable: *"Was kannst du, armer Teufel, geben!"* (Poor devil, what more can you give me!) Sometimes he had prevailed against Holstein, but he still was given to declaring "that it was hell" (E. 2, 380). Moreover Holstein's down-fall could only enhance Eulenburg's still powerful influence with the Emperor—so Bülow decided on ejecting the alchemist.

But with the most exquisite precautions! If Bismarck himself had not dared to get rid of him "lest he should blab in foreign parts," how much more must Bülow have feared him, being—according to that dark saying of Eulenburg's —personally to some extent in his power. What Bülow now succeeded in—the achievement of ruining Holstein, and yet retaining him as a friend—is his masterpiece, enough in itself to rank him high among diplomatists.

A pretext was soon found—attaching itself to the person of the then Secretary of State, von Richthofen, whose removal from office Holstein after various intrigues had vainly demanded of Bülow. Upon Bülow's refusal Holstein tendered his resignation for the dozenth time. But on this occasion he also wrote to Hammann (*Bilder aus der letzten Kaiserzeit*, 29) in a most astounding strain, of course for Bülow's eyes:

For more than a quarter of a century I have sat in my office, never gone to Court, and never asked to play any prominent part in affairs. . . . During this period numberless exacting tasks have been carried out by me, which one might have supposed would have led the Emperor to regard me as a useful member of the Foreign Office Staff. But what became of all my . . . memoranda? It was only very exceptionally and very rarely that any one of them reached the Emperor's eyes as confidential minutes . . . the majority went straight to the Archives. It is no wonder that the Emperor seems to have come to the settled conviction that this unproductive Ministry is in a state of ossification. . . . The acceptance [of my proffered resignation] is a matter-of-course in the prevailing circumstances. as are the attacks and dishonouring conjectures which will be directed upon me from notoriously hostile quarters. I shall defend myself to the utmost, with all the means I have at my disposal. No personal considerations need now deter me. . . . The prestige of Germany has been destroyed in recent years, and our enemies are at present occupied in forming a ring against us. Complicated situations will arise, for which I would rather not assume the degree of moral responsibility attaching to every active functionary—therefore I prefer to bid you Farewell.

Here is the complete Holstein. After having persistently shunned the light of day, he complains of inadequate recognition from the Emperor he despised; because for once he is not able to get rid of an uncongenial Chief, he not only offers to resign but turns his official letter into a farce by his unveiled menaces, wherein he—the super-blackmailer— threatens to reveal secrets about highly placed personages, and addresses these threats not even to those concerned but to a third person; at the same time once for all declining any responsibility for the consequences of his own decisive steps. In these letters the German people can read not only the character but the modes of thought and action of that Baron von Holstein who for fifteen years so deeply affected the destinies of the Empire.

Bülow's retort was masterly. He wrote to Hammann:

Since Bismarck's dismissal there has been nothing—from the non-renewal of the Russian Treaty and the Far Eastern Triplice to the handling of the Morocco question; from the so-called Urias Letter to Vienna to the publication of the Swinemünde Telegram; from the coolness with England in 1896 to the differences of opinion with her about Shanghai—nothing of any importance in our Foreign Office procedure which was not advised by Holstein.

By the compilation of this catalogue, which is a summary of Germany's foreign policy from 1890 to 1904, Bülow may be said to have clutched at the coat-tails of the evasive Privy Councillor, while seeking to exonerate himself. The resignation was not accepted; but Bülow left the letter unanswered, so that it might hang over Holstein's grizzled head. After the holidays the Privy Councillor reappeared in the Foreign Office, resumed work and intercourse as before, and believed that all was well—for he felt sure of his ground.

His eccentricities were extravagant in the succeeding year. While Bülow was working for agreement in Morocco, Holstein was setting the Press by the ears and promulgating his so-called Hostage-Theory, according to which the French would be German hostages in a war with England. As this increased the tension with Bülow and Hammann, editor-in-chief of Bülow's Press, Holstein tried to insure himself officially against the future—played the house-tyrant pure and simple, and at the end of his career for the first time transgressed the inmost law of his being. For in the New Year of 1906 he demanded, with fresh threats of resignation, his immediate appointment to be Director of the Political Department, with control of the Press-service.

Bülow, who was ill in bed, refused to grant this comptrollership; but Holstein wheedled it out of him by promises of unswerving support. The next day Bülow said to Hammann: "I perfectly understand your moral prejudices against that blackmailer. When the Conference is over I will get rid of him, but I must keep him on now, for he might seriously injure the national interests by getting up wrangles in the Press" (Hammann, *Bilder*, 36). But when the question was to be brought before the Reichstag and a "Holstein-Debate" seemed imminent, by which the nation would for the first time have learnt something of their most influential official, Holstein's horror of the light of day once more prevailed over his autocratic inclinations, and he withdrew his demand.

The couple were still pulling along despite this disintegration of friendly feelings and common purposes and motives, when Bülow received information from Paris that France was prepared to fight if things went on as they were. His energy was now put to the test, and it magnificently answered. That March of 1906 gives us the measure of what he could have achieved in the July of 1914. From one day to another he wrested the documents of the Conference, which for months had been dominated by Holstein, from the omnipotent wizard's hands, fell upon them himself, and worked day and night to liquidate the Conference and clear up the threatening situation. That month of March, in which he displayed the full force of his capacity, was harassed throughout by the daily conflict with Holstein, still in office and still unestranged, due for dismissal not to-day, but to-morrow; and Holstein's letters and threats of resignation must, as Hammann writes, have completely broken down the Chancellor's nerves.

At last, in the beginning of April, the Conference came to an end. The Entente had been put to the initial test at Algeciras, and was now a settled thing. Germany had lost at the Conference, but it was declared to have been a great success; and on the fifth the Chancellor was to lay the results before the Reichstag. Now was the moment for getting rid of the Unbearable. His last resignation was still in Bülow's desk, the Emperor was forewarned, and on the morning of that session Tschirschky, the new Secretary of State (violently objected to as such by Holstein), carried the latter's offer of resignation to the sovereign "by order of the Chancellor." The Emperor countersigned. Instantly Bülow informed Hammann that the Emperor had "gladly acquiesced in the resignation" (Hammann, *Vorgeschichte,* 151). Then he betook himself to the Reichstag, and half the Foreign Office followed him—it was to be a Grand Field-day.

Holstein sat solitary in his den, unwitting of the event. After wellnigh thirty years of strenuous activity he sat there for the last of days that day, a retired Privy Councillor with a pension and an Order. To-morrow and henceforth the flood-gates might be closed or opened—his hand would not be upon the levers. Maybe he felt uneasy. These last weeks had not left much doubt that he would have to go—and now to whom should he most usefully complain? Who was the most powerful of his friends? Was it not the English Ambassador? And while his Moroccan policy was being criticized in the Reichstag, and nothing (he knew) was to be looked for from Bülow's sapient lips but a speciously glittering obituary, the destroyer summoned the Englishman to his presence, told him of all the internal intrigues, and never reflected that his listener would not only write all home next day, but would recount the entire interview to the Secretary of State. So profound was Holstein's knowledge of human nature.

In that very hour, while Bebel was setting forth his indictment, the Chancellor suddenly fainted dead away in the Reichstag.

This fainting-fit was one of Bülow's happiest accidents—and inspirations. Of course his nerves and brain were overwrought, of course it was no put-up job; but that just then, in full tide of debate before a crowded House and galleries, precisely as the criticism took its most critical turn, this distressing accident should have come to pass, and not an hour sooner or later . . . that he should have demonstrated so publicly how much he was the victim of his zealous labour, literally broken-down at last—this is proof of such a sense of situation as could permeate not only the Governmental, but the nervous, system. Such subtlety of perception is rare even among diplomatists—among William the Second's diplomatists existent in none but Bülow.

For when next day that swoon became known to the public, not only were millions of unpolitical Germans led to look more kindly on the results of the Morocco policy, but even Holstein was obliged to believe Bülow guiltless of having let him go. His first thought on receiving news of the mishap by telephone had been: "This may lead to his retirement. Another Chancellor may be more submissive to me; in any event I must get back the old offer of resignation." But he was six hours too late. When he learnt next morning that he was relieved of office, Holstein stood incredulous before the incredible sheet of paper. When had the dastardly deed been perpetrated? A soothing falsehood was allowed to leak out: Tschirschky had fished out the letter while Bülow lay helpless, and had taken the responsibility of getting the Emperor to sign it. And Tschirschky *was* Holstein's chief. . . .

But Bülow came out of his swoon with a smile on his lips. How easily he could now insist upon his innocence to his old friend! Had he not been prostrate, victim of his zeal? How should he, how *could* he—? And as he dreaded Holstein's enmity and needed his practical advice, he left his relegated friend to ponder mutely over the question whether he would not prefer to retain some indirect influence in affairs and incidentally Bülow's friendship, to the execution of a revenge whose consequences were uncertain.

Holstein, always averse from any show of power, must have felt in his heart that the desire to continue on the lines of his former activity would prevail. If Bülow's share in his downfall was imponderable, Holstein's share in Bülow's decisions would be ponderable enough—so it would be well to say nothing about the former that he might retain the latter. And besides, a revengeful man needs one victim—not two; and one was ready to his hand. How very promptly Holstein, once suspicious, could change sides, we have seen in the instance of Marschall and Bülow. Now he clung to Bülow, to whom he had sworn allegiance nine years before over a glass of wine with Eulenburg; but on Eulenburg he directed the full force of his hatred and vindictiveness, and did not hesitate (nor was entirely unjustified) in stigmatizing this friend—long since estranged—as his mortal enemy, who had paved the way for his downfall with the Emperor.

When they had thus defined their positions Bülow, victorious and undespoiled, was master of the field; Holstein was officially defeated but indemnified by influence to come; the only one to lose—lose all—was Eulenburg. His doom was sealed.

3

Ever since his young days as attaché, Eulenburg had complained in his diary and to his friends that politics came between him and his art, and said that only for his beloved Emperor could he have made such a sacrifice. When he retired after twenty years' service to the Empire, he depicted himself as seriously ill and caring little for recovery unless, removed from all the turmoil of a heartless world, he might live for his muse and his dearly loved family in tranquil Liebenberg. But no sooner was he restored to private life than he seemed all agog to place himself again at the Emperor's disposal, "so as to spare him any disappointment." He was with him during June 1903 in Norway, in September at Rominten, and received him as a guest at his own castle in the following November. In this and the immediately succeeding years he was the only diplomatist in the Emperor's entourage, and as such played a decisive part in the imperial counsels. Just as in his younger days, he conveyed the sovereign's wishes to the Foreign Office from yacht or shooting-butt, and saw him every autumn from 1903 to 1906 at Liebenberg, where on every occasion important questions came up for decision.

As the favourite pure and simple, he now used his unofficial influence almost exclusively in personal matters. Not that there were many old friends left to place. Most of them were already in the highest offices of State, and the new ones were not of courtly complexion; so it became chiefly a question of displacing. Why not, then, take a hand in deposing a slippery friend whom one had assisted to his throne ten years before? At any rate, Bülow felt himself to be menaced, felt that Eulenburg desired his downfall. And how should he not have been suspicious, when—still addressed as "dearest Bernhard"—he found in Eulenburg's letters from Rominten hints of the Emperor's disapproval of his policy, and read in that familiar writing how the Emperor had said: "If Bülow really puts his back into this business, it will show that he's still what he was"? And Eulenburg went on to say: "One thing is certain—he knows of absolutely no one that he could put in your place. I'm convinced of that, by the way he speaks of you in spite of this displeasure."

"Still what I was?" thought Bülow, and wondered only

if Emperor and Eulenburg were still what *they* had been. When later on he read in the Press of the Liebenberg camarilla, he said no word in the Reichstag to repudiate its existence, but merely one of warning—that this poisonous foreign weed had never been planted in German soil without great injury to prince and people.

The Morocco affair had drawn Eulenburg again into the sphere of high politics. One of his friends, who was on the secret list of the Berlin police as a pervert (Treskow, *von Fürsten und anderen Sterblichen,* 152), the Councillor to the Embassy, Lecomte, had been deeply initiated by his familiar circle into political conditions—that is, so far as his friends themselves were; and to him at the Foreign Office in Paris went Eulenburg's information as to the Emperor's pacific tendency. This was designed to discredit the Holstein mischief-making; and Lecomte was transferred to Berlin in the autumn of 1905, that he might be nearer to the source of information.

In the thirty years before the World War there was a rhythmic alternation of anxieties and menaces between all the great Powers; it was as the alternation of day and night in the two hemispheres—when one was in light, the other was in darkness. And so in this Morocco crisis, the declaration of a single Power: "The ruler of the State is in fact peacefully inclined," was enough to avert an immediate collision. In that respect, Eulenburg's influence was indubitably a thing to be thankful for. As Holstein, who had insistently maintained the contrary, saw that his influence must inevitably be destroyed by this pacific policy, it added a keener edge to his desire for revenge when the hour of his retirement sounded. Had he not always kept his hand in at assassinations? Now was the moment for the expert to bring down the amateur;

now, in their sixties, the two friends were ripe for mutual slaughter. It was only a question of pluck, and that neither of them had yet had an occasion to display.

Neither the misanthrope nor the dilettante had ever welcomed such occasions. Holstein was risking nothing when immediately after his fall he despatched to Eulenburg on 1st May 1906 an unspeakable letter: ". . . After many years, you have attained your end—my removal from office. And the base attacks upon me ought to be equally to your liking. . . . For certain reasons, it is undoubtedly dangerous to have anything to do with you." Eulenburg reads this; hurries to Berlin, selects Varnbüler as a dashing second, they hold hurried counsel—it is to be exchange of shots till disablement or death. The Foreign Office is informed; Bülow is still lucky enough to be ill; Tschirschky sinks on a chair and foresees "one of the greatest scandals the world has ever known." The letter, of which only the above-cited words have hitherto been made public, was in the opinion of Baron von Reischach, who was consulted, "Such as I have never before read the like of—full of the most vulgar insults. It threatened to make public the Prince's obliquities if he ever again attempted to obtain an official position."

Reischach inquired: "Will the Prince defy the worst consequences, and fight?" Varnbüler's answer was: "Anyhow, we must get him up as a hero."

These words from his friend and champion go some way to explain a protocol, signed by Holstein that same afternoon: "Prince zu Eulenburg having assured me, on his word of honour, that he had neither hand nor part in my dismissal, and has been in no way concerned in any of the attacks made upon me in the Press, I hereby withdraw the offensive remarks I made upon him in my letter."

The more decidedly one deprecates the duel as the mere "cannibal-courage" of Napoleon's derision, the more ludicrous must appear the offer and the acceptance of this explanation in an affair between two aristocratic officers and Excellencies, of whom the one insulted was Prince, Ambassador, and Guardsman. It was the disavowal of a private code of honour which these very men and their fellows preached incessantly at the expense of peace-loving communities. Such insults as these would justify a war of annihilation, if regarded from the usual international standpoint—yet we see them suffered by a Prince and unretracted by a Baron, so that before the sun went down on his wrath, as the cliché has it, the Prince's honour might be whitewashed by a purely farcical "explanation."

But not yet was the revengeful Baron appeased.

For immediately afterwards Eulenburg received the Black Eagle as the one favour still owed him by his imperial friend. It was the last he ever was to have. He received it ostensibly as acknowledgment for a pretentious book about the Hohenzollerns which was on sale, with a preface by Eulenburg, in the format of a Romish mass-book, including a desk to read it on. In point of fact the Order was conferred for his services in the Morocco Peace, which could not, since he was now a private individual, be officially acknowledged. But when Holstein saw that, despite the mud-slinging, his enemy was still so secure in the imperial favour—he who had promised away nothing, and now was being given everything—his next step was to say and write to as many people as he could think of that Prince Eulenburg, Knight of the Black Eagle, had been called to his face a despicable person, and had not resented it. Court and Society were soon talking of the affair, but nothing actually happened.

Then Holstein, who despite his shrewdness had little force of intellect, hit upon the expedient of seeking force of intellect elsewhere.

He found it in Harden, who had long opposed Holstein's influence, but in the Morocco affair had approved his aggressive policy, and besides had been attacking the camarilla in every form for twenty years. Harden, indeed, was better acquainted with matters of the Court than Holstein was, and may possibly now have received a few first-hand data or documents from the alchemist's kitchen as confirmation of his attacks—but these would not have been the first.

At the end of the year Harden opened the campaign in his newspaper—at first by dark hints comprehensible only to the initiated. So the group in question were alone in pricking up their ears, and they turned pale indeed when they found themselves called by the intimate names used in strictest privacy by Eulenburg and Kuno Moltke, Town-Commandant of Berlin, and their friends. Eulenburg was the most terrified of all. The very first article, a purely political one, which appeared under Holstein's auspices in the *Zukunft*, left him in no doubt of the doom now hanging over him. "The campaign concocted between Holstein and Harden opens a most disturbing vista. I see in this not only revenge but something far graver, and cannot conceal my anxiety." So strong was his consciousness of being, certainly not a criminal, but a man punishable by a reactionary law as a pervert. He at once left the country, and caused Harden to be requested to discontinue the attacks. Harden promised silence if Eulenburg's political influence came to an end, thus demonstrating that he was working for a cause, and not, like Holstein, pursuing a victim. At Court everyone was overjoyed and excited—at last he was to go under, the eternal favourite! Only his friends knew that the situation could be saved by his accepting political oblivion.

And now Eulenburg took such a false step as reflects upon his powers of perception. Swiftly and completely he had realized Holstein's implacable enmity, and the means that would be taken to gratify it; as completely he now went wrong in estimating the degree of William's affection for him. He knew that his enemies held proofs of his guilt, and reckoned both the personal and the political opponent as inexorable; so that his return, after only a few weeks of self-banishment and without any official necessity, to the Emperor's side at Wiesbaden—posing as a pronounced invalid who was independent of office and henceforth devoted to art alone—can only be explained, when taken together with his manipulation of the Press, as the action of one who had disastrously miscalculated the Emperor's capacity for friendship. Eulenburg, who in this dilemma as in that with Holstein, had no desire to fight, was confronted in the New Year of 1907 with the choice of a final renunciation of politics and Emperor, or reliance on the loyalty of his lifelong friend. He chose reliance, and he lost the game.

For instantly the attacks increased in violence. The group of friends were soon designated, not by enigmatic pet-names, but by their actual titles; at home and abroad the scandal swelled, and now at last the Emperor's subjects learned what manner of men had been the anonymous rulers of their ruler. Of offences against the penal law, such as Holstein's letter to his foe had cast in his teeth with immunity, nothing was said; for, as a politician, Harden had no desire to go beyond the psychical effects of abnormal susceptibilities—he had not the least intention of opening up the question of infraction of a penal law which every doctor

held in derision. From the *Zukunft* the public learnt only
the same kind of thing as Bismarck had said of Eulenburg
and his group: "Effeminate natures, transcendentalists,
visionaries, phrase-mongers—particularly dangerous for the
Emperor's temperament." Everyone in the country, no one
at the Court, was amazed; nor did anyone at Court come forward in defence of men whose failings were known to be cor-
rectly set forth. Yet not a single one of them dared tell the
Emperor. It was not until May that the Crown-Prince
brought him the articles, and information as to their effect.

Was the Emperor, in truth, the only one at Court to be
surprised? A few years before this the Criminal-Inspector,
von Meerscheidt-Hüllessem, had bequeathed him a sealed
packet in which, as an enclosure stated, he would find a
card-index, ranging over decades, of the names of over a
hundred homo-sexuals belonging to the highest circles, together with the documents in proof—a most momentous
legacy from a police-official to his sovereign. But when Lucanus delivered the packet and the Emperor had read the
covering letter, he left the seal unbroken and merely said
abruptly: "Police-business. Send the packet to the Chief
Inspector" (Von Treskow, p. 115; who then received it). It
was thus that the neurasthenic avoided knowledge which
would, he divined, prove a trial to his feelings—and it is testimony to both his cowardice and his folly. For that knowledge would have enabled him to purge his Court *sub silen-
tio;* there would have been no Press reports, no scandals, for
all the aristocratic names which were afterwards compromised appeared—with the spies and blackmailers involved—
upon that unread list.

But in the last analysis, of what was the Court to be
purged? The Emperor was not ignorant of any phase in

the interrelated phases of perverted practices and unnatural tendencies. One Prince had been banished from Court, another had become a favourite there—simply because the one was at the end, the other at the beginning, of a long psychical development towards abnormal sexuality. And, moreover, is it conceivable that with his susceptible nerves the Emperor, after twenty years' experience, was unaware in what respect the men of his choice differed from those of his antipathy? Is it conceivable that he could not account for the difference between Eulenburg's languishing grace and Kiderlen's angular sturdiness, between the elegance of Kuno Moltke and the virility of Tirpitz, or that he should not have perceived that between a crudely perverted Colonel and a subtly abnormal artist there runs a devious path whereon no woman sets her foot? Had not Eulenburg often handed him those letters to read, in which the friends called one another "Beloved Phili, dearest Kuno," and sang the praises of friendship in sweetly plaintive tones?

But if it is certain that he must have divined these relationships, it is no less certain that he chose to overlook them. Of such packets he did not break the seal. And now his own son brings him an unsealed one. What! Before his Guards, his subjects, before King Edward and the Tsar, is *he,* the greatest gasconader of them all, to stand as the friend of effeminates? Has he fought down the secret consequences of his outward infirmity throughout his life only to be unmasked at fifty as the associate of ephebes with whom he has never had anything whatever to do? Because a man sings beautifully, must he necessarily be unclean? Better lose a battle than the campaign of a life-time!

And speedily he acts. Friedheim of the Police is summoned; he will know all about it (Von Treskow, 164). "This

Harden is a damned scoundrel," says the Emperor. "But he would not dare make these attacks if he had not the material to go on. Bring me your Secret List." Next day he reads a part of the "material" he had shunned in other days; and there is very much more to be read there than ever came out in the *Zukunft*. In the evening he says to Bethmann Hollweg, whom he sends for as Home-Minister: "It has come to my knowledge that Eulenburg, Hohenau, Kuno Moltke, are perverts. I have no further use for them." Then to Zedlitz: "This must be made a moral example of before all the world, and without any consideration of persons."

No one is happier on this day than Count Hülsen-Haeseler, whom Eulenburg had of yore removed from Vienna by means of a malignant report; and who, lately appointed Chief of the Military Cabinet, had come across this letter among the documents and sworn vengeance on his favoured foe. Hülsen's appointment itself had been an affront to Eulenburg, whose influence was even then on the wane. . . . And now vanish, at a gesture, nearly all the persons named by Harden; some dismissed on the spot, some to appear before a military Court of Enquiry—two Counts Hohenau, both of them aides-de-camp, one a colonel in the Cuirassier-Guards, sons of Prince Albrecht; together with Count Lynar, a third aide-de-camp, a Prince of Prussia, whom the Emperor deprived of his military rank; Kuno Moltke, Commandant of Berlin; and later, one Count Wedel, Master of the Ceremonies.

And Eulenburg? The only man whom in all his life he had ever called his bosom friend? The man for whom he had "glowed" in his youth? To whom quite lately he had given a free hand in criticism of his advisers? Whom he had made first a Prince and then a Knight of the Black Eagle?

What was the first thing any decent friend—nay, even any sensible President of an Association—would have done? Had he not learnt from the rash accusation of Herr von Kotze that slander cannot be obliterated with Easter-eggs? In those days he was still young. Now he was nearly fifty; a long succession of officials, many individuals and private acquaintances, had been put to the proof in the meantime, and not one of them had he ever chosen with so confident a heart as this man, nor had he ever stuck so long to any favourite—it was exactly thirty years since they had first found one another. The Emperor was on his trial now— here was the crucial moment.

William the Second was not equal to Fate's crucial moments. In one short hour he abjured the man he had proved a hundred times. He never sent for him that he might ask him, face to face, to assert his innocence against these documents, which after all might have been forged; but even though they were genuine, how was it that he did not, after all the intimacy of their dialogues, long for one more—the last—in which to hear the confession of an abnormal, and therefore wholly guiltless, man; and having heard it, answer as a friend would have answered?

Now, because Fortune has heaped favours on you, you are being put to the torture; and even I, constrained by the world's slandering tongues, must let you go. Leave the country, keep a place in your heart for me, and though I should never see you again, be assured of my friendship.

What did he do, instead of this? He sent an adjutant, an enemy of Eulenburg's, to Liebenberg with a demand for resignation (the Prince was only *en disposition*) and forthwith signed it. . . . The scandal was stupendous. When

Harden wrote a few days later that he had never alleged perverted practices, Zedlitz remarked: "How horribly we have given ourselves away! How recklessly and monstrously compromised the most prominent persons and the sovereign's best friends!" There was a momentary lull in the tempest, outside the Court; then the wind veered right round, and with it veered the sovereign—he who should have directed it. "I don't believe it either," he said then; "but Eulenburg didn't show enough fight." Not even then did he send for him to exculpate himself—he merely demanded, and that harshly, an assurance that Eulenburg was "uninvolved," otherwise he was to leave the country. His apostasy was complete.

And now began a series of lawsuits, trials in camera, self-advertisements—to all of which the Emperor had opened the door, when for human, political, and dynastic reasons he ought to have prevented them at any cost. "These lawsuits are the stupidest things the Hohenzollerns have done yet," remarked King Edward. Instead of being salutary in effect, their result was an explosion of noisome and disgusting venom. The rôle of injured innocence was re-assumed by the instigator, Holstein; public opinion was equally hostile to him and to his victims; the monarchy lost all prestige, without the smallest advantage to democracy; and there arose such a chaotic complication of sympathies and enmities that ultimately a Prince, assailed for his political influence, was driven into a corner and forced to deny things which Harden, his very modern-minded assailant, had always been foremost in pronouncing to be private and beyond the cognizance of the law. Eulenburg was forced by the logic of the process into perjuries which neither Harden nor the Emperor desired.

And after all, the Emperor's environment was fundamentally unchanged—for Zedlitz, who saw everything at close quarters, declares "that the lawsuits did nothing whatever towards removing homo-sexuals from about the Emperor." The fluctuating course of these lawsuits was closely followed by the Emperor, himself as fluctuating as they. This time he read the newspapers—read the reports from beginning to end.

He has moments [writes Zedlitz in that November] of profound dejection, in which he is convinced that the whole thing was an ineptitude. Then, in an impulse of affection for Eulenburg and Moltke, he conceives the fantastic idea that he is bound to rehabilitate them. . . . This plan has now taken firmer hold on him (I write in December), and I am convinced that he means to carry it out . . . or at another time, when he is very much infuriated by an article, he will quite seriously think of demanding direct satisfaction, and say in complete good faith: "If the newspapers don't stop this kind of thing, I'll send an aide-de-camp to blow the editor's brains out!" In short, he may be said to have lost his nerve.

In the beginning of 1908 he was so relieved that he "would have dearly liked to embark upon an instant rehabilitation of a kind unparalleled in social history; but so far there have always been influences to prevail upon him, by warnings against such an exposure of the royal personality" (Z. 171).

This degree of instability, unusual even in him, demonstrates his affection for his bosom friend, together with the bad conscience to which Philip of Spain once gave expression in the words: "We have acted too hastily." It also shows a decidedly womanish susceptibility to any immediate influence. At any one of these moments the Emperor could have rescued his friend; and as nobody failed to foresee and expect the resort to perjury, he was the more bound to attempt it—nor, after all that he had done and said against democracy for the last twenty years, could he take his stand upon the principle of "no respect of persons before the law," for he had always upheld class-superiority in every department of the national life.

When it came to the indictment for perjury, it was too late for him to act. The Prime Minister was obliged to give an order of arrest; bail was refused, certificates of illness obtained, the Prince was incarcerated in the Charité, later to be—in the most horrible circumstances—carried in an invalid-chair and even prostrate in his bed, into court, there as a man of sixty to put a good face on his relations with young fishermen and soldiers, with whom he had had unlawful intercourse ten, twenty, thirty years before. He was saved by frequent swoons, nervous in origin, and therefore indirectly volitional; the further hearing was indefinitely postponed; and he returned to his castle, where he lived a leisurely life for twelve years longer, without, when his health improved, making any further attempt to rehabilitate himself. He survived not only Holstein's death, but the abdication of the Emperor, which he had prophesied.

And Bülow's fall—that likewise he survived. Bülow, ten years before the scandals, had warned his friend of a secret protocol from Vienna, very injurious to him, and already handed over by Holstein to the police (E. 2, 323). Simultaneously with this warning, though, Bülow is said to have got the police to let him have this material about Eulenburg (Treskow, 130). When the Harden affair began, it is true that he advised his friend to go abroad—for he had knowledge of the documents; but he is said by those in the know to have looked favourably on the law-proceedings; later, he signed his name to the order of arrest.

The part played by Bülow in the affair is to this day obscure; he may yet think well to clear it up himself. But it is not difficult to imagine it—it would be easily explained by an atmosphere in which true friendship could not draw breath. The Emperor, Bülow, Eulenburg, Holstein had held the reins of government for ten years; and if Holstein insulted Eulenburg and challenged him to a mortal combat —if Eulenburg complained of Bülow's having a hand in his dismissal from office—if Bülow could suspect Eulenburg of being his secret enemy with the Emperor—if the Emperor could abjure first Holstein and then even Bülow, and sacrifice Eulenburg, his truest and oldest friend, on mere suspicion, without turning a hair . . . was Bülow bound, in such a region of mistrust and treachery, to any such duty as rescuing a very questionable ally from a hopeless situation, by a gesture of personal devotion?

When in the September of 1908 the legal proceedings came to an end, only two men were left standing on the field of battle—Bülow and Tirpitz. In Eulenburg and Holstein —who had literally assassinated one another—not all, but the most important, were politically dead of those who had governed Germany without responsibility for what they did. At Court and in the Cabinets others had gained predominating influence; of these but little has been here set down, because the narration of so many intrigues would have made difficult reading.

Holstein, remarkable as a specialist under a leader, victim as he was of his suspicious temperament, could do nothing but injure the Empire as a leader unconfessed; Eulenburg, erratic in thought and feeling, knew his limitations better, never desired to lead, and did the Empire much more good by his frequent admonitions of the Emperor, and even by the nomination of Bülow, than he ever did it harm by the advancement of his other friends, and his infatuation for the Emperor. So that our desire for poetic justice is appeased by Holstein's downfall, while the Emperor's betrayal of Eulenburg stirs us to sympathy for so tragically disastrous an end to so brilliant a career.

Only a few weeks after his friend's catastrophe, the third and last—Prince Bülow—was himself to receive his death-blow.

4

For England the nineteenth century had come to an end in gloom and anxiety. First, when Chamberlain had taken the initial step towards a European alliance and held out a hand to Germany, only to receive a cold douche from Bülow; next, when the Emperor advised the Tsar through the Russian Ambassador to utilize the moment for an attack upon England in Asia, guaranteeing him the protection of his Western frontier by Germany.

Together with his exultant condolences, exaggerating the already considerable English losses in the Boer War, the Emperor sent to his uncle in London, in December 1899, some pages of "stray thoughts" and wrote: "I send a *précis* of various discussions in military circles here about the Boer War, in the shape of some reflections which will give you an idea of what our Army is saying and thinking. I have set them down without commentary or partiality. Do what you like with them. Chuck them into the fire if you choose" (Lee, 755).

Although only a curt cold acknowledgment was returned, the Emperor, in the beginning of February 1900, when the English troops were in a better position, sent a second col-

lection of such stray thoughts—this time as entirely his own
ideas, and with more pretensions to actual advice. "They
may possibly be . . . of some use, if you think so . . . for
they are set down by a man who has been in active military
service for three-and-twenty years, and has organized and led
the German Army for twelve." The last of these reflections ran:

> In the existing situation a military decision is not to be re-
> garded as attainable. So that unless the absolutely indefeasible
> guarantee in question can be obtained by political pressure, it
> would surely be better to come to a compromise. Even the crackest
> football-team, when it is beaten after a plucky game, puts a good
> face on it and accepts defeat. In the great match England v.
> Australia last year, England took her beating quietly, and
> chivalrously acknowledged her opponents to be the better men (A.
> 15, 553-7).

This was quite the worst of William the Second's stray
thoughts. A dynasty related to his own was conducting an
arduous campaign; the Emperor's position, as evidenced by
the Kruger Telegram, had at first been on the enemy's side,
and had afterwards altered only in appearance. He had
gone so far as to advise an attack upon the British Empire
while it was at war, and to promise assistance to Russia in
the event of such an attack, at the same time declining the
offer of an alliance with England. Nation and Emperor
were at one in their sympathy for the Boers; and now, just
home after a freezing reception in England, he not only
sends unasked-for amateurish advice, pretends to be helpful,
boasts of his long experience and sums up with a hint to
"give up the game—you are done for!"—but he uses the
terms victory and defeat as if he were writing of a campaign
already decided, and incidentally compares it to a football-

match. What can the old Queen have said behind locked doors to her son of the unaccountable nephew whose letter lay before them, full of gratuitous insults? It was rather too little than too much for the uncle to answer that he repudiated the analogy of the football-match, for, "as you ought to know, the British Empire is at present fighting for its existence."

Seven years later, when the Emperor was paying a few weeks' visit to Colonel Stuart Wortley, he told his host of all he had done for England and how he had been misunderstood there; and when he saw the Colonel again during the Alsace Manœuvres in September 1908, at a time when English feeling against Germany was again exacerbated, he "expressed his personal desire that the utmost possible publicity should be given in England to anglophile views held by himself and his House" (A. 24, S. 167f.; and also as source for the following statements). From what he further said, the Colonel immediately composed the rough draft of an interview with an unspecified interlocutor, which he proposed to publish in the *Daily Telegraph* as an attempt to pacify the Press and public opinion, submitting it beforehand to the Emperor. The Emperor pronounced the "article to be well written, and a faithful report of what he had said"; and sent it through the Ambassador von Jenisch to Bülow, that he might "suggest any desirable alterations on the margin of the existing English text." Bülow was to be sure to send it straight back to him, not through the Foreign Office, "keeping it a secret from as many others as is at all possible." This was to be done as quickly as might be. Jenisch—a diplomat indeed—fought shy of reading the article, confined himself to penmanship, and did as he was told.

When Bismarck, as a man of over seventy, had made

protracted stays at Friedrichsruh, the youthful Emperor and the old Foreign Office officials had been wont to complain of the delay thus caused to business. Here was the beginning of October, yet no one was in Berlin; and while the Emperor was shooting at Rominten, Bülow bathing at Norderney, Secretary-of-State Schön climbing at Berchtesgaden, a document in its locked attaché-case was liable to undergo some strange vicissitudes. True, it consisted merely of a few typed pages, and the Emperor had designated it as confidential; but the contents—merely a "Kaiser-speech"—seemed so hackneyed that the Chancellor was not tempted to read them; so off with it to Berlin with the superscription "Confidential" and the instruction "Revise carefully," any corrections to be written on the margin. In Berlin it was opened by the deputising Under-Secretary Stemrich, who simultaneously opened his eyes at the covering-letter, took very good care not to read the typescript, and gave it to a Privy Councillor, saying, "It seems to me rather rocky—however, you'd better take a look at it and see what's to be done."

Councillor Klehmet was a conscientious person. *He* read the typescript, and at first felt "very dubious about the advisability of publication"; but quickly took refuge in the reflection "that the Foreign Office as such is not entitled to place itself in opposition to the Emperor's express wish, when the Chancellor, on his side, has conveyed no sense of uneasiness. . . . Such being the circumstances, I assumed that the Imperial Chancellor had already decided, or would decide, what was to be done." Thus thought Klehmet; he studied the document, corrected two important mis-statements of the Emperor's, and suggested, besides, a change in the diction.

Back it went to Herr Stemrich, who stuck to his resolve not to read it, but signed his name; thence back to Norderney, where the Ambassador von Müller, the Emperor's right-hand man, received it and in his turn recoiled from reading. Taking a copy of Stemrich's letter, he packed the whole thing back to Bülow. Bülow bestowed but a cursory glance on the typescript; signed it, however, as it stood with Klehmet's corrections, describing these officially "as alterations which strike me as desirable." Back to Berlin went typescript and all; the Secretary of State received it, marked "Urgent"; but being just then summoned to the Chancellor, had nevertheless "no time to take cognizance of the contents," and handed it over yet again to Bülow, who remarked that he had seen to it himself. So back with it to Jenisch, from him to the Emperor, from him to the English Colonel—and behold it in the London newspaper!

So that the typescript had been read by Emperor and Councillor only—by the former with the paternal emotion of its author, by the latter with the detachment of a philologist; while in the meantime it had passed through the hands of five diplomatists whose moral duty, as politicians, it was to read it—a Chancellor, two Secretaries of State, two Ambassadors, of whom not one had been urged by a sense of responsibility, official zeal, or even mere curiosity, to examine what a fortnight later all Europe was to read as the authenticated words of the German Emperor:

You English are like mad bulls—you see red everywhere! What on earth has come over you, that you should heap on us such suspicion as is unworthy of a great nation? What *can* I do more? I have always stood forth as the friend of England. . . . Have I ever once broken my word? . . . I regard this misapprehension as a personal insult! . . . You make it uncommonly difficult for a man to remain friendly to England. . . . During the Boer War, German public opinion and the Press were decidedly hostile to you. But what did we do? Mark my words! When the Boer delegates were seeking friends in Europe and were received with acclamations in France—who was it that called a halt and put an end to their proceedings? I alone refused to receive them.

Then, when the campaign was at its height, we were invited by Russia and France to force England to make peace—we were told that the moment had come to humble England to the dust. But what was my answer? That Germany would draw the sword to prevent so base an action! . . .

And that is not all. In your Black Week, when disaster followed disaster, I received a letter from my revered grandmother, which showed that her health and peace of mind were being undermined by grief and anxiety. Instantly I wrote her a sympathetic answer, but I did more than that! I told my aides-de-camp to draw up the most accurate statement in their power of the numbers and positions of both armies, as they stood at that period. I worked on these figures to the best of my ability, drawing up a plan of campaign which I submitted to the criticism of my Staff; then I sent it to England, where in Windsor Castle it awaits the impartial verdict of history. And let me remark on an extraordinary coincidence— my plan almost exactly corresponded with that which Lord Roberts ultimately adopted and carried through to the successful end. And now I ask you—is not this the behaviour of a man who wishes England well? Let England give a fair answer.

Then he went on to speak of the Fleet, which he was not building against England, but for great contingencies to come "which are impending in the Pacific Ocean, and are not so remote as some believe. . . . Japan now has the upper hand. China's awakening is imminent. When that time comes, only great naval Powers will have a voice in the decision of events" (*Daily Telegraph,* 27th Oct., 1908).

This document began by commanding England to be friends: "And will you not my brother be, I'll break your head—so trust in me!" Then a false colouring was put upon the escape of England from her critical position; no reference was made to the fact that the Emperor had proposed to the Tsar not merely a joint mediation but an attack on the British Empire, and afterwards only refused to follow up that suggestion because he was afraid of the consequences. Next he designated a collection of commonplaces by the resounding title of a Plan of Campaign, upon which he invited the verdict of history; fibbed about the approval of his Staff, who had never seen the papers at all; and plainly hinted as his trump-card that his imposing "Plan" had enlightened the English Staff, and that Lord Roberts had conquered by following up William the Second's suggestions—in short, the German Emperor's ingenuity had saved England in her direst need.

When Metternich, whom no one had consulted, opened the *Telegraph* at this article, he said to the members of his Embassy: "Now we may shut up shop." His despatches regarding its effect translated this speech into the language of diplomacy, and the full measure of his despair was compressed into one sentence: "We shall have to pursue an unequivocally pacific policy for a considerable length of time, if we desire to efface the impression." English Ministers and Generals at first refused to express any opinion whatever about the article; the fury of the Press equalled that over the Kruger Telegram—twelve years of improved relations seemed to have gone by the board. From excited Tokio came similar despatches; in Paris, Rome, and Petersburg every pen was against the Emperor. But these were old stories. The effect at home was something new.

For the first time the German people revolted. For twenty years it had been silent, while the Emperor spoke:

now it spoke, that he might learn to be silent. A torrent of such deep-drawn wrath broke forth as was not equalled in directness and sincerity between 1870 and 1914. Truly, the miraculous had come to pass—the most submissive nation on earth had uprisen against its sovereign, and claimed redress. At that moment it could have demanded and obtained his abdication; not the Republic, but the Emperor's son; for the movement was not socialistic—it affected all classes. It came to this: the subjects revolted against their sovereign, not on account of a lost campaign or a tyrannous ordinance, not even as against some particular encroachment seen to be injurious in its consequences; they revolted against his very nature, against the irrepressible loquacity which had now manifested itself in a manner that enabled them to estimate it as his duplicities had hitherto prevented them from doing. For *this* was as good as a story—every citizen, every peasant, could see his Emperor drawing up the Plan of Campaign for his grandmother under the midnight lamp. It was both dangerous and ridiculous; and so the first storm broke upon the Emperor, precisely ten years before the second.

That the political Left should explode was less surprising than that the comic papers were allowed to tear the Emperor to pieces, without being torn to pieces themselves by the censorship. In *Simplicissimus* the old Emperor was seen pleading for God's mercy towards his grandson: "After all, he is 'by the Grace of God' "; and God's reply was: "Now you want to put the blame on me!" A drawing by Zille showed a boy, "Little Willy," with the Emperor's features, squatting on a writing-table and smearing it and himself with ink, while Mother Germania and Father Bülow cried: "Didn't we tell you you weren't to play at writing letters any more?" In a third sheet a Court-Chaplain was lifting up his hands to heaven with the Bible-words: "O that I could put a lock to my mouth, and a seal to my tongue!" Again, on New Year's Eve a comic paper showed him giving himself a muzzle as a present. All this was permitted in German lands; and a lampoon had the refrain:

> Majestäts-Beleidigungen
> Tanzen auf Geheimratszungen.[1]

In November 1908 the Germans might have been taken for a free and independent nation.

But the idea of abdication was much too revolutionary; it was mooted only by those who were conscious of their strength—by the Royalists themselves. "The Royal Idea is undoubtedly a precious possession," wrote a Conservative organ. "But the richest of heritages can be dissipated by wanton extravagance. . . . The sovereign's rights are counterbalanced by duties which to neglect is to undermine the very foundations of the monarchy." In these circles, but only in these, they went further still: "Among the German Ministers, convened for a session of the Federal Council's Committee on foreign affairs, there was talk of persuading the Emperor to abdicate" (State-Secretary von Schön, *Erlebtes,* 100). Eleven years earlier similar schemes had been among the secretions of Holstein's brain, and therefore confined to his own narrow circle; now the aristocracy of Bavaria and Saxony, of Oldenburg and Württemberg gathered in the embrasures of windows, biting their lips and talking of rough justice. They could have saved Germany!

Bülow stood in the midst, and did forthwith what he

[1] Insults to the Emperor-King
Even Councillors' lips can sing.

was bound to do—tendered his resignation and those of the responsible Secretaries of State. The Emperor was within his formal rights: he had not departed, this time either, from the path assigned him by the written word; he could with a good conscience have let the Chancellor go. But he kept him, though he need not have kept him—not out of loyalty, but fear. To stand forth naked now—too frightful was the prospect! Besides, here was the Chancellor's opportunity; he could clothe Emperor and catastrophe with his approval. And he did it, next day, in an official explanation which set forth the case for the Emperor in all its tragi-comic verity. The tug of war had still to be faced in the Reichstag. The Emperor, ill at ease, left Berlin. From the 4th to the 16th of November he was away; and having brought down the English bull, was occupied in doing the same for stags with Franz Ferdinand, and foxes with Prince Fürstenberg.

But amid all the fun he cast a lingering look behind.

The two days here [he wired to Bülow from Vienna] have gone off very harmoniously and gaily. . . . The shoot went off splendidly; I brought down sixty-five stags. . . . I remember you in all my prayers, morning and evening. When has He ever failed to help us, though hate and envy might pursue! There is a silver lining to every cloud. God be with you! Your old friend, William I.R.

How cleverly he pushes home the guardian's position between God and friendship; how blind is this nation-arraigned monarch to any gleam of salutary perception! No—it is he who is despised and rejected of men; and in the meantime he enjoys himself and brings down sixty-five head of game.

On 10th November the Reichstag met, with all the appearance of a national court of justice on the sovereign. That day anything might have happened—solemn pledges, constitutional modifications, probably even the abdication, as already envisaged by the members of the Federal Council. And not one of them happened! The Germans, after a fortnight of agitation, were already their submissive selves again; no one ventured on the fatal word, not even the Socialists. The Emperor, whom custom forbade to attend the debate, was indeed phantasmally present, but the party-leaders did no more than sermonize him. The sternest reproofs came from the group of his Paladins, from Heydebrandt and Hatzfeldt. Others laid the blame on that Byzantinism which for twenty years they had fostered; motions for modification of the Constitution proved futile; the Reichstag did not even venture on the most deferential form of protest, an address—much less dared hint at the parliamentary system!

After that day the Emperor had no more to fear from his people. But Bülow had, from his Emperor. For in truth Bülow was, so to speak, the tragic hero in that Tenth of November drama. He was now to be punished for always pretending to be more of a fool than he was. He should either have championed the Emperor or abandoned him. He was in duty bound either to tell the Reichstag in Bismarckian fashion: "The Emperor acted with the best intentions, and constitutionally too; he has refused the Chancellor's proffered resignation, and so we intend to proceed as before, whether the nation likes it or not"; or else to have thrown in his lot with the Reichstag and the nation, left the Emperor in the dock, indicted him, and passed out of favour next day. That way was closed to him, by reason of his deep-seated loyalty; so he decided on the other, and had prepared a speech in the Emperor's favour, in which, as Hammann states, he unequivocally defended him.

But at the last moment the statesman in Bülow—or perhaps merely the patriot—prevailed over the courtier. He over-estimated the Germans, when he feared to strain the bow so soon unstrung. By choosing this *via media* he lost ground with both the nation and the Emperor. He criticized the Emperor, said his expressions had been too strong, reduced the Plan of Campaign to a few commonplaces, made no mention of the Staff, and finally undertook to promise that the national uneasiness would

lead the Emperor henceforth to lay upon himself, even in his private conversations, those restrictions which are indispensable for consistent policy and the authority of the throne. . . . Were it not so, neither I nor any successor in office could accept responsibility for the consequences.

A murmur of dissent from the Left—but the House was satisfied with this lame statement; no more was said.

On the same Tenth of November the Navy received the following minute:

His Majesty's orders are that the cheering on all ships is to be absolutely simultaneous with the raising of the caps. . . . At the command, "Three cheers for His Majesty," the flags will be hoisted. At the same moment those on parade will remove the right hand from the rails, and grasp the cap. On the first "Hip-hip-hurrah" the flag-signal will fall; the cheer will then be repeated, the cap being held up by lifting the right arm at an angle of about 45 degrees, and as soon as that cheer has ceased to resound, the cap will be carried on a sharp bend of the arm to the middle of the chest. . . . At the third cheer, the cap will be smartly resumed and the right hand replaced on the rails. These instructions are to be followed on the forthcoming occasion of His Majesty's presence at the swearing-in of recruits.

Everyone who read these orders in the weekly service-gazette, and knew them to be if not actually inspired, at any rate approved, by the Emperor, instantly felt happier and more at home than during the perusal of the nagging Reichstag speeches. Cheers for the master, "all together," at an angle of 45 degrees—that was the natural way for self-respecting subjects to behave; very different from un-fruitful criticism of the good pleasure of that eternal boy —their Emperor.

He, on that same Tenth when they were all making speeches about him, opened the day by making a speech himself. Zeppelin's flying-experiments had hitherto been scorned by the Emperor, the War Office had refused to examine his plans and models, officers in general were for-bidden to take any part in the Count's fantastic proceedings; only three months earlier the Emperor had called him "of all South-Germans the greatest donkey" (Z. 196). On this day he addressed him thus:

Our Fatherland may well be proud of possessing such a son, the greatest German of the twentieth century, who by this invention has opened a new epoch in the development of mankind. It would not be too much to say that we are living to-day through one of the most pregnant moments in the evolution of humanity.

In Friedrichshafen, that is to say—not in Berlin, for there the mountain had brought forth a mouse.

At Donaueschingen, whence the Zeppelin flight started on the Tenth, lived the Emperor's new friend, who inherited Eulenburg's intimacy without his intelligence.

His established friends . . . now Prince Fürstenberg and General von Kessel, owe their favour to their funny stories. They are the sort of men who can keep it up, not only by the hour but by the day. The intellectual level is not a high one, and one must grant to Eulenburg that his conversation was decidedly more intelligent. But all these gentlemen's stories are so banal and coarse that they degrade the narrators, and still worse are the idiotic pranks to which they lend themselves (Z. 231).

It was in this circle that the Emperor spent the most critical days of his reign. Zedlitz, who was on personal service with him, states that the Emperor shed tears when he read the speeches in the Reichstag.

This dejection very soon took the form of reading nothing more about the crisis, and seeking distraction from his troubled thoughts. He took an early walk, breakfasted with us at nine o'clock, stayed talking till half-past eleven, drove to the shoot, came back about five, took part in general conversation till nearly seven, then lay down awhile, appearing for dinner at half-past eight, and afterwards spent the evening with us till half-past twelve.

On one of these evenings a music-hall troupe performed for the illustrious party, and soon the German people were reading its newspaper puff:

A performance, lasting two hours, took place before the German Emperor, Prince Fürstenberg, and Count Zeppelin, with sensational success, finishing at half-past twelve. The Emperor and the distinguished company applauded enthusiastically, and personally expressed their appreciation of the brilliant programme and its faultless execution.

If the reader turned the page, he came upon the report of how enthusiastically the Reichstag had applauded *its* orators, and how a Ministerial Council, too, had lasted until half-past twelve.

But parting had to come—duty called, the recruits at Kiel were waiting to take the oath, and cheer according to

the new regulation. The farewell-evening at Castle Fürstenberg was a magnificent occasion—the ladies in all their brav-
ery, the gentlemen in green-and-black dress-coats with black
knee-breeches, and as there had been a meet in the vicinity,
some in hunting-pink.

The brilliance and elegance of the party was really most remarkable [writes the Court-Marshal]. They assembled after dinner
in the stately hall of the magnificent castle, an orchestra playing
on the staircase landing. Suddenly Count Hülsen-Haeseler appeared, dressed as a ballerina (as he had done once or twice before)
and began to dance. Everyone was vastly delighted, for the Count's
dancing is superb, and there was something quite out of the common in seeing the Chief of the Military Cabinet, got-up as a woman,
perform a *pas-seul*. The Count had just finished a dance, and
retired to the adjoining gallery to get a breath of air. I was standing within a few feet of the entrance when suddenly I heard a heavy
fall. I hurried to the spot, and saw the Count lying full-length
on the floor with his head in the embrasure of the window.

It was a heart-attack. The Emperor, who was standing
talking by the fireplace, was informed, and hastened to the
dying man's side. They tried to restore him; the music
went on a while; a second doctor was summoned—in vain.
The body was taken to the great dining-room; Kiel had to
be abandoned; a telegram sent to the Empress: "Have lost
my best friend"; then there were other telegrams, together
with preparations for a mourning-service next day. The local
clergyman, an old man, was sent for; and in the small hours
appeared shivering before the Emperor, who was impressing
upon him what he was to say in the morning when, from
nervousness and the long standing, the clergyman suddenly
fell fainting at the imperial feet.

The priest recovered; the General lay dead upon the improvised bier. They had hastily transformed him from a

ballerina into a soldier—it was Dürer's Dance of Death come true. But the Emperor did not read the writing on the wall. He did not see that once again a mightier hand than his had pointed threateningly to follies and frivolities. Encircled by the anger and resentment of sixty millions of tranquil active fellow-creatures, one man sat, inactive and provocative, drowning his mortifications in music-hall songs and jokes, in shooting-parties and ballets, and allowing exasperating tales of Court-life to circulate among the people. Now, when finally one of his most prominent Generals had appeared as a ballerina before the highest society, disgracing the most illustrious class in the land, behold! the hand of Heaven was put forth; it struck the abject courtier to the earth—upon the wall of the castle at Donaueschingen flamed the great Mene Tekel, that now at last the roistering King might look into his heart.

But the King was looking into quite other places. How, for instance, was the great dining-room to be transformed in one night into an imposing mortuary-chapel? What were to be the travelling-arrangements in these altered circumstances? And when in the middle of the night he upset all these arrangements for the third time, and was obliged to hear the deferential voice of the Court-Marshal, warning him that another postponement of two special trains would create difficulties, the mountebank he was took cover behind his simulated grief, looked wounded to the heart and said, with tearful eyes: "And it's at such a moment that you make difficulties for me!"

5

At home, the tutor was waiting with his lecture. *Simplicissimus* portrayed the Chancellor in mourning, stagger.

ing under the weight of a huge padlock, and murmuring: "How am I to explain it to my Emperor?" Bülow made his second mistake on this occasion. He could have got anything he liked just then, if he had turned the mood of dejection to good purpose, for "the Emperor's nerves are not equal to any serious emergency." But instead of intimidating him, Bülow confined himself to a courtly adumbration of the consequences likely to result from these rash exploits. The Emperor, in his enforced quietude, returned monosyllabic answers, showed no sign of desiring amendment or seeing any necessity for it; and finally gave a reluctant consent to the insertion of a statement in the *Reichsanzeiger* (which he later denied having given)—setting forth that he had granted the Chancellor an audience, for consultation on public opinion and the Reichstag speeches.

His Majesty listened very gravely to the Chancellor's exposition, and expressed his desires as follows. While undisturbed by the—in his opinion—unfairly exaggerated strictures of public criticism, he regards it as his proudest imperial duty to ensure the stability of national policy through the exertions of constitutionally responsible functionaries. His Majesty therefore expressed approval of the Imperial Chancellor's remarks in the Reichstag, and assured the Prince of his undiminished confidence.

The German people breathed again—now it was all right, signed and in order. Few were the anxious patriots who looked at one another and asked: "Is that all? Undisturbed? Unfair? Exaggerated? Constitutional?" Even the minimum demanded by the nation, a promise of amendment, was imperceptible behind the waving banners of the autocrat, just as were the shuttered windows of the Francophiles at the entries in Alsace. All that it amounted to was that he had expressed approval of the Chancellor's speech, and had listened very gravely—this latter so prominently set forth that its effect was rather insulting to him than otherwise.

That was all Bülow asked. But that was quite enough to shatter a monarch who had been invariably pampered, on whom the sun had always shone; and there was more to come. The Emperor was informed of the Federal Council's plan, which had gone further than the Reichstag's attacks, even as far as abdication; and he collapsed, as neurasthenics often will, at thought of a danger past and gone: On the 24th the old Chamberlain Schulz came panting into the aide-de-camp's room and stammered out:

His Majesty—has commanded me—to ring up the Imperial Chancellor immediately. I am to inform him plainly—His Majesty wishes him to know—that His Most High has been so completely unnerved by the recent incidents that he is compelled— to abandon all business of any kind, and entrust it to the Crown-Prince (Z. 194).

A frightful moment for the aide-de-camp! A Chamberlain announces the Most High's withdrawal, the Chancellor is to be informed, the heir-apparent summoned. Had the officer sufficient sense of humour to savour this immortal scene? He merely said that Schulz could not possibly carry out this behest, and sent for the Court-Marshal, whereupon ensued a consultation between the Chancellor and the two Cabinets. When, next day, the Crown-Prince arrived, his tearful mother told him what had happened, and was to happen. He found his father in bed, soothed him, and in a few days all was as before.

But why did the Crown-Prince refuse? Why did he not grasp the hand then—and never again—offered him; he who had had his fill of groaning over the Emperor's behests, and must have known that he would probably, his father's constitution being what it was, have to wait twenty years for the crown? He, too, was wanting in manful resolution—nowhere was to be found the courage that seizes the rope thrown by fate to plucky swimmers once, and only once; nowhere the spirit that is quick to accept responsibility, nowhere the love of action. That moment in November 1908, seized by a gallant-hearted Prince, might possibly have been of service to the Empire—certainly it would have been to the Emperor, who could then have resigned as a voluntary martyr, a wise man yielding to his wiser self; and thus, not only in the eyes of history, have greatly bettered his position.

Swift as the collapse was the recovery. Both were of the nerves; neither was fruitful. At the end of November he ordered a speech of the Chancellor's to be handed to him in the Berlin Guildhall, and ostentatiously "recited" it himself. There was more of contempt than of anything better in this gesture—a mere demonstration, at the best. Before a month was over, oblivion covered all. The eyes of his sycophants pleaded with him for return to the old groove. "If no one will protect me," he wrote on the margin of a cutting, "I shall have to protect myself!" By this womanish argument he very adroitly steered himself out of the troubled waters into the haven of autocracy where he felt most at home; and was soon threatening: "If anything like this occurs again, I shall not act constitutionally, I promise you!" (Z. 239). That he was in no sense altered, Zedlitz could report at Christmas-time from daily observation.

In real essentials the Emperor is just the same as before. . . . On our quiet evenings, when he often reads diplomatic despatches aloud to the ladies and aides-de-camp, he particularly delights in making farcical scenes out of anything mistaken or ridiculous that is done abroad, and describing them as "very good" or "quite right." But if anything occurs that may recoil unfavourably on us, he writes in the margin: "How foolish!" or something of the kind. He specially enjoys, nowadays, any attack from England; insists on seeing all anonymous letters, and feels that the famous interview is justified as regards the Fleet when he reads that the English advise him to give up his position as the head of a nation of sixty millions, to be instead the President of a Football-Club or Cricket-Club. . . . He really had the mortification of reading that (Z. 199).

Immediately after Christmas came tidings of diamond-fields in South-West Africa; and he repeatedly declared that they were forty kilometres long and two broad, adding many other figures "which got bigger every time, and his fantastic dreams correspondingly dazzling." At this time he said, before some chance guests and the servants:

Only a fortnight ago those mutton-heads [in the Reichstag] refused to believe the first news—they said it was impossible. Now we can see what rubbish these owls talk . . . and people whose ideas they can't comprehend, and without whom they couldn't stir a step, they throw mud at! . . . I'll read no more newspapers; it's nothing to me what those mutton-heads write! [Before the same witnesses he made such remarks about the Germans in America that Zedlitz dared not commit them to paper:] If only a quarter of what he said were to become known, the alarm would more than equal the excitement over the Kaiser-Interview.

His nervous temperament could not have achieved such oblivion of the past if he had not found a scapegoat. Hülsen was dead; but dozens of newly helmeted heads had sprung from the Hydra, and a hundred forked tongues were hissing: "Bülow has betrayed his King." The watchword at Potsdam was: "Bülow was lying: he knew all about the interview, he passed it; and then abandoned his master to the storm." Thenceforth he was never spoken of but as one guilty of high treason. It was not until March 1909 that he succeeded in bringing the Emperor to speak out with him in the picture-gallery of the Palace, where he earnestly begged to be allowed to resign (Hammann, *Um den Kaiser*, 30).

The Emperor: "No, I have forgiven you. But you did not stand up for me properly in November. You had approved my interview both by letter and word of mouth."

Bülow: "I will ask Your Majesty to show me those letters."

The Emperor: "It—it was by word of mouth as well, when I came back from Rominten."

When Bülow reminded him of earlier rashnesses, the Emperor said he knew nothing about them; afterwards he declared that Bülow had admitted his error and begged for forgiveness; the Press even reported that Bülow had shed tears. In confidence, though, the Emperor said:

"I've done with that fellow Bülow. But he must put through the financial reforms for me."

Bülow spent his time in almost incessant consultation with Holstein, who was seriously ill, but still exercised considerable influence with him and with the new Secretary of State, by giving advice on high politics, sometimes even over the telephone. His practice in the composition of ostensible offers of resignation now bore some of its last fruit, for he drew up one for Bülow, eight pages long, in January 1909. Nevertheless at the end of April, immediately before his death, he conjured the Chancellor to remain in office: "If you go, war will be inevitable." This was Holstein's only true prophecy.

But when in July the Probate Duties, and with them the

bloc in the Reichstag, came to grief, Bülow took leave of office on the "Hohenzollern," the spot and the day of the year being identical with those on which he had formerly undertaken the management of affairs. In Berlin the Emperor discussed with him the question of his successor, walking up and down in the well-overlooked Palace Garden, and dismissed him with a kiss and an embrace.

"Bülow shall be my Bismarck," the Emperor had once rather boyishly exclaimed. Bülow *had* been his Bismarck —that is to say, he was as much the superior of his master as Bismarck had been of the grandfather; only the degrees of greatness were different. Bismarck's passionate energy had graven clefts and folds in his countenance; Bülow's elegance had gone no deeper than dints and wrinkles.

His departure was the greatest of the four catastrophes. The downfall of Holstein and Eulenburg, the crisis brought about by the Emperor—these altered little in the usual course of affairs; but Bülow's elimination "made war inevitable." The best summing-up fell from Zedlitz senior in a letter: "To have kept the coach from overturning for so long, and to have skirted such abysses, was a service to be grateful for."

When the attacks in the imperial Press increased by reason of the Emperor's false representations about Bülow, he tried to obtain redress from his successor, and wrote a retrospective statement:

I knew as little about the interview beforehand as I had formerly known about . . . the Swinemünde despatch to Bavaria, or the telegram to the Prince of Lippe-Detmold . . . or the Hun-speech of the summer of 1900, or the pessimist-speech during the manœuvres of 1906. . . . I implored His Majesty never to say a word to the English which the Russians and French, the Japanese and

Americans, might not hear. Over and over again I warned him that a susceptible and distrustful nation like Japan must not have its suspicions roused. I remember wiring to suppress a letter despatched several days before by His Majesty to Roosevelt, because it seemed to me to contain incautious references to Japan. . . . I was obliged to waste much of my time and energy in retrieving the rashnesses and indiscretions which had been committed.

For twelve years it had indeed been so; and even those who blame Bülow's English policy and much of his interior policy as well, are bound to pay tribute to his brilliant capacities and indefatigable zeal—the Emperor most of all, since he worked him harder than any one else could. What did he do after his friend's departure, on whose remaining he had made his life dependent four years earlier?

All the blame for the Eulenburg scandal is Bülow's, for . . . he had personal as well as other motives for desiring it. If at that time he had persuaded Eulenburg to remain abroad, there would have been no scandal at all. Even his famous speeches were written for him by Hammann, and he learnt them by heart, and Europe thought him a wonder. . . . Since Cæsar Borgia there hasn't been so hypocritical and perfidious a man! (Z. 237).

And, as Kiderlen writes, when he was showing the King of Württemberg a picture of the Palace Gardens, he pointed to the spot where he had kissed and embraced Bülow, and said: "There's where I gave that sweep the boot!"

BOOK III

RETRIBUTION

"I pray God that I may not live through what I see coming."
Waldersee's Last Entry in his Diary.

CHAPTER VII

GATHERING CLOUDS

WILLIAM the Second's heyday was over.
He had reigned for twenty years, and was now fifty. His hair was beginning to turn grey; and though his subjects had not yet perceived that change, there was a corresponding greyness in the atmosphere around him. The coruscations which had made him interesting were dying down, yet there was no sign of a calmer, clearer evening-glow. His friends had been banished, and with them went his wisest counsellors—the brilliant Chancellor and the tender intimate, who had been with him in his early conflicts and his later splendours. The Court, with its cold glitter, seemed deserted—more than one of the Federal Princes now kept away from Berlin. Shooting-parties and entries, even journeys, had become monotonous—the same thing over and over again. It was a perpetual fourth act, as it were, for the man who had hitherto been so easily pleased and excited; and while loneliness grew, while a sense of the disillusionments of friendship weighed upon his spirits, he did not indeed cease to be an optimist, but the gestures by which he sought to convince himself and the world how richly God had blessed him did become less frequent.

He had lost the two great encounters in his reign of twenty years. When he looked downward from his heaven-kissing throne, he saw in the far depths the third part of his subjects working and plotting in discontent and hostility. His young ambition, product of fear and impetuosity, had not been fulfilled; for there below, unreconciled, the labouring millions swarmed—an amorphous mass, an insoluble enigma, a subterranean portent luridly revealed in restless flashes. In the twenty-five years of his reign, Social Democracy had gained strength; from three-quarters of a million votes it had increased to four-and-a-quarter million—that is, from nine to thirty-five per cent of the electors.

Even upon the aristocracy, who had always stood by the monarchy, even upon the Princes of the Empire, he could no longer rely. The former objected to the autocratic methods by which he perverted the doctrine of *primus inter pares;* the latter had repeatedly made an open stand against him and, grouped around the bellicose Crown-Prince, presented a threatening front when the sovereign failed to be sufficiently forceful and Pan-German—for in their view he was poor-spirited. But while the Reds were clamouring for a change from Cæsarism to parliamentary government and even the republic, while the Blues wanted an aggressive instead of a pacifist King—while the former demanded a better understanding with their French comrades and ultimately with all Europe, and the latter would be satisfied with nothing less than a Greater Germany, which could not be obtained without a war . . . the *bourgeoisie* stood firmly by their Emperor, under whom they had grown prosperous, and grew more prosperous with every year.

And in truth the Army and the aristocracy had good cause for becoming more and more estranged from their Emperor. As that greatest army in the world's history grew more and more formidable, as the armour of the German paladin grew more and more ponderous, the caution of their Supreme War-Lord correspondingly increased, till everyone was whispering, "He is afraid." The blustering gestures, the provocative speeches, the whole arsenal of phrases seemed neglected or forgotten; their eternal boy had learnt his lesson, and was circumspect at last.

This was no change of heart, for never did conviction of one single error come to this man. What he beheld around him now, he interpreted as the rancour of an evil world, as the envy of kindred Houses, the rivalry of caballing dynasties; but that it *was* around him, he no longer denied. Terrified—and assuredly more terrified than even to himself he was fain to admit—he felt that William the Second was encompassed by enmity; and the consciousness could have no other result on him than to strengthen his belief that he had done all a man could, and was but broken on the wheel of the world's callous cruelty. Had he not helped the Tsar in the war with Japan? Had he not shown unfailing courtesy to France? Was it not he who had provided his grandmother and uncle with plans of campaign, when England was in peril? Had he ever flinched from the fatigues of distant journeys, that he might knit up the bonds of political friendship in person at Rome, Damascus, Athens? With furtive thankless glances the false friends had gathered behind his back, had craftily surrounded him, the noblest quarry in all Europe, hoping in the end to bring him crashing to his fall. The father of his people misunderstood by the Socialists, the pacific sovereign misunderstood by his Russian cousin and his English uncle—there he had to stand, the martyr of his own good-will, and watch the circle closing round his realm.

Perhaps he was guiltless before God, though not before

of the counter-insurance treaty, but was not now to be obtained. And the spectres rose again; behind the Reval entente, concluded ten years after Bismarck's death, his spirit hovered ghost-like—the spirit which all those eighteen years ago the Emperor had driven, with the man himself, from the Foreign Office, when he refused to renew the Russian treaty.

That year of 1908 seemed a year of belated punishments. Three months after Reval came the chastisement of a second masterpiece of the Emperor's policy; and this time it was not his enemy, but his ally, who frightened him.

It was ten years since the Emperor on his second Eastern cruise—dazzled by pictures, cheers, and presents—had turned his attention to the Turk, and envisaged a German Dominion in Asia Minor. The Bagdad Railway, which he soon afterwards embarked upon, calling it "My Railway," and which was described by his sycophantic Ambassador as "Your Most Exalted Majesty's own undertaking," pointed to developments in international politics—the green flag of the Prophet was to be unfurled in the World-War of the future, a Holy War declared, England annihilated by revolts in India and Africa. Hence Germany became involved in the Balkan question, from which Bismarck had always contrived to keep her isolated; and a railway, which but for the Emperor would never have been constructed, drew her into the sphere of her two principal European rivals, and that in the most precarious of regions. Marschall was soon maintaining that Bismarck's phrase about the bones of a Pomeranian Grenadier had lost all relevance, that the Emperor's Damascus speech had resounded through the Mussulman world; the Sultan was induced to grant the Austrians a railway through the Sandjak, whereby it was their intention to cut off the Serbians from the sea and from their kindred races. This would drive the Russians, Austria's old rivals in the Balkans, to seek new friends—and suppose that meant England!

Even in those days the Emperor was nervous about these results of his Turkish policy. He was very far from being a devotee of Austria; he clung to her Emperor only as to the last of his allies, and it was not he who either invented or particularly affected the slogan of *"Nibelungen-Treue"*—that was Bülow's inspiration. Bülow had either taken over from Holstein, or really shared with him, the creed of unconditional loyalty to Austria; and never in his whole career did he make a greater mistake than when he handed Germany over, without any sort of limitation, to the most ramshackle of Empires. "For our attitude in all Balkan questions the requirements, interests, and ambitions of Austria are the ruling factor." So he wrote, and impressed it on his Ambassadors as their principle of action, in the summer of 1908. When did the most insignificant of States give Germany such a promise—when had Austria herself made any equivalent advances? Was not the natural relation of the powerful German to the feeble Austrian Empire completely reversed by such a thesis? Here, too, the predominance slipped through Germany's fingers; twenty years after Bismarck she was actually the subordinate partner in the Triple Alliance, and was committed to that very Balkan adventure of Austria's which he had dismissed with the sardonic words: "The Triple Alliance is not an unlimited liability company."

No wonder that Vienna, whose diplomats knew their business better, should take advantage of the German subordinate! When Aehrenthal, Franz Ferdinand's creature, seized upon the Turkish Revolution as a pretext for the long-desired annexation of Bosnia, and voluntarily opened up the whole Eastern question by this display of force, he did not take much trouble to ensure Germany's adherence, but was solicitous about Russia's. The Berlin Congress, without the consent of whose signatories no such dismemberment was supposed to take place, was apparently forgotten— it was not until everything was ready that Aehrenthal revealed the morrow's secret to the allies. Indeed, Vienna had evidently reckoned with the modern German fashion of interminable holidays, for so many days intervened between the announcement to Secretary-of-State von Schön at Berchtesgaden and Bülow at Norderney, and *their* communication with the Emperor at Rominten, that this last knew nothing of the arbitrary annexation of two provinces by his allies until the very day of the deed, 5th October. His information synchronized with that of horrified Europe—the French President, however, had been earlier communicated with.

The Emperor was beside himself, not only because of the betrayal of faith. "A raid on Turkey!" he wrote, with shrewd premonition, on Bülow's despatch. "Material for cheap suspicions in England about the Central Powers. . . . Austria won't be able to shake off responsibility for the Bulgarian Declaration of Independence" (which resulted on the same day).

Vienna will incur the reproach of double-dealing, and not unjustly. They have duped us abominably! . . . This will probably be the signal for the dismemberment of Turkey. . . . Personally, as an ally, I am most profoundly wounded. . . . Pretty gratitude for our help in the Sandjak affair! . . . So I am the last person in Europe to hear anything whatever about it! Such are my thanks from the House of Hapsburg!

This explosion is interesting from three standpoints. It shows a just political judgment in the Emperor when taken by surprise, possibly because he was at a distance from his various mentors; it shows his fear of developments, and his impotence against the offending Hapsburg. He could not take any practical steps as a result of his anger, for hindered as he was by the isolation he had brought upon himself, he could not well disavow the only allies he now possessed. But his anger lasted, and included Bülow. It is true that he wrote on Bülow's renewed exposition that they would eventually be obliged to recognize the annexation; but "what I deplore is having been put into this awkward fix by Aehrenthal's horrible levity. I fear that I shall not be able to protect my friends, now that my ally has wronged them. . . . Henceforth King Edward will inscribe Protection of Treaties on his banner. . . . A great score over us for Edward VII!" This was the underlying sore. Meanwhile his Chancellor wrote out the following neat blank cheque for the Austrians in the event of war: "I shall regard any decision to which you may ultimately come as influenced by our mutual relations"; and in confidential letters he expressly confirmed this attitude, with Holstein's authority behind him.

When simultaneously the *Daily Telegraph* affair exploded, it was easy for Isvolski to make the Tsar, whose own treachery dated from 1899, believe in another breach of faith by the Emperor in this Bosnian affair. Serbia's acquiescence, on a hint from Isvolski, then—in March 1909 —prevented war; for on Germany's decisive declaration that she would stand by Austria, Isvolski held his hand. But from that day forward the Tsar himself reckoned on "an unavoidable collision"; in Paris they talked only of an alliance and retribution; and if Austria had gained nothing but distrust and hostility by the annexation, Germany was regarded, and the Emperor above all was regarded, by Europe as the instigator, the receiver of stolen goods, in an affair which had taken him by horrified surprise.

The Turkish Revolution he accepted wonderfully soon after the first shock. He reconciled himself to it by the reflection that the moving spirits were "German-trained officers," and that after all the Sultan had long been ready to grant a Constitution. At that time Marschall wrote in a despatch:

> Every day makes it clearer that those who had most influence with the Sultan . . . are branded as traitors. A heavy indictment against the monarch who chose such advisers! And of these people, who were indebted to the Sultan alone for their positions and emoluments, not one stood by him in the decisive hour (A. 15, 622).

The Emperor's comment on this was: "Court-parasites are always like that! Not only in Turkey—with us Christians too."

Written in the autumn of 1908, ten years before his own calamity.

3

It was a Judas-kiss—a dual one—that the Emperor and his uncle exchanged on the Anhalt station platform. After years of postponement, the English royal couple had at last made up their minds to come to Berlin; but acrimony and frigidity had infected even the weather and the horses. Neither the reception nor the entry was a success; the horses jibbed, the escort—nay, the mere subjects—had more than once to shove the carriage on its way to the Arsenal where the two crowned ladies were to alight. An arctic downpour chilled the mood of family reunion; at the English Embassy the King had an alarming heart-attack. Still, they assured one another of their mutual affection. It was only "at the last moment before their departure," as the Emperor wrote to Bülow, that politics were touched upon; and then the Emperor took his stand upon the approved Naval Estimates, which were, he said, unalterable. "They will be adhered to and exactly carried out, without any restrictions." That was all; and it meant a definite refusal of any sort of understanding.

Bülow worked upon the slightly melancholy mood of the Emperor, when after the November scandal he returned from Corfu in a more subdued frame of mind; and ventured on yet another attempt at some fleet-building agreement with England, which was the sole means of ensuring European peace despite all that had happened. "In the summer of 1908," writes Brandenburg, "it would probably still have been possible, by a concession with regard to fleet-building . . . to persuade England to assume a friendly attitude towards Germany on every question." This was near the time of the Reval meeting, when Edward and the Tsar—three years after Björkö—with no sham treaties, no grand-sires looking down from Heaven, but merely a responsible Minister, laid the foundations of an understanding. Thus came to pass at length what Bismarck had feared and avoided, but William had provoked throughout twenty years —England joined hands with the hostile group. At Reval, Germany's doom was sealed.

Now, in April 1909, when Bülow met the Emperor in Venice, and the weather-eye of Tirpitz was not on him, he did at last obtain permission to make a deal with London on the question of building, and at the same time to propose a commercial treaty, even an alliance. The summer before, a fleet-arrangement had been regarded as nationally dishon-

ouring; an alliance had been twice refused by Bülow be=
tween 1898 and 1901.

And now it was too late. The curse that lay upon Prussian policy—of nearly always, throughout a century, being
too late—fulfilled itself once more. What the Emperor had
rejected at Friedrichshof, his diplomatists in London were
now unable to retrieve for him—Reval, Bosnia, the *Daily
Telegraph* had altered the English mood. "Europe is hence·
forth divided into two camps," said Grey to Metternich; "it
is only from time to time that we shall be able to speak
frankly." Tirpitz then became more insistent than ever.
While Bülow declared him responsible "to His Majesty, the
country, and history," because his deceptive programme had
shaken London's faith in Germany's trustworthiness—while
at the great Conference of June 1909 not only Metternich,
but even Moltke, spoke out for an understanding—Tirpitz
only asked for more, and declared that he would go on building from then to 1920.

Even Bethmann-Hollweg tried to slow down fleet-building. As if to emphasize the loss of his own gifts, Bülow had
suggested this functionary as his successor, and Ballin went
so far as to say: "Bethmann is Bülow's revenge." Bethmann brought to his high office only what Caprivi had
brought—a strong sense of duty and discipline; he lacked
precisely what Caprivi had lacked—knowledge of affairs and
foreign countries, of human nature in general, of those he
had to deal with in particular; and besides, had none of the
plain common-sense which Caprivi had frequently displayed.
He had the advantage of Caprivi in a fairly good education,
of which he made but little use; and as a civilian he was
necessarily less imposing in the Emperor's and the German
people's eyes. Bülow could play the Hussar when he con-

fronted the Generals, but Bethmann always had a touch of
Don Quixote about him; nor did his democratic ideals exceed
the level of the text-books. The depth and clarity of thought
ascribed to him by the intellectuals bore no perceptible fruit;
and would, anyhow, only have been acceptable to his sovereign if presented in the artistic shape of which he was incapable.

In point of fact, Bethmann was craftier and more ambitious than he allowed to appear. When in September 1909
Bülow, his advocate for the Chancellorship, besought an official denial of the slanders against him, Bethmann advised the
Emperor against that mere obligation of chivalry; and then
wrote to Bülow that he was sorry to say the Emperor had
"quite spontaneously" refused (A. 24, 210). When the
Emperor, during the War, reviled Bernstorff because America had come in, Bethmann offered up his Ambassador,
whose policy he had prescribed, as a victim to the Emperor's
vexation. He flinched before the cardinal test of his existence when, in the middle period of the War, he continued—
against his convictions—to officiate as a dummy Chancellor.

The first thing he did on being called to power was to
provide himself with a right-hand man; for before Kiderlen-
Wächter became responsible for foreign policy, Bethmann
was advised by him on fundamentals, and in special instances
received long letters of dogmatic counsel. Later he would,
as Kiderlen states, write despatches at his dictation, so that
the handwriting might leave no doubt of their being his own
intellectual property—so crafty was Bethmann-Hollweg.
The Emperor's tardy appointment of Kiderlen, whom he
had banished from his sight for years, was one of the signs of
a certain listlessness and secret despondency which had been
growing on him since the fall of Bülow and of Eulenburg.

"Well then, take Kiderlen," he said to Bethmann. "But you don't know what a louse you're taking on you, till you've got him." Kiderlen was, in truth, about the only man whom, before the War, the Emperor suffered to be near him against his own desire.

With more good sense than his predecessor, though often led astray by his native brutality, Kiderlen was hampered throughout his term of office by three particular circumstances. He did not possess the sovereign's confidence; the promotion came, both practically and personally speaking, too late, for meanwhile he had been prematurely worn-out by the endless waiting and a most unprofitable manner of life. Those heavy hands of his had been well able to grip and stun; but now, when the decisive battle was lost, had forgotten how to mould and bend. And above all he lacked, as did Bethmann, Bülow's skill in guiding the Emperor, whose vanity he had severely wounded by the malice of some long-ago intercepted letters. That under Holstein's spell he had of yore been Bismarck's enemy did him no good with the Emperor, who now brooded secretly upon all he might have learnt from the veteran; that he had broken with Eulenburg could only injure him, for the Emperor secretly pined after his friend—he said so to an intimate when they were once driving past Liebenberg. Kiderlen's roughness, his incapacity for honeyed phrases, made him uncongenial company for the sovereign.

This was why these two politicians could not make any headway against the swashbucklers on land and water, either with the Emperor or the *bourgeoisie*. True, Kiderlen was less pliable than Moltke, but Bethmann was more pliable than Tirpitz—and if the Emperor did not love the latter, he did fear him; moreover, Tirpitz had a resonant cast-iron programme to set against the flabby policy of the Wilhem-strasse, to which the two Epigoni of a sensational period were condemned.

The Emperor was peacefully inclined. "This wretched Morocco-business must be disposed of, quickly and once for all. There is nothing to be done there—the French *will* have it. So let us get out of the affair with decency!" But Kiderlen was keener than that. Now that the French were tackling Fez, he was meditating on another intervention in Morocco, on obtaining "material guarantees" in the shape of the best harbours, on a threatening gesture which should wipe out the lamentable consequences of the first, and squeeze some new Colonial territory out of the negotiations. For the second time the Emperor was right in Morocco—that is to say towards France—and his advisers were wrong. As in the past he had never for a moment wished to land at Tangier, and only yielded on Bülow's pressure, so in this summer of 1911 he opposed Kiderlen's plan of despatching warships. Now as then, one glance at the abyss was enough to deter him. In the earlier year he had been hypnotized by the ironworks of a German industrial; now he was paralysed by the iron circlet of a European alliance. A fatality which one might almost describe as logical, always tempted his advisers to a *coup de théâtre* when it was the last thing he desired.

Not that Kiderlen, either, wanted a war. He did not conceal from himself that it was impossible to prove any actual French encroachment in Morocco; but he was aping Bismarck's manner when in the July of 1911 he said to his Chancellor, who was almost completely in the dark: "Our prestige has suffered badly; if it comes to the worst, we shall have to fight" (Hammann, *Bilder*, 88). He merely

wanted "to remind the French that Germany still exists.
. . . Perhaps some German will be patriotic enough to get
slaughtered in Morocco, so that we can step in to avenge
him" (*Deutsche Revue,* 46, 201). His idea was to imitate
the Tangier gesture, and he forgot to consider that France
would not sacrifice a second Delcassé, that this time she
could reckon on new and powerful friends. Kiderlen wanted
to extort compensations at the point of the pistol; and at last
dragged from the reluctant Emperor at Kiel the command
to send the small cruiser "Panther," which carried 150 men,
to Morocco, where the French and Spaniards had over
100,000.

When, after this, some laconic negotiations between
Kiderlen and Cambon resulted in nothing, the Emperor
wrote:

What the devil is supposed to be going on now? It's a pure
farce! . . . If we let all this precious time go by, the British and
Russians will stiffen the backs of the frightened French, and dictate to them what they are to be most graciously pleased to concede us. This sort of diplomacy is too fine and large for my poor
brain!

He was right, and was right again when soon afterwards he
forbade Kiderlen to make any threats. For all the consequences, for the suspicion and ridicule poured by Europe on
the ill-considered policy of his two statesmen, the Emperor
must be absolved of any personal responsibility.

Only when the problem of England raised its head in all
its kaleidoscopic immensity, was the Emperor unchanged in
this more tranquil period. Throughout these years the documents are crammed with imperial fulminations against England: "Lies! The dog is lying! England! Uncle! A most

charming fellow, this King E. VII! Ineffable cheek! Phari-
see! Rot! Twaddle! Bunkum! Hurrah, we've caught the
British scoundrels out this time!"

The question of the fleet, again acute in the years
1911–12, culminated in a duel between Metternich and Tirpitz; the former wanted to stop, the latter to proceed indefinitely with building. Metternich spoke out more plainly than
ever:

> There is an idea in our naval circles that once we have taken
> some decided step towards the further construction of our Fleet,
> England will submit to the inevitable, and we shall become the best
> friends in the world. . . . It is a disastrous mistake. . . . Fear
> will have quite different fruits. It will set England in arms against
> us. . . . The alternatives are—slow down, or strike the blow.
> For the latter there is national objective.

Tirpitz, on the other hand, provided himself with reports
from the naval attaché in London which pointed to an attack being imminent, and easily contrived to win the Emperor over.

The Emperor wrote in August 1911: "A better tone
towards Germany will only be obtained by a larger fleet,
which will bring the British to their senses through sheer
fright." The better tone, the sheer fright—his old motives!
To win the respect of that one eternally unconquerable
family—that was it; for when the Emperor wrote "the British," he was always thinking of his grandmother, his uncle,
and later of his cousin George. While the Navy group were
tackling him at Rominten, Kiderlen wrote to one of his
jackals there, in a fuming rage:

> The Emperor must not listen only to one-sided advocates of the
> interests involved, but to all his appointed representatives; for we

stand now at the parting of the ways, and the position is too serious for him to decide upon at such a distance from his capital, and without giving any audience to his chosen advisers.

But these forcible words, when he read them over, frightened the new Bismarck. He struck them out of the draft.

Metternich alone kept his head, and reiterated his warnings. The Fleet-party attacked him; he was soon to pay the penalty.

If I had followed his advice at that time [wrote the Emperor on one of his despatches] we should now have no fleet at all! His argument implied the arbitration of a foreign nation in our naval policy, which I, as Supreme War-Lord and Emperor, could not now or at any time consider for a moment—and which, moreover, would be humiliating to our people! We stick to the Estimates.

Metternich read the comment, but on 11th December repeated his warnings. Then the Emperor openly derided him: "The poor man is past praying for! His parrot-cry is 'Don't arm at home, and then England will go on being in a good temper.'" But with admirable resolution Metternich still pressed on, and soon wrote:

I am very conscious that my attitude . . . does not meet with support from Your Majesty. . . . But I should depart from the truth if I reported otherwise, and I cannot barter my conviction even for my sovereign's favour. Moreover, I doubt if Your Majesty would be better served by smooth and optimistic communications persisted in until we suddenly found ourselves facing a war with England.

If only half a dozen Excellencies had thus manfully opposed the Emperor, he would be the Emperor still.

Neither Bethmann nor Kiderlen ever dreamed of resigning unless an Estimate which they regarded as pernicious was postponed; all they did was to send Ballin to London, where he talked with Churchill and Cassel. Churchill said: "This persistent competition in armaments must lead to war within the next two years." But when Metternich verbally reiterated his arguments, Ballin replied: "It's no good; the Emperor's nerves won't stand the strain much longer."

Metternich's answer was: "I had thought we were speaking of the Empire, not of the Emperor." Here we perceive once more that even Ballin, pacifist by conviction and interest, was at the service of the Emperor's personal feelings, which he deplored.

In February 1912 Lord Haldane, the War-Minister, came to Berlin to make a last attempt. Haldane spoke for the Cabinet, and with his King's approval, to the Emperor and Tirpitz—dangled before their eyes an African colony, suggested elimination of one ship each, but obtained no more than postponement of the German Estimate for one year. There followed written negotiations about crews and guns. But when Grey said to Metternich that he had no fears while Bethmann was Chancellor, but would have to reckon with other persons in the future, the Emperor, mortally offended, broke off the negotiations on various pretexts, and wrote furiously on the despatch: "It is the first I have heard of people making arrangements with one particular statesman, independently of the reigning sovereign. From the above it is evident that Grey has no notion who is really master, and that *I* govern!" This, and an affected speech of Churchill's in which he talked about the German "Luxury-fleet," were sufficient to produce a decided rupture. Even the Empress was drawn in by Tirpitz: "Your Majesty, the throne of your children is at stake!"—whereupon she drove straight to see Bethmann, and urge a decision upon him.

Metternich fell, because "he had failed in his duty." Tirpitz stood triumphant.

"And that *I* govern!" In those words William the Second once more asserted his innate consciousness of autocracy. This was not the mere cant-phrase of a Roi Soleil, of a Most High behind whose back his Ministers smiled; but the expression of a definite purpose. The Emperor, urged by three political advisers to an understanding, was perfectly free to fix, with Haldane or through Ballin, that "Fleet-Holiday" of which England was desirous; Lloyd George, Grey, Haldane, even Churchill, were once more striving to get rid of the monstrous expense of naval competition. No majority in the Reichstag, no overwhelming expression of public opinion, demanded an accelerated programme from the Government; nobody was putting pressure on the Emperor beyond a dozen naval men, supported by a few hundred thousand whooping civilians. Tirpitz once dismissed, the Emperor could have appointed any of his moderate men from one day to another—and a sigh of relief would have gone up from his people, more audible far than the trumpeting of the Pan-Germans. The English would not have decided against Germany in July 1914, and the War would have been avoided.

But the Emperor could not do these things; his nature forced him to the other course. Too deeply it was felt—the bitter, ever-renewed jealousy, the old unsilenced outcry of his wounded, susceptible spirit: Never to yield an inch to this one power, never to strike sail before England; or rather never to strike cannons, bristling as they were from out the neatly drawn-up lists, from out the pale-blue plans of the armoured turrets! That they might never go off was his hope; but that they should enforce respect from that haughty dynasty was his determination.

All his secret love of England, forever thwarted by hate and spite and jealousy, was made manifest when his uncle died. He was immeasurably relieved by the death of his mortal enemy; a few hours after the tidings came he wrote beside the Chancellor's condolences:

The . . . system of intrigue which kept Europe on tenterhooks, will come to an end. . . . I believe that European policy as a whole will be more quiescent; even if that were all, it would be something. Edward VII's chief mourners, besides his own people, will be the Gauls and the Jews.

But immediately afterwards, at the funeral, all sorts of old memories were revived—a human heart was filled with reminiscences of young untroubled days; and between Court-gossip, naïve delight in the approbation of the populace, and the weary round of politics, we find this, in the many-paged descriptive telegram to the Chancellor (A. 28, 327):

I found that my parents' old apartments in Windsor Castle, where I often played as a little boy, had been assigned to me. . . . Manifold were the memories that filled my heart. . . . They awakened the old sense of being at home here, which attaches me so strongly to this place, and which has made the political aspect of things so personally painful to me, especially in recent years. I am proud to call this place my second home, and to be a member of this royal family. . . . And they had kept my memory green, as a child who was so much addicted to pudding that he once was violently sick! Kindest regards.

When he concludes his long account of the obsequies with this smiling reminiscence, reaching back into the very mists of childhood, we cannot but be struck by the extraordinary destiny of a man who was driven by his dæmon to hate what he wanted to love.

4

Throughout the whole summer of 1912 the menace of a world-war hung over Europe. For the first time, the Balkans confronted Austria as an entity—that great antagonism which for thirty years had been far more unsettling for the Continent than the Alsace-Lorraine question. The conflict between Russia and Austria seemed once more acute, but no one dared to draw the sword.

Least of all the Emperor. Even in the year of Bosnia, when his Ambassador reported a renewal Panslavist agitation in the interests of military prestige, he wrote on the margin of the despatch: "Haven't they had misery enough? Incredible folly—to sacrifice hundreds of thousands just to save their face!" If this had represented his earnest conviction, it would be his redemption in the eyes of history; but it was like the rest, it was as deeply, or as superficially, felt as any of his hundred threatening speeches—it represented the mood of a moment, vanished with that moment, and in the decisive hour was lost in uttermost abysses of the heart.

The Balkan War of October 1912 convulsed the European Powers. They all lied freely, differing only in the manner of it—which in Petersburg was brazen, in London cautious, in Vienna frivolous, in Berlin stupid. When the war ended in the speedy defeat of the Turks, and they besought Germany's mediation, the Emperor forbade any joint action which could be construed as inimical by the Quadruple Alliance, "even at the risk of giving umbrage to some of the Powers in the Concert" (4, 11, 12). It was not until all were inclined for mediation that he acquiesced.

At the Conference he was more reasonable than his own Ministers, and told the Viennese Count Berchtold, who again wanted war with Serbia, that he had no right to cut the Serbians off from the sea. "I am still less inclined to embark on war for this question than I was for the Sandjak. The Triple Alliance covers only the actual possessions of the Powers concerned, not subsequent claims. I could not answer either to my people or my conscience for anything more." And when Bethmann warned him of a possible rupture of the Alliance, he earnestly reiterated his pacific admonition to the truculent Austria, rejecting all idea of a war,

in which everything would have to be risked, and which might mean the downfall of Germany—and all this for Albania and Durazzo! There is nothing whatever in the Treaty of Alliance to say that the German Army and the German people are to be pressed into the service of another State's political caprices, and be, so to speak, at her disposal for any and every purpose.

Golden words! Repeated two years later, they might have prevented the World-War.

But only two weeks later, a "shooting-visit" from the Austrian heir-apparent, Franz Ferdinand, produced a change of mood. Suddenly the Emperor declared the moment to be "too serious for us any longer to take the responsibility of hindering Austria from striking her blow." Such a revulsion, due to the suggestions of the allied Prince during a shoot or an evening-talk, is yet another testimony to the womanish instability of the Emperor's temperament. The political results were not long in following—a Conference of the allied Generals at Berlin, simultaneous advance guaranteed, a speech from the Chancellor about loyalty to the Alliance, great risk of war. Nor until this was over was it perceived that Vienna had duped them all, had never wanted the contest, but only a personal diplomatic success. Count Berchtold was merely toying with the idea of a world-war.

But the Emperor had been tuned up, and now demanded that his people should be enlightened by the Press "upon the vital needs of Austria; for otherwise, when the war comes, no one will know in whose interests Germany is to take up arms." But Russia once more drew back decisively; and Poincaré, "in great consternation," racked his brains to discover the "secret grounds" for this *volte-face*.

Again the Emperor turned a deaf ear to England. Great inducements were held out by Grey on the Eastern question, but were brought to naught by exaggerated claims and suspicions, precisely as in Holstein's year of opposition to Chamberlain; and immediately after the German refusal an agreement with France—this time, that known as the Cambon Correspondence—was concluded by England. "Now," wrote the Emperor, "we know what we have to expect. . . . Any Power we can get to help us is good enough now. It is life or death for Germany" (8, 12). So low had his pretensions fallen. The Empire was isolated, and now its Emperor had at last realized that, he would go in with any Power that offered itself. They must beware all round! And the Emperor wrote in March 1913: "Vienna's Serbian policy was a failure. Let her be advised . . . to retreat. Austria must share the Slavonic waters, else all the Slavs will be driven into Russia's arms."

With such pacifist reflections the Emperor sought to overthrow Berchtold; but he did not succeed. Nevertheless he had not failed to perceive, even then, the dangers attendant on the levity and ambition of a few aristocrats in Vienna. And when Serbia came out of the Peace of Bucharest with enhanced authority, and the policy of Vienna grew more aimless even than before, with internal affairs revolving in an endless chain of ineptitudes, it became clear to everyone, including the Emperor, that alliance with a tottering Empire meant that he was irrevocably and disastrously bound up with her fortunes. He felt "the battle between the Slav and the German" (as he always called it) drawing nearer and nearer, and could not but own to himself that the "Germans" were fettered in that conflict by a national covenant with a semi-Slavonic State.

Holstein's thesis of the inviolability of that covenant, so utterly and so swiftly refuted by history (like his other one of the eternal enmity between England and Russia), together with the Emperor's unstable policy—symbolized in the zigzag of his journeys—had ended by so isolating the Empire that it was too late for recognition to be of any service. Even Tschirschky, for many years Ambassador in Vienna, wrote so late as May 1914, in doubt whether it was "really worth our while to have identified ourselves so closely with a structure which is giving way at every point, or to persist in the heavy task of trying to drag it in our wake." Yet for all that, they did not even feel sure of Austria at Berlin, and in the last war with Serbia had been relieved to know that at least Vienna must be the first to show fight!

The Emperor was entirely conscious of the situation which in point of fact his own decisions had imposed upon the Empire, and was not urged by any sentimental motives to over-prize the Alliance. He had no very excessive respect even for the old Emperor—he only affected that cult because it seemed to him becoming; and as to the Archduke, *he* was as wholly alien as the difference in the shape of their heads would indicate. Hard, savage, entirely without charm, he

was a morose and scornful misanthrope, sullen and dare-
devil, brutal and rapacious, neither an orator nor a linguist,
but an impassioned sportsman and gardener, tender only as
husband and father, and unacquainted with pretence in any
form.   Franz Ferdinand's and William's characters were
poles apart. The only trait they had in common was an autocratic temper; their only bond of union was a pact to which
they stuck as to a tedious half-hearted marriage.

The more the Emperor distrusted Austria, the more he
sought, especially at the last, to make sure of the Balkans.
He had supported Serbia against Vienna at the Conference;
the Bulgarians he pronounced to be "the nation of the future, and as little to be checked in their development as of old
the Prussians."   To the Greeks, whose Queen was now his
sister, he handed over Kavalla in time of peace against
strong opposition, and concluded that Greece was a rich
country because he had seen for himself how prosperous was
Corfu. As to the Turks, suspended between life and death,
he insured himself for either event. He wrote: "Preparations from the partition of Turkey, which apparently is more
imminent than is generally thought. . . . N.B.:—No partition without us!" and mentally reserved Mesopotamia for
Germany. But at the same time, in the November of 1913,
he sent General Liman von Sanders there as Commander of
the First Army Corps, with almost unlimited powers of control and punishment. This enraged the Russians and perturbed the English, who were by way of assuming the command in that quarter, though it were but from on board
their ships. Ultimately the Emperor had once more to
yield the cardinal point in this rash undertaking.

Only about the Fleet was he unchangingly intransigeant.
The roots of this had been planted in his youth. And yet

he had known now for the last five years that, encircled as he was, only the greatest prudence would avail to preserve him and his Empire.

5

The Kiel Week was at its height. The Emperor as Admiral, under the ensign of the "Hohenzollern," was conducting the Regatta. The date was 28th June 1914, and it was three o'clock. If he looked eastward, he could see a couple of swart ships silhouetted against the sunlit sky; these flew the Union Jack. Churchill had wished to be present, but there had been difficulties about the form of the invitation; and so this last opportunity for a quiet discussion had been let slip on the characteristic ground that the Englishman must give official expression to his privately conveyed desire for an invitation. But Briand too was absent, though he had been bidden by the Prince of Monaco. Why was that?

And now, while the Emperor is heart and soul in the Regatta, a motor-boat is seen approaching. Those on board convey their desire to lie-to; the Emperor signals "No, he will not be disturbed"; but the officer in the boat persists; he flourishes a despatch—then puts it in his cigarette-case and hurls it on board, so that the sailor standing nearest has to pick it up and present it to his sovereign. Woe betide someone, if the tidings are not worth such powder and shot as this!

Three hours ago—the Emperor reads—the Archduke and his wife had been assassinated at Serajevo. "Now I've got to begin all over again!" Those were his first words. Then flags half-masted, Regatta and Kiel Week broken off; and he returns to Berlin.

The Serbian marksman, who under the doubly symbolic

name of Gabriel Princip let lose the world-cataclysm, shot the Emperor straight through the heart. Not because of the chief victim, who had never been his friend, and for whose memory no word of grief escaped him even in the earliest moment of the tidings. Much more than friendship had been pierced in him; the Serb had blown out the very nucleus of his outlook on the world, of his most cherished faith. "By the Grace of God"—that was the profoundest consciousness in William the Second's soul, sincerely, guilelessly alive in him, both source and vindication of his self-esteem. By that consciousness alone he felt himself enjoined to dominate his fellow-men, to cling no less than religiously to the ancient conceptions of King and Subject.

Princes are hallowed, because God holds direct communion with them—that, in its antiquated fullness, was his article of faith; and even the most antagonistic of princes, even King Edward, was in personal intercourse at any rate more congenial to him than Roosevelt, whom he courted for the sake of his powerful country. Though he despised the Tsar as a weakling and a dreamer, that monarch's life was of much more importance in his eyes than the life of the "woodcutter Fallières." When Carnot was assassinated, his heart was entirely unmoved; when King Humbert fell, all the Emperor's spectres rose and gibbered round his head. Not only was his whole foreign policy one of alliance with dynasties, so that he lamented over the blood-sprent ruins of the French monarchy a hundred-and-twenty years after Louis XVI had been beheaded, and thought of Jaurès as enthroned where Kings had sat; not only did he feel that semi-republican England with her changing majorities was no stable partner in a covenant; but in Germany, that faith in kings determined his Thirty Years' War against the Socialists, whom he lumped in with anarchists, and thought of as mere regicides.

With his intense class-consciousness, the news from Serajevo could not but assail him in his dignity, his sense of a divine mission, and likewise in his ever-wakeful fear of a kindred fate; so that his markedly pacific attitude in the recent emergencies altered in the twinkling of an eye to a burning desire for atonement and intimidation. In the last five years the Emperor's veto had been chiefly instrumental in averting three Serbian conflagrations; but now at last the fire-eating Viennese Counts and the Berlin Pan-Germans, the Parisian *revanchistes* and the Petersburg war-lords, with their respective militarists, had their long hoped-for, glorious Day. The World-War which had been smouldering for thirty years, and even in Bismarck's time had threatened to break out over the Russo-Austrian quarrel—that is to say, over the paradox of the Hapsburg Monarchy—could not have exploded more logically than upon the pretext of this Serbian affair.

Neither Poincaré's pretensions nor William's provocations, neither the whooping of a few thousand Lorrainers on the boulevards, nor the arrogance of as many Pan-Germans, will avail, in the eyes of history, to fix the crime of this war upon the respective nations. The situation had existed for decades, the danger had been increasing for years, and with it the caution of all concerned; but there was not one ruler who dreaded, and therefore avoided, war so much as the Emperor did. Had he kept quiet, as in the three recent emergencies, Europe might have been saved once more by statecraft, even though he had incurred the enmity of England, the deciding factor in this crisis. Only the most profound emotional disturbance could divert his essentially timorous nature from the chosen course; and even so only for a brief period.

In the beginning of the July of 1914—the history of which is no more to be recounted here than that of the War —an adept in human nature could have foreseen the Emperor's attitude, and that in both of its phases. First, punishment for regicide, swift, violent; but then, with growing sense of his encompassment, cessation of any sabre-rattling. All his affectation of domineering masterfulness revived at the sound of the fanatic's pistol-shot, but only for a moment; and just as on that January morning of 1896 his megalomania had been diverted from letting loose a war with England in the Transvaal to sending a congratulatory telegram to Kruger, so, these eighteen years later, the bleeding head of that one Serbian would have availed to stay his wrath.

Three students of human nature, with a sense of their responsibility upon them, at the head of the Petersburg, Vienna, and Berlin Cabinets, could, on that First of July, 1914—despite all the bellicose militarists of Europe—once more have conjured the tempest, precisely as had been done thirty, and then five, years before. Witte, Tisza, and Bülow could have achieved it. But Isvolski and Berchtold toyed criminally with the idea of war—the former to avenge himself for his failure at Buchlau, when he abandoned Bosnia to the Austrians; the latter to wipe out the Serbian checkmate of the preceding years, which he sullenly ascribed to the Emperor William's desire for peace.

Three Emperors, avowedly opposed to war, were driven by the ambition, vindictiveness, and incompetence of their Ministers into a conflict whose danger for their thrones they all three recognized from the first, and if only for that reason tried to avoid. Their three peoples were, like all the others

eventually to be involved, pacifically inclined; and only by
the universal propaganda of lies were they ever goaded into
hate—for not trade-rivalry nor race-antagonism, not material nor moral causes, made this Cabinet-War a necessity
in any one of the European States. The life-blood of ten
millions of her sons was shed by Europe, not under any
"tragic necessity," not through any "fatal concatenation" of
circumstances; the sacrifice was extorted from her only by
her wrangling statesmen.

The first of the many words written by the Emperor on
the margin of the 879 German documents of the days preceding the War, were these, two days after the assassination:
"Now or never!" (D. 7). When it came to the settling of
accounts with Serbia, and his Ambassador in Vienna wisely
wrote: "I seize every similar opportunity of advising, very
quietly but very decidedly and earnestly, against any rash
steps," the Emperor broke out furiously in the course of
perusal: "Who gave him any such instructions? It's idiotic!
he has nothing to do with it. . . . Later on, if it comes to
blows, they'll be saying that Germany wasn't inclined!
Tschirschky, if you please, is to have done with that nonsense! The Serbs must be wiped out, and at once!" In the
days immediately following he insisted, in all despatches,
that Vienna's demands on Serbia should be made without
delay.

On 5th July he received an autograph letter from his ally,
which informed him that Count Hoyos had declared for the
dismemberment of Serbia. On this, without consulting his
Chancellor, he gave the Austrian Ambassador, after lunch
at Potsdam, the *carte blanche* which he had refused him before they sat down to the meal. Without this promise Austria could not have stirred a step; with it, Vienna could

carry out her plans. On the 5th and 6th, as all the chiefs were on leave, the Emperor consulted with their delegates over military and naval preparedness for war. This was inevitable at a crisis; but he summoned no Crown-Council. Then he started—fatally—on a Scandinavian cruise, in some sort urged by those who hoped for war and dreaded his timidity.

Three years ago, in July 1911, the mere intimation that Kiderlen was desirous to take strong measures against France had so disturbed him on the Scandinavian cruise that he had written, quite rightly:

Then I must come home at once. For I cannot allow my Government to take such a step without being on the spot myself, so as to have a clear idea of the consequences, and some control over them. It would be unpardonable to do anything else. . . . *Le Roi s'amuse!* And meanwhile we're heading towards mobilization! That sort of thing shan't go on in my absence.

Now, for three weeks, he sprinkled the telegraphed reports with comments which reveal his moods as clearly as a journal could have done. Everything that was more than an emotional outburst, everything that represented purpose and conviction, was wired to the Ambassadors, in order that "their tone" should be in accordance with the imperial will. By these orders, dashed on to the paper by an excited man on board ship, to whom neither individual nor national counsel or admonition could be directly conveyed, the decisions of the Allies were, in those three weeks of July, shaped, authorized, or at the very least unhindered.

In the Viennese despatch of the 10th the Emperor read the intolerable demands which it was proposed to make upon Serbia, together with the following comment on them:

"Should the Serbians accept all the conditions, it would be a solution very unwelcome to Count Berchtold; and he is still considering whether further demands cannot be made, which would render it quite impossible for Serbia to acquiesce." Beside this diabolical suggestion the Emperor wrote: "Clear out of the Sandjak! So then the fat is really in the fire! Austria must have that back at once, so as to prevent the union of Serbia and Montenegro, and Serbia's access to the sea!"

A year and a half ago he had said:

I am still less inclined to embark upon war for this question than I was for the Sandjak. The Triple Alliance covers only the actual possessions of the Powers concerned, not subsequent claims. I could not answer either to my people or my conscience for anything more. . . . A war in which everything would have to be risked, and which might mean the downfall of Germany—and all this for Albania and Durazzo!

So blind had fury made him now. At the same period he wrote beside the remark that Count Tisza was for prudence and moderation: "Towards murderers, after what has come to pass? Imbecility!" And underneath: "As in the time of the Silesian War: 'I am opposed to councils of war and deliberations, since in these the chicken-hearted party always has the upper hand' [Frederick the Great]" (D. 29).

Suffering from his sense that the sanctuary had been violated, impelled by the desire to stand forth before his people in this swiftly sharpening crisis as the guardian of the royal idea, surrounded only by the sea and his gasconading fellow-voyagers, represented at home by two incompetent statesmen—he forgot all the prudent arguments which had hitherto made him so sceptical about the Viennese War-Counts' adventure, and insisted on avenging the assassination. Indeed, it seemed that he was the one who could not wait; for on two Viennese despatches of the 14th, intimating a desire to postpone the ultimatum until Poincaré's departure, he twice wrote: "What a pity!"

A decisive factor in this vehemence was his fixed belief that the Tsar could never take the part of "regicides." That old delusion of his—that nations were still, as of yore, ruled by their sovereigns, the exaggerated regard for dynastic influence which he derived from the fact that his own was far too preponderant in Germany—affected his calculations throughout these weeks. For him, the Tsar "by the Grace of God" represented the Government of Russia; and though he knew by experience that Nicholas was a weakling, he continued to repeat in writing that never could the Tsar take the Serbians' part—those "active and vicarious regicides." Hence it was, once more, the royal idea which caused him to believe that Russia would tacitly suffer the humiliation of Serbia, instead of reckoning on her intervention, and its consequence—the World-War.

This note was recurrent as against England also—of whose hostile intervention Prince Lichnowsky urgently warned Germany from the earliest day. He, Bernstorff, and Wangenheim were the only men who, before Germany's enemies declared themselves, saw and said how things would go. And when he read such warnings, the Emperor's sense of the Elect of God assailed took on a dual form. Just as no king could possibly take the part of regicides, so no voice might be raised against the Hapsburg's right to decide as he pleased.

Why should *I* undertake [wrote the Emperor beside Grey's suggestion] to smooth down Vienna! Those dogs have added murder to rebellion, and must be made to knuckle under. . . . This is a piece of monstrous insolence on the part of Britain. I am not called upon to write His Majesty the Emperor prescriptions for the preservation of his honour, *à la* Grey! . . . Let this be conveyed to Grey, very seriously and explicitly, so that he may see I am not to be played with. . . . The Serbians are a pack of criminals, and should be treated as such. I will not interfere in matters which are the Emperor's business, and his alone. . . . This is the typical British attitude of condescending authority, and I wish to put it on record that I entirely repudiate it! William I.R.

Even to its pompous signature this outburst resembles the most frantic documents of his middle-period; yet while he thus refused to tranquillize his ally, he ordered that Paris should be requested to smooth down hers. This was written under the heights of Balholm on 24th July, before he had any knowledge of the ultimatum to Serbia. Of its purport the Emperor then had no idea at all, and his Ministers were informed—to their consternation—only twenty-four hours before it was delivered. The excitement which England had always been able to stir in him now awakened all the old impulses and foibles, all the old defiance and uneasiness; and while he played the chivalrous ally who had promised the "venerable sovereign" in Vienna his lance and shield, and scorned to inquire for what sort of an adventure, he was at the same time pitching into the Englishman as if he were a schoolboy.

Higher and higher mounted his martial ardour—nothing that was done in Vienna seemed enough, in his eyes. Again on the 26th he wrote (D. 145) on a despatch from Paris: "Ultimata are either carried out or not! But there's an end to discussion! Hence the name!" and on one from Vienna (D. 155) which reported that Berchtold had disclaimed to the Russian Ambassador any idea of acquisitions, and had even spoken in a somewhat conciliatory tone, the Emperor wrote:

> Quite superfluous; will give an impression of weakness . . . Which is entirely untrue as regards Russia, and must be avoided at all costs. . . . The matter cannot now be referred to discussion behind our backs. . . . The ass! Austria must get back the Sand-jak, else the Serbians will come down to the Adriatic!

And: "Serbia is not, in the European sense, a State at all," he continued on the same day (D. 157), "but a community of brigands!" When Grey in the same despatch conveyed his view that a European war was "staring us in the face," the Emperor's only comment was: "That's a certainty"; and when the Englishman for the fourth time suggested a conference for arbitration with a view to avoiding war: "Superfluous. . . . I will not co-operate, unless Austria explicitly asks me to do so, which is improbable. One does not confer with others over vital questions of honour."

These words, which on the night of the 26th were wired to Berlin, and next morning wired on to London, put an extinguisher on the suggestion of Grey, who wanted (precisely as in the preceding year) to patch up the quarrel at a Conference of Ambassadors; but who, it must be said, had delayed to inform Petersburg of neutrality, or Berlin of England's readiness for war—which, officially conveyed, would have acted as a deterrent warning.

On that 26th, while all Europe was in suspense about the reception of the ultimatum, the Emperor's vehemence increased to boiling-point. By this time he had lost all faith even in Russia's attitude to kings, for he wrote: "Since her fraternization with the French Socialist Republic [she has] let that go!" In another place: "This comes of an alliance between an absolute monarchy and an absolute socialistic *sans-culotte* Republic." Finally, on Sasonov's threat that if Austria exterminated Serbia, Russia would fight, he wrote in the Berlin vernacular: *"Na, denn zu!"* (Well, come on then!"). On the same day, under a monitory despatch from Rome: "This is sheer bunkum, and events will soon prove it to be so"; and on a warning from the Chancellor to stop the homeward-bound Fleet, he wrote furiously: "Incredible suggestion! Not to be thought of! . . . Our civilian Chancellor has not yet grasped the [general situation]" (D. 182).

In those July days all the Emperor's good angels deserted him in mid-ocean.

Even in the days immediately following, when Bethmann warned him against precipitate mobilization, again referred to England's mediation, and asked for a pacific attitude (D. 197), the result was open derision. "To be pacific is the first duty of the citizen! Peace, peace—nothing but peace! A peaceful mobilization, too, strikes one as something new"; and Bethmann in his despatch having inquired where the Emperor meant "to land," the Admiral of the Atlantic made game of the land-lubber in two exclamation-marks, because the Chancellor, in the stress of affairs, had not wired in nautical language: "go ashore."

The Emperor and the Serbian answer reached Berlin almost at the same moment. The answer was very nearly that unconditional acceptance which Berchtold had so sorely dreaded. The Emperor read it—and in a trice his mood completely changed. Was it the anxious faces of his subjects, which this time he had searched upon his way from the coast to the capital? Was it the change of environment? The too long-delayed contact with his responsible advisers? Or was it perhaps only the recognition that no more *could* be asked? Anyhow, on the 28th he wrote under the Serbian reply:

A brilliant solution—and in barely 48 hours! This is more than could have been expected. A great moral victory for Vienna; but with it every pretext for war falls to the ground, and [the Ambassador] Giesl had better have stayed quietly at Belgrade. On this document, *I* should never have given orders for mobilization!

Indeed, he actually spurred himself to write a long autograph letter to his Secretary of State, instead of the usual marginalia or oral behests which had long taken the place of such efforts. It stated: "The most submissive of capitulations is what this signifies, and no possible pretext for war now remains." In the meantime, though, Belgrade must be held as a material guarantee for the execution of the demands, so that the Army, thrice fruitlessly mobilized, might have its *satisfaction d'honneur* and the consciousness of having at least set foot on alien soil. . . . Otherwise, with the abandonment of the campaign, there might arise considerable discontent against the dynasty, which would be most deplorable.

In case Your Excellency shares this view, I would suggest saying to Austria . . . that we congratulate her. That of course there are no further grounds for war. But that certainly a guarantee is necessary, until the claims are satisfied. . . . On this basis I am ready to negotiate for peace with Austria. . . . This I will do after My own manner, and with all possible consideration for Austria's national sentiments and the honour of her Army. . . . The Army must have a tangible *satisfaction d'honneur*—that is to be understood as a condition of My mediation. . . . I have ordered Plessen to write to the Chief of Staff in the foregoing sense.

A return to reason—very slightly masked. Can we not hear his sigh of relief—the civilian eternally condemned to the uniform? The storm has cleared off; there is no more talk of war, the bandits need not be wiped out, the Sandjak need not be invested, Serbia need not be cut off from the Adriatic; conquest and general conflagration have turned into a military parade; the only questions are the honour of the Army, the prestige of the dynasty—and the regicides are extolled for their "brilliant solution." All that was moderate in him was counting on peace.

Too late. Pandora's box was opened.

6

Everything that ensued in the decisive four days was born of his will to peace; and if sometimes the Emperor belied that earlier impulse, it was only the result of a nervous temperament which forgot one mood in the excitement of the next. All the recklessness with which Berlin had sanctioned the proceedings of its ally and subscribed beforehand to what was later exacted, was authorized by the Emperor's marginalia; if the dissuasions, exhortations, and warnings, which poured into Vienna from 28th July onwards, had been despatched in the preceding fortnight (as Grey had urged upon the Emperor), if he had been as collected on board ship as he was now, Vienna would never have rejected the reply to the ultimatum, London would have obtained the Conference, Petersburg could scarcely have drawn the sword.

In these latter days, when all Europe was laying, and unjustly laying, Vienna's rejection of the ultimatum to Germany's charge, the Emperor was whole-heartedly ready for any retreat from the position. Though so recently as the 26th he had repudiated all reliance on Russia since her fraternization with the Republic, he now declared (D. 288): "This was not known to me [that Russia would support Serbia]. I could not foresee that the Tsar would go in with bandits and regicides, even at the risk of a European war. Such a mentality is inconceivable in a German—it is Slavonic or Latin."

By any means he now sought to put on the brake. His urgent telegram of the 28th to the Tsar crossed a precisely similar one from the Tsar to him—two cries for help, which symbolically passed each other on the singing wires; though the tone in which he dealt with the Russian telegram was collected. But, on the other hand, he fulminated against his own subjects with a terrible energy of hate: "The Socialist crew is making anti-military street-demonstrations—that must not on any account be suffered, especially now. If there is any repetition, I shall proclaim martial law and have the leaders, one and all, imprisoned."

Beyond the frontiers an army of a million was assembling; from one day to another the Emperor's functionaries informed him, not only from Petersburg, that Russia was mobilizing. That did not dismay him. But that the people, or some of the people, in Berlin had risen to avert the disaster if their utmost effort could achieve it—this was for him the call to arms. William the Second, throughout his life, was less afraid of the coalition without, than of the revolt within, the realm.

For England alone he was as full of hate as ever; and while the other marginalia of the 28th were suddenly invested with a calm common-sense style (only occasionally

enlivened by "Swine" and similar zoological amenities)
against England there was a hailstorm of invectives and
harangues. Indubitably he was right, that Grey "by one
stern, energetic expostulation with Petersburg . . . could
quiet them both down"; but then he worked himself up into
an outburst which, coming from Germany, had the effect of
an amazing paradox: "A common scoundrel! England
alone is responsible for war or peace—*we* are so no longer!
And that must be publicly proclaimed!"

Then, like a thunderbolt, fell the tidings—dreaded for
years, foreboded for days. It had come true. Russia was
mobilizing her army of a million along the whole length of
the frontier. And now it was as though the Never-Silent
stood speechless before the embodied spectre. Seconds
passed away; and then with his last hope his nerves, too,
broke in pieces. How suddenly they seemed to darken the
sun—the awful meshes of that net invisible till now, though
so long felt! He was caught in those meshes . . . and now
the heaped-up waters of his rage rushed forth in torrents.
The insulted, the betrayed, the blameless Prince, whose good
intentions he was conscious of, whose errors he ignored, and
so could feel subjectively absolved from blame! In a genuinely impressive composition the floodgates of his forebodings were opened at last:

My function is at an end. . . . Wantonness and weakness are
to engulf the world in the most terrible of wars, the ultimate aim
of which is the ruin of Germany. For now I can no longer doubt it
—England, France, and Russia have conspired . . . to fight together for our annihilation. . . . That is, in a nutshell, the naked
truth of the situation which was slowly and surely created by
Edward VII . . . and is now to be put in use. The folly and
incompetence of our ally is the snare in which we have been caught.

. . . And so the notorious encirclement of Germany is at last an accomplished fact. . . . England stands derisive, brilliantly successful in her long-meditated, purely anti-German policy—a superb achievement, stirring to admiration even him whom it will utterly destroy! The dead Edward is stronger than the living I! We ran our heads into the noose . . . in the pathetic hope of appeasing England!!! All my warnings, all my prayers, fell on deaf ears. And here are our thanks from England! Through my dilemma of loyalty for the venerable old Emperor a situation was created for us which gave England the desired pretext for annihilating us. . . . Our Consuls in Turkey and India, our agents, and all such, must inflame the whole Mohammedan world to frantic rebellion against this detestable, treacherous, conscienceless nation of shopkeepers; for if *we* are to bleed to death, England shall at all events lose India! W.

Never in all his myriad utterances did William the Second give forth so elemental an outcry; never in his life did he call down fire and flame upon an enemy with fervour like to this. Only from a genuine passion does such blind wrath blaze forth, and only once in a lifetime. This malediction was written under a threatening despatch from Petersburg which never once mentioned England. With the Russian mobilization, the Emperor saw the War to be inevitable which for five years he had tried to hinder. England's attitude was menacing, but was not yet decisive; the conflict was Russian; the mobilization, the betrayal, were Russian; yet the Emperor's bitterness and fury, mortification and horror, were directed neither on the trickery of his ally nor the rancours of the Russian Court, nor even on the English Premier. In the hour of this Passion, only the ghost of that loathed enemy whom he had thought to overcome through death, appeared before him, while the images of mother and grandmother hovered vaguely around him. The rending of a

family-tie was, in William the Second's belief, the origin
of the World-War. As a despairing man he entered that
conflict.

Nevertheless, he assumed in every way the attitude of an
absolute monarch. Amid the turmoil he was solicitous for
all the knightly procedure which his historical sense of etiquette demanded; and while everywhere the Parliaments of
the Twentieth Century were deciding the issues of war or
peace, the three last Emperors were flinging down their
gauntlets as in the troubadours' tourneys, without in any one
instance riding into the lists themselves for life or death.
They turned over ancient parchments to find the best-
rounded formula for gauntlet flung and challenge issued;
and so the Wilhelmstrasse wrote (D. 542): "S.M. l'Em-
pereur, mon Auguste Souverain, au nom de l'Empire relève
le défi et Se considère en état de guerre avec la Russie."

It was thus that the crazy old machine creaked for the
last time through the earliest clatter of weapons; and while
Emperor and Tsar were exchanging anguished appeals—
which were genuine on both their parts, since each was trembling for his throne—they were both caught up against
their wills by the vast engine whose mighty arm had such
centripetal force as no king had ever so much as imagined
until now. Even with England, the family rancour was
veiled in cousinly affection. Like antiquated puppets, Prince
Henry and King George assured each other of peace and
amity; and George and Willy, even on the First of August,
were exchanging telegrams which it must be owned were
chillier even than the martial farewells of Nicky and Willy.

Though the Tsar's troops were already discharging their
guns, the Emperor's heart was much more sorely stricken
by the King of Italy, who now at last began to chaffer with

him. "Scoundrel! Blackguard!" (D. 700) said the marginalia; and the King of Greece, who pleaded his alliance with Serbia as an excuse for neutrality, was hectored in true Frederician style: "You are ordered to advance against Russia!"

With the beginning of the conflict, a sense of pride in Germany took chief place among the Emperor's emotions; and though all the sovereigns were cousins and in nearly every instance had a common grand- or great-grandmother, he dissociated himself from them, and talked of "Slav treachery, Latin arrogance, native British duplicity." Marginalia to remarks by Tyrrell and Bunsen ran thus: "The son of a German, yet he lies like this!" and "A German, and he puts his hand to such lies!!" (D. 764). Yet in particular instances he perceived German errors sooner than anyone else did; and though he cast all blame for the War on Russia and England, never on Paris nor even on Vienna, he wrote on a report of the 4th of August which confirmed the defection of the Roumanian confederates: "Our allies are falling like rotten apples, even before the War begins! A total defeat for German, and consequently Austrian, foreign diplomacy. This could, and should, have been avoided" (D. 811).

These classically formed phrases, which are the last of any interest among his marginalia, afford us a glimpse into his inmost soul on the afternoon following the speech in the Weisser Saal. It was a brief moment of insight wherein he perceived, not his own errors indeed, but at any rate those of his functionaries. The terrible isolation which his personal policy, his nervous temperament, had brought upon him and his Empire in the space of twenty-five years grew more and more alarming as ally after ally deserted him. Then he could fully realize what it meant to be burdened with a corpse which stank to heaven, and—a worse lot than Hamlet's with the dead Polonius—to be obliged to drag it on the stage with his own hands. "I never," said an intimate, "have seen so tragic and ravaged a face as the Emperor's is in these days" (T. 238).

William the Second was confronted by the first and last ordeal of his life. Now, before the nation and history, he was called upon to justify his system of autocracy and the Divine Right of Kings; now, too, within his heart to play the winning hazard of his life—show courage, strength of will, decision, and collectedness: all that through thirty years he never had exacted from himself. For now the measure he had set so arrogantly for the Emperor—the measure of omnipotence—was given him in all its length and breadth, and he must answer to it.

Now or never he must show that he was master.

CHAPTER VIII

WAR

1   1914–1918

THE Emperor, during the War, refused to face facts, and entrenched himself in optimism. . . . The contrast between the masterful personality which he tried to assume (and indeed was obliged to assume), and the absence of any real force of character, grew daily more glaring until the bitter end. It was his and Germany's misfortune that it could not be said of him as of his grandfather that he was no mere War-Lord, but a true soldier (Freytag-Loringhoven, *Menschen und Bilder*, 276).

This verdict from an aristocratic General epitomizes the Emperor's attitude throughout the War.

The selection of his commanders in the field was entirely his own. It was he who then urged on the excellent younger Moltke the command of an army of a million—a task which demanded nerves of iron, and accorded ill with a tendency either to agoraphobia or humanitarianism, both of which afflicted Moltke. With the appointment he took over the Emperor's own plan of campaign, which had been unprotestingly acquiesced in by Schlieffen. It led, as we saw in Waldersee's account, to a great diminution of the Eastern Army for the Western—thus contravening old Moltke's scheme. For a moment chance seemed to be going to turn everything topsy-turvy. A misapprehension in London, whereby it was believed that France might remain neutral under an English guarantee, revealed the inflexible nature of warlike organizations even to lay perceptions. "Then," said the Emperor to Moltke on 1st August, after this fallacious news had reached him, "we will simply advance in the East, with the whole Army!"

Moltke: "That is impossible, Your Majesty. An army of a million cannot be improvised. It would be nothing but a rabble of undisciplined armed men, without a commissariat."

The Emperor, tartly: "Your uncle would have given me a different answer!"

Moltke: "It is utterly impossible to advance except according to plan: strong in the West, weak in the East."

On this the Emperor wired to the King of England: "For technical reasons the mobilization on two fronts ordered by me for this afternoon, which entails the advance already arranged for on the Eastern and Western frontiers, cannot now be countermanded. I hope France will not be uneasy." To tone down the inevitably menacing effect of an advance on the frontier, the Emperor then—at Bethmann's desire, and without consulting Moltke, who was present— gave orders to his aide-de-camp: "The Sixteenth Division at Trier will not be transferred to Luxembourg."

Moltke, who describes this scene, confesses:

I felt as if my heart would break. Here was yet another risk of complications in our advance. When I got home, I was like a broken man, and shed tears of despair. . . . I sat in my room, doing nothing, utterly dejected, until at eleven o'clock at night I was again summoned to His Majesty.

The mistake had been cleared up; there was to be war with France; the advance was to be as arranged. "I have not been able to get over this experience. It was as though something in me had been irretrievably shaken. My confidence and self-reliance were destroyed."

From this account of a mistake which had no tangible results there is more to be learnt than from the report of a battle. The logic of the machine checkmates its constructor and makes him its slave; the war with France would inexorably have broken out, even if it had been really inhibited by England's guarantee, and despite the will to peace of both combatants (in so far as that existed in Paris)—and that because the artful mechanism of the advance must not be meddled with, and a million soldiers could not possibly confront another million on the frontier without a warlike incident of some sort. And simultaneously this narrative reveals the character of a Field-Marshal who, on the decisive day of his life, at the outbreak of the War for which he and his Army have been preparing for decades, sits for hours gloomy and inactive in his room, because international necessities have upset the arrangements for his advance—and yet, when publicly and personally ignored, has not the pluck to resign his office there and then.

Beside him stands an Emperor who indeed had ventured, in his youth, to contravene the fundamental principle of this advance, and therefore is to be regarded as an authority on the art of war—but who now, when the bomb has exploded, betrays entire ignorance of the laws of his machine, and imagines it can make a sudden revolution which had never been provided for. But when the whole thing reveals itself as a mare's-nest, the Field-Marshal is a broken man—not because the war is after all to be on two fronts, but because for a moment it threatened to be on only one. His tears of despair were for the system over-ridden; and though we cannot but look upon a weeping Prussian General with some distaste, we can certainly understand his forebodings of the autocracy which the Supreme War-Lord was apparently going to exercise over his Chief of Staff.

It was not so, in the event. This event surprised those who knew the Emperor only from the outside—which means, the entire nation.

For twenty-six years he had accustomed his people to "our royal will and pleasure"; he had meddled in all departments of the national life, had prided himself on a personal authority which over-rode the Constitution. Now, free of the detested Houses, sole arbiter in all decisions of the War, invested with such power as none other in Europe possessed (for Tsar and Hapsburg were too weak or too old), now, when autocracy was the order of the day—*now* the Emperor would have none of it. With our recognition of this, the last link in the chain is forged—in the chain which from his childhood, from his princely youth, to the days of November and the days of July, it has been the aim of this book to link up with the infirmity which was the source of every action of his life. In the stern hour which called for energy—and all his intimates had foretold it—the mainspring of his nervous temperament snapped, and he stopped dead.

The Emperor [writes Ludendorff (*Kriegserinnerungen*, 203)] was Supreme War-Lord. Over Army and Navy his was the unquestioned power of command. The Army and Navy Chiefs were his subordinates. The Chief of Staff personally conducted operations in the field, but under His Majesty's orders. Vital decisions had to obtain the imperial sanction; the Chief of Staff did not possess supreme authority.

Falkenhayn makes a similar statement; and Schwerdtfeger (S. 12), from whose masterly diagnosis we take the following quotations, repeatedly and emphatically declares that "the responsibility of the Sovereign was supreme, and as a consequence the whole extent of the various failures, or even the final defeat, is primarily attributable to him." And so says Hindenburg (*Aus meinem Leben,* 170) : "On vital matters I interviewed the Emperor myself and besought, when necessary, the imperial sanction for our measures."

Thus omnipotent, the Emperor could have created his masterpiece—could have given daily and nightly consideration to the welfare of the Army, which was at once the welfare of the nation and his own interest; at a stroke he could have concentrated his lifelong craving for excitement on the single aim of learning war from war, of being the father of his troops. But scarce six months had passed before he was the prisoner of his own Headquarters; in two years all power of decision had left him.

At first, when he realized that instead of a resolute soldier he had, in Moltke, a tormented intellectual at his side, he did make an effort to assume command. But in Falkenhayn's time he was quick to abjure an active part. Ultimately he was not the commander, but the subordinate, of Hindenburg and Ludendorff, of whom the first hypnotized him by a national reputation, the second by an iron will.

He was partly responsible for the result of the Battle of the Marne. That decrease in the Eastern Army which was the Emperor's, not Schlieffen's, idea, and which had been described as perilous by Waldersee fifteen years before, was quickly visited upon him by the irruption of the Russians. The President of East Prussia arrived at Headquarters, imploring aid. He demanded from the Emperor in person the despatch of two divisions, by which the Western advance was suddenly depleted, and the fatal gap in the flank of the

Second Army created. Even the second and more determin-
ing cause of that defeat—the inadequate transmission of
orders on the decisive 8th and 9th of September—can be
traced to the position of Headquarters, which "by the Emperor's command" were in Luxembourg, and therefore too
far behind the lines; this, entirely for the sake of personal
safety from air-bombs, for resolute men there were urgently
desirous of a more forward position.

Criticism of the Emperor became more rife than ever
among his highest officers immediately the War began. So
early as that August, Moltke calls it "heart-rending to see
how entirely he fails to comprehend the gravity of the situation; already there is a certain 'Hooray!' sort of mood which
I hate like hell." And during the Marne days: "The Emperor must go to France and be nearer the troops; he *must* be
on enemy soil like his soldiers" (M. 388). Tirpitz writes,
in the first winter:

I came home after seeing the Emperor, much depressed. . . .
Imagine his grandfather in the same situation! . . . The chief
mark of his character is that he will make no decision, take no
responsibility. . . . Yesterday evening again, it was very dismal;
the conversation dragged on interminably. The Emperor sees colossal victories in every direction, but I think it is only to allay his
uneasiness. . . . The Staff-Surgeon says that the Emperor definitely begged to be relieved of his responsibility; but then he was
brought up short by the wall he has built around himself, and ran
his head against his sense of personal dignity.

By 15th March it had gone so far that Tirpitz pointed
out to a General in the entourage that the Emperor, for the
sake of unity of command, would have to delegate his authority for some time—say, to Hindenburg. His anxiety increased; soon the Admiral was writing decidedly:

I see only *one* way out—the Emperor must give out that he is ill for eight weeks or more. He must go to Berlin to begin with. Kessel . . . too was in a fright about the Emperor, and suggested that the King of Bavaria should be persuaded to ask him to let it be supposed for some time that he was ill. If we could contrive it, it ought to come from himself—the Empress might help us there. . . . It seems as if only a still greater disaster would bring about any change in him, but then it would be too late.

Had Tirpitz but shown himself so good a prophet about England as he did about this!

So—between fear and over-confidence, passive and yet not single-minded enough to delegate his authority, afraid of responsibility, afraid of that questioning look which more searchingly than in peace-time met him now in every eye— a civilian to the marrow, yet at the head of the strongest of all armies, lacking the soldier's virtues, and for that matter most of his effectual vices as well, oppressed by a tradition which had placed his fathers in the field, though not indeed as commanders—so did he live the life of camps, unsoldierly, aloof, wellnigh inactive, and with nothing in the last resort to stay him but an almost religious conviction of martyrdom, of being misunderstood by the world.

For when presently a chorus of hundreds of millions broke forth from every quarter of the globe, and exalted this unstable, pacifically-minded being into an Attila; when whole continents were snowed-under with caricatures and lampoons, of which even in his sheltered corner he must have had some inkling; when the walls around him crackled with the flaming maledictions of the universe . . . no wonder that so monstrous a misjudgment of his purpose caused him to forget the errors which had made it what it was; and that, knowing himself no Attila, he never remembered that he had once commanded his troops to emulate the Huns.

Now and not till now, confronted by the terrible results of that eternal boyishness of his, the Emperor begins to show as a tragic figure; for what Nature had done to him in the hour of his birth, and what he was forced by the soldier-king tradition of his House to conceal throughout a lifetime under the uniform-coat, was fatality; it was not guilt.

2

But there was guilt in the self-indulgence which swayed those around him only to flattery and deception. It did not cease with danger, it grew worse.

An unexceptionable witness [writes Tirpitz], the Staff-Surgeon, said lately that all three Cabinet-Chiefs blindly obeyed the Emperor in everything he said. . . . I have gone through two years of watching this aimless truckling; I have seen how . . . everyone looked only to "Him," confirming him in the belief that he alone was master, from whom so many good things were to be had. Byzantinism! And here we are, landed in a desperate war; and . . . yet they all keep a furtive eye on the Emperor, who is sur-rounded by triflers. . . . The Emperor sat there, filled up with news of victories—nothing else may be conveyed to him; and they talk, among other things, of "a gigantic upheaval in India," whereupon everyone sings Hosanna. . . . It may be that he pur-posely deceives himself.

"To keep up this mood," writes Count Stürgkh, Con-rad's liaison-officer at German Headquarters, and fre-quently the Emperor's guest, "he was told innumerable stories of the trenches, in which the German soldier always appeared in the best light towards the enemy. . . . When he visited the troops, care was taken that he got only the most favourable impressions." When Erzberger, coming from Rome in March 1915, was about to inform the Emperor whether Italy would take the field or not, the aide-de-camp said pleadingly: "You won't tell His Majesty anything but good news, will you?" His own librarian's book, *Der Kaiser im Felde,* which told of nothing but motordrives, luncheon-parties, addresses, decorations, and beaming looks, all in a tone of unpleasing adulation, the Emperor presented to Count Czernin and others, with his own inscription.

Remoteness inspired optimism. After the fall of Antwerp Tirpitz writes: "The Emperor of course in the rosiest of moods. . . . The cardinal point, that the garrison might have moved north, appeared to trouble him very little. . . . He is not a bit changed, and one cannot talk to him seriously at all, though I have tried." In this temper the allies got the same sort of treatment as the courtiers. After only three weeks of war he trod on Count Stürgkh's toes with the remark (*Im Deutschen Quartier,* 31): "Well, we're getting on at last, boys! Fritzie [the Archduke Friedrich] is actually to advance." Later he retailed to the same officer the opinion which his youngest son had brought back from a visit to the Austrian front—it was a biting criticism, after a short inspection, of commanders and officers. Though the Austrian regrettably confined himself to answering that the Prince knew very little about these officers' qualities, the Emperor took even this mild protest in bad part.

All these blunders were, in war as in peace, the outcome of the deceptive selection and presentation of news. "The Hydra"—Plessen, Müller, Treutler, whose portraits reveal their outlook on the universe—guarded the Emperor's pillow. "The orderly from Turkey was anxious to see His Majesty: but Plessen would not let him, saying His Majesty

did not wish to hear anything more about Turkey just now."
This little incident, recorded by Tirpitz in March 1915, is
typical of a hundred more important; for in those very weeks
everything depended on Turkey's holding-up Russian corn
and powder. An early decision of the World-War might
result from the fight in the Dardanelles; and a conscientious
War-Lord should have cross-examined this orderly (who
ranked as an officer and had seen many things of import),
thereby acquiring some knowledge of how things had stood
in the critical quarter less than two days earlier.

What did he do instead of this? "The Emperor traces
the progress of the war upon the maps. . . . The whole
company around him," writes Tirpitz in July 1915, "gradually falls asleep." His activity lasted one hour daily. The
German Army, the German nation, sixty millions, were
achieving the impossible; thousands behind the Front were
breaking down from overwork, tens of thousands gradually
collapsing from exhaustion; what was done and endured at
the Front it would be presumptuous to touch upon in these
pages. The Emperor alone spent the morning (as all the
memoirs testify) "mostly in reading reports and talking" in
the garden, "to which he was obliged to confine his walks, by
reason of the undeniable danger." Then an interview with
the Chiefs of Staff from twelve to one; and of this Hindenburg has to say that, "Much of the time appointed for the
submission of papers in the morning would perhaps be devoted as well to consultation with the leaders of the Government"—so that the Generals were in this way cut short for
the politicians, all to get sooner rid of the work. At a critical
conference with the Emperor at Pless, in August 1915, when
the question was: "America or no America," Tirpitz relates:
"At our preliminary meeting we had all been of different

minds, and papers were laid at once before the Emperor, who cut the time short because the waiting luncheon-table could be seen through the open folding-doors."

At table, in a room which seated no more than sixteen or twenty persons, things were extremely simple; in the hunger-years there were "only three courses with white or red wine, and afterwards cigars and beer." As guests who would have had personal experience of the scarcity in the land were ineligible, those who could be invited were much struck by the simplicity of the imperial table; but as he always lived moderately himself, there was a good deal of pretence about all this self-denial. After lunch he would sleep, then take a walk—"either," reports Stürgkh (74)

in the charming neighbourhood [of Charleville] or to visit an old castle, of which there were many close by, or else to follow the great events of 1870 on the battlefields of Sedan, which was near at hand. It was the business of the entourage to discover a pretext for these excursions—something that would interest him and keep him in good spirits.

Then supper, "guests on most evenings"; and conversation until eleven o'clock.

As in that convivial hour the most important news was apt to come in, Hindenburg had once for all excused himself from table; but it was then that the Emperor liked best to read the latest despatches, which he opened himself.

The disability in his left hand, which was to some extent paralysed, and like the left arm withered, made this somewhat difficult for him; so he used to manage by taking the despatch first in his right hand, then thrusting it between the fingers of his left, when he would break the envelope with the right, draw out the despatch, and unfold it.

Into this little scene we may read the entire symbolism of that tragic simulation of a soldier's life. Far off, there is a welter of heroism and horror, of human beings and inhuman things; five million Germans are fighting to save five-and-fifty. Behind the lines their Supreme War-Lord sits at table. After killing time upon a bygone field of battle while his people were being killed upon a new one, he now, after the fatigues of the day, sits with his boon-companions —cheery souls, or pretending to be so—who tell him anecdotes of heroism at the Front; and when the heliograph flashs fresh tidings, the poor disabled man must make shift with the acquired skill of a lifetime to open the reports which are to put new heart in him.

While in Brussels the German Command was requisitioning the brass handles and the weather-cocks and commandeering every scrap of copper—while millions of German housewives were emptying their kitchens of the glittering utensils handed down to them through generations—the Emperor ordered from Belgian craftsmen a bath for the royal train in pure copper, to be made in the workshops of the Brussels State Railway. This can only have been at his own behest, considering that the bath was for his private use. Yes—they had long gone by, the days of the iron camp-bed wherein the old Emperor had sought repose after long hours of toil, and had found his final rest at last. His grandson, after thirty imperial manœuvres, in the course of which his bath and those of all his Princes had been "carted after" them by sappers, could inhabit only villas and castles in time of war—and that was why Headquarters were always 200 kilometres behind the lines, and battles lost in consequence.

Sometimes he did go near his struggling people. "The Emperor himself," writes Stürgkh (114), not without admiration, "had been on the spot, following the fight at Soissons through a telescope. He was able to watch the operations of his artillery; he saw the enemy in flight and his own brave soldiers pressing forward; then he could extol them and their leaders, and deck their breasts with the Iron Cross." So the Most High had his compensations, after all; and even this Count, who always seems to see him crowned with stars, calls the pleasure he took in the distribution of decorations, "almost childish."

His detestation was England. His purely dynastic view of the War and its origins was very early, and very angrily, expressed; for when the Western advance began he was so furious at having fruitlessly wired in a pacific sense to his cousins, that he "frequently banged his fist on the dinner-table" (Stürgkh, 20). For him, writes Ballin (Huldermann, 297), the case stood thus: "He had been betrayed by his English relatives, and therefore had to fight with England to the bitter end." Even the extremely pacifist Empress was seen by Ballin later on "to cry with both hands clenched and lifted: 'Make peace with England? Never!'" The dynastic idea went so far as solicitude for his enemy's person. To the Emperor it was an unwritten law that Kings by the Grace of God do not shoot at one another. And when the first air-bombs fell at Charleville, Tirpitz declares that the Emperor was furious. "Because now Buckingham Palace is not immune. He really believes in a tacit understanding between the monarchs to spare one another—a quaint sort of notion!"

This feeling about England led to decisions of vast import. Though some might have failed to perceive it in the earlier course of his reign, there could now be no mistake— the treatment of the Fleet by its Supreme War-Lord was the outcome of that old jealous, wounded sense of repulsed affection. A burning hatred, fomented by the idea of having been attacked and betrayed, would now have found its satisfaction in a swift assault; but the Emperor's jealousy flinched before the "emergency," his secret admiration of the greatest Sea Power made him regard a naval victory as impossible; from abysmal depths there rose a desire for that understanding after the fight, which before it he had perpetually obstructed; and in war he never played the card for whose sake he had in peace drawn down the enmity of England—the Fleet remained in harbour.

There stood Tirpitz, its creator, and had to see that verified which he had put forth as the pretext for his Fleet. It was not to be used for fighting, but as a material guarantee for negotiation—the World-War was to be an intermezzo for the Fleet. This was the punishment of Tirpitz the Story-Teller; for that he should now have desired to let loose at last his crews and his torpedoes, his cannons and his iron-plated vessels, and show what *his* armaments could do, is what no one can blame in a fighting-man. There he stood, and tried to persuade the Emperor; found that he could not, gave it up—and went.

"As a result of the war-news . . . I have for the present ordered a defensive attitude on the part of the High Sea Fleet," was the Emperor's command to Admiral von Pohl on the fifth day of mobilization. Pohl, Tirpitz, Ingenohl, made horrified protests against this order; but beside the Emperor as Chief of the Cabinet sat Admiral von Müller, a smooth-tongued courtier, who was a total abstainer, a Christian Scientist, artistic, effeminate, in that respect another Eulenburg—and who talked only of prudence, even of forbearance. "As against the English, the Commanders must await 'the Day' in patience. No forward action, until I give orders for it. W." This, on the 30th day of August, was promulgated as Emperor's orders by Pohl; and Moltke "could not believe it possible." On the 4th of September: "Admiral Tirpitz informs me that he has not been able to persuade the Emperor to rescind his order, and that the Navy-Chief is not to take any decisive action without his instructions." At the same period Tirpitz writes: "It is the Emperor who has put the brake on Ingenohl. He won't take any risks with the Fleet. He wants to hold back until the winter, if not altogether. . . . All would be well if we only had an Iron Chancellor, and an 'Old Emperor.'" It was thus that the paladins expressed themselves.

For his passivity in the command of the war on land, whose leaders, plans, and camps he daily saw, he made up to himself by his determination to be Chief in the war on sea, from whose base he was distant, whose daily fluctuating fortunes were made known to him by no submission of papers, but only very incompletely by telegrams. Thus from his remoteness he paralysed the action at sea, while in his proximity to the action on land he was far from an inspiring influence. For both these things the reasons were profoundly psychological; their results were the appointed fate of Germany.

"I will not have anyone between me and my Navy," said the Emperor; and to Müller: "I need no Chief; I can do this myself." In these reiterated refusals he betrayed, by the very words he used, how he regarded the Fleet as his creation, his own special sphere. That the clique of flatterers confirmed him in this view, poor Tirpitz could but lament. "Of course there were plenty of people on the spot to confirm the Supreme War-Lord in the illusion that he was himself operating with the Fleet, by consulting him in the lesser actions even to the smallest details." By this insistent show of authority he soon prejudiced vital strategical and national questions. The suggestion made by Tirpitz in November 1914, to blockade England by U-boat warfare, was rejected by the Emperor; but possibly, after the War, he may have read the British Admiral Scott's report that at that time the blockade "would have meant an immediate collapse for England. In Scapa Flow we never knew, on any day, whether we should be alive next morning."

How it must have told upon the *morale* of the Navy when Ingenohl in December 1914 was obliged, despite the most favourable conditions for an engagement, to turn tail before an enemy squadron, and return to Wilhelmshafen! "The feeling," writes Admiral Scheer, "of having let slip an unusually good opportunity was not to be effaced; the likelihood of another such was scarcely on the cards." And Tirpitz says straight out: "On 16th December Ingenohl had the fate of Germany in his hands."

When later, in the Skager-Rack, Admiral Scheer wanted to sail out on the second day of battle, and everything was in his favour, the Emperor forbade a fresh advance. If the inclinations of Emperor and Admiral had been reversed, this would have meant a Court-martial for the latter. And even when Falkenhayn, pressed upon by English artillery at Verdun about this time, asked for the U-boat warfare as a method of defence, the Emperor refused his request. It was then that Tirpitz resigned. A few months later the U-boat warfare was decided on after all; Bethmann remained in office instead of going, but Tirpitz, instead of seizing the opportunity to return, stayed out.

With this *chassez-croisez* of his advisers the Emperor's

first war-phase came to an end. In the second he completely abjured his authority.

3

The advent of Hindenburg and Ludendorff in the middle period of the War put an end to the political control of the Empire. If the Emperor had made a constitutional arrangement co-ordinating the civil and military authorities, the balance of power would have been preserved; but as he—a talker, not a doer—failed at every point, these two departments, everywhere and always antagonistic in time of war, were perpetually at odds, and there was no single overruling will to bring them to their bearings. From the throne, before which Chancellor and Generals bowed as before a deity whose word was law, the watchword "Silence!" fell with discouraging persistency.

Once more the cause lies evidently in the peculiar psychology of the man. The fear of his overwhelming adversary which had possessed him since the encirclement (that is since 1909 or thereabouts), and simultaneously a shrinking from critical decisions, a vague premonition of the internal revolts which would follow on external defeats, fostered his tendency towards the defensive. But as for a lifetime he had confused activity with an offensive bearing, thereby keeping the civilized world on tenterhooks, he had no other conception of the defensive than a passive attitude, and was incapable of action when it included forbearance and patience. Hence a just political point of view led to the complete extinction of his influence, and the strong men did as they pleased.

Chancellor and Vice-Chancellor, Bethmann and Helfferich, who at once foresaw from Bernstorff's agitated despatches on the unrestricted U-boat warfare that America would come in and ensure the defeat of Germany, nevertheless consented to the course urged on them by the despairing Generals. They did this on the contemptible pretext, pleaded by all unscrupulous and ambitious placemen, that the country stood in need of their services. As nobody besought them to remain, not even the monarch, they had themselves to vouch for their indispensability. At Pless, on 10th January 1917, the Chancellor handed over the whole political authority of the Empire to a couple of Generals, who bore no responsibility for their actions.

The Emperor was all for the supremacy of the soldier in war-time. Bismarck (vol. ii, chap. 23) had written: "The establishment and limitation of the ends to be obtained by war, and the advice thereon to be given to the sovereign, are and remain in war as before it, a political function; and the tenor of these decisions cannot be without its influence upon the conduct of the war." The Emperor wrote angrily upon a similar representation by the *Frankfurter Zeitung*: "Let this fallacy be instantly and publicly stamped out by the Wilhelmstrasse. . . . Politicians hold their tongues in war-time, until strategists permit them to speak!"

But now that Ludendorff was master of the Army and the Empire, the Emperor began to chafe under the fetters he had riveted on himself. The man whose "sergeant's face" he reviled among his intimates, he now felt to be more and more his despot, and so he was. The Emperor fled from him to the milder atmosphere of the Field-Marshal, though he was aware of the latter's subjection to the General. Under such a tyranny the last vestiges of his authority disappeared. "His Majesty," writes Hindenburg cautiously, "was usually content, at a submission of papers, to acquiesce in my arguments. I do not remember any difference of opinion with my War-Lord which was not removed during these interviews"; and the Crown Prince (*Erinnerungen,* 94) says still more emphatically: "During the War his self-suppression went so far as to be an almost complete abnegation of his personality with regard to the . . . measures taken by the Chief of Staff."

Along with this went a growing dread of hearing any bad news. Hence he opposed a passive resistance to Count Czernin (*Im Weltkriege,* 75) whose duty it was to lay some important matters before him, in the royal train.

He invited me into the dining-car for the first breakfast, and there we sat surrounded by about ten gentlemen, so that there was no possibility of entering on a serious conversation. The meal had long been over, but the Emperor did not rise from table. I had several times—and the last time very explicitly—to beg him to let me speak to him in private, before he got up at last—and then he brought in a gentleman from the Foreign Office, as if for protection against anticipated exigencies.

This scene, which belongs to the January of 1917, bears witness to the collapse of his nervous system, which preceded the political breakdown.

When there was no longer any escape from seeing the representatives of his struggling people face-to-face, he was requested to meet them together with the party-leaders. On that evening William the Second saw a Social-Democratic member for the first time in his life. No one, least of all Ebert, could have imagined on this occasion that he was so soon to be the Emperor's successor. Bethmann had been relegated at last. The Supreme Command, in the person of Colonel Bauer (as he himself relates), had brought down the Chancellor directly the Government was threatened with democratization. Erzberger, at the same time, had obtained a majority for a peace by mutual agreement, but had firmly refused to consider a "guaranteed peace," as Ludendorff wished the offer to be phrased. It was in this temper that the people and the Crown were to meet. But what came of it?

It is very satisfactory [said the Emperor to the assembled representatives] that the Reichstag should desire a guaranteed peace! The word guarantee is excellent. . . . Guarantees mean this, that we are to deprive the enemy-forces of money, raw materials, gun-cotton, and oil, and transfer them from their pockets into our own. That is a really admirable word.

"The listeners," writes Erzberger (*Erinnerungen,* 52), "were shocked to perceive that not only was the Emperor misinformed as to what they wanted, but that he was actually deriding them by these remarks."

Then the Emperor proceeded to unfold his own war-aims.

England will be disposed of in two or three months. . . . My officers inform me that they never by any chance encounter an enemy-ship on the high seas nowadays. . . . The Lower Danube will in time have to be diverted to the Black Sea—then the Danube-Commissioners will be high and dry. . . . At the end of the War we shall enter into a far-reaching agreement with France; and ultimately all Europe, under my leadership, will begin the real war with England—the Second Punic War.

He added a pleasantry about the Balkan peoples, and uttered an aphorism on a victory of the Guards: "Where the Guards are, Democracy is not."

With this he laughingly closed the session, which he had entirely monopolized. "The consternation among us members," writes Erzberger, "got greater and greater. . . . Grey-haired deputies, who hitherto would have nothing to do with the parliamentary system, discussed it openly that evening."

Incapable in every fibre of being the people's representative, he yet felt quite as alien to his powerful opponents in the Reichstag as to the two Generals; and now, secretly pining for Bethmann, in whose fall he had been forced to acquiesce, he stood completely alone between the two opposing forces. His intimates advised him against the appointment of Count Bernstorff, to which he was inclined; but Bülow, whom the Generals wanted, was even still, eight years after his departure, the man "guilty of high treason." So the Emperor, having obtained the Supreme Command's express permission, made some insignificant official his Imperial Chancellor; and after the swift downfall of that personage, forced the appointment on the aged Count Hertling.

The only solution [writes Schwerdtfeger (88)] would then have been for the Emperor to come into the foreground and undertake the Supreme Command himself, and that with a firm hand. The development of events positively called for some such authoritative concentration of the Supreme Command. . . . He remained in the background, gave the Command the utmost liberty of action, and himself relied increasingly on his personal influence. . . . It was not the fault of the German people, but their disaster, that in the severest armed encounter in their history they had not a man at their head possessed of the qualities of Frederick the Great.

At the beginning of 1918 there was talk in the operations-section of arresting the Emperor. Even Hindenburg, always technically loyal, presented the following threatening ultimatum in a memorial of the 7th of January:

It is Your Majesty's supreme right to decide; but Your Majesty will not command true-hearted men who have loyally served Your

Majesty and the Fatherland to take part, with your authority and in your name, in transactions which their inmost convictions assure them to be injurious to the Empire and the Crown. . . . I beg Your Majesty . . . to reflect before deciding.

As this concerned the Peace of Brest-Litovsk, Hinderburg's authority was in no way endangered—he was a Field-Marshal, posing the question in a Cabinet-affair, a political affair, which the Chancellor should properly have been alone in handling. In his answer the Emperor explicitly took the part of an umpire in conflicts between the military and political administrations, and therewith not only constitutionally but personally, the whole responsibility for the events of the closing year of the War.

For all that, the two Generals forced him to dismiss his friend of many years and his Chief of Cabinet, as "preventing the Supreme Command from working with cheerful confidence"; and by his desire for an understanding with the enemy "most seriously endangering the dignity of the Crown." The Emperor revealed all his impotence in a marginal comment which he wrote in those days on a Berlin article. "In the conditions now prevailing among us" (this ran), "it has come to pass that the equilibrium between political and military authority has been disturbed, and that the predominance—by its very nature the right one—of the Foreign Office in political questions can scarcely be said to exist." Beside this he wrote: "Because on both sides the Emperor is ignored."

For thirty years he had annotated the documents and cuttings with thousands and thousands of behests and menaces, with words of derision, of ill-will, of autocratic wilfulness—by turns clamant, insistent, satirical; and now what a confession of failure in eight words! Was not this the real abdication? He who stood as the cynosure of his people, of Europe, much reviled but more belauded; he who had never wearied of disturbing the face of the earth; who had written *Regis Voluntas;* who had exclaimed, "Here there is only one ruler, and that is Myself!" he without whom no great decision might be taken anywhere in the civilized world, before whom the Russian Minister was to stand with heels together—*he,* William the Second, ignored? Manipulated by his Ministers and his Generals, urged to dismiss his closest intimates, degraded into a decoration, only fit to hand out decorations?

It was even so. While the great Battle of the Marne in the West was still undecided, the sovereign, under the stress of his ennui, bestowed on Hindenburg the Iron Cross with the Crown in gold—only once before bestowed, instituted indeed to be bestowed on Blücher as a thank-offering for the victory at Belle-Alliance, when he assisted in the overthrow of Napoleon after twenty years of despotism. . . . Three days later the German onslaught was repulsed. But not until thousands more had been sacrificed, not until the final repulse on the 8th of August, did the Emperor realize the situation. "I quite see now," he said after Ludendorff's report (Niemann, *Kaiser und Revolution,* 43) "that we must strike a balance. . . . The War must be brought to an end. . . . I will expect you, gentlemen, at Spa within the next few days."

At the Session of 14th August at Spa, when the Crown Prince, the Chancellor, and the new Secretary-of-State Hintze were present, and when those very steps were declared to be necessary, for advocating which Kühlmann had been turned out of office, the Emperor said (White Book, *Vorgeschichte des Waffenstillstandes*):

There is too much unrest in the interior. . . . Moreover, our home-reserves are of inferior calibre. . . . We might institute a Commission for Propaganda with the aim of reducing the enemy's confidence and enhancing that of the German people. Influential men, such as Ballin—but there should be some statesmen as well— might make stirring appeals. Adequately gifted men should be appointed to this Commission, not officials.

Now, when it might have been of service for the sovereign to carry his gift of eloquence from one German city to another, breathing that fire and flame with which of yore he had perturbed the halcyon days—now, and withal four years too late, he suddenly held forth about Commissions which like iron cranes were to uplift the sinking spirit of the nation. The "speech of warm good-will," which in 1890 he had demanded for his edicts from Bismarck, was now demanded in the form of "stirring appeals" from men unspecified, till then disdainfully regarded.

This address, however, was the beginning of the "new era." True, this time too the Emperor began with the customary demands for political power over his subjects, for the despatch of better cannon-fodder; but he began too by calling upon private persons instead of officials—for the first time his emphasis was laid upon capacity, not upon titles or blue blood. Is he contemptible or pathetic—this unstable, distracted spirit, hovering on the threshold of a new epoch, hearing the mighty door grind on its hinges, and hoping he may enter unassailed because compliant? At the latter end, this anti-democrat was like a miser who should seek to conciliate Heaven by little offerings before he dies.

What does a Supreme War-Lord do, when he sees the end approaching? Hurriedly he forsakes Head-quarters; goes, while by day and by night the most critical of situa-

tions arise, to Wilhelmshöhe—there to receive Ballin. As
no one had anything helpful to suggest, they put forward
the clever Jew—perhaps *he* would tell the Emperor how
to act. The Emperor had long relied on him, and in the
past had appeased his own anti-semitism by snubbing (as
he himself relates) a gentleman of his Court who protested,
"But Ballin—!" with the retort: "Ballin a Jew? No such
thing! Ballin is a Christian!"

But to-day, instead of their talking intimately as on
other days, Ballin was unpleasantly surprised to find his
visit described as one "for report," so that the new Cabinet-
Chief might be present to keep an eye on him. For still
these parasites obscured their sovereign's outlook with their
chains of paper-roses. "It was infinitely difficult," writes
Niemann in the Eulenburgian manner, "to give the Emperor
a clear idea of the situation, without disturbing his mental
equilibrium"; and when Ballin advised mediation through
Wilson,

Herr von Berg adroitly interposed, and explained to me, when
the Emperor had left us, that we must not make him too pessimistic.
. . . The Emperor talked about a Second Punic War. . . . I
thought he seemed very much misled, and in the arrogant mood
which he affects in the presence of a third person. . . . The poor
monarch is so humbugged that he has no idea how catastrophic
things have become.

The equilibrium of a nation is disturbed, and it is justly
pessimistic; but its Emperor must have sunshine even though
the sun has long gone down. He must be sheltered from
the thunder of the cannons; his equilibrium must not be
disturbed, endangered by harsh truths; and when the independent private person, capable and trusted too, comes
to him and would urge him to make a speedy end, the

courtier adroitly interposes and lets his sovereign go on talking about the Second Punic War, his favourite theme through these four years. . . . Perhaps he was right; for when on 2nd September the English Tank-attacks resulted in imminent peril for Germany, the Emperor was so shattered by the news that he fell ill "not uncritically," and those around him feared that "his excitement and exhaustion might lead to a mental and physical collapse." Quite as in the Eulenburg year; only of less consequence, for, in the interval, excitement and exhaustion had reduced sixty millions of innocent people to a state of "collapse."

While at the Front a nation was fighting its last battle with traditional devotion, its Emperor sat in the picturesque background, where, according to his aide-de-camp (Niemann, 65),

all concerned did their best to distract the monarch's thoughts from the pressing anxieties of the day, and to start a discussion on some interesting artistic, scientific, or technical question. When the subject attracted the Emperor, and (as not seldom happened) impelled him to bring forth something from the positively inexhaustible store of his own experience, the long hours would go by like winking, and were a real refreshment to him.

So at the end it was the same as it had been for thirty years—again he held forth "under the soft light of a standard-lamp." There, at Wilhelmshöhe, it seemed to him the fitting moment to uphold the candidature of a German Prince, his brother-in-law, for the throne of Finland. Three weeks of holiday had gone by, when the Emperor obeyed an urgent recall to Head-quarters.

On the way there, on 9th September, he made a speech at Essen, where he had never before made one—he addressed the men at Krupp's Works. They stood round him in a circle, 1,500 of them in the vestibule, the enemies of his long royal career, whom he hated more fiercely than they hated him, because it was he who must fear, not they. The Emperor, in his field-grey uniform, confronted them; vulnerable, but as yet unwounded, he spoke of the German nation. The atmosphere was stifling; there was no throne—only a tribune as for a demagogue. He spoke for half an hour. Would he, like Coriolanus, gain "their most sweet voices"?

"My dear friends of the Krupp Workshops!" ("Friends?" thought the men. "Since when?") "My friends, which of us has any hate in his heart? The Teuton knows not hatred. Hatred belongs to peoples who have the sense of inferiority. He who knows the temper of the Anglo-Saxons knows how unrelenting they can be." ("'Teutons'? What is all this?" thought the men.) "Last year I said: 'Boys, make no mistake—this war is like no other; this is a long long fight for life!'" ("*By Christmas we'll be home!*' Didn't he say that four years ago?" thought the men. "Now he's going to pretend he foresaw all this.") "You will have read of the recent events in Moscow. The English Parliamentarians have tried to overthrow the ultra-democratic government which the Russian people have now begun to form, because that government, watchful of the national interests, wished to obtain for the nation that peace for which it clamours. But the Anglo-Saxon wants no peace as yet." ("And when did William the Second begin to be enthusiastic about Communists?" thought the men, grinning.)

"That is because he is out to win, and our enemies have the deepest respect for the German Army—so they are trying to foment disturbances in our land, that discouraging rumours may cause us to lose heart." ("Disturbance in

the land?" growled the men. "That's a hit at us!")
"Everyone who listens to such rumours is a traitor and
worthy of condign punishment, whether he be noble or
working-man. . . . To every single one of us his task is
given—to you with your hammer, to you at your lathe, to
me upon my throne!" ("Ho-ho!" thought the men, and
smiled.) "We are at peace to-day with Russia and
Roumania; Serbia and Montenegro are disposed of; only
in the West are we still fighting, and is the good God going
to forsake us at the last moment? . . . God be with us;
and now farewell, good fellows!"

A heavy silence. The speech had lasted half an hour,
but all it had produced was sullen criticism and furtive
laughter. The orator's adjutant and adorer, Niemann,
writes as an eye-witness (p. 80): "The intimate contact
established at the beginning of the address was gradually
lost. The men's faces were expressionless, and the more
eloquent the Emperor became, the more apparent was the
coolness. . . . We all felt that he had missed fire." For
once something depended on his words, and that once the
man missed fire. Why? Because William the Second lived
aloof from his people. The men divined the coldness of
his heart, and he had scarce an inkling of their resentment.

After only a few days his restlessness drove him once
more from Head-quarters—there were inspections, bestow-
als of decorations at Colmar, Kiel, the Baltic Provinces.
Suddenly arrived the news of Bulgaria's defection. He
then returned to Head-quarters.

Came September 29, at Spa. Fully six weeks had gone
by since the last political session in that room; and despite
the Emperor's acknowledgment that they were at the end
of their resources, those precious weeks had been thrown

away, and could not now be retrieved. For four years they had wasted time in every direction; now, when all was over, it had to be hoarded—every day counted, as at the beginning. For as the number and value of the young American troops, who were now hammering at the fortress, increased with every day of those six weeks, so day by day dwindled the hope of deceiving the enemy with the fiction of a still unshaken German Army; and while the onslaught gathered force, the spirit behind the battlements sank lower and lower. The nation was wasted to the bone; it needed no internal shock—of itself it went to pieces.

Too late as always, but with secret tremors, the Emperor now read the earliest reports, couched in courtly euphemisms, of the unrest at the Front. The things said to each other by uselessly sacrificed men, out there—said for a year now in face of the gradually hardening resistance—he knew nothing of; he had heard but little of the mutiny of January 1918. Now all he learnt from his Generals was that here and there exhausted troops had met those returning to the Front with the cry: "Strike-breakers!" But a few such reports were enough to darken his soul with a fear which the world in arms against him had not hitherto instilled.

Thenceforth, through all the last six weeks, his gaze was exclusively fixed on his land and his subjects—not any more on the Front and the foe. The downfall of the Tsar had given his whole outlook, even his religious faith, a staggering shock which he could parry only by remembering how his cousin *would* go in with that French Republic, despite his many warnings. All that kind of thing was inconceivable in Germany! Had he not just fraternized with the men at Krupp's? A few hundred misguided individuals could never get the upper-hand of millions of loyal subjects! It was inevitable that the Emperor should feel in this way—he who in these four years had known nothing of the temper either in the Army or at home; who was fed only with the official substitute for the truth, and whose egocentric nature never could submerge itself in the feelings of others.

And yet, from afar he did hear the low mutterings. It was time to yield. The session in the forenoon of that 29th of September began with the demand of both Generals for immediate overtures to the enemy both for an armistice and peace: "every hour of delay is perilous." This resolve, conditioned solely by the situation at the Front, not by Bulgaria's defection nor by unrest at home—this blow which was to fall upon the nation to-morrow or next day, was a "complete surprise" to the Ministers, even to the Emperor, as the Crown Prince testifies. But it did not dismay him. His eye was fixed on the interior only of his realm; and he requested the Foreign Secretary to describe the situation at home (Hintze's report of the Commission of Enquiry, p. 409).

Hintze, who had been only two months in Germany, pointed out that the Chancellor was expected that day with his report. The Emperor insisted, for this alone—this question of revolt—absorbed him. Then Hintze told all he knew, advised that "the threatened Revolution should be canalized," and said that one way to that end was a dictatorship. "Dictatorship—nonsense!" interrupted the Emperor. Thereupon Hintze suggested the alternative—an immediate democratization of the Government; this, in order that the blameless nation might share in the responsibility for a bad peace. "His Majesty listened to the statement which suppressed emotion, with kingly dignity, and declared himself in favour of the programme suggested."

His attitude was logical. At the end of his career, the defeated sovereign demolishes his most cherished conception of his rank and influence, renounces the dictatorship at which he had incessantly snatched in the moment of its being actually a possibility, and admits into the ranks of Government the very men whose claims he had always laughed to scorn—real, live Socialists; and all this for fear of the masses who, as it now appeared, were really venturing to make themselves felt. Half a century ago—and it was his grandfather who had stood as he stood now, and how had *he* argued? "I take my leave, and abdicate," he said to Herr von Bismarck-Schönhausen; it was September then as now, and in the Park at Babelsberg the leaves were yellow as here at Spa. He too had no will to fight, but he had the will to go—yet he had no war behind him, and (after waiting for thirty years) had enjoyed his crown for barely two. His grandson, who for thirty years had governed with a hundred per cent. of his being and had ended by losing the World-War, was so faint-hearted that he proposed retreating step by step. Surrounded by swords and cannons, he was not tempted to sally for life or death, such as Bismarck had obtained from his grandfather—but it is true that there was no one at Spa to look lightnings at him from under bushy brows.

To retreat step by step—that was his programme. When Hertling, Berg, and Rodern came in the afternoon—the Foreign Secretary being unrepresented at this further conference over the fate of the Empire, "because no one asked me to go in with the rest of them" (Hintze, p. 410)—they calmed him down again; but laid before him a proclamation, dated for next morning, which ran:

It is my wish that the German people should take a more active part than heretofore in deciding the fate of the Fatherland. It is therefore My Pleasure that men who are supported by the confidence of the people should have a larger share in the rights and duties of the Government.

Issued two years earlier, this document might have led to endurable peace-terms, might have saved the dynasty. But even now it seemed premature to the Emperor; for after an hour and a half he sent for the waiting Foreign Secretary, who found him visibly relieved. "This Revolution-business hasn't gone so far, after all, the Chancellor tells me. So we can wait awhile about the New Government and the Peace. We'll stay here quietly in Spa for a fortnight, and think things over."

Hintze, dismayed, reminded him of the two Generals' demand for an immediate armistice, of their fear of a sudden collapse.

His Majesty listened quietly, but did not seem inclined to make up his mind just them, and turned to the door. On the table lay the proclamation drawn up by the Imperial Chancery in His Majesty's name, for the 30th. I followed H.M. to the door and again said that the formation of a new Government was a preliminary condition of the armistice and the offer of peace. The Emperor turned, walked to the table, and signed the edict.

Thus cornered, the Emperor established German Democracy. In no scene of his life is his character so transparently revealed. For four years war had raged; on this day his tenacious Generals had for the first time declared it lost, and demanded an armistice from the Reichstag, without a day's delay. For four years his subjects, in Prussia and in Germany, had clamoured for the right to a voice in the decisions. For four years it had been refused them. To-day the people were admitted to a share in the government, not because they were ripe for it, but because the ruling class was bankrupt, and had every reason to believe it would do better with a democratic Germany than with the Generals who till now had dominated policy. A new Cabinet with Socialists was seen to be a condition for successful peace-overtures. A people in arms had been obliged to fight for bare existence, in order that at the appalling end they might snatch at a corner of the purple mantle which symbolized authority in this State. The man in that purple mantle was obliged to grant what for thirty years he had refused. How did he go about it?

"This Revolution-business hasn't gone so far, after all; and we can wait a while about the new Government. We'll think it over during the next fortnight." Had he got off? The door was there—who was going to force him to sign the paper? Besides, with that endless session it was nearly seven o'clock, and he had not changed for dinner. The Secretary-of-State barred the way, courteously indeed, but would not let him leave the room. He exhorted him once more—nay, he conjured him by the words of despair which had come from the Generals that day, and which seemed to have escaped the sovereign's memory. What was to be done? It was a dilemma—and perhaps it might exorcise the danger at home if one let the Socialist rascals nibble at the manger, for that was all they wanted.

So he turned, and signed for the new Germany, in a hurry to dress for dinner.

CHAPTER IX

EXIT

Oct.–Nov., 1918

FIVE continents were demanding that one man should leave the stage. The most level-headed of the victors could not see any end to the War without the sacrifice of that ruler to whom it was falsely attributed; a great nation could not expect justice from the most merciful of its enemies unless it parted with the man whose words for thirty years had kept Europe on tenterhooks. A system which he was held to have devised and ruled by, though he had only inherited it and was incapable of working it, was now to be ended—both abroad and at home the best minds were resolved on that; representatives of peoples, allies, adversaries, joined in the chorus: "The man must go!" Even those statesmen who knew all about the manifold causes of the War, their own share in it, and the names of those who were really most to blame, could no more indict Isvolski before the world at large than they could indict Count Berchtold or Nicholson—nowhere would the man in the street have known what they were talking about. The Emperor was to be deprived of power, because it was he who had once gone sabre-rattling all over Europe.

No one wanted his head; no one even wanted his crown. No one demanded the Republic from vanquished Germany, for many kings were averse from it; not even Germany's own Socialists demanded it. All they wanted was that he should give the crown to another, possibly a kinsman; this was indeed the heartfelt desire of the most royalist Germans, who were trembling for their dynasty. In the interior there was little hatred for the Emperor; walking unprotected with Ludendorff down any street in the land, he would even now have been in no more danger than his General. How should a nation which in thirty years had failed to fathom its sovereign and so had borne with him, have blamed him for a war which he had not let loose, which he had never wished for, and had several times prevented? All he had done was to make war easier for the swashbuckling leaders in every country of Europe, by the thirty years of his characteristic attitude and its effect. In the autumn of 1918 it was still only a skin-deep knowledge that the Germans, as a nation, had of their Emperor.

Hence it was reason, not passion, which urged part of the nation to join in the cry for abdication; and moreover the idea of a sacrifice, a martydom for the people, flattered the German spirit, always in love with tragic endings. Nor was it now too harsh a demand—two of his friends, Ballin and Max von Baden, testify to that. At heart he would have been glad to escape responsibility for the evil days that were inevitably to come.

He was sixty now, and had reigned for thirty years. After that comment on the newspaper-cutting in January, after his two years of complete relegation, it was psychologically speaking quite on the cards that—despite his former autocracy—he would be the first to abandon a forlorn cause with a flourishing royal gesture for all the world to wonder at.

With night in his heart, Prince Max von Baden—one of the last real paladins—suddenly drawn into the vortex, took over the Chancellorship with its dread implications. As a friend and cousin, he could not but perceive that no one so well as he could set the stage for the withdrawal he was to press upon the Emperor. The Prince himself was risking everything, for he was of royal blood, his father's heir, and a General; and if he leaped into the breach to beg for endurable peace-terms, his only hope was in the effect of some speeches which had shown him to be more modern-minded than his colleagues. There had been hundreds of fine phrases about sacrifice for the Fatherland—this Prince was the first to act upon them when he, who had never talked about sacrifices, took the much-coveted Chancellorship. Immediately before the downfall of the reigning Houses of Germany he gave history to know that there was at least one Prince who could spring to the helm of a foundering vessel, if at worst he might steer the wreck into harbour. Foreseeing the odium that would be his only thanks, this Prince of the House of Zähringen once more confronted the Kingdom of Prussia. He was like another Mirabeau.

First, for three days he opposed the two Generals' demand for simultaneous peace-overtures and armistice; then, for five weeks, their pernicious influence on the Emperor. He was clear-sighted enough to perceive the ultimate possibilities—of bargaining with the Emperor's person for endurable peace-terms, but along with those, for the continuance of the dynasty. Loyal sentiment unfortunately prevented him from saying this straight out to his cousin, though his colleagues advised him to do so. If Prince Max had been even more emancipated at heart than he actually was, if he had sacrificed traditional feeling to the tradition itself, he would (so all the actors in those weeks declare) have brought the Emperor to abdicate.

The Emperor was as little desirous as the Chancellor of continuing the fight. When on 2nd October, after his return, he sat beside Hindenburg (Ludendorff absent) in the Imperial Chancery, and heard his cousin urge that no precipitate overtures for an armistice should on any account be made before a speech in the Reichstag had prepared the political world for the will to peace, he entirely misconceived the probable effect of a sudden cabled appeal for help to Wilson, and so sealed his own fate.

With full conviction he declared (S. 298) that no obstacles ought to be put in the way of the High Command with regard to this question. He thus, as War-Lord, took the entire personal responsibility, at this critical moment, for the despatch of an offer of armistice.

Nevertheless, the new Chancellor made a further attempt; and next day ventured, as the chief civil functionary, to confront the Generalissimo with five bluntly-phrased questions, expressly restricting his answers to the military situation. Hindenburg stuck to his demand for an immediate armistice. On the 3rd the Prince even took upon himself to father a pious fraud—he told the world that the German front was unbroken, thus incurring the odium of acting on his own pacific inclinations instead of the necessities of war. In these October weeks he had to contend with the Generals, the Socialists, and President Wilson; and was further entrusted with the task of persuading the Emperor to abdicate. He naturally believed that he would prevail upon that unstable nature in its present state of depression, and had even prepared the Reichstag speech in which he proposed to give the people the cue for the sacrifice of their Emperor.

For Wilson had written:

If the Government of the United States must deal with the military masters and the monarchical autocrats of Germany now, or if it is likely to have to deal with them later in regard to the international obligations of the German Empire, it must demand not peace negotiations but surrender. Nothing can be gained by leaving this essential thing unsaid (23rd October).

Capitulation or negotiation—the Germans were thus given to understand that the alternatives were bound up with the Emperor's person. This had been known to the German Government since Wilson's first Note of the 14th, and also by confidential communications from all the capitals of Europe; and it was only the Supreme Command who indignantly declared they must fight on in defence of their military honour, although so early as 17th September they had known that these conditions were imposed by England and America (*Kommentare zum Waffenstillstand,* Nrs. 76c and 86c).

From Brussels the German Ambassador advised immediate abdication; otherwise Germany would be playing the French and English game against Wilson. This was to invade Germany. The Ambassador at Berne wired in the same sense, and could even quote similar advice from the Federal Council. Prince Max and his adherents proposed that the Emperor should recommend his grandson to the loyalty of the nation and the Army, the protection of the Field-Marshal and incidentally of God—thus retaining the Socialists in the Government, and depriving the Spartacists of their strongest argument. Every day the telegrams from German representatives abroad grew more urgent, their import being that unless swift action was taken Wilson's position towards the Chauvinists in his own country would be made impossible. So the Ambassador at Berne reported, and voices from all countries reached his ears. On the 25th the Prussian Ambassador at Münich wired in the same sense.

But the Emperor, who might have flinched before the threat of coming responsibilities, was bound by his nature to regard any external pressure as an outrage; and Wilson's first Note inspired a mood quite as stubborn as that of ten years ago, when they had told him of the Conservatives' desire for his withdrawal. "Don't you see?" he said furiously to Niemann. "The object of this is to bring down my House, to set the Monarchy aside!" After the second Note, by Niemann's account, "the imperial couple's indignation gradually turned to ineffable contempt." Solf, the new Secretary-of-State, said to the Emperor when he demanded protection against the Press that the highest circles had long been speaking freely of the abdication; and if the Emperor recalled the November days of ten years back, he must have remembered how on a far less insistent and exclusively German cry, he had been ready to abdicate. As he relates in his Memoirs, "the rolling-up of this question of abdication" had no sort of "effect in upsetting the apple-cart with the Cabinet." His old friendship with the Chancellor, who himself kept silence, tended rather to make official relations more agreeable.

As the Emperor—deprived of authority in every direction—sat through these weeks in the New Palace, he was ruled (as one of the principal actors testifies) by one sensation only—boredom. Politics he left to the Left; with the new Ministers, when he received them, he spoke only of their native towns and their sons at the Front. To his first Socialist Minister he did say, on his appointment: "With Herr Ebert too I should be glad to co-operate. . . . I have nothing whatever against Social-Democracy except its name. The name, you know, *must* be changed." Step by step, at the expense of all dignity—that was his plan.

But it was precisely these improving relations with the *bourgeoisie,* this giving-in, which made the Generals kidnap him.

For it was a kind of kidnapping, when the Emperor left Berlin with his Adjutants-General on 29th October. The secretly meditated step was unknown to the Chancellor until six o'clock that evening. He instantly, though ill in bed, offered to go to Potsdam at once; despatched Solf to the Home-Secretary, to Prince Augustus William, to Delbrück, the new Chief of the Civil Cabinet, who all three sheltered behind official and other reasons for taking no active part. On this occasion the Chancellor's pedigree was accountable for a grievous shortcoming—now was the moment to keep the Emperor in Berlin, though it were by force. If he was to be the prisoner of Head-quarters, why not the prisoner of the Government? The nation would have heard as little about the one as the other.

Meanwhile the Emperor had been infected with distrust for the Prince's "South-German" point of view. He took refuge in bitter remarks that no one had any use for him here, and that he ought to be putting things right at the Front, now Ludendorff had been dismissed. Disastrous! For the metropolis, staggering towards Revolution, believed that the Emperor was going to set his troops on Berlin, while others said in print that he was running away like Louis

XVI. In reality it was no flight, for he had lost all power of decision; it was the imprisonment of the Supreme War-Lord by his Generals.

Vainly did the Chancellor, next day, implore him to return to Berlin. Then it was decided to make an official request for abdication. When a Grand-Duke and a Count had proclaimed themselves ready to undertake this mission and then drawn back, the citizen Home-Secretary, Drews, went alone by order of the Cabinet to Spa. The Emperor received him in the garden of his villa, leaning on a crutch-stick like Frederick the Great, and interrupted him at the first word. "You ought to have remembered your oath, and refused to undertake such a commission!"

The Minister: "As Minister it is my duty to keep my Sovereign informed even of disagreeable matters."

The Emperor: "I don't need that! I am alive to the entire situation."

The Minister: "May I then regard my task as accomplished, or does Your Majesty command me to speak on?"

The Emperor: "Speak on!"

This garden-dialogue was something new for William the Second. Again he had thought to intimidate his opponent by a show of energy; but on this occasion he was confronted by an upstanding man who knew how to answer him. And so what Eulenburg and Moltke had experienced happened over again—instantly the Emperor gave in and listened. In case of need he ordered Plessen to follow them as they walked up and down—three paces off. While the Minister spoke, and he spoke for half an hour, the Emperor grew calmer, interpolated questions, then stood still and said: "All my sons have given me their word of honour, that they will never take over a Regency. . . . As a Prussian King and a successor of Frederick the Great, it is my duty to remain at my post."

With these words, which betrayed his fear of his own sons, he left his Minister standing and turned away. Practical reasons, such as solicitude for the Army, the retreat, his distracted people, swayed him far less than tradition, a royal gesture, like that of the great ancestor whose crutch-stick he had borrowed for support. But for all that, he spoilt his exit of the moment—this Drews knew more than he would tell, so almost instantly he came back to him. Drews was now conferring with the Generals; the Emperor inquired: "Do you anticipate violent outbreaks?"

The Minister: "Beyond all doubt. Their success will depend on the steadiness of the troops."

On this question all three Generals were quite easy in their minds—six able regimental commanders had been ordered to Berlin and "where the Guards are, Democracy is not." After a hot argument between Drews and Gröner, who to the Emperor's delight impugned the Government, Drews begged to take leave.

The Emperor, jovially: "Certainly not—do stay! This plain-speaking has been very good for us all. Won't you dine with me?"

This cordial invitation, which the Minister could only get out of on the plea of pressing business at home, was an appropriate climax to an interview begun in true Court-theatre style—an interview in which the Minister sought to induce the monarch to go because he was no longer trusted, and the monarch assured the Minister that *he* was —and stayed.

Meanwhile, at the end of a war which had begun with the defection of allies, the last of these were likewise falling

away, and making overtures for separate peace-terms. The
Poles, the Alsatians, announced their defection from the
Empire in the Reichstag; every day the Front was pushed
farther back; in Kiel there was mutiny because the troops
would not let themselves be sacrificed to the Fleet in an
aimless war of prestige; Munich and Stuttgart were calling
upon their kings to abdicate; and on the 6th the German
representatives were received by Foch in the forest of Com-
piègne with the insulting words: "What do you want?"
On the 7th the Socialists laid down an ultimatum demanding
an abdication, on the expiration of which they would leave
the Government—in other words, would head the Revolution.

The Chancellor, sending this news to Spa, took the opportunity of also tendering his resignation, and warned those
at Spa of the danger of a military Dictatorship, which must
ensue and would inevitably lead to civil war. By every
means he sought to gild the pill of withdrawal for the Emperor—first, there was to be a general election, a National
Assembly; then the abdication, which need not at the moment
go beyond a promise—in the meantime a delegation of
power, the struggle confined to the voting-booths instead of
spreading through the streets, the Royal Idea rescued by a
democratic cutting of the Gordian knot. Bavaria and Württemberg, he said, would become Republics either to-day or
to-morrow. Answer from Spa on the 8th: "His Majesty
emphatically declines to consider the dynastic question raised
in Your Grand-Ducal Highness's proposals, and regards it
as your duty to remain at your post."

On the evening of the 8th at Spa, there was a Council of
War between Hindenburg, Gröner, and Plessen on the
march to Berlin. Plessen in favour of it, the other two

against. According to the official memorandum, the Supreme Command had even then knowledge of disobedience to orders among certain units, "which are reckoned as the flower of the troops, and to whom was entrusted the task of protecting the rear of Head-quarters against the mutineers." All the highly placed officers, summoned from the Front to report, spoke of this temper among the armies. Yet neither of the two Generals dared to tell the Emperor these facts: silently they acquiesced in his command "to begin an operation in the interior." It makes one think of a surgeon preparing to operate on himself for cancer. For this mood of the Emperor, resolute on sacrificing neither his authority nor his person, but on marching against the revolutionary capital, the responsibility is solely the Field-Marshal's, who had counselled him for two years and had now brought him back to Head-quarters. Although he regarded the "operation in the interior" as impracticable, he did not advise against it; although he felt that all was lost, he did not counsel abdication. Torn between his emotions as a General loyal to his Emperor, the head of a defeated army, and a German averse from shooting down Germans, he let the whole day pass without a word of counsel, for he did not realize that the Chancellor's cry was that of a drowning man.

The latter got into telephonic communication with the Emperor that evening; their dialogue lasted twenty minutes.

Prince Max (9th November, p. 7):

The abdication has become a matter of necessity, if civil war is to be averted, and the Emperor's peace-mission to reach a favourable conclusion. If that succeeds, Your Majesty's name will be revered by history. If it fails, the Reichstag's demand will be made and carried. We can no longer rely on the troops; Cologne is in the hands of Councils of Working Men and Soldiers; an

Your Majesty's daughter's castle at Braunschweig the red flag is flying; Munich is a Republic, in Schwerin a Council of Soldiers is sitting. I see two alternatives: abdication, renunciation of the throne by the Crown Prince, and a Regency for your grandson; or abdication, nomination of a Regent, and a National Assembly. The Committee of the Reichstag demands the latter, and it seems to me the better of the two, because it offers any chances there still are for the Monarchy. Whatever is done must be done quickly; the effect would be lost if blood had been shed. With the Socialists' help the situation might still be saved in this way—otherwise the Republic confronts us. The sacrifice must be voluntary—so only will Your Majesty's name live in history.

Thus, through the telephone, spoke the Spirit of History; thus were politics and pathos, regimental numbers and historical renown commingled in the dialogue of one Prince with another, the object of which was that the listener at one end of the wire should be induced to renounce the authority which he had delegated to the speaker at the other. The desire of sixty millions was concentrated in this one voice, which could address the Emperor as that of a kinsman. But at the far end sat the Emperor, pale, biting his lips, as Eulenburg had seen him do for lesser perturbations; and he spoke back: "Nonsense! The troops will stand by me. To-morrow we march against the interior!" Even on this last of royal evenings William the Second did the wrong thing, because he had taught those around him to palter with harsh truths. "If," writes Prince Max, "the Supreme Command had told the Emperor on the 8th of November the truth about the Army which they kept from him till the morning of the 9th, I do not doubt that the Emperor would have promised to renounce the throne on the evening of the 8th."

In the course of that night four members of the Reich··

stag gave the Supreme Command to understand what was
to be expected on the morrow. If the abdication was not
known in the morning at Berlin, the leaders would not be
able to keep the workers in the factories. All this was, at
Spa, either not believed or looked on in a personal light.
Prince Max was distrusted, as opposed to the Hohenzollerns, as heir in reversion to the throne; and his "weak-
kneed Cabinet" was derided.

On 9th November, at ten o'clock in the morning, the
Imperial Government was informed that the Alexander-
Regiment and the Jüterbog Artillery had gone over to the
workers; likewise even the Naumburg Rifles, who had been
drafted into Berlin expressly for protection. These reports
followed hard on one another to Spa—where in the Emperor's villa one telephone, it is true, was "always engaged,"
but the other "was disconnected." That disconnected telephone was the last false kindness shown by a dense-witted
Court to its sovereign. Weakly the grotesque symbol of a
disconnected authority wavered and swung there—the imperial instrument declined to receive the tidings of that
Ninth of November.

At that very hour Hindenburg, Gröner, and Plessen
were with the Emperor, together with the hastily summoned
Count Schulenburg and two officers. The topic to be discussed was: "Statement on the operation in the interior commanded by the Emperor." A garden-room, a wood-fire in
the grate, and the Emperor (Niemann, 134), "who was
shivering, leaning against the chimney-piece." Uniforms
sprinkled with stars, well-drilled attitudes, practical serious
faces, list of numbers—a session like a hundred sessions presided over by the Emperor throughout the War; only this
time the Front was east, though the standing army was west.

While in Berlin soldiers who were working-men were fraternizing with working-men who to-morrow would be soldiers, while men who for four years had been throwing fire-grenades were joining hands with the men who had fashioned them in a general impulse which had more of the heaviness than the excitement of intoxication—each and all driven by the craving to see peace once more around them—the great ones on whom yesterday their lives had depended were considering how best they might shoot down the rebels. Among these great ones stern composure reigned. Nobody's voice was louder than usual. Nobody spoke out for the unity of the nation which now, after all that had been, it was proposed to lacerate afresh. Not a single one of them! Outside the door hung the disconnected receiver.

The only disagreement was about the methods. Hindenburg begged to be released from the conference, because "it was inexpressibly painful to him to be obliged to dissuade his sovereign from a course of which he most gladly and sincerely approved, but of whose successful accomplishment he could only say, after profound reflection, that he held it to be impossible." Less feelingly, but in the same sense, spoke General Gröner. But Plessen was now, as in Eulenburg's time, "all for gun-fire"; with him was Schulenburg, though out of sixteen representatives of his Army-Corps twelve had yesterday replied in the negative to the question of the troops' reliability, and none had given a positively affirmative answer. Schulenburg sketched out his scheme of advance to the Rhine, and for an incentive suggested that "the Army should be told that its sister-service, the Navy, had attacked it from behind under pressure from Jew-profiteers and shirkers, and was holding up supplies." The Emperor, at first in favour of the tussle, grew irresolute after Hindenburg's statement and, true to himself, sought for a compromise: "I want to spare the Fatherland a civil war; but after the armistice it is my desire to come home to peace at the head of the returning Army."

Had he not solved the problem? No bloodshed, no danger for the Empire, none for the Emperor; but instead, an entry through the Brandenburg Gate. But behold! Gröner quietly stood up—Gröner whom that very day the Emperor had approvingly called "Brave Suabian!" and clapped paternally on the back; and Gröner told the truth at last. "Under its leaders and Generals the Army will march quietly and steadily home, but not under the command of Your Majesty. It is no longer behind you."

A terrible moment. Had the revolt reached even to the sovereign's writing-table? He made a few steps towards General Gröner: "Your Excellency, I demand a written statement of this opinion! In black and white I will have the announcement from all the Generals commanding that the Army is no longer behind its Supreme War-Lord. Have they not sworn it me in their military oath?"

Gröner: "In such a situation the oath is a mere fiction."

When the truth of those words broke over him, the Emperor's world fell to pieces in his heart. For thirty years he had been intent on strengthening the iron cordon around him; in thirty days it was shattered. There had not been a word of abdication in that session, though this was a preliminary condition of the Armistice.

Meanwhile the session had been interrupted by the incessant wires from Berlin to the Supreme Command. The officers were consulted; from three selected Army-Corps came the anticipated negative. One of the Colonels informed the Emperor. While he was speaking there came a message from the Commandant of Berlin: "All troops de-serted—completely out of hand." It was eleven o'clock then.

There he stood, hard-pressed between the thronging wires from Berlin, and the dispassionate No of his officers. The hour had come—long-dreaded, held in check by all the arts of rhetoric. The paladins were wavering; no soldier sprang forward to shield the heaven-throned Prince from his rebellious subjects. Was Bismarck's ghost not seen to hover in that room? It had been his last of warnings to the Emperor; twenty years ago it was: "So long as you have these officers around you, there is no doubt that you may do exactly as you please. But if ever that should not be so, it will be quite a different matter." They had been drink-ing champagne; after that dinner they did not again see one another. And not till now, in this last inglorious moment, did the Emperor, hemmed in, decide to lay down his arms. "His Majesty was profoundly affected by these statements, and evidently resolute to make a personal sacrifice for the sake of averting civil war." But Count Schulenburg pre-fered his own scheme for the salvation of the monarchy. He now propounded the fantastic idea that the monarch should abdicate as German Emperor, but not as King of Prussia. As Hindenburg and even the Crown Prince, who now ar-rived upon the scene, approved the grotesque suggestion, the Emperor caught at this way of escape—neither imperial nor royal though it was—like a gambler who should hope with his last throw to win back all that he has lost.

The Chancellor spoke again from Berlin. He would be obliged to resign, the monarchy was not to be saved unless the abdication came without an instant's delay. The Em-peror ordered Hintze to answer by the announcement of his semi-abdication. Schulenburg again interfered, insisting on a formula for this momentous step, to be signed by the Emperor. Meanwhile the movement in Berlin was gathering force; no one in the Wilhelmstrasse could be sure that in ten minutes the mob would not be upon them with machine-guns. One more anguished appeal to Spa: "It is a question of minutes!" Schulenburg replied: "So momentous a decision cannot be made in a few minutes. His Majesty is resolved; he is at this moment formulating his resolve on paper; it will be in the hands of the Imperial Government within half an hour." Not a word did the Count say of his own scheme for destroying all the effect by the retention of half the sovereign's authority. "Of an abdication only as Emperor and not as King of Prussia," writes Prince Max, "not one syllable was said in the telephonic conversations of 9th November, nor on any previous occasion." Nor could anyone in Berlin have had any inkling of such a wanton destruction of the German Bund, which would have deprived the Constitution of all meaning and the abdication of its essential significance; for it was not of the German Emperor that men desired to be rid, but of William the Second.

The Chancellor sat in his house with the rest of the Cabinet, and waited for the announcement; the Socialists had departed—they were leading the masses. At any moment Unter den Linden might hear the Republic proclaimed. The announcement came not—three Generals, a Minister, and a King, found it too hard a task to put those two or three sentences together. Now the Chancellor was confronted with the choice of leaving the first step to the streets, or himself formulating the officially conveyed intention to abdicate, his one aim being to save the dynasty. So he did what as Chancellor, Prince, and friend, he was bound to do. He formulated the officially declared intention of his sovereign as an unequivocal resolve, and in doing so overstepped his province only in one respect, namely, under the pressure of necessity he also announced the Crown Prince's renunciation of the throne:

The Emperor and King has resolved to relinquish the throne. The Imperial Chancellor will remain in office only until . . . the questions connected with the abdication have been regulated by the establishment of a Regency. His intention is to propose to the Regent the nomination of the deputy Ebert to the Imperial Chancellorship, and to lay before him the draft of a Bill for immediately proclaiming a General Election for the National Assembly, which will provide a Constitution for the country, and will apply itself to a final decision on the form to be henceforth taken by the German State.

Prince Max could not now help the dynasty by this proclamation; it came four weeks, four days, four hours, too late. Scheidemann had in the same hour proclaimed the Republic. Only to one person did the Prince, doing this, render the greatest of services—the Emperor. When all had forsaken him, this Chancellor alone stood by him; here at last was the scapegoat he needed for all his errors. It was Prince Max who procured the Emperor a tranquil eventide of life.

The Emperor had no sooner heard of the Prince's edict than he was possessed, for all his impotency, by a momentary mood of resistance. "Treason! Barefaced, outrageous treason!" he cried out, for this was the Fifth Act (Niemann, who was an eye-witness, p. 140). Then "the monarch in feverish haste filled one telegraph-form after another with a manifesto of protest." His telegraph-forms had not deserted him—they were his last adherents. He proclaimed that he remained the King of Prussia. Admiral Scheer and Rear-Admiral von Levetzow depict the scene. Its irony needs no underlining.

"Before the Emperor stood the Field-Marshal, General Gröner and General von Marschall being a little to one side. On our entrance the Emperor said: 'Field-Marshal, will you please repeat to Admiral Scheer what you have just said to me.' "

Hindenburg: "The Army and the troops are no longer behind His Majesty. There are no loyal troops left. Would to God, Your Majesty, that it were otherwise!"

The Emperor: "If it is as the Field-Marshal informs me, I cannot well allow myself to be arrested! There is nothing for it but to abdicate as Emperor. I remain King of Prussia. But that the gentlemen may learn how I am served by my Chancellor—Prince Max von Baden proclaimed my abdication both as Emperor and King this morning, without my knowledge and without my authority. That is the way I am served by my last Chancellor!"

Scheer: "The effect on the Navy will be incalculable, if it has lost its Supreme War-Lord."

The Emperor, gloomily: "I have no Navy now!"

He went out, with a shake of the hand for everyone. Not a word about leaving Spa; he had elected to stay with the troupe.

The whole confused, pathetic scene, with its theatrical climax, could only have fittingly ended with a shot behind the scenes, or else a ride to the battle-front; for between this 9th and the 11th, hundreds more were slaughtered there. Delbrück came rushing over on purpose to die at his sovereign's side; the Junkers of Pomerania told the Empress, that day, of "a similar intention," and Solf had ere this felt sure that they must count on the Emperor's doing something of the kind. When later on the Emperor, in conversation with Niemann, repudiated equally, on moral grounds, a challenge to the Almighty and self-murder, he was speaking privately, and no one has any right to criticize his views; but his second argument is extremely interesting: "What would be the good of playing the stage-hero? The days are gone when the Royal General could lead his Triarians to the field of slaughter with his sword in his right hand."

Were these the lips which for decades had boasted of that battle with the sword in the right hand, which had promised himself that "stage-hero's" part, for four years now imposed upon his subjects, lying on the field in hecatombs? Had he not perpetually appealed to the Great Frederick? Frederick had always carried poison about him.

Every one of his subjects was free to prefer life to an heroic death, but not He, not on that day. William the Second only was not free to choose on that Ninth of November.

He stood helpless before reality. A bad exit or death—those were the alternatives. Though Hindenburg and Hintze warned him of his danger with the Army, he persistently clung to the thought of a storm-battalion which was supposed to be still reliable—there was talk of an officer's guard. "I will fight to the last moment," he said towards nightfall, "if even a few of my friends stick to me—even if we're to be slaughtered, every one!" In the most primitive fashion, as he had seen done upon the stage, he ordered munitions and arms to be brought into the villa, as if he proposed to entrench himself there. On receiving news of the Empress he exclaimed: "My wife is sticking it out—

and they want to persuade me to go to Holland! I never will. It would be like a captain deserting the sinking ship!" (Niemann, p. 143).

Suddenly, even as he was provisioning his little fortress, he caught sight of the royal train standing outside, or perhaps he only remembered it. Had it not carried him through all countries, an ever-obedient steed? And there it stood, dazzling in its white and gold, spotless, well-oiled, well-coaled, on feather-springs, noiseless, ever-ready—the Emperor's true home. Only when in movement, in gliding rocking motion, only when faring onward, was life a thing of beauty. . . . And he flings everything to the winds, and goes to the train to sleep; and Hintze is heard to say that he will leave for Holland to-morrow. At nine o'clock he summons Hindenburg to the train—no, he does not intend to go; the Crown Prince is to be told; he will speak to him to-morrow morning.

When Niemann, whom Plessen had summoned to the train "in case they left that evening," arrived with his baggage—how did he find his War-Lord?

In the train I found the Emperor already at dinner with his suite. I had been afraid that the excitement of the previous hours would have made him lethargic. But not at all. He looked up at me with all his animation; his face was calm and resolute. They told me that the Emperor had quite changed his mind about going to Holland.

By this time the whole suite had known for twenty-four hours that he would take flight; but decorum was preserved. So that when at ten o'clock Grünau, "by order of the Field-Marshal," pleaded in common with Plessen and Marschall for "Holland without delay," there was no more beating about the bush. "After brief reflection, the Emperor consented." But to show himself master just once more, to let no one be able to say that he was "afraid of his life," he found the fitting phrases: "Well, if it must be so! . . . But not before to-morrow morning!"

What else could the Field-Marshal, who loved the Emperor, have advised when all was over? After the crawling, the despicable, retreat from power there was only this back-alley left for escape. But would not the uniform speak—the uniform he had worn for fifty years? Would not the spirit of his forebears cry out for the wildfire deed, the hot-headed splendour, the old Hohenzollern knightliness? A thousand speeches in the past—now one speech in the living present! Ten words to his assembled officers: "To the front! To battle!" and with the Old-Prussian Hurrah! a human rampart would have closed around him in a minute. A prince in arms would have done honour to the dead, and saved the living.

But he only took a sheet of paper and wrote to his son, to whom he had given his promise to stay. "Dear boy." . . . After all he had made up his mind to go. . . . Quite simply, quite unaffectedly. But when he came to the signature it occurred to him that the scene was historic; and with ceremonial stiffness he signed the artless page: "Your stricken father." When his son came to see him next morning, he was gone. Nobody held the Emperor back—the saddest of all epilogues.

In the grey of dawn he and a few of the faithful had driven westward in motors. There was no time to make any arrangements, nor did they dare to use the wires, already tapped in every quarter. And so it was virtually the first and last escapade of his life.

The frontier was not far away. The cars drew up. The frontier-guard in his Dutch uniform refused to let German officers pass. His officer was sent for. For a moment he thought he must be dreaming; then he knew what to do: Telephone to The Hague. For the present he conducted the gentlemen to a little iron waiting-room. But before those at The Hague—the Ministers and the Queen—could make up their minds, six hours went by.

The Emperor had never before had to wait six minutes. Possibly a train with a crowned guest might be a few moments late, or a message at the manœuvres might fail to arrive on the tick of the clock. That day he was pent in that iron box for six hours; and if he had much to atone for, in those six hours part of the pilgrim's burden of sin fell from him.

The window of the little waiting-room looked east. Directly outside, he could see the Dutch colours, the frontier-posts; four paces farther on, the Black-White-and-Red of Germany. The Emperor looked at the posts; then looked backward at his land, at his life.

There, beyond those frontier-posts, a great people is groaning. Those are the Germans, Emperor William, whom you have governed for so long. Pacific and mighty, rich in thought and rich in music—so they have always been; so they still are at heart. But over them was flung a glittering veil of illusion; their eyes were dazzled by the sheen of gold and gems; they learnt ambitions, jealousies —ambition for predominance and jealousy of other lands; these thirty years have swept them, breathless, from their steadfast course. Too soon they took the semblance of their youthful Emperor—too well he pleased them; and they urged each other ever farther onward, ever growing

richer, till there came the days of *Hubris*. Flatterers all,
they thronged about their sovereign's throne; each would
be first to snatch the quick-won prize, and for their folly
they are called upon to pay—for the arrogance which set
all Europe against Germany.

The land is groaning now. More than a million of her
sons—the half of her youth—lie prostrate, rotting in alien
soil. Hark to the mothers' tears, the fathers' execrations;
see this brave famished people cower to the victor's lash!

Are these the glorious days you vowed to bring your
people? Which of your promises have you kept? Though
Nature and upbringing wronged you, what have *you* done
with your many gifts in that festival you made of life?
In the service of your phrases, your pretensions, this great
people has been led astray; and when for once it warned
you, you derided it.

After four inactive years—four years of sacrifice for all
but you—you have refused your people the last service
which, in history's eyes, might still have saved you; and for
scurvy life are breaking now the soldier's oath you swore
before your grandsire—the oath inviolate; you dinned that
in their ears a thousand times. Now, in their direst need,
you wash your hands of them—wife, children, subjects; in
your craven fear you cast away the honour of your fathers.
Chaos is upon your land; and while millions stare privation
and slavery in the face, one man, the man who stands for all,
steps into his luxurious car and rolls away to ease and com-
fort in a neutral country.

At last! The officer, saluting, comes into the waiting-
room. "The gentlemen may pass." With leaden heart the
Emperor goes to his car; he even forgets, to-day, to hide

his withered arm under his cape. A soldier sits in front, escorting the distinguished prisoners. The engine throbs— the car drives on into the alien land from which there will be no home-coming.

Fainter, ever fainter. . . . Soon the Emperor can scarcely hear the groaning of his land.

INDEX